A HISTORY OF
San Juan County

A HISTORY OF

San Juan

County

In the Palm of Time

Robert S. McPherson

1995
Utah State Historical Society
San Juan County Commission

ISBN 0-913738-01-8
Library of Congress Catalog Card Number 95-61770
Map by Automated Geographic Reference Center—State of Utah
Printed in the United States of America

Utah State Historical Society
300 Rio Grande
Salt Lake City, Utah 84101-1182

Contents

Acknowledgments

No history is written in a vacuum, and this history is no exception. A number of organizations and individuals have freely given of their time and energy to assist in making this work representative of the many facets of the county's experience. Starting on the broadest level, gratitude is expressed to the Utah State Legislature for the wisdom and financial backing that allowed the massive undertaking of commissioning a written history for each of the twenty-nine counties in Utah. The legislature and their workhorse, the Utah State Historical Society, are to be commended for their depth of vision and expert guidance. Two people in particular, Kent Powell and Craig Fuller, bore the greatest burden in assisting with the direction, research, editing, and publishing of this manuscript, yet they always had the patience and grace to pleasantly encourage the author. The Utah Humanities Council, one of the most helpful and professional agencies I have had the pleasure to work with, funded a number of Native American oral history projects over the years. Part of the results of these grants has found its way into the manuscript, providing a Native American perspective that would have otherwise been impossible to achieve.

Two other professional historians read and critiqued this work. Thanks go to Stanford J. Layton, editor of the *Utah Historical Quarterly*, for his comments. As an "outsider" to San Juan history, he provided a broad contextual critique that helped insure a balanced treatment. Gary L. Shumway viewed the manuscript as an "insider." Born and raised in San Juan County, he was able to speak to the local concerns regarding both content and feeling. His expertise helped the author avoid some embarrassing mistakes and omissions.

On a local level, appreciation is expressed to San Juan County Commissioners Ty Lewis, Bill Redd, and Mark Maryboy for encouraging the writing and for funding the publication of the work. They never questioned the need for a broad-based history of the county. The San Juan County Historical Commission, led by such enthusiastic leaders as LaVerne Tate and Corinne Roring and backed by a capable advisory committee, have spent many hours reading and commenting on the manuscript. Their direction has helped maintain the "heart" as well as the intellect in the writing. While they realize there is much more that needs to be said about the county, they also understand that the broad scope of this work makes it impossible to tell it all in one volume. The College of Eastern Utah—San Juan Campus and my supervisor, Kay Shumway, also have been supportive. Without this encouragement and assistance, the book would not have been possible.

About four dozen readers critiqued parts of or entire chapters of the book. There are too many to name, but their assistance helped me to clarify events and attitudes of which they had particular knowledge. As for the technical aspects of writing, a special thanks goes to Merry Adams, who knows just where to put each comma and can explain why a certain word does not "feel" right. In both writing and content, if there are errors, they are my own.

A final word of thanks goes to unsung heroes: family and friends. My wife, Betsy, and children—David, Jonathan, Daniel, Elizabeth, Heather, and Michelle—provided that special type of support and love that is so necessary in life. Their understanding of the goal was one more aspect that made this project possible. I hope they keep the red sand of San Juan in their shoes for many years to come.

General Introduction

When Utah was granted statehood on 4 January 1896, twenty-seven counties comprised the nation's new forty-fifth state. Subsequently two counties, Duchesne in 1914 and Daggett in 1917, were created bringing the number of Utah counties to twenty-nine. These twenty-nine counties have been the stage on which much of the history of Utah has been played.

Recognizing the importance of Utah's twenty-nine counties, the Utah State Legislature established in 1991 a Centennial History Project to write and publish county histories as part of Utah's statehood centennial commemoration. The Division of State History was given the assignment to administer the project. The county commissioners, or their designees were responsible to select the author or authors for their individual histories and funds were provided by the state legislature to cover most research and writing costs as well as to provide each public school and library with a copy of each history. Writers worked under general guidelines provided by the Division of State History and in cooperation with county history committees. The counties also established a Utah Centennial County History

Council to help develop policies for distribution of state appropriated funds and plans for publication.

Each volume in the series reflects the scholarship and interpretation of the individual authors. The general guidelines provided by the Utah State Legislature included coverage of five broad themes encompassing the economic, religious, educational, social, and political history of the county. Authors were encouraged to cover a vast period of time stretching from the geologic and prehistoric times to the present. Since Utah's statehood centennial celebration falls just four years before the arrival of the twenty-first century, authors were encouraged to give particular attention to the history of their respective counties during the twentieth century.

Still, each history is at best a brief synopsis of what has transpired within the political boundaries of each county. No history can do justice to every theme or event or individual that is part of an area's past. Readers are asked to consider these volumes as an introduction to the history of the county and it is expected that other researchers and writers will extend beyond the limits of time, space, and detail imposed on this volume to add to the wealth of knowledge about the county and its people. In understanding the history of our counties, we come to understand better the history of our state, our nation, our world, and ourselves.

In addition to the authors, local history committee members, and county commissioners, who deserve praise for their outstanding efforts and important contributions, special recognition is given to Mr. Joseph Francis of Morgan County for his role in conceiving the idea of the centennial county history project and for his energetic efforts in working with the Utah State Legislature and State of Utah officials to make the project a reality. Mr. Francis is proof that one person does make a difference.

ALLAN KENT POWELL
CRAIG FULLER
GENERAL EDITORS

SAN JUAN COUNTY

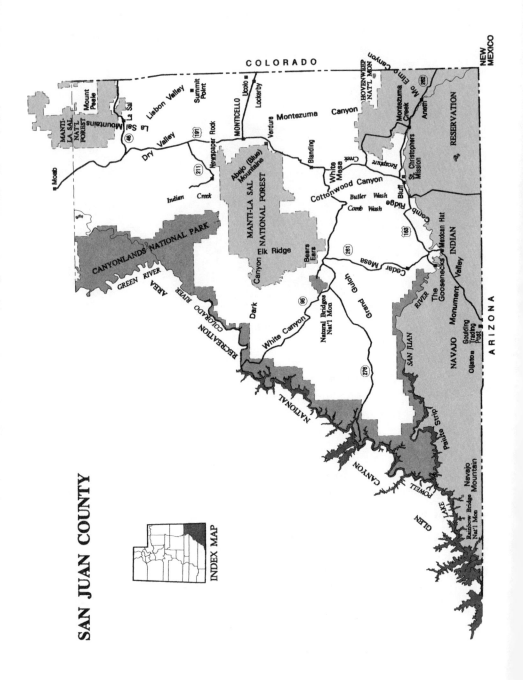

INDEX MAP

In the Palm of Time

UNDERSTANDING THE SAGA OF SAN JUAN

Navajo elders, speaking of a mythic past when the world was "soft," use the phrase "in the palm of time." Encapsulated in these words are the feelings that this mystical period was something remembered, cherished, almost sacred. It was a time when important things happened and the Navajos began to establish their identity and life patterns. The gods were very much present, guiding the people in understanding as both moved about the land and experienced life in this world. The holy beings provided the spiritual landscape for the Navajo, who planted their roots in the soil of the Four Corners region in preparation for a journey through history—a history filled with discovery and growth as well as denial and death. But always there was the land and the people's past to assure their identity.

History has a way of doing that—of tracing the roots of people while strengthening the main stalk of life today. The Navajos were not alone. Utes, Paiutes, Hispanics, and Anglo-Americans also sank their roots into the Four Corners area. In San Juan County, Utah, this becomes particularly apparent after studying the area's prehistory

1

and history. From the earliest travelers and explorers through its settlers and developers to its citizens of today, the land has served as a magnet to draw a variety of people from many walks of life. Each has his or her own unique story to tell, each with its own interpretation.

Indeed, writing a history of San Juan County is actually telling the story of three distinct groups—the Ute, the Navajo, and the Euro-American. Their stalks intertwine and at times support each other, at other times compete, but always remain individual and different, nurtured by dissimilar understandings and ideas of the same world. For this reason, their stories are told here separately, with chapters dedicated to each group; other chapters share a common theme among all three societies. It is hoped that no single point of view dominates the entire work, but rather that the differing perspectives evoke a feeling of shared events and ideas that allows for greater understanding.

A few words about what this history is and is not. A Chinese proverb says, "He who wins the war writes the history." In a sense, this has been true of previous works about San Juan. Although there are many partial accounts, the first writer to attempt a full-fledged history of the county was Albert R. Lyman. Born in 1880 (died 1973), he was fortunate enough to have lived during many of the early events following the initial Mormon settlement. Lyman also performed the yeoman's task of collecting oral histories, diaries, and journals from participants and then transferring this knowledge onto the printed page for public consumption. He was prolific. His books, articles, and essays span three-quarters of a century and were widely circulated both inside and outside of the county.

Lyman was also an accomplished storyteller. Indeed, it is difficult for a writer of San Juan history to come out of the shadow he still casts. Dramatic accounts flowed from his pen as he interpreted what he believed to be the personalities of protagonists and antagonists. He wrote in the spirit of his times, a time when the wild West held a charm all its own. Both fictional and real characters were clearly framed in a "good guys-bad guys" scenario. These fruits of his interests and efforts insure that his legacy cannot be ignored.

His faith motivated his efforts, and "Uncle Albert," as he was known by many local people, was a staunch advocate of a Mormon point of view. He did not wince when it came to proselyting, and he viewed events through the religious eyes of a devout Mormon. His vision never changed. Even as the editor for the short-lived *San Juan Blade*, a newspaper springing from Blanding's soil and lasting for less than two years, Lyman could not let go of the main theme that courses through all of his works. He wrote in the first issue that the paper's origin grew "out of a keen interest in the long fight made to redeem its rich prairies from wilderness. . . . We have watched the pioneers of San Juan batter down the barriers of the wilderness, making a breach so wide that people have come from far and near to enjoy the opening."[1] In later years, he published a long-standing column entitled, not surprisingly, "The Old Settler" in *The San Juan Record*. Uncle Albert was first and foremost a spokesman for the "sturdy pioneer" point of view.

What this has done for San Juan history is to cast a mold that is difficult to break. Until recently, it was hard for local history to move very far beyond the story of the Mormon pioneers. Cornelia Perkins, Marian Nielson, and Lenora Jones wrote *Saga of San Juan*, published by the San Juan County Daughters of Utah Pioneers. The authors depended heavily on Lyman's work. So too did other local historians. Not until Charles S. Peterson published *Look to the Mountains: Southeastern Utah and the La Sal National Forest* (1975) did an outside view of white settlement come into print. Peterson's excellent scholarship and balanced approach laid a historical foundation for the county's history while concentrating on the evolution of government control over the forests and mountains in southern Utah. Yet this work does not pretend to be a county history.

In 1983 Kent Powell from the Utah State Historical Society edited *San Juan County: People, Resources, and History*. This book, organized around such themes as roads, education, mining, and Indians, offered a scholarly approach tempered by local responses. The result was illuminating but incomplete. For instance, an honest attempt to obtain a Navajo point of view resulted in a chapter written by Clyde Benally; but by necessity it was brief and did not examine many aspects of Navajo experience. An equally short and sympathetic treatment also was given to the Utes and Paiutes, who until this time had been typecast as outlaw factions with no claims to the land or reasons for being disgruntled. There were some excellent chapters in the collection, but others were uneven and raised issues never answered. With few exceptions, because of a readily available written record, the authors followed the paths already blazed by the white community.

Except for the early history of Bluff, an outside reader of these early writings might think that San Juan County started just a little south of Blanding. Much of the activity of the Native American populations was ignored because of the need for archival research or because those writing the history did not understand the people and culture or because the Navajos and Utes cast a negative light as a counter to white expansion. The absence of historical writings about Native Americans said as much as what was in print. Only two books, besides those written by Lyman, attempt to elucidate part of their experience. The first, *The Last of the Indian Wars* (1961) by Forbes Parkhill, centers around the 1915 skirmish in Bluff. The Utes and Paiutes receive a more sympathetic treatment than usual, but the author, a retired reporter, depended heavily on newspaper accounts and tended toward the dramatic. The second book, *The Northern Navajo Frontier 1860–1900: Expansion through Adversity* (McPherson, 1988), follows a topical approach. Chapters on Navajo/Ute relations, trading posts, boundary changes, and resource competition add pieces to the puzzle of Native American activities in San Juan County but do not create a cohesive framework for a full picture. This book also spans a relatively short period of time, cutting off at the beginning of the twentieth century.

What then does this new county history propose to do? First of all, it is an overview. The reader should understand that, without exception, there is no chapter in this book that could not be expanded to at least the size of a monograph and, in many instances, to a book of its own. One of the biggest challenges in writing this history was to pare down the available information. Much of the material came from state and federal government records, the Utah State Historical Society, universities on the Wasatch Front, and previously published sources. Oral histories with Native Americans helped provide another view beyond the written word, as did the interviews gathered in the white communities at an earlier time by Gary Shumway.[2] There are still many stories waiting out there to be told, and, like Uncle Albert, I hope to get three-quarters of a century to continue my work.

To make the vast kaleidoscope of San Juan County history manageable, certain decisions had to be made. The number of pages of this book were predetermined, a time schedule established, and a contract agreement signed. It would have been easy to fall into the pit of storytelling, never to reach the rim of understanding with its broader view. The identification of general patterns in history became the ladder by which this vista could be achieved. Thus, in each chapter, an organizing theme ties at least one, and sometimes two, topics together. Those who would like to take their own romp through the source material are referred to the endnotes of each chapter.

Some readers undoubtedly will be disappointed. Those who are expecting a long string of stories or a detailed retelling of events already in print will not find them here. Space just does not allow that. There will be others who feel that a certain personality or event should have been included or that too much space is devoted to something they consider unimportant or irrelevant. I have tried during the writing process to incorporate suggestions or make corrections from the roughly four dozen people consulted. These people ranged from professional historians and government officials to county residents who experienced a particular aspect of San Juan history. Their help was invaluable. Mistakes, although unintentional, are bound to have crept in. I accept full responsibility for any that exist and for the interpretations derived therefrom.

What the reader will find is an honest attempt to tell a very complex story of three groups of people as they worked, struggled, played, and philosophized in the lands of San Juan County. Each of them has its own genesis, its own "palm of time," that establishes its origin and identity. They all share a common denominator in the land, which each invests with its own significance, whether it be social, economic, historic, or religious. To each group, San Juan is special, and to each this book is dedicated.

ROBERT S. MCPHERSON, WINTER 1995
COLLEGE OF EASTERN UTAH—SAN JUAN CAMPUS

Endnotes

1. "Introduction," *San Juan Blade*, 10 August 1917, 1.

2. Gary Shumway, an historian born and raised in San Juan, directed the collection of oral histories in the county at different times for more than twenty years. He began in 1963 to record general histories and then later held interviews on Navajo history (1968), the uranium industry (1970), more general history (1971–72), and Mormon polygamy (1980s). Most of this work was a collaborative effort between California State University—Fullerton and the University of Utah (Navajo interviews of the Doris Duke Project and the Uranium Industry Project), or, in the case of the Southeastern Utah Project, with the Utah State Historical Society. The Mormon polygamy interviews were funded by the Charles Redd Center at Brigham Young University. Some of these projects are continuing to this day. Most of this work is bound, indexed, and covers a broad range of topics associated with white settlement, lifestyle, and economic development of southeastern Utah.

1

Land of Contrast, Land of Change

THE GEOGRAPHY AND PLACE NAMES OF SAN JUAN COUNTY

In 1934, Everett Ruess, a twenty-year-old vagabond philosopher, made his third visit in as many years to the geographic wonderland of northern Arizona and southern Utah. His intense love for the land's beauty caused him to pen some of the most lyrical poetry of the soul, describing mountain and desert through the eyes of an artist. That June, he sat upon Navajo Mountain and tried to describe his feelings towards the landscape:

> The perfection of this place is one reason why I distrust ever returning to the cities. Here I wander in beauty and perfection. There one walks in the midst of ugliness and mistakes. . . . The beauty of this country is becoming a part of me. I feel more detached from life and somehow gentler. . . . I have some good friends here, but no one really understands why I am here or what I do.[1]

Five months later, he disappeared forever in the wilderness near Escalante, Utah, a victim of the land he loved.

Ruess's vision of this part of the world and his mysterious death encapsulate a dichotomy, an irony that pervades the region. Call it a love-hate relationship, contrasting elements, or opposition in all things, but in this land so filled with promise of growth, wealth, and new life there also abounds dramatic possibilities of destruction, poverty, and death. Success may be temporary and illusory, giving rise to a boom that will be followed by a bust of equal or greater proportion. The only thing a person can count on is that the land will eventually render an accounting of the natural and human activities that play across its features.

In no place is this more true than in San Juan County, Utah. Nestled in the southeastern corner of the state, where Colorado, New Mexico, and Arizona join with Utah to form the Four Corners area, this land offers dramatic evidence of nature's ceaseless efforts to shape and change the earth's surface. Wind, water, temperature, and chemical activity have combined to flake, crack, scour, melt, and create some of the most picturesque scenery in the world. Lone sandstone spires protrude from a desert floor; a roiling, silt-laden river courses through a narrow floodplain before passing between canyon walls hundreds of feet high; cedar-covered mesas give way first to ponderosa pine, next aspen, and finally the naked rocks of a towering peak, while grass- and sagebrush-clad plateaus serve as home to herds of sheep and cattle. The land is as diverse as the geological prehistory that helped to create it.

San Juan County lies in the Canyonlands portion of the Colorado Plateau, in what is known as the Upper Sonoran ecological zone. It is high desert country, ranging through an elevation of 4,000 to 6,000 feet. But that is an average. The highest peak in the county, Mount Peale in the La Sals, stands at an elevation of 12,700 feet, while Abajo Peak on Blue Mountain reaches 11,360 feet. If a person traveled to the top of Abajo Peak from Monument Valley (4,900 feet) that person would experience approximately 6,500 feet of elevation change in two hours. He or she also would have traveled through five different ecological zones, starting in the lower elevations with blackbrush, ricegrass, sagebrush, juniper, and pinyon (Upper Sonoran), next ponderosa pine (Transition), on to Douglas fir and quaking aspen (Canadian), spruce and fir (Hudsonian), and finally, above timberline, the small mat-like plants and lichens of the

Alpine Tundra Zone.[2] The view, once one reached this height, would be of a land filled with deserts, canyons, and mountains so diverse that contrast appears to be its only unifying theme.

Consider what this is all built upon—its rock formations. Underlying San Juan County are vast stretches of sandstone and limestone beds resting in horizontal layers that tilt slightly north. The development of these strata started four and a half billion years ago during the Precambrian period. Geologists have identified a series of succeeding periods, all of which added variety in color and texture to the different layers of stone and shale beneath. As the Pacific Ocean, inland seas, jungle plants, and animal life evolved through eons of time, these elements came under the physical and chemical forces of evaporation, lifting, faulting, erosion, and volcanic activity to form a colorful and varied landscape.[3] The principal constant over the thousands, millions, and billions of years was inexorable change.

The layered deposits held various elements that would greatly affect human beings. For instance, the forces of nature created Spanish, Lisbon, and Big Indian valleys by either pushing down or eroding away the less stable salt deposits underlying those depressions. Streams and swamps helped form the Chinle and Morrison layers which, between the two, contain uranium, vanadium, copper, petrified wood, fossils, and dinosaur bones. Unexplored coal deposits lie east of Monticello, oil wells pump their valuable liquid out of the land south of La Sal and in the southeast corner of the county, while small amounts of gold and silver are present in the mountains and in the streams that flow from them.

One of the newest uses of this oldest resource—the land—comes from the ever-expanding tourist industry, as thousands of people flock each year to view the sandstone plateaus, mesas, and monoliths of canyon country. Nature began the process hundreds of millions of years ago by providing wind, water, sand, and pressure to form the large blocks of stone compacted during the Paleozoic era. Lateral forces squeezed Elk Ridge and Comb Ridge from the desert floor; erosion then washed and blew away material surrounding the exposed edges of the uplifts to create a knifelike rim. The desert lands in the southern third of the county also were uplifted when faulting rejuvenated the area west of Bluff, a region extending all the way to

Blue (Abajo) Mountain, one of the most prominent landmarks in the county. Showing on the right side of the mountain is the "horse head," formed by trees and open areas. (San Juan Historical Commission)

Monument Valley, while the land to the east remained unchanged as an old age desert. After millions of years, the land and its rock formations reveal the continuing effects of differential erosion caused by exfoliation, wind, and water on the surfaces of varying degrees of hardness. Strange shapes tantalize the imagination and beckon camera-laden tourists. Equally attractive are the reddish hues derived from iron oxide in the sandstone, and the black streaks, called desert varnish, from manganese oxide. Today, Canyonlands National Park, Dead Horse Point, Valley of the Gods, Monument Valley's Navajo Tribal Park, Natural Bridges National Monument, and Rainbow Bridge National Monument hold just a few of the spectacular forms and colors spread throughout the county's 7,884 square miles.

Yet nothing stands as a greater testament to the change and variety found here than the three large laccolithic intrusions known as Blue (or Abajo), La Sal, and Navajo mountains. Formed an estimated average of twenty-four million years ago, these mountains slowly bulged upward as magma from beneath pushed the sandstone strata above. Erosion later exposed the subsurface igneous rock. Based on the amount of remaining uneroded sandstone on top, geologists believe that Navajo Mountain is the latest arrival, with Blue Mountain next. The La Sal Range is the senior citizen of the three because it boasts the least amount of sedimentary rock.

These mountains, in addition to their mineral and plant wealth, provide something of even greater value—water, the bond between life and death, settlement and abandonment. It is no exaggeration to say that what has or has not been used or developed in the county depends to a large extent on that location's relation to water. Without this resource, no people can remain.

There are three major sources of water in the county, all of which are affected in one way or another by the mountains. The first and most important is the moisture that comes from the winter snows or the summer thermal currents formed by heated desert air pushed upward to cool and fall as rain on the peaks. Billowing thunderheads, marble-sized hail, and zigzag lightning testify of both life-giving power and destructive force. Residents of San Juan County—whether Anasazi, Ute, Navajo, or Anglo—have looked to the mountains and the waters that come from them as a necessity to sustain life.

A second source of water is the creeks, intermittent and perennial streams, and rivers that flow through red rock country. Dozens of small tributaries pour off the mountains each spring, swelling the waters of the Colorado River as it meets the Green in Canyonlands National Park, or the San Juan River moving westward to Lake Powell. Known as "exotic" rivers because their major source lies outside of the dry land through which they run, these bodies of water push heavy loads of pebbles, rocks, and boulders; carry large suspended loads of clay, silt, and sand; and transport dissolved loads of minerals. As rain, snow, and irrigation waters pass over the land, they accumulate more salts and other minerals, making the water less desirable for human use. Farming settlements had to make the choice of either staying by the San Juan River, whose water originates in the San Juan Mountains of Colorado, or moving to the base of the Blue or La Sal mountains in order to utilize their water. Generally, the most successful towns were those that were closest to their source of moisture, the mountains.

Pioneers who settled Bluff and Montezuma Creek learned this lesson the hard way, as each year they cleaned their ditches of sand and braced their headgates for the onslaught of spring and fall floods. Just how great fluctuations of water levels could be was recorded in the autumn of 1941. Between 9 September and 14 October the San Juan River changed from a placid, shallow stream three feet deep, 125 feet wide, flowing at 635 cubic feet per second, to a raging torrent twenty-five feet deep, 240 feet wide, gushing at 59,600 cubic feet per second. The results were obvious. The river ravaged hitherto protected floodplains, with only the highest banks containing the water. Few irrigation facilities and bridges survived the onslaught.[4] Now, however, with Navajo Dam controlling the capture and release of runoff, this type of flooding is no longer a problem.

Underground aquifers in the county serve as the third source of water. Even those are affected in part by water that flows from the mountain through subterranean streams. Until recently, springs and seeps were the only visible means by which humans could avail themselves of this precious commodity, but with the introduction of drilling techniques and pumps, wells have allowed people to settle in areas never before suitable. Shallow wells to approximately 130 feet deep are heavily dependent upon subsurface mountain water, and their output can be greatly diminished by adjacent pumping. Deep water pockets and domes at depths of about 1,700 feet appear to be more stable, though this source has only begun to be utilized in the deep coal mines at Black Mesa south of San Juan County.

Thus, abundance or dearth in this region depends heavily on the availability of water and on the weather that brings it. Averages of rainfall and temperature can be misleading. Blanding, for instance, receives twelve inches of precipitation and has an average annual temperature of fifty degrees Fahrenheit.[5] Twenty-five miles to the south lies Bluff, which receives an annual rainfall of about seven inches and has an average temperature five to ten degrees warmer than that of Blanding.[6] Important storms generally come from the southwest or west, bringing water from the Pacific Ocean in the form of clouds that leave their most significant loads of moisture on the cooler higher elevations.

San Juan County has a semiarid climate; as a result, there are few clouds, little water, and scarce vegetation. The rocks and soil absorb and release the heat from the sun quickly. Consequently, warm days, cold nights, and low humidity characterize the Colorado Plateau, providing an environment that is ideal for preserving the remains of historic and prehistoric sites.

Plants have adapted to the regimen of feast and famine caused by elevation, precipitation, temperature, and type of soil. Their root systems follow three different forms, each of which solves the same problem of obtaining, storing, and utilizing water. The Utah juniper tree, for instance, has a relatively shallow fibrous system that extends over a large area, radiating out from the base of the trunk. Any moisture not trapped by its leaves or retained in its shaggy bark falls to the ground, where it is collected by its network of roots. Most desert plants cannot compete with this plant's efficiency and find another place to grow. An alternate way for a plant to collect water is to head straight down and deep, through one main taproot. Sagebrush and rabbitbrush are adept at locating water this way. Plants with bulbs or expandable exteriors provide a third type of survival system, by storing collected water. Cacti not only expand and shrink according to the moisture available but, like many desert plants, have sharp thorns as a means to protect and keep it for themselves. Adaptation is the key. Settlers may have chained the junipers, burned out the sagebrush, and made jam out of the cactus; but, when it came to persisting in the region, the plants often won out in the long run, as humans literally sought greener pastures.

Yet even when the people moved on, they left behind a colorful legacy of place-names to record the feelings, personalities, and events that were once there. Donald Worster, an ecological historian, believes that man's propensity to name a place is one of the natural things he does to create and organize his landscape. Worster says,

> Find a label for something and you have discovered it. Say the Word, and whole planets, solar systems, galaxies—light itself—spring forth out of darkness. . . . Words are like empty balloons, inviting us to fill them up with associations. As they fill they begin to gain intrinsic force and at last to shape our perceptions and expectations.[7]

San Juan County has had the good fortune of being a palimpsest of history, as Native Americans and later Euro-Americans traveled, worked, played, and labeled features within its far reaches.

To the Indians who live in this area, the land is more than just a physical place of survival. It is all part of a spiritual universe, imbued with power to protect or harm, according to how it is treated. Archaic and Anasazi Indians were among the first to record their ideas and leave their calling card, which they did by means of inscriptions on hundreds of rock walls, cave sites, and water holes that dot the land. Pictures of animals such as desert bighorn sheep, elk, deer, snakes, and lizards speak of the environment; carvings of men with weapons, in council, on migration, hunting, and at war tell of human activities; drawings of the humpbacked flute player associated with fertility, of pregnant women ripe with birth, and the ubiquitous handprints of adults and children suggest family life and individual personalities beyond the depiction of great events and mythology.[8]

Exactly what these pictographs and petroglyphs mean can only be conjectured, though a number of people have tried to interpret them. Most archaeologists take a conservative approach, spending much of their time dating or classifying the rock art. They come at odds with someone like LaVan Martineau, who views these symbols as writings that follow a system that can be read.[9] He believes that many of these drawings serve as trail and water markers, outline boundaries, express clan relationships and migrations, and record identifiable prehistoric events.

Jane Young, an anthropologist, spent three summers living with the Zuni Indians, trying to unlock a satisfactory interpretation of their ancient rock art. What she discovered suggested that the pictographs and petroglyphs followed a pattern of cultural ideas and ideals that tied the people religiously and historically to the land. In her words:

> Rock carvings and paintings and other features of the landscape are especially important elements of Zuni cultural symbolism because they are visual records, constant and immediate reminders, of the past; . . . in some cases they are "messages from the ancestors," rarely explicitly understood but signs of the ancestors' involvement with and concern for contemporary Zunis.[10]

And so it is with the Anasazi, believed to be the forerunners of a number of the historic pueblo tribes living in the Southwest today. Rock art panels such as those at Sand Island, Butler Wash, Montezuma Canyon, and elsewhere remain among people's first recorded attempts to express a relationship with the lands of San Juan County.

Historic Indian groups have preserved through writing and oral history this same affiliation. Not as much ethnographic work has been done with the Utes' lore concerning geographic place-names as has been done for the Navajo. Though it may have existed in a richer form, at present the Ute naming system appears to have been less complex or very literal. For instance, Montezuma Canyon is simply called Sagebrush Canyon, the San Juan—Water Canyon, and Mount Tukuhnikivats (La Sals)—Where the Sun Sets Last.[11] Many other place names existed, but have since been lost.

Just beyond the southeastern boundary of San Juan County lies Sleeping Ute Mountain, another large laccolithic intrusion. The Utes believe this was one of their deities. Angered by his people, he collected rain clouds, put them in his pocket, and then went to sleep. When a storm arises, the Indians say that it is only the clouds coming out of the rain god's pocket. Some say that when the end of the world is imminent, the Sleeping Ute will awaken to fight his people's enemies.[12]

The Navajos, or Dine, have a more complex system of mythology about the land.[13] The San Juan is viewed as one of four sacred rivers and serves as the northern boundary of their territory. Known as Old Age River, Male Water, One-With-a-Long-Body, and One-With-a-Wide-Body, the river is often described as an old man with hair of white foam, as a snake wriggling through the desert, as a flash of lightning, and as a black club of protection to keep invaders away from the region of the Navajo.[14] The being within the river has served as a guardian for a long time. As early as 1865, Manuelito, one of the last Navajo war chiefs, claimed that he could not surrender to James Carleton because "there was a tradition that his people should never cross the Rio Grande, Rio San Juan or the Rio Colorado."[15] Today this tradition of protection is still in force. When older people cross the San Juan, they sprinkle corn pollen to the holy being and ask for

Totem Pole Rock, Monument Valley. To the Navajos the formations hold religious significance representing a line of prayersticks, a frozen god held up by lightning, and the home of the mirage people. (Photo by author)

safety in their journey and accomplishment of their goals. The spirit hears the plea and wraps its power like a shield or rainbow around the supplicant.[16]

Because the San Juan served as a geographical boundary for hunting expeditions and war parties, certain observances came into play when Navajos crossed the river. For instance, Blessingway ceremonies of protection pertain to events and places within this area, while beyond the Colorado and San Juan rivers, Enemyway and Evilway measures apply. Traditionally, the stick used in the Enemyway ceremony embodies many of the values important to the people and should never cross the river; however, now that many Navajos live north of the San Juan River, this proscription is no longer observed.

The Navajos are also attached to their land through the place-names they give to it. A great deal more work needs to be performed in gathering information about their names for the land, but if a person takes just one area, say the Aneth-Montezuma Creek region, and studies it closely, he quickly realizes the rich heritage bestowed upon the land just through its names. Multiply this understanding over hundreds of square miles, and the strong bonds that Native Americans feel toward their land become apparent.

Aneth played a key role in the history of this section of the San Juan. McElmo Creek empties into the river at this point, and because of the wide floodplain suitable for planting crops and travel, it was natural that Navajos bestowed a variety of labels to the area, each originating from an important incident or personality. *T'aa biich'iidii* ("In-the-Form-of-a-Ghost") is its most popular name, applied to the government farmer Herbert Redshaw, who lived there in the early 1900s. He walked slowly and deliberately, in an almost robotlike fashion; hence, one explanation of his name is that it is "just his devil or ghost within." Another is that he used to cuss and tell people to "Go to the Devil," while a third is that he was as "slow as the devil." Whatever the reason, the name stuck and has become the official title of the Aneth Chapter district.

Another place-name for Aneth which some Navajos descriptively applied to a trader was "Big Ears" or "Wiggling Ears." Still other names such as "Barely Enough Pep to Make It" and "A Good Place to Stay Away From" tantalizingly suggest stories. The area is also known as "Black Mountain (Sleeping Ute) Wash (McElmo Creek) Joins In."[17]

Montezuma Creek is called "Where the Sagebrush Wash Drains into the River" but also has other names including "Black Hat," given because of Bill Young, who established a post there, *Mosi,* or "Cat," after an earlier trader called "Old Cat," "Flew Back Out," and "Large Eyes." Some places in the Aneth-Montezuma Creek area are associated with economic activity. One is "Among the Prairie Dogs," named because Navajos transplanted these animals to add to their food resources. Other locations include "Clay" (used in ceremonies), "Spring in the Sour Berry [Squaw] Bush," "Gather Yucca," and "Corn Bush."

Place-names between the Four Corners Monument and Montezuma Creek also mark events: "Soldiers' Crossing," given during the 1906 *Bai-a-lil-le* disturbance; "Reclaiming the Horses," for a woman who caught Utes stealing her stock and so whipped and scolded them; and "To Look at One Another," given to a trail on a hill that was so narrow it caused passersby to look at each other.[18]

As Navajos settled this area, geography helped define limits on land-use rights. One Navajo told of how her two relatives, "Woman From Blanding" and "Old Gray," came atop a hill overlooking Montezuma Creek and outlined the boundaries where they would live. Woman-From-Blanding declared, "From that juniper covered hill to White Point, down the gray ridge to Stair Formation Rock and across to Fallen House—this is how big our land will be."[19] Thus from mythology to subsistence activities, from events to people, the land holds special significance for the Navajo, teaching, through naming, the things of importance.

In this same area, even though it is Navajo land, the majority of places on the map bear names of Anglo derivation. Aneth has had a variety of titles, including Riverview (1878–85), Holyoak (1886 to around 1895), Guillette, and finally Aneth, a Hebrew word meaning "The Answer," given by Howard Antes, a Methodist missionary who lived there beginning in 1895.

Peter's Nipple, a rock formation south of Aneth, was named after Peter Shirts (sometimes spelled Schurtz), who settled in Montezuma Creek in 1877; Allen Canyon took its name from John and Peter Allen, who raised their families at its mouth.[20] Names of other long-gone settlements along the river such as Noland's, Berlin, and Peak City have likewise disappeared.

Yet hundreds of place-names throughout San Juan County still provide stories, sometimes two or three to each title. A sampling suggests categories that range from the simple to the sublime, as history, values, and folklore thread through the names. Take Jailhouse Rock in Dry Valley, for instance. One of its stories tells of a man who wanted to go on a drinking spree and left his three children in the tall sandstone hole for a number of days until he returned sober, ready to assume his parental duties; another version relates how a cowboy, married to an attractive wife, had similar alcoholic desires and used the excuse of marauding Indians to lure her into the deep recess, where she remained until he satisfied his craving. Once free, she got a divorce from him. A third story relates that a trapper used to keep pregnant coyotes in the hole until they had their litters. He allowed the pups to reach maturity then killed and skinned them for profit.[21] Whether believable or not, each of these tales adds color from the past to the heritage of the county.[22]

People traveling through this region are often struck by the colors and in the past have labeled places like Red Mesa, White Mesa, White Rocks, Blue Mountain, and Green Water Springs. Anyone who has hiked or ridden horses in those areas can testify that Deep Canyon has high sides, that Dark Canyon does not receive a full day's direct sunlight (claimed by one person to be so deep that "the sun don't come up until the next morning"), that Verdure lies in a grass-filled valley, that Long Canyon stretches a number of miles, that the Green and Colorado rivers still meet at the Confluence, that the entrance to Lost Canyon is well hidden, and that Trail Canyon is still helpful to cowboys moving a herd. Other names tell of plants and minerals present in the particular area—Alkali Canyon, Cottonwood Canyon, Brushy Basin, Copper Canyon, Gypsum Canyon, Cedar Mesa, Clay Hills, and Coal Bed Canyon—or they describe a feature of the terrain such as Boundary Butte Mesa, Grand Gulch, Upheaval Dome, Arch Canyon, Bears Ears, Lake Canyon, Still Water Canyon, Rincon, Monument Valley, and Summit Point (dividing the San Juan and Colorado drainages).

But it took imagination to describe other rock formations, canyons, and escarpments: Paul Bunyan's Potty, Six Shooter, Cheesebox, Venus's Goblet, Mexican Hat, Train, Looking Glass, Elephant, Rainbow, Goosenecks, Snake, Castle, Navajo Blanket, Rooster's Comb, Seven Sisters, the Monitor (Butte—a Civil War battleship), Jacob's (Adams—a local cowboy) Chair, Zeke's (Johnson—early custodian of Natural Bridges) Bathtub, Alhambra (a medieval Moorish castle in Spain), and Woodenshoe. Perhaps one explanation for this rich legacy of place-names lies in the variety of Euro-American people who have tramped its canyons for various reasons.

Some of the oldest place-names originated with the Spanish and Mexicans who first came into the territory. The Dominguez and Escalante expedition in 1776 recorded names for some of the region's major geographic features, such as Sierra de la Sal, "Mountain of Salt," "because close to it there are salt beds where . . . the Yutas [Utes] who live hereabouts get their salt." They also mentioned seeing Sierra

The Goblet of Venus was located near Cottonwood Wash on the road leading to the Bears Ears and Natural Bridges. Stories ranging from dynamite to
rifle target practice tell of how pranksters toppled this unique rock formation around 1948. Next to it stands Zeke Johnson, the first caretaker of
Natural Bridges National Monument. (Kathryn Shumway Collection)

de Abajo (Blue Mountain) "four leagues" to the west-southwest, an
interesting fact since some historians have tried to ascribe bestowal
of the name to the Ferdinand V. Hayden survey party of 1875.[23]

The San Juan (Saint John) River (called by Escalante the Navajo River) obtained its name later, with the most likely derivation coming from the biblical Saint John the Baptist. Others have suggested it was named for Don Juan de Onate, first colonizer of New Mexico, or Don Juan de Rivera, an explorer of this region in 1765. No doubt exists that the Colorado River took its title from the red silt suspended in its waters, but it is not known who first applied it. Dominguez and Escalante crossed this river at Vado de los Padres (Crossing of the Fathers), known to local Indians as the Ute War Trail, which now rests under the waters of Lake Powell. The Spanish had also placed the Bears Ears (Orejas del Oso) on their maps by the late 1700s, while other Hispanic names given by travelers, traders, and, later, stockmen, include Rincon (a horseshoe bend or corner on the San Juan), Cajon (box canyon) Mesa, Tuerto (crooked) Canyon, Arido (dry) Creek, and Casa del Eco (home of the echo) Mesa.

San Juan country mythology suggests that Montezuma Creek received its name from Peter Shirts, who is said to have believed that Montezuma (Moctezuma II), the famed Aztec ruler in the days of Hernando Cortez, escaped his captors, was overtaken in Recapture Wash, and then brought to Montezuma Creek where he was killed. Reports of the Hayden survey, however, indicate that this name was already known before Shirts used it, thus leaving the origin of the title a mystery. Other names that may relate to this story are Aztec Butte, Montezuma Canyon, and, in Colorado, the city of Cortez.

Recapture Canyon is also said to have received its name from the apprehension by the law of an outlaw who had escaped his initial arrest; another story tells how horses and mules from the Hayden party were retrieved there from Indians who had stolen them.[24] Later, when Anglo Americans traversed the land, they named some places after the Indian peoples they found residing there. Hoskinnini (Hashkeneinii) Mesa and Kigalia (K'aayelii) Spring took their appellations from two Navajo head men who roamed the territory during the nineteenth century. Mancos Jim Butte, Bridger Jack Mesa, Johnny Benow Canyon, and Posey Canyon were named after Ute leaders residing in the county during roughly the same period.

One of the most prolific groups to provide names was the cowboys who ranged their herds through the canyons and over the mesas.[25] Many provided their own personal handles: (Al and Jim) Scorup Canyon, (John H.) Schafer Basin, (Arthur) Taylor Canyon, (Alonzo) Hatch Point, John's (Oliver) Canyon, (Zeke) Johnson Creek, (Donald) McIntyre Canyon, and (Jim and Parley) Butts' Point. Also of interest are the cattlemen's names for activities that occurred in these places. Bull Valley, located between the Confluence and Dark Canyon, is where Al and Jim Scorup temporarily separated male from female cattle; newborn animals went to Calf Canyon, not far from Beef Basin, the jumping-off point for the long drive to market. Elsewhere, Steer Gulch served a similar purpose.

Other livestock-related names include Hog Canyon near Hart's Point, Horse Canyon in Canyonlands, Mule Canyon west of Comb Ridge, Studhorse Peak (so named because a stallion reportedly stood there to watch his mares graze), Wild Cow Point, Mustang Mesa, Dead Horse Point, and Slickhorn Canyon. Cowboys frequented Tank Mesa because of the water stored in a rock formation. The League of Nations on Bluff Bench was so named because many individual ranchers ranged stock there; Sweet Alice Spring at the head of Dark Canyon was named because of the moaning wind that reminded a cowboy of a song about a woman named "sweet Alice Ben Bolt"; and Hurrah Ridge was the place where cowboys stormed down the hill with guns blazing for a dramatic entrance into Monticello. Bluff settlers named Milk Ranch Point for their dairying enterprise with cows at the summer pastures below the Bears Ears.

Men seeking mineral wealth and archaeological treasures also left their names behind. (Dobe) Brown's Hole, (James) Douglas Mesa, (John) Duckett Ridge, (Charlie) Fry Canyon, (E. L.) Goodridge, Camp (George W.) Jackson, (L. B.) Lockhart Basin, Kirk (Puckett) Basin, (Henry) Honaker Trail, (Charles H.) Spencer Camp, (Ernest) Mitchell Butte, and (James) Merrick Butte are all examples of sites honoring men of the mining industry. Archaeologists and their associates named some locations because of prominent features there; these include Ruin Canyon, Defiance House (because of a pictograph of three figures with shields and weapons), Poncho House (because of a mummy wrapped in a cotton blanket), and Anasazi Canyon. They also left behind their own names, including (C. C.) Graham (now called Bullet) Canyon in Grand Gulch and (Byron H.) Cummings Mesa near Navajo Mountain.

Settlers also took their turn at giving the landscape new names. With a heavy influx of Mormons, it is not surprising that Salvation Knoll, Angel Arch, Church Rock, Mormon Pasture, Little Zion, and Red Temple are found; but the Devil has his own canyon, with Hell's Kitchen, Babylon Pasture, and Devil's Lane to boot. Many of the places Mormons and gentiles (the Mormon name for non-Mormons) inhabited have followed the cycle of establishment, growth, and then either abandonment or full-fledged development. A surprisingly long list of settlements—some of which may have had only a handful of people at their height—have sprung from the soil of San Juan. Some of the less successful of this boom-and-bust breed are Gingerhill, Horsehead, Carlisle, Fry Canyon, Goodridge, Ucolo and Urado (derived from their proximity to the state's border with Colorado), Torb (named after Tomney, Oliphant, Roring, and Boyd, Blake, or Brubaker), Bug Point, East and West Summit, (A. E.) Lockerby, (Ira) Hatch (a trader to the Navajo), (Charles) Halls Crossing, and Boulder.

Some of the more permanent settlements include Bluff, Blanding, Monticello, Eastland, La Sal, Oljato, Red Mesa, Mexican Hat, Navajo Mountain, Montezuma Creek, and Aneth. The earliest of these towns was Bluff, founded in 1880 and named for the cliffs surrounding its floodplain. Monticello took the name (but not the usual pronunciation) of President Thomas Jefferson's home during a formal meeting at which the three suggested titles of North Montezuma, Antioch (of Bible fame), and (Francis A.) Hammond, a local Mormon stake president, were all rejected. Near Monticello lies Piute Springs, a popular camping point for wayfarers, while farther east of town sits Eastland.

Twenty-two miles south of Monticello is Blanding, whose name was changed in 1914 from Grayson, named after Nellie Grayson Lyman, the wife of Joseph Lyman, a brother of Walter C. Lyman, the founder of the town. Thomas W. Bicknell, a wealthy easterner, offered a thousand-volume library to any Utah town that would adopt his name. Grayson vied with Thurber (now Bicknell) for the prize; the two towns split the books and Grayson assumed Bicknell's wife's maiden name—Blanding. The people of Blanding were somewhat disgruntled to find many of the books dated and relatively useless (being legal tomes), but the name stuck.[26]

Blanding had other appellations, such as Edge of the Cedars, given to where the sagebrush plain changed to junipers, located roughly around where First North is today. This same wooded area, also known as "the Jungle," became home to a number of Mormon settlers, some of whom moved in from Mexico.[27] Four miles south of town is Shirttail Corner, named in 1917 when two cowboys, sleeping near the S-bend in the dirt road, awoke to the glare of the headlights of Zeke Johnson's Buick. Afraid that their herd would start to move, one of the men sprang out of bed in his shirt and underwear and set about quieting the livestock. The car did an about-face, leaving a trail of dust and a new name on the landscape.[28]

So goes the unending process of human interaction with the land. San Juan County is fortunate to have such a dramatic landscape and variety of people to claim as its own. Whether Anasazi, Ute, Navajo, Spanish, or Anglo, each made their contribution, as they collectively named and recorded what they believed to be significant at that time and place. They have bequeathed a legacy that is evident today as the names on the land speak of its rich heritage.

ENDNOTES

1. W. L. Rusho, *Everett Ruess: A Vagabond for Beauty* (Salt Lake City: Peregrine Smith Books, 1983), 160.

2. Leslie P. Arnberger, *Flowers of the Southwest Mountains* (Tucson: Southwest Parks and Monuments Association, 1982), 2–3.

3. For detailed information about the geologic history of San Juan County see Donald L. Baars, *The Colorado Plateau: A Geologic History* (Albuquerque: University of New Mexico Press, 1983); Stephen F. Mehls, "Canyonlands National Park, Arches National Park, and Natural Bridges National Monument Historic Resource Study," unpublished report to National Park Service, 1986 (located in the Utah State Historical Society Library, Salt Lake City, Utah), 24–28.

4. Robert J. Foster, *General Geology* (Columbus: Merrill Publishing Company, 1988), 124.

5. Richard D. Poll, Thomas G. Alexander, Eugene Campbell, and David

E. Miller, eds., *Utah's History* (Provo: Brigham Young University Press, 1978), 720.

6. Anonymous, "Information on Aneth and Bluff," n.d. (located under "Bluff" in Subject File, Utah State Historical Society Library, Salt Lake City, Utah), 1.

7. Donald Worster, *Nature's Economy: A History of Ecological Ideas* (New York: Cambridge University Press, 1977), 191.

8. For a handy reference to San Juan rock art and its interpretation see Winston B. Hurst and Joe Pachak, *Spirit Windows: Native American Rock Art of Southeastern Utah* (Blanding: Spirit Windows Project, 1989).

9. LaVan Martineau, *The Rocks Begin to Speak* (Las Vegas: KC Publications, 1973).

10. M. Jane Young, *Signs from the Ancestors: Zuni Cultural Symbolism and Perceptions of Rock Art* (Albuquerque: University of New Mexico Press, 1988), 231–32.

11. E. L. Hewett, "Field Notes 1906–09," unpublished typescript, photocopy on file, Edge of the Cedars Museum, Blanding, Utah; John W. Van Cott, *Utah Place Names* (Salt Lake City: University of Utah Press, 1990), 264.

12. Florence Begay interview with author, 29 April 1988, manuscript in possession of author; Ira S. Freeman, *A History of Montezuma County* (Boulder: Johnson Publishing Company, 1958), 166–67.

13. For a lengthy treatment of Navajo sacred geography in the county see Robert S. McPherson, *Sacred Land, Sacred View: Navajo Perceptions of the Four Corners Region* (Provo: Brigham Young University Press, 1992).

14. Washington Matthews, *Navaho Legends* (New York: Houghton, Mifflin and Company, 1897), 211; Charlie Blueeyes interview with author, 28 August 1988, manuscript in possession of author; Ernest Nelson, as cited in Karl Luckert, *Navajo Mountain and Rainbow Bridge Religion* (Flagstaff: Museum of Northern Arizona, 1977): 113, 117; see also 40, 24.

15. "General James Carleton to Headquarters Department of New Mexico, 21 March 1865," in U.S., Congress, War of the Rebellion, Series I, Vol. 48, Part I, 1232.

16. Blueeyes interview; Tallis Holiday interview with author, 3 November 1987, manuscript in possession of author; Florence Begay interview; Andy Natonabah, at the Navajo Studies Conference, Tsaile, Arizona, 3 November 1988.

17. Robert W. Young and William Morgan, *Navajo Historical Selections* (Lawrence, Kans.: Bureau of Indian Affairs, 1954), 38; Charles Kelly, "Aneth," Charles Kelly Papers, Special Collections, University of Utah, Salt

Lake City; Ben Whitehorse interview with author, 30 January 1991, manuscript in possession of author.

18. Billy Smiley interview with author, 14 January 1991; Margaret Weston interview with author, 13 February 1991; Jerry Begay interview with author, 16 January 1991; John Norton interview with author, 16 January 1991; Isabelle Lee interview with author, 13 February 1991; Jane Silas interview with author, 27 February 1991; manuscripts in possession of author.

19. Isabelle Lee interview.

20. Van Cott, *Utah Place Names,* 8, 256, 311, 292, and 3.

21. Tara Perkins Jones, "Geographical Landmarks in San Juan County: The Stories Behind the Names," *Blue Mountain Shadows* 7 (Winter 1990): 69; Anonymous, "Jailhouse Rock" (located in Subject File, Utah State Historical Society Library, Salt Lake City, Utah), 1.

22. At least one person, Melvin Young, takes issue with these stories, saying the hole is too deep, the climb too impractical for these types of activities. He adds, however, that his father, who homesteaded the 660 acre tract of land upon which "Jail Rock" sits, heard stories of Indians using the hole as a place to put prisoners. For further discussion, see "Letters to the Editor," *Blue Mountain Shadows* 8 (Summer 1991): ii–iii.

23. Herbert E. Bolton, *Pageant in the Wilderness: The Story of the Escalante Expedition to the Interior Basin, 1776* (Salt Lake City: Utah State Historical Society, 1951), 148, 151.

24. Albert R. Lyman to Maurice L. Howe, 4 March 1937 (located in "Place Names" file, Utah State Historical Society Library, Salt Lake City, Utah); Perkins et al., *Saga,* 70.

25. Many of the following names come from Van Cott's work, previously cited.

26. Van Cott, 256, 39; Walter R. Buss, "The Fascination of Utah Place Names," *Encyclia: The Journal of the Utah Academy of Sciences, Arts, and Letters* 63 (1986): 196.

27. William Riley Hurst interview with author, 23 January 1992; J. Glenn Shumway interview with author, 23 January 1992; manuscripts in possession of author.

28. "Breaking into the Limelight," *San Juan Blade,* 12 October 1917, 1.

2

Academics, Amateurs, and the Anasazi

AN OVERVIEW OF THE PREHISTORY OF SAN JUAN COUNTY

A hiker in San Juan County cannot move far beyond the paved streets and watered lawns of a town before encountering some type of prehistoric remains—potsherds, mounds, projectile points, or rock art. The Anasazi and other Native American groups who left these remains contributed to a fascinating, frequently studied aspect of heritage of the San Juan Basin of the Four Corners region. The literature relating to this interest is voluminous, generated by a hundred years of exploration, mapping, digging, and investigating. While new information surfaces continuously, enough is already known to piece together some of the puzzle of the origin of these people, how they lived, and what were some of their beliefs and concerns.

This chapter will provide a brief overview of thousands of years of Native American prehistory as well as some of the history of those who have studied this early human life in San Juan County. Many interesting connections outside of this specific area will not be discussed, such as the regional ties beyond the Anasazi epicenter of Mesa Verde; Meso-American trade and influence; and the florescence of other groups in Arizona, New Mexico, and the southeastern United

States during roughly the same time period. Instead, the primary focus will be on the early inhabitants of San Juan, their adaptation to ecological changes in the environment, and the subsequent migrations of these people, who created a rich heritage of adaptation, based upon the inherent need of survival.

The earliest group of Native Americans to enter San Juan County is called Paleo-Indians. They are believed to have hunted and gathered throughout the Southwest from about 11,500 to around 8,000 years ago.[1] The Paleo-Indian lived at the end of the last great Ice Age when temperatures in the region were cooler, lush vegetation abounded near rivers, and wooly mammoths, huge bison, and other large animals roamed the earth. Most of what is known about these people is learned from their scattered hunting and butchering sites as well as their dispersed spear points that range in location from Alaska to Tierra del Fuego and from Massachusetts to California.[2] Archaeologists have categorized these distinctive projectile points according to shape and age, the oldest being Clovis, followed by Folsom, and then Plano.

In San Juan County, Clovis points have been found in Montezuma Canyon, Lisbon Valley, and on Lime Ridge near Bluff. This latter find was in a campsite overlooking the confluence of Comb Wash and the San Juan River where Paleo-Indians could watch for mammoths and other animals attracted to the water below. Six point fragments, nine end-scrapers, and three notched tools lay amid numerous chips of agatized wood and quartzite spread over an area of approximately 100 square meters. This is the "first known Clovis site on the northern Colorado Plateau documented with chronologically distinctive artifacts."[3]

Archaeologists have found other types of Paleo-Indian projectile points in San Juan. For instance, Folsom points have appeared in Montezuma Canyon, Lime Ridge, Sweet Alice Spring, and near Moab, while Plano points have been located in Comb Wash, Hovenweep, and the Moab area.[4] One explanation suggests that the changes in spear point forms were caused by a shift in the type of game animals that were hunted due to a general warming trend and decrease in vegetation. This, in turn, helped bring about the subsequent extinction of first the mammoth and, later, large bison, camels, and horses. Whatever the reason, the day of the large-game hunter ended, making way for the next phase of Native American development, known as the Archaic Stage.

With the advent of warmer weather and a general drying trend, the entire Indian population in North America has been subdivided by archaeologists into two major categories—the Eastern and Desert Archaic traditions. The latter is found in the West and Southwest where the inhabitants of the region adapted to a more arid environment that featured precipitation and temperatures similar to those experienced today. Archaeologists have further subdivided the Archaic peoples into "traditions," "complexes," and "phases," based on local variations; but, for our purposes, these variations will not be delineated. In general, the Archaic Indians roamed San Juan County as hunters and gatherers who sought small to medium-sized game such as deer and bighorn sheep and became increasingly dependent upon such wild plant food as ricegrass, dropseed, and goosefoot.

Starting around 6000 B.C. and ending with the widespread adoption of maize (corn) horticulture in the Four Corners area by approximately 1000 B.C., these people depended on foraging for plants and animals still common to our contemporary environment.[5] Their tool kits included traps and snares, baskets and cordage, atlatl and dart, mano and metate, and a wide variety of stone knives and points. They probably lived in small bands of twenty-five to fifty kin-related people, migrated to different elevations seasonally to harvest plants and animals, and inhabited rock overhangs or other temporary shelters for protection from the elements.[6]

In San Juan County, Archaic campsites and artifacts range from Sand Dune and Dust Devil caves near Navajo Mountain in the west to the Montezuma Creek/Aneth area in the east, and from Monument Valley in the south to Lisbon Valley and the La Sal Mountains in the north. While remains from these campsites may be mixed with later cultural material and the projectile points and other artifacts carried off by a Navajo medicine man or an avid Anglo collector, one of the more ubiquitous indicators of the Archaic presence is often found nearby—rock art. The two most common styles of Archaic art—either pecked (petroglyph) or painted (pictograph) on rock surfaces—are called "Glen Canyon Linear" and "Barrier

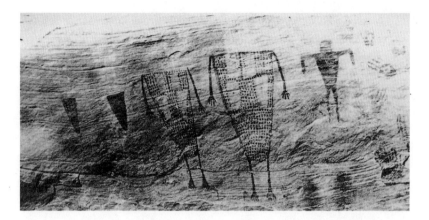

Pictographs from the Green Mask ruin in Grand Gulch. (National Museum of the American Indian, Heye Collection)

Canyon" styles. Examples of the first are found along the Colorado and San Juan rivers in Glen Canyon, near Sand Island, within Butler Wash, on Newspaper Rock, and in the Needles District of Canyonlands National Park. The figures are pecked into the rock and are characterized by long, box-shaped bodies with small, round heads in association with faces or masks, bighorn sheep, deer, snakes, zigzag lines and circles, and a "rake" motif among other abstract forms.

Although many of these petroglyphs are no taller than a meter, this is not the case with the art of the Barrier Canyon Style, whose painted figures often loom larger than life. These forms are also elongated and feature prominent bulging eyes, simple heads, and no arms or legs, giving them a ghostly appearance. Animals and geometric shapes are also present but are not as prominent as they are in other rock art styles. The Abajo Mountains appear to have served as the southern limit of this form of art in San Juan County; examples of it are found in Canyonlands National Park, along the Colorado River, and in the La Sal Mountains and Moab area.[7]

Archaeologists are unsure about the meaning of all the regional and different rock art styles. In some instances, the presence of Paleo-Indians overlapped that of the Archaic groups, although material remains leave little record of the relationship between contemporary factions. Rock art has helped to show that changes occurred, but what caused them is still unknown. Attempts at decoding the meaning of these pictures on canyon walls and prominent boulders have not found universal acceptance, though more sophisticated techniques of dating and analysis hold promise for the future.[8]

The next group, the most famous of all the prehistoric groups in the Four Corners region, was the Anasazi, whose homes and material remains are found throughout much of the San Juan landscape.[9] Anasazi culture, which started approximately 1000 B.C. and persists today in the historic pueblos, has been generally subdivided into two major categories—Basketmaker (early and late) and Pueblo (periods I, II, and III; examples of the later periods IV and V are not present in the county). This classification scheme is based on changes in technology, art styles, and subsistence patterns.

The relationship between the late Archaic and the early Basketmaker groups is unclear, some archaeologists dating the start of Anasazi culture earlier than 1000 B.C. By that date, the single most important element differentiating these two cultures was now present—corn (which would also serve as the basis for the entire Anasazi civilization). This plant had been domesticated thousands of years before in the highlands of Middle America, giving rise to important civilizations like the Olmec and other precursors of the Maya and Aztec groups. In the Four Corners area, where the scarcity of water, plant, and animal resources results in a harsher ecosystem and reduced carrying capacity of the land, the effects of corn providing a staple source of food were significant. Slowly the culture of the hunting and gathering population gave way to a sedentary lifestyle dependent on crops.

Early Basketmaker life flourished in, but was not limited to, the canyons of the lower San Juan and Colorado rivers. Shallow pithouses, circular storage pits, skillfully crafted baskets and sandals, feather and fur robes, and a greatly expanded tool kit characterized these early dwellers, who made their homes and stored their food in the rock overhangs of the canyon floors or amid the juniper and pinyon groves of the lands above. Archaeologists have excavated early pithouses at the head of Grand Gulch, in Castle Wash, around Hovenweep, near La Sal Junction, and in the Aneth area.

The lifestyle of the early Basketmaker Anasazi still reflected a partial orientation to the hunter-gatherer tradition in that the people seasonally moved to various sites to harvest their foods (although they returned to care for their crops), continued to use the atlatl for hunting, and foraged for wild plants as a supplement to their main diet of corn and squash. Bell-shaped underground chambers and shallow slab-lined storage cists located in protective rock alcoves held not only food supplies but also the Anasazi dead, some of whom met a violent death. The first of these burial sites was uncovered in 1893 and yielded more than ninety individuals with smashed skulls, bodies pierced by knives and spear points, and severed body parts. Subsequent excavations have provided supporting evidence that life was not always peaceful for these people.

The Late Basketmaker period started around A.D. 450 and is distinguished from the earlier phase by the introduction of pottery and the use of larger, more elaborate pithouses with internal storage facilities and antechambers located to the south or east of the main room. These houses may be found alone, in small clusters, or in groups of a dozen or more dwellings. Some of the larger communities, such as the one along Recapture Creek where the reservoir now stands, contain a large structure that may have served as a community meeting-house. Other Late Basketmaker sites are spread throughout San Juan County, including Milk Ranch Point, Comb Wash, White Mesa, Alkali Ridge, and Montezuma Canyon.

Another significant addition to the growing Anasazi culture was the introduction of beans to the economy. Not only did this plant provide the amino acid lysine for more efficient digestion of corn protein and a better regulated diet but it was a natural addition in the planting cycle. Corn, beans, and squash are known in some Native American groups as the "three sisters": corn served as the main bulk of the diet because of its better ability to be stored, while beans and squash added nutritional variety. Corn removed vital nitrogen and other minerals from the nutritionally weak soils of the Four Corners region, but beans replenished the soil as they sunk their nitrogen-fixing roots downward and twined their tendrils up the cornstalk. Squash plants provided shade for the cornstalks' roots and thus helped conserve water. Garden plots were either irrigated by a system of small check dams, were planted on the moistened floodplains of a river, or were nurtured by pot irrigation with water carried in jars to the plants. For over a thousand years this agricultural system supported a generally expanding Anasazi population base.

Other innovations that entered into the Late Basketmaker phase were the appearance of pottery—gray utility and black-on-white painted ware—as well as the introduction of the bow and arrow to replace the atlatl. Arrowheads supplanted dart points as one of the primary stone implements, facilitating the hunting of small and medium-sized game. At a site west of Bluff, archaeological remains reveal that rabbits, birds, and waterfowl were most of the meat eaten by the Anasazi there; deer and bighorn sheep made up only four percent of animal remains. Another innovation, occurring around A.D. 700, was the use of wooden stockade fences around village sites, presumably for protection.

Basketmaker rock art also underwent significant change. Characterized as being more "representational" and "realistic," the human forms have body decorations such as necklaces, arm bands, belts, and other items of clothing, while the faces appear masklike. Other objects painted and pecked in association with these figures include bags, crook staffs, atlatls, handprints, various animal forms, and full-face scalps with attached handles. Rock art specialists have suggested that some of these forms may represent shamanistic elements of spiritual "flight"; others see symbols of fertility; most agree that the figures are more personalized than the Archaic forms. Large panels and individual representations of this phase of Anasazi culture can be found in Butler Wash, along the San Juan River, on Cedar Mesa, near Hovenweep, and in the Navajo Mountain region, just to name a few.

A variation in Basketmaker/Pueblo I rock art found in Canyonlands National Park and near the La Sal Mountains is called the Abajo-La Sal Style. Apparently a result of the mixing of Anasazi culture with the Fremont culture to the north, this rock art type features broad-shouldered humans with long slender necks and fringed and horned headdresses. There are also flute players juxtaposed with a line of figures holding hands. Rock art specialists have linked other elements in these panels with specific Fremont and Anasazi imagery.[10]

By A.D. 750 the Anasazi had reached the next stage of develop-

Anasazi artifacts from the Butler Wash-Allen Canyon area collected in the 1890s by Charles Lang, a Bluff resident. (Courtesy Ryerson Collection, Field Museum of Natural History)

ment, that of Pueblo I. As the name suggests, there were some significant changes in their dwellings, though elements from earlier phases persisted. For instance, the Anasazi now built their homes above ground in connected, rectangular blocks of rooms, using rocks and jacal (a framework of woven saplings and sticks packed with mud) for construction materials. One or more deep pit houses have been found in each of the building clusters and may have served a ceremonial function. These rooms were equipped with a ventilator shaft that brought in fresh air, deflected it around an upright stone placed between the shaft and the firepit, and then evacuated the smoke by the entryway in the roof, a technique utilized by the Anasazi for the remainder of their stay in the Four Corners region. In Pueblo II times this structure became the common kiva, which will be discussed later.

Generally, Pueblo I communities were located along major drainages at elevations of 6,000 feet or higher. Evidence of prolonged drought and a warming trend suggest that the Anasazi moved to areas where the growing season and water were adequate. Village clusters are found on Alkali Ridge, Elk Ridge, Blanding, Bluff, Montezuma Creek, Aneth, McElmo Canyon, Ismay, and Recapture, South Cottonwood, Butler, and Comb washes.

An important innovation of this time, harkening back to the end of the Late Basketmaker period is the introduction of thin-walled, finely crafted pottery classified as Abajo Red-on-Orange and Bluff Black-on-Orange, with continuing variations of black-on-white wares. Many other pottery classifications are found beyond the boundaries of San Juan County, the two strongest impulses coming from Mesa Verde in Colorado and Chaco Canyon in New Mexico. However, based on the identification of clay-types and patterns, archaeologists suggest that a major manufacturing site for this type of pottery was located between Cottonwood Wash and Montezuma Canyon.

The Pueblo II phase started about A.D. 900 and lasted for the next 250 years. A change in climate provided an increase in precipitation, higher water tables that affected springs and seeps, and temperatures conducive to agriculture in most parts of the county. The Anasazi reacted by moving from a pattern of clustering populations in strategic locations to a far-ranging decentralization. Satellite work-and-living sites fanned out from the larger concentrations of people. At no previous time had there been as many people spread over so much of the land.

An apparent link that unified different areas is evidenced by a new phenomenon—clearly constructed roads with associated specialized building sites. The most dramatic examples of road activity are found in Chaco Canyon, New Mexico. Several of the Anasazi's roads converge on "great houses" (multistory room blocks) and great kivas—large, semisubterranean ceremonial chambers—whose roofs were supported by pillars and spanned by long-beam construction. Unlike the smaller kivas found with most habitation sites, the great kiva had a specialized ritual function not totally understood by Native Americans and researchers today. These structures were located where significant concentrations of people lived and worshipped, with satellite communities on the periphery. Great kiva/great house sites in San Juan County are located in Montezuma

Canyon, Bluff, Cottonwood and Comb washes, the Edge of the Cedars, and in the Natural Bridges/Cedar Mesa area.

The Anasazi road system, though faint and in some areas badly marred by historic activity, is spread throughout the canyons and washes just mentioned. The roads are designed for foot travel, generally in a straight line either over or cut through various land features. The width of the roads is from fifteen to forty feet, steps to surmount rock faces have been pecked in the stone, and horseshoe-shaped structures from twelve to twenty-five feet in diameter have been found at the top or bottom of some steep slopes or cliffs. Explanations of the roads' economic, religious, and social importance, and even the dates of construction are still unclear and await the gathering of further information.[11]

Construction of smaller sites also underwent changes. Homes, now built of stone masonry instead of jacal, were above ground, while rock-and-mud storage granaries perched high in cliff recesses. Underground chambers, first introduced in Basketmaker times, now served as kivas, with one associated with each household. A typical structure followed the Mesa Verde pattern of a rounded chamber with a shaft-deflector-fire pit configuration, a small hole (sipapu) representing a place of emergence from the worlds below, and a three-foot-high bench that encircled most of the room. Upon this bench stood three-foot-high pilasters that supported a cribbed roof through which a ladder extended to the world above.

The final stage of Anasazi occupation, Pueblo III, in San Juan County occurred between about A.D. 1150 and 1300. Ruins in the Hovenweep/Cajon Mesa area, Allen Canyon, Westwater, Montezuma Creek, and the neighboring Yellow Jacket complex in Colorado all exemplify this phase. Although extensive remains of this period have not been excavated within the county, the neighboring dramatic cliff dwellings of Mesa Verde, Betatakin, and Keet Seel offer a good picture of the buildings and lifestyle of this era. The general pattern of events is characterized as a shrinking or gathering of the dispersed communities into a series of larger villages in areas that were more defensible. Large, communal plazas, tower clusters around springs at the heads of canyons, less carefully crafted building techniques, evidence of decreased regional trade relations, and the introduction of

This Pueblo III Anasazi ruin was inhabited during the A.D. 1200s but still has well-preserved jacal and masonry walls. (Courtesy Daniel Spotsky, Edge of the Cedars Museum)

the kachina cult prevalent during the historic period among the pueblo peoples are all indications that Anasazi society was undergoing rapid and stressful change.

Archaeologists argue about what caused these cultural shifts and the subsequent abandonment of the area by the Anasazi. Some people place the cause on environmental factors such as prolonged drought, cooler temperatures, arroyo cutting, and depleted soils. Others suggest that the area was invaded by nomadic hunters and gatherers, precursors of the historic Ute, Paiute, and Navajo peoples. Pueblo mythology points to internal strife and the religious need to purify the group through migration and pilgrimage to a new land in the south. No single explanation satisfactorily answers all of the questions, but by A.D. 1300 the Anasazi had left the San Juan drainage and moved to their pueblo homes along the Rio Grande (Eastern Pueblos) and to the areas where the Acoma, Zuni, and Hopi villages (Western Pueblos) now stand.

Besides their ruins, artifacts, and rock art, the Anasazi left behind much for us to ponder. Starting with the historic tribes and ending with twentieth-century archaeological investigation, a fascination with the Anasazi persists. Some of these beliefs are fairly simple and to the point; others are elaborate and complex. For instance, the Utes' perception of the Anasazi is not clearly defined other than an avoidance of some Anasazi sites and respect for the dead, whereas the Navajos present a fully developed series of stories with variations and explanations to account for who these people were and what happened to them.[12] Even the name, "'anaasazi," comes from the Navajo and is interpreted as "ancestral aliens or enemies."

According to tradition, Navajo relations with the Anasazi started in the mythological worlds below this one. They shared a friendship that included the Anasazi giving the Navajo corn following the two groups' emergence into this world. One story tells that after a dispute the two peoples agreed to break an ear of corn in half, and the Navajos were allowed to choose between the two pieces. Coyote, the trickster, selected the tip of corn and ran away, leaving the fuller stem behind, "and this is the reason the Pueblo Indians have today better crops than the Navahoes. But the Pueblos had become alarmed at the threats and angry language of their neighbors and moved away from them, and this is why the Navahoes and Pueblos now live apart from one another."[13]

Some Navajo clans such as the Salt, Towering House, and the Water's Edge clans, well-represented in San Juan County, had relations with the Anasazi following the separation of the two groups. In general, the stories indicate friction and portray the Navajos as an impoverished, downtrodden people enslaved by the Anasazi but liberated through the help of the holy beings. A number of these stories center around sites in Chaco Canyon, but one local version told by Manuelito, a famous Navajo leader born five miles south of the Bears Ears, tells of a man who came from the east, appearing to "rise out of where the sky and earth join together. . . . When he came amongst the Dine, he saw how they were being treated by the people who dwelt in the stone houses in the cliffs north of the San Juan River and he was very much displeased."[14] The stranger sent the Navajos to instruct the Anasazi to change their ways, but they ignored this advice. He then told the Navajos to prepare a feast along the southern banks of the San Juan and Little Colorado rivers, invite the Anasazi to it on an appointed day, and await their destruction. All went as planned. The man separated the waters so that the Anasazi could cross with dry feet, waited until they were midstream, and then closed the waters over them, turning them into fish. Those who had remained in their dwellings were struck with lockjaw and paralysis and died within four days.

Other stories tell of how the Anasazi were killed by a strong wind that sucked the air out of their lungs, a great fire that swept through the canyons and left black streaks (desert varnish) on the rocks and near the dwellings, an ice storm that crushed the people and drove their homes into the ground, or a flood that destroyed everything in its path. All of these different forms of destruction came about because the Anasazi had offended the gods by abusing the supernatural powers given to them. Older Navajos today still caution their youth against this type of misconduct, warning that living in harmony and respect with the natural surroundings will prevent a similar fate.

The sites left by the Anasazi are considered to hold strong supernatural powers because of the events that occurred and the spirits that still reside there. Many Navajos avoid these places, but medicine men who know how to work with the powers use them to heal, protect, and bless those in need. Part of a ruin may become a place of worship, old arrowheads are used in medicine bundles for healing and protection, ancient potsherds are crushed for temper in newly formed pottery, replicas of Anasazi gourds and rattles are shaken during ceremonies, and a piece of Anasazi bone may be used in the Enemyway ritual to exorcise evil from a patient. None of this can be done without the proper ritual knowledge, which may be as simple as a prayer or as complex as a lengthy ceremony.

Navajo beliefs concerning the Anasazi are centered within the realms of religious teaching and respect. To walk on a path used by the Anasazi, to place one's hand in a pictograph, or to see an ancient bone or scalp may have an adverse effect that requires a supernatural cure. Because of these beliefs, many of the ruins and artifacts had been left substantially untouched until the coming of white men into

San Juan County. What followed, commencing in the late nineteenth century, was a veritable ransacking, by today's standards, of the ruins and remains. Considerable destruction occurred in the name of preservation.

The earliest Anglo-American investigations of the Anasazi occurred with travelers passing through San Juan County for various reasons—exploration, government surveys, and, by the late nineteenth century, the cataloging of remnants of the "dying race" of American Indians. Thus, the William Huntington expedition (1854), the J. N. Macomb/J. S. Newberry report (1859), John W. Powell's records (1869 and 1871), and writings of William H. Jackson as part of the Hayden surveys (1874, 1875, and 1876) all reported ruins and noted their locations. Scientific accuracy reflected the current but sometimes misinformed beliefs of the time, but the reports and spurred interest.

Beginning about 1880 there was also a growing population of settlers from central and southwestern Utah and southwestern Colorado who ventured into the isolated San Juan country looking for homes. Joining them were cattle companies that sought out grass and water in the canyons and plateaus once inhabited by the Anasazi. A more detailed discussion of these different groups will be found in later chapters, but the net result of their incursion into the area was to increase the deterioration of the ancient sites.

The 1890s saw a marked increase in individual and group exploration of Anasazi ruins. A growing awareness of the rich archaeological treasures located in the Four Corners area, the search for unique elements of American heritage for national exhibits such as the Columbian Exposition (1893), the government's laissez-faire approach towards private enterprise in the avid pursuit of wealth, and the availability of investment capital combined to encourage people to ransack the ruins for items that could be exported for sale or show. What had started in Mesa Verde was now spreading to the isolated canyons of San Juan.

The most famous of these exploring entrepreneurs were the Wetherill brothers—Richard, John, Win, Al, Clayton, and Benjamin—who are credited with discovering Cliff Palace in Mesa Verde, excavating in the ruins of Chaco Canyon, and exploring as far

In 1893 an expedition led by Richard Wetherill into the Cottonwood Wash drainage discovered at this site the remains of ninety-seven men, women, and children who had been massacred during the Basketmaker period. (Courtesy Frank McNitt Collection, New Mexico State Archives)

west as the Navajo Mountain area. The Wetherills were also the first to use the title of "basket maker," based on their observations of the earlier Anasazi culture.[15] In San Juan County, Richard Wetherill led an expedition into Grand Gulch in 1893, though in the two preceding years other explorers had photographed and dug in some of the ruins there. The Wetherills conducted subsequent digs each year from 1895 through 1897. From these trips came artifacts that went on display in Colorado, at the Chicago World's Fair, and in Pennsylvania, New York, and Europe. Some documentation regarding what was found and where it went does exist, but much of the archaeological record was inadvertently destroyed.

Expeditions into San Juan County became increasingly popular. Some of the more important excursions during the 1890s included those headed by Don Maguire representing the State of Utah in the World's Fair Commission, by Reverend C. H. Green and Charles

McLoyd from Durango, and by Warren K. Moorhead, an archaeologist from Ohio. One well-documented account, published for a more general reading audience, is that of the Illustrated American Exploring Expedition's travels from southwestern Colorado into southeastern Utah, recorded in *The Illustrated American*. The members of the expedition came from Ohio to explore, map, and sketch the ruins along the San Juan River and its tributaries. Although their stated goal was impossible to fulfill given the number of sites and vast territory involved, they did succeed in providing accurate information and sketches of some of the sites and were the first to map and describe part of the Hovenweep ruins.[16]

The beginning of the 1900s saw the development of professional archaeology and the growth of a more ethical, scientific approach to studying the past. This featured better research techniques and documentation, though by today's standards there was still much left to be desired. A number of famous men made their way to the ruins of San Juan County to begin their careers in archaeology. Some later went elsewhere (such as Sylvanus Morley, who studied the Maya in Central America), but others remained and became famous for their work in the American Southwest. Scholars like Alfred V. Kidder, T. Mitchell Prudden, Edgar L. Hewitt, Jesse Nusbaum, Neil Judd, John Brew, and Byron Cummings all worked on the ruins in San Juan County and helped provide a better understanding of the Anasazi.[17]

Byron Cummings, though perhaps not as thorough as some of the other archaeologists, has become an important figure in the county. He began his work in 1906 and returned the next four summers, as his teaching duties at the University of Utah allowed. Cummings directed the excavation of a large Pueblo I complex on Alkali Ridge but is given even more credit for the official discovery of Rainbow Bridge in 1909. Perhaps his greatest contribution was in the training of many good, young archaeologists who would return to San Juan in years to come.

In 1929 Charles Bernheimer, affiliated with the American Museum of Natural History in New York, led a group that included John Wetherill and Earl Morris, a famous southwestern archaeologist. They traveled into Butler and Comb washes, camped in Arch Canyon, and roamed through Kane and Grand gulches and beyond.

Byron Cummings, founder of the archaeology program at the University of Utah, standing outside of John and Louisa Wetherill's Oljato trading post in 1909. (Special Collections, University of Utah Library)

Their field notes indicate that they investigated both Basketmaker and Pueblo sites, took wood samples for tree-ring dating, found what they believed to be a calendar and a weaving loom, and recorded numerous burial sites with associated artifacts. Their writings also contain excellent information about the land and people of San Juan County.[18]

Still other surveys followed, including the Rainbow Bridge-Monument Valley expeditions of the 1930s, and others in Glen Canyon, Natural Bridges, Alkali Ridge, and Monument Canyon. From the 1940s through 1955, however, there was a decrease in archaeological work on Anasazi sites with no accompanying increase in quality. In summarizing this era of investigation (1900 to 1955), Paul Nickens, a professional archaeologist, believes that in spite of the at times almost feverish activity, the end results were minimal. "Indeed, in a majority of the cases, little meaningful published information resulted, and often, simply adding to museum collections was viewed as being sufficient to justify a given expedition."[19]

By the mid-1950s the federal government had become increasingly responsive to the calls for protecting cultural resources and making information more accessible to the public. What this meant in economic terms was that before a site could be permanently destroyed by constructing a new road or building, establishing an oil pad, creating a reservoir, or damming a river, an extensive archaeological research study needed to be launched at taxpayers' expense. The Glen Canyon Dam project provides a dramatic example of the extent of this type of study.

Starting in 1957, an eight-year survey of prehistoric and historic sites was conducted along the Colorado and lower part of the San Juan rivers because of the anticipated reservoir waters that would be backed up behind the Glen Canyon Dam at Page, Arizona. The University of Utah assumed responsibility for the study along the Colorado River and Northern Arizona University for a study on the San Juan. This geographical area had appeared to be a meeting place between the Mesa Verde and Kayenta Anasazi groups, and so evidence of cultural relationships between the two groups was a primary concern. Other studies looked at the Fremont culture as well as Navajo, Paiute, Hopi, and white occupation and use of the area. Mounds of information and dozens of publications resulted, some of which outlined cultural phases, social organization, and demographic information about the San Juan Anasazi.[20]

The project, however, had been both time-consuming and expensive. In a county with so many ruins, this type of site mitigation—even on a greatly reduced scale—appeared to many residents to be more of a hindrance than a help. Calvin Black, a county commissioner, snagged front-page headlines in another instance charging the Utah State Division of History with "gross irresponsibility, waste of taxpayers' money in the name of archaeological salvage, and improper use of public vehicles." He claimed that "the archaeologists have forced the expenditure [waste] of up to a million dollars" to mitigate ruins on the proposed site of the Energy Fuels uranium-processing plant.[21] Although his charges were refuted by those involved, Black's prominent and oft-heard voice spoke for many local people who concurred.

Indeed, since the passing of the Antiquities Act of 1906, there have been some who have prided themselves in flouting the law by digging "Mokis" and selling the fruits of their labors as a supplement to their income, almost as if it were a family tradition. Often the only ones to feel alarm at this black-market trade were the scholars who saw the irreplaceable past being vandalized. Julian H. Steward, head of the Department of Anthropology and director of the museum at the University of Utah, in 1931 decried what he saw, claiming that the people of Utah were being deprived of "archaeological treasures of inestimable value . . . [only] one one-thousandth [of which] has found its way to Utah museums," and the rest of which had been taken by people from out of state.[22] No one seemed to listen.

Sixty years later, the same problem still exists. Rock art panels have been vandalized, isolated sites have been illegally dug, and in at least one instance part of a ruin under excavation was ransacked right under the noses of the archaeologists involved when pot hunters visited a site in Montezuma Canyon one weekend. They did not find much of value but obliterated a carefully preserved strata of floor deposits during their search.[23]

There are an estimated 100,000 Anasazi sites in San Juan County, ninety percent of which either have been disturbed or obliterated through this type of illegal activity.[24] Even though the Archaeological Resources Protection Act of 1979 established stiff penalties of as much as five years in jail and fines of up to $100,000 for second offenders, the looters still find it profitable enough to take the risk. Some artifacts can sell for as much as $30,000 to a wealthy black-market client. In a county where unemployment and poverty are consistently among the highest in the state, such figures serve as a strong enticement.

The federal government in the form of the Bureau of Land Management, National Park Service, National Forest Service, and special task forces prowls the ruins looking for violators, but with limited success. Vast distances, two-way radios, night operations, and the criminals' years of experience in evading capture have frustrated the efforts of law-enforcement officers to capture the vandals. In May 1986 a state and federal task force raided some of the homes of suspected poachers and seized artifacts, but authorities had a difficult time proving that what had been taken did not come from private land. The action drew even sharper divisions between the local people and "outsiders," with some suggesting, tongue-in-cheek, that the county secede from the union. Although the dust from that particular incident has settled, many residents still feel distrust and frustration over continuing government regulation of what they consider to be a county resource.

There has never been more interest about the Anasazi than there is now. Tourists come in droves to roam among the ruins and ponder the meaning of rock art; archaeologists methodically excavate sites and wrestle with the mounds of paperwork generated from painstaking research; Navajos use the artifacts in ceremonies and point to the Anasazi's destruction as a lesson to the younger generation to keep traditional values alive and strong; local people with one breath express admiration for the Anasazi but in the next breath complain about the hindrance that the ruins create in building the infrastructure of a modern economy. Although these early inhabitants could not have had an inkling of the furor they would create, they have succeeded in providing a fascinating aspect to the heritage of San Juan.

ENDNOTES

1. Literature concerning Paleo-Indians in the Four Corners region is scattered throughout archaeological reports and a few published sources for the lay reader. The following list is composed of some of the more easily accessible texts that cover general prehistory through to the Anasazi. See John C. McGregor, *Southwestern Archaeology* (Urbana: University of Illinois Press, 1965); E. Steve Cassells, *The Archaeology of Colorado* (Boulder: Johnson Books, 1983); Linda S. Cordell, *Prehistory of the Southwest* (New York: Academic Press, 1984); Sally J. Cole, *Legacy on Stone: Rock Art of the Colorado Plateau and Four Corners Region* (Boulder: Johnson Books, 1990);

and *Handbook of North American Indians—Southwest,* Volume 9, ed. Alfonso Ortiz (Washington, D.C.: Smithsonian Institution, 1979).

2. Arrell Morgan Gibson, *The American Indian: Prehistory to the Present* (Lexington, Mass.: D.C. Heath and Company, 1980), 18–20.

3. William E. Davis, "The Lime Ridge Clovis Site," *Utah Archaeology— 1989* (Salt Lake City: Utah Statewide Archaeological Society, 1989), 66–76.

4. Winston Hurst, "The Prehistoric Peoples of San Juan County, Utah," in *San Juan County, Utah—People, Resources and History,* ed. Allan Kent Powell (Salt Lake City: Utah State Historical Society, 1983), 23.

5. Cassells, *Archaeology of Colorado,* 113.

6. Paul R. Nickens, "A Summary of the Prehistory of Southeastern Utah," *Contributions to the Prehistory of Southeastern Utah* (Salt Lake City: Bureau of Land Management, 1982), 10–12.

7. Cole, *Legacy on Stone,* 60–79; Winston B. Hurst and Joe Pachak, *Spirit Windows—Native American Rock Art of Southeastern Utah* (Blanding: Edge of the Cedars Museum, 1992), 3–4.

8. For an interesting attempt at uncovering the meaning of rock art symbols see M. Jane Young, *Signs from the Ancestors—Zuni Cultural Symbolism and Perceptions of Rock Art* (Albuquerque: University of New Mexico Press, 1988).

9. The following discussion of both the Basketmaker and Pueblo phases of Anasazi archaeology is drawn heavily from the writings of Winston Hurst, whose many years of research in San Juan County has centered on these people. Mr. Hurst has graciously allowed me to liberally refer to his work without having to refer to all of the citations that he has so painstakingly made in his own publications. For a far more detailed and scholarly treatment of this topic see Mark C. Bond, William E. Davis, Winston B. Hurst, and Deborah A. Westfall, *Cultural Resource Inventory and Evaluative Testing Along SR-262, Utah-Colorado State Line to Montezuma Creek, Navajo Nation Lands, San Juan County, Utah* (Bluff: Abajo Archaeology, September 1992), 11–74; for a more general overview of San Juan prehistory see Hurst, "Prehistoric Peoples . . . ," previously cited. Unless otherwise noted, the following information is derived from these two sources.

10. Cole, *Legacy on Stone,* 109–30, 151–64.

11. For more information see Winston B. Hurst, Owen Severance, and Dale Davidson, "Uncle Albert's Ancient Roads—Anasazi Formal Trails in Southeastern Utah," *Blue Mountain Shadows* 12 (Summer 1993): 2–9; for a general overview and discussion of the roads' significance, see Kathryn Gabriel, *Roads to Center Place—A Culture Atlas of Chaco Canyon and the Anasazi* (Boulder: Johnson Books, 1991).

12. For a more complete account of the Navajo view of the Anasazi, see

Robert S. McPherson, *Sacred Land, Sacred View—Navajo Perceptions of the Four Corners Region* (Provo: Brigham Young University Press, 1992).

13. Berard Haile, recorder, *The Upward Moving and Emergence Way: The Gishin Biye' Version* (Lincoln: University of Nebraska Press, 1981), 78.

14. "The Third Arizona Expedition," Don Maguire Papers, Utah State Historical Society, Salt Lake City, Utah, 166–69.

15. See Frank McNitt, *Richard Wetherill: Anasazi* (Albuquerque: University of New Mexico Press, 1957); Frances Gillmor and Louisa Wade Wetherill, *Traders to the Navajo: The Story of the Wetherills of Kayenta* (Albuquerque: University of New Mexico Press, 1953); and Maurine S. Fletcher, ed., *The Wetherills of the Mesa Verde: The Autobiography of Benjamin Alfred Wetherill* (Norman: University of Oklahoma Press, 1977).

16. "In Search of a Lost Race," *The Illustrated American,* serial, 2 April to 13 August 1892.

17. For an excellent overview of the archaeologists who worked in the San Juan area during the twentieth century see Paul R. Nickens and Anthony L. Klesert, *Cultural Resources Overview for BLM Lands in South San Juan County, Utah,* Volume I (Montrose, Colo.: Centuries Research, 1982), 46–67.

18. Charles Bernheimer, "Field Notes of the 1929 Expedition," unpublished manuscript, Utah State Historical Society, Salt Lake City, Utah, 1–31.

19. Nickens and Klesert, *Cultural Resources Overview*, 58.

20. Ibid., 60–61.

21. "Commissioner Charges Archaeology 'Rip-off,'" *San Juan Record,* 1 May 1980, 1.

22. "Utah Being Robbed of Archaeological Treasures," Moab *Times-Independent*, 16 April 1931, 1.

23. "Vandals Destroy Pictograph Panel at Arches," *San Juan Record,* 8 May 1980, 1; "Vandals Invade Indian Diggings," *San Juan Record*, 31 July 1969, 1.

24. Carol Ann Bassett, "The Culture Thieves," *Science* 249 (July/August, 1986): 24.

3

Utes, Paiutes, and Navajos Come to San Juan

SETTING THE FOUNDATION, A.D. 1100 TO 1880

According to the 1990 U.S. census, over half the population of San Juan County is now Native American. Their burgeoning numbers indicate not only better health care, greater statistical accuracy, and more abundant personal resources but also older, historic trends of mobility and expansion. Indeed, in a little more than one hundred years, there have been four major additions of land to the Navajo Reservation in San Juan County. This chapter is concerned with the entrance into the county of the three historic tribes—Ute, Paiute, and Navajo—and some of the early reports of their activity in this area until around 1880, at which time major Anglo-American expansion in the region began.

Close to the time of Anasazi abandonment of the Four Corners region (roughly the year 1300), there arrived a new group of Native Americans who were Numic speakers. Where these Native Americans came from is still open to anthropological debate. Most scholars agree that the initial homeland of Uto-Aztecan speakers was in the area of Death Valley in southern California. Approximately 3,000 to 5,000 years ago this large Native American language family started to subdivide into nine smaller groups. Numic speakers composed one of these divisions, which includes today's Utes and Paiutes. Fanning out from southern California, they moved in a northeasterly direction but remained on the edge of the Great Basin until about 1,000 years ago, when they moved rapidly into the Basin and eventually onto the Colorado Plateau. Their language became increasingly diversified as groups split from each other, one anthropologist suggesting that the Utes separated from Southern Paiutes 400 years ago as they settled in the Four Corners region.[1]

Today, the two languages are still mutually intelligible. Southern Utes and Southern Paiutes recognize dialectical differences in speech, one Ute informant saying that the Paiutes' language is more "clipped" or abbreviated, and that the Paiutes accused the Utes of "talking fancy." This is part of a general pattern: the Southern Paiutes consider the Utes to be their "fancy" cousins, who went off to the plains and learned "everything."[2]

The archaeological and ethnographic record of Ute and Paiute entrance into the Four Corners area is vague. Campsites and material remains are difficult to find and differentiate from those of previous people because of the small amount of pottery, nondescript dwellings, and the limited technology of a hunting-and-gathering lifestyle. The waters are further muddied by the Utes' practice of utilizing other peoples' camps and material remains.[3] Robert Euler, a noted Paiute historian, suggests that there were two migrations of Numic speakers into Nevada and Utah. The first one took place around A.D. 1, the second around A.D. 1150—this last movement possibly causing the resident Anasazi to withdraw into larger, more defensible sites. At this same time, Paiute culture became very stable, with few changes in lifestyle and technology until well into the late nineteenth century.[4] Some archaeologists, however, place the date of entry later—during the early to late 1300s.[5]

The San Juan Band Paiute and Southern Utes were part of this eastward movement that entered San Juan County. The effect it had on the Anasazi is questionable, but some authors suggest that the sudden expansion of Numic speakers into the Great Basin and onto the Colorado Plateau occurred because of the severe droughts in what is now the western United States during the twelfth and thirteenth centuries. Anthropologists believe this could have caused first relocation within and then evacuation of these areas by the agriculturally oriented Anasazi. Numic speakers, better adapted to surviving the rigors of a desert environment, occupied the areas left by the migrating Fremont and Anasazi cultures.[6] In support of this theory, it is interesting to note that the Anasazi abandoned a well-developed community at Navajo Mountain by A.D. 1270, suggesting not that the Paiutes forced a withdrawal but that they could have been present when it occurred.[7]

The way that Southern Utes and Paiutes view the Anasazi helps to partially support this theory. They call the Anasazi the "muukwitsi," meaning the dead, and believe that the dead, their spirits, and spiders are interrelated. This explains why spiders often haunt the ruins. Utes use a similar name to refer to the Hopi, "Moqui" (pronounced Mokwi, not Moki)—a term applied only to this Pueblo group, and one which seems to have entered general usage following the Dominguez-Escalante expedition, which depended heavily upon Numic speakers for guides. According to some informants, there was never any Ute conflict with the Anasazi, and the two groups developed a shared language that could be somewhat understood. The modern Utes also tell how their forebears would see their neighbors only sporadically because the Anasazi appeared "like phantoms and would be seen at a distance or be heard to scream, but would disappear into the pinyon when a Ute approached."[8]

Early white travelers recorded different stories from various sources. One tells of how the Hopi lived a peaceful life until "about a thousand years ago," when the ancestors of the Utes arrived to prey on their farms and attack them. Once the invaders came to stay, the Hopi abandoned their defensive positions high in the cliffs and "stole away during the night [to] wander across the cheerless uplands." Their pursuers fought them for "one long month," until "the hollows of the rocks filled to the brim with the mingled blood of conquerors and conquered, and red veins of it ran down into the canyon."[9] One of these battles was said to have occurred near Battle Rock in McElmo Canyon, Colorado, near the San Juan County boundary.[10] The Hopis retreated south with their families and took up defensive positions on the three mesas where they live today. In support of this

story, some archaeologists suggest that the Anasazi fortified themselves in large defensible cities for protection from Numic-speaking
invaders—the Utes and Paiutes—who eventually drove the
puebloans out by disrupting and preventing their farming activity.[11]

Other scholars, however, argue that the Utes and Paiutes were not
even in the region at this time. One theory of migratory trends places
Numic speakers in southwestern Utah 430 years ago and in southeastern Utah and southwestern Colorado 370 years ago. These people
began moving along the Rio Grande 330 years ago and out onto the
midwestern Plains—their easternmost expansion—300 years ago.[12]
All of these dates are tentative, but few people would argue with the
point that by at least the late 1500s, the Utes and Paiutes of San Juan
County were in their general historic setting.

By the early 1600s, Spanish reports indicated that there were Utes
living in northwestern Arizona, north of the Colorado and San Juan
rivers, and in eastern Colorado.[13] Early accounts do not provide exact
distinctions between different Numic speakers, the Utes, Paiutes, and
Chemehuevi all being designated as "Yutas." Today, however, there is
a clearer understanding of the three bands that compose the
Southern Utes. Starting from the east there were the Muache, living
in the Denver area; the Capote in the Sangre de Cristo Mountains of
Colorado and south to Taos, New Mexico; and the Weenuche, who
ranged from the Dolores River in the east to the Colorado River in
the north, and west and south to the San Juan River.[14] All of these
groups were highly mobile and visited far into the Great Basin,
throughout the Colorado Plateau, and onto the Great Plains.
Although their name has a variety of spellings—Wimonuntci,
Weminutc, Guibisnuches, Guiguimuches, Wamenuches, and
Weeminuche among others—the Weenuche Utes were the band of
Southern Utes that inhabited (and continue to inhabit) San Juan
County.[15]

The second group of Numics in the county is the San Juan Band
Paiute. Historically, they have been a little-known segment of an
already amorphous group. Southern Paiute territory centered in
southwestern Utah and Nevada, with its easternmost extension pushing into the Monument Valley region of the Utah-Arizona border.
Sixteen identifiable bands compose the Paiute tribe, with the San

Juan being the only group to occupy lands south and east of the Colorado River. Perhaps this is why their name has been translated as "people being over on the opposite side," or as the "San Juan River People."[16]

William Palmer, during his interviews with Paiutes around Cedar City in 1928, found only a slight knowledge of the Paiutes living in southeastern Utah, his informants indicating that these people were called "Nau-wana-tats which to the Pahutes means fighters or wrestlers. If there is a tribe of this name, the Indians interviewed think they are in the San Juan Country."[17] This vagueness underscores the fact that there was little cohesion between certain bands and that the area of southeastern Utah was peripheral to major Paiute activity. The San Juan Band may be subdivided into the Tatsiwinunts, who ranged over the area between Tuba City and Navajo Creek, and the Kai-boka-dot-tawip-nunts in the Navajo Mountain area.[18]

The major distinction between the Utes and Paiutes living in this area was cultural, not linguistic, and was affected by the environment and accompanying technology. Paiutes operated in family groups and, when resources allowed, came together as bands. They hunted and gathered in an austere desert land, had no central chieftain, no collective religious practices, and no common goal (other than survival) to unite the different groups. The Utes started from similar cultural roots, but with the acquisition of the horse in the mid-1600s, began to adopt elements of Plains Indian culture, beginning with those groups farthest east. The Weenuche, farthest west of the Utes, were the last to adopt buffalo-hunting, the sun dance, and other recent practices of their relatives.

Another group to arrive in San Juan County during prehistoric times was the Navajo. Unlike the Utes and Paiutes, the Navajos spoke a different language—Athabascan—and left more distinctive material remains. There is a large body of literature that argues origins and chronological sequence. A short perusal of this information indicates how varied and detailed the debate becomes.

A basic assumption underlying most of the research associated with the origin of the Navajo is that they came from the north. Most scholars place the ancestral Athabascans in northwestern Canada/Alaska by the time of Christ. Using a technique called glottochronology to measure language change between groups over time, anthropologists have determined that various Athabascan-speaking peoples split off from their ancestors at different times. Linguistic differences between Navajos and other Athabascan speakers can also be measured. For instance, the Hupa, now living in California, separated from the Navajo about 1,100 years ago; the Kutchin and the Beaver groups in Canada 890 and 690 years ago respectively; the Jicarilla and San Carlos Apaches 300 years ago; and the Chiricahua Apache 170 years ago. If these dates are relatively accurate, the Navajo separated from their ancestral stock roughly 1,000 years ago.[19] Since there are many variables that enter into language change, not all scholars agree with these figures, but they do help provide an understanding of differences among groups.

Another concern is the route these people took. A number of explanations offer a variety of routes either going down the west coast and then into the Southwest through the Rocky Mountains in order to utilize a cold climate technology, or going down the eastern side of the Rocky Mountains, or a combination of these routes. Most anthropologists now agree on the more westerly route.[20] Clyde Kluckhohn, one of the most respected Navajo scholars, believes the forefathers of the Navajos could have been in the Southwest by A.D. 1000, while David Brugge, a famous anthropologist, summarizes his view by saying that "by 1300 the Apacheans must have been close to the northern periphery of the Anasazi region."[21] If mythology is an accurate indicator of events, the Navajos had extensive contacts with the Anasazi, as outlined in their rich body of lore.[22]

Others do not agree that the Navajo were in the Southwest that early, although the dates of occupation are being pushed back from the long-accepted date of A.D. 1500. For instance, recent excavations north of Farmington, New Mexico, and just south of the Colorado state line have yielded twelve sites with twenty-three radiocarbon dates that predate the 1500s, the earliest going back to the 1300s. Because of this new information "it appears likely that the Navajo were in the Four Corners region by at least A.D. 1400. . . . The period of time between the last Anasazi occupations north of the San Juan River and the earliest Navajo sites is now only about a century, suggesting the possibility that future research may establish contemporaneity between the two cultures."[23] This is particularly important, since the area producing these early dates is considered by the Navajo to be the area of their oldest habitation once they emerged from the worlds below this one.

Recognized Navajo archaeological remains in San Juan County are from a much later time. This is partly because far less excavation has been done here, but there may also be fewer sites because of Ute and Paiute occupation of the area. Whatever the reason, the earliest-dated Navajo structure in Utah is in White Canyon, with a tree-ring date of a.d. 1620. Five other dates exist for the Navajo Mountain area, going back to the last quarter of the 1700s; and sixteen dates, ranging between the years 1700 and 1800, come from Butler Wash, Montezuma Creek, White Canyon and the Bears Ears.[24]

The Navajo (who call themselves "Dine"—The People) have their own explanation of their origins. There is nothing in their myths that tells of a migration from the north, but rather of a journey through four worlds beneath this one. As each world was destroyed because of the wrongs of the people and human-like animals, a small group of survivors traveled to the next world to start anew. When they finally reached this, the fifth, or glistening, world, they emerged either in the La Plata Mountains of Colorado or in the Navajo Dam area near Farmington, New Mexico, and started their wanderings to the Pacific Ocean. This was the time that Navajo clans originated, shared new experiences, and met other peoples. When they finally returned to take up residence in their homeland, "Dinetaa," historic events were starting to take shape (approximately 1500–1750).[25]

Spanish documents first referred to the Navajos and Utes in the 1620s and early 1630s.[26] For the next two centuries, Spanish and, later, Mexican writers chronicled their struggles with both of these groups of "wild" Indians, who raided Hispanic and Pueblo groups alike, stealing livestock and crops, capturing women and children, and killing or harassing those who pursued them. The military power of the Indians was enhanced by the adoption of the horse, gun, and evolving tactics; their economy also changed due to the introduction of sheep, goats, and cattle. Social and political practices also altered, caused by the slave trade and changing alliances, all of which created a dynamic frontier. By 1675, the Utes and Navajos were well-mounted and aggressively assaulting the Spanish and their sedentary Indian allies.

A brief sketch based on fragmentary Spanish and Mexican reports of this fluid situation shows how fickle the protagonists could become. By understanding what happened in these alliances, later events in San Juan County fall into a clearer perspective. The early relationship between the Navajos and Utes with the Spanish was characterized by a jockeying for position to gain an upper military hand. The Spanish and their Pueblo allies were stationary, profitable targets for mobile forces who could descend from a canyon and desert wilderness at random. Although the Spanish took hundreds of Navajos captive and used them either as domestic servants or in the silver mines of Zacatecas, Mexico, there were still too many enemies operating in fragmented bands to force the Indians to the bargaining table.

Throughout the 1600s, Spanish power ebbed and flowed. Friction with "wild" Indians, like the Navajos, caused the government periodically to send expeditions north in pursuit of raiders. Imprecise geographic references make it difficult to determine how far these forces penetrated into the Four Corners region, but the record is clear that the Navajos and other hostile tribes served as an unintentional lure, drawing their enemies into new lands. For instance, in September 1660 Governor Bernardo Lopez de Mendizibal sent forty Spaniards and 800 Indian auxiliaries to destroy the homes and ripened crops of Navajos living along the San Juan River. His forces reported many enemies killed and captured.[27] Maps published five years later located Navajos on Black Mesa north of the Hopi villages. In July 1678 Governor Antonio de Otermin again attacked Navajos on the San Juan River, destroyed crops, took fifty prisoners, and rescued two women captives. Similar scenarios unfolded in 1705, when Spaniards launched two successful punitive expeditions in northwestern New Mexico.[28] The Four Corners area was becoming increasingly familiar terrain to these first Euro-Americans.

By 1720 the Spanish hit upon the plan of turning the Utes and Comanches against the Navajos and achieved this with telling effect. For the next fifty years, the Spanish enjoyed an uneasy peace with their arch rivals. Indeed, by 1749, some 500 Navajos willingly entered two Catholic missions at Encinal and Cebolleta, New Mexico, to escape the intense pressure placed on them by their neighbors. Three years later, a group of Utes attacked Navajos in a rocky, fortified position so successfully that the defenders "stacked their arms and carried a wooden cross above which was a [Franciscan] almanac on a pole. . . . Thereupon those who before were lions became lambs."[29] By 1754, the Navajos abandoned the area of Dinetaa in northern New Mexico and took up residence farther south in places removed from the Utes.

Therefore, it is not surprising that when Fray Francisco Atanasio Domínguez and Fray Silvestre Vélez de Escalante traveled on the borders of San Juan County in 1776 they encountered no Navajos. They recognized the San Juan River (or, as they called it, the Navajo River) as the northern boundary of this tribe and the southern boundary of the Utes, yet reported no Athabascan presence.[30] Of Utes and Paiutes, there were plenty.

The padres' account of the Indians living in or near San Juan County is informative. They encountered Utes who warned them about running into a Comanche war party and being killed, but the fathers replied that God would protect them. They also obtained some guides to lead them to the north by paying each a blanket, knife, and beads. One of the Utes overindulged and became so sick that he accused the Spanish of poisoning him until he lost his burden through vomiting. Other Utes willingly sold the party food and listened to the fathers' preaching; but they also often tried to impede the move to the north. Later, the fathers learned that some of their Indian companions who started out with them from Santa Fe were telling the local Indians to do this because they did not want to go farther. All this was to no avail—the padres moved on to Utah Valley.[31]

After Domínguez and Escalante continued down the western side of Utah and turned east to return, they once again neared San Juan County. They described the Indians they encountered, this time Paiutes, some of whom undoubtedly belonged to the San Juan Band. The fathers noticed how reticent these Indians were to approach them, no doubt in part because of the slave raiding and intertribal warfare that were common. The Paiutes were happy to learn through an interpreter that since their enemies—the Navajos, Comanches, and Apaches—had not been baptized, they could not enter heaven and would "burn forever like wood in the fire."[32]

The fathers made special note of a group of Paiutes, whom they called the "Payuchi Yutas," east of the Colorado River. These people were members of the San Juan Band Paiutes, who spoke the same language as the surrounding Paiute groups and the Utes to the east. The padres used some of their trails, built up with "loose stones and sticks."[33] Thus, Domínguez and Escalante were the first to provide an accurate ethnographic report of some of the inhabitants of San Juan County.

Utes, Navajos, and Spaniards continued their mutual hostilities right through to the time of Spanish withdrawal from the Southwest in 1821. These relations generally were characterized by the Spanish currying the favor of the Utes in order to use them against the Navajos. However, during the time the Mexican government faced the problem of controlling its "wild" Indians (1821–48), the Navajos had formed a friendly alliance with the Utes, much to the dismay of the settlers of New Mexico. Reports filtered in to Santa Fe of Navajos and Utes working together to steal horses, forming alliances for slave raiding, living together in the La Plata and Sleeping Ute mountains, and working to quell disturbances between members of the two groups when minor troubles erupted.[34]

The Mexican reaction to this was misguided frustration. Like their predecessors, they sent out expeditions to attack the Navajos. These forays were almost totally ineffective; to the Navajos and other "wild" Indians, these invasions did little except intensify the Indians' raiding efforts. For instance, in June 1823 Jose Antonio Vizcarra set out from Santa Fe with 1,500 men to punish some Navajo recalcitrants and bring them to the peace table. Vizcarra skirmished his way through the Chuska Mountains of northern New Mexico to the Hopi mesas in Arizona and then headed north toward Utah. Near the present site of Cow Springs Trading Post, Vizcarra attacked two different Paiute camps, "believing they were Navajos; for having taken up arms, there was no one to warn me they were Paiutes."[35]

Vizcarra's soldiers killed four warriors and captured seven slaves, this action based on the rationale that the Indians possessed goats—

"which only the Navajos have." He released the Paiutes after they corrected this mistaken impression. A day later, Vizcarra had a running
fight with Navajos fleeing before him. He captured livestock—87
cattle and over 400 sheep and goats—but lost five horses and inflicted
no casualties. The soldiers slept that night near Oljato Creek, within
the boundaries of San Juan County.[36]

A separate column of men under Colonel Don Francisco Salazar
headed towards the confluence of the Colorado and San Juan rivers
in search of the Navajo. Like Vizcarra, they attacked a group of
Paiutes, later were convinced of their mistake, and freed them. Salazar
then trudged east to Laguna Creek near Kayenta, where he crossed a
fresh livestock trail heading towards the Bears Ears. The next day he
followed the trail toward the Ears, entering San Juan County, then
turned south to Chinle Wash. He skirmished all day long with
Navajos who had begun "harassing the party, hoping to impede the
march; they continued the harassing, striking a flank and drawing
back, causing the soldiers to chase them."[37] By 18 August he had
rejoined the main body of soldiers under Vizcarra and departed for
Santa Fe.

A Navajo account of this incident or one similar to it tells of how
Mexicans chased the Navajos to the mouth of Copper Canyon. The
Indians fled across the San Juan River with their livestock and then
headed towards its confluence with the Colorado River. The
Mexicans in the meantime gathered all of the livestock they could
find and moved toward El Capitan in Monument Valley, skirmishing
as they went. Navajos fired into their camp at night, killing five men,
who were buried at El Capitan. They stampeded and recaptured half
the stock near Teec Nos Pos and fought a pitched battle in which thirteen more Mexicans were killed without the loss of a single Navajo.
According to the person recounting this incident at the turn of the
century, bones still lay around the site, "the trees nearby were still full
of arrows, and handfuls [of arrowheads] could be picked up on the
ground, with part of the Mexicans' saddles."[38]

A joint expedition sixteen years later under Manuel Chavez and
Don Juan Andres Archuleta penetrated into the areas of Black Mesa
and the Carrizo Mountains of Arizona and, simultaneously, to the La
Plata and Animas rivers in Colorado. Parts of these excursions very

possibly entered Utah in pursuit of Navajos. The end result of this
three-month task force expedition netted only thirty-four enemy
dead, twelve prisoners, 222 captured horses and mules, and 9,253
sheep and goats.[39] By the time the Americans took control of the
Southwest in 1848, the Mexicans were no doubt ready to have someone else make an attempt at controlling the "wild" Indians.

The U.S. army, a larger organization with greater resources,
wisely returned to the earlier Spanish policy of letting Indian fight
Indian. Starting in the mid-1850s, the fragile Ute-Navajo alliance
began to splinter beyond repair. In 1856 a Navajo war party decided
to raid the Utes. They killed three principal chiefs—Surdo, Cumabo
and Sobeta—near Abiquiu and stole livestock. Other Navajos heard
of the attack and went to the Utes with horses to pay for the wrong-
doing, but they were killed despite their peaceful intentions.[40] About
a month later, reports trickled in that Utes had killed eight Navajos
in the northern part of the Chuska range. Navajos retaliated by killing
five Utes.[41]

Events, however, were starting to turn against the Navajos. In
addition to increased conflict with U.S. troops, the corn harvest of
1857 was a total failure due to drought and early frosts. The Navajos
also realized that the San Juan River and its tributaries provided a
major planting area for crops, and if hostilities increased, use of this
region could be denied through Ute hostility.

At about the same time, Mormons in southwestern Utah were
feeling the effects of Colonel Albert Sidney Johnston's attempted
invasion of Salt Lake City. The Mormons, fearing the worst, encouraged the uniting of Navajos, Utes, and Paiutes to serve as auxiliaries
in their militia—the Nauvoo Legion. Some Utes attended meetings
with Brigham Young in Salt Lake City and then sent emissaries to the
Navajos, encouraging a peace conference. One Ute appeared at Fort
Defiance with a certificate of membership and baptism in the
Mormon church, alarming government authorities with this suspected tampering in Indian affairs. The Mormons scheduled a large
meeting of Paiutes, Utes, and Navajos in the Navajo Mountain area,
at which time the settlers reportedly handed out guns and ammunition to the Indians.[42] The effects of these rumors were twofold. First,
the Utes received increased annuities from the government as bribes

to keep them peacefully tied to their agency. Second, agents and military authorities were alerted to new concerns in the tangled web of conflict between the Navajos, Utes, Mexicans, and Anglo-Americans.

In February 1858, some principal chiefs of the Navajos arrived in Santa Fe for a conference with the Utes. The Navajos claimed that they would be lost if they did not have access to their San Juan River planting grounds. "They were already in a pitiful and deplorable condition . . . being forced by the groanings of hunger to sell their horses and stock, or steal."[43] But before the meeting could be held, nine or ten Navajos stole 2,000 sheep from Abiquiu. Utes and Mexicans went in pursuit, killing five and taking three Navajo prisoners, none of whom had been involved in the robbery.

When Navajo and Ute leaders met again on 11 March 1858, the Utes swore vengeance as soon as the weather cleared, claiming that they would join with other groups to chastise these inveterate thieves. They also denied accepting any support from the Mormons, insisting on their allegiance to the federal government in Washington, D.C., though the Navajos claimed the Utes were obtaining arms and ammunition from the Latter-day Saints.[44]

By the summer of 1858, Utes were operating in large numbers in the heart of Navajo territory. The U.S. military encouraged these forays, one report saying that the Utes "appear to have inspired the Navajos with a dread not to be gotten over." When the Navajos asked officials what would happen if the Utes came into their country, they learned that the government would help whichever tribe was its best friend.[45]

The government also used conventional military force to bring the Navajos under control. This military activity has been heavily documented elsewhere and so will not be dealt with here other than to point out that much of its effectiveness depended either on Indian scouts, Mexican allies, or people like Kit Carson who understood how best to neutralize or counter the enemy.[46] General James H. Carleton, as the commander of these forces, charged his troops with bringing the Navajos to Fort Sumner on the Pecos River, in east-central New Mexico. This they did. For four years, between 1864 and 1868, approximately half of the tribe (over 8,000 people) spent a nightmare existence at Fort Sumner before returning to their homes in Arizona, New Mexico, and Utah.

On a more local level and as part of the plan to force the Navajos to surrender, military commanders encouraged general raids by Utes, Mexicans, Jicarilla Apaches, and Pueblo peoples against their old enemy. In General Dixon Miles's words, "Let loose on these Indians all the surrounding tribes and inhabitants, particularly the Utahs and Mexicans, the two they seem to dread the most."[47] Soldiers reported finding large Ute trails made by herds of captured horses headed north, and Utes started scouting for the army as "spies and guides."[48]

As pressure increased, some of the more settled Navajos came to Santa Fe to meet with the Utes and seek peace. The Navajos wanted to obtain their old planting grounds along the San Juan River and to stop the loss of their livestock. They reached an agreement, touted by Indian Superintendent of New Mexico J. L. Collins as a permanent peace, but within two months Ute Indians at Abiquiu reported to subagent Albert H. Pfeiffer that the Navajos had broken the treaty, saying they did not want peace but only Mexican livestock.[49]

The obvious solution, and one with which the Utes heartily agreed, was for Ute Indians to continue as hired auxiliaries to the regular U.S. Army forces. Colonel Thomas T. Fauntleroy, working with Kit Carson, suggested that a band of 300 to 400 Utes could augment the six to eight available companies of Mexican volunteers and spearhead a thrust into Navajo territory. Nothing would be more effective than to use these forces to ferret out the enemy from their camps in the deep recesses of the Chuska and Tunicha mountains, Canyon de Chelly, and areas as far west as the Little Colorado River. Indeed, field reports indicated that camps in the Navajo Mountain region and Carrizo Mountains in Arizona already had been abandoned.

Carson guaranteed the eagerness of the Utes, "the best riflemen in the world," to wage war. He continued:

> I desire that I may be allowed to employ them, as they do not
> require pay as soldiers, but only to be supplied for a short time
> with provisions, until they can get well into the Indian country. I
> cannot but recommend this plan as it will at once have the effect
> to get the cooperation of a most valuable force, and at the same

time employ these restless people, who otherwise must foray upon our own settlements.[50]

This was a most agreeable solution: it occupied the Utes while providing for their welfare at the expense of the Navajos. They also rendered a service that was difficult, at best, for the conventional military.

As a result, Navajo enslavement boomed as never before, with Rio Arriba, Abiquiu, and Taos serving as markets for Mexicans to purchase their human merchandise. By January 1862 at least 600 Navajo women and children were held captive in New Mexico through a system described as "worse than African slavery." The number of unreported slaves can only be guessed; however, by 1865, Carleton estimated that at least 3,000 were living in Mexican households.[51]

Southeastern Utah and northern Arizona served as a gathering place for some of the Navajos looking for a sanctuary from the pressures of war. Navajo oral tradition is rich in stories of battles, slave raids, and flights into the wilderness.[52] One of the most detailed accounts, as told by his son Hashkeneinni Begay in 1939, concerns a leader named Hashkeneinni, who lived in the Kayenta-Monument Valley area in the early 1860s. The Utes and U.S. soldiers, part of Kit Carson's efforts to round up the Navajo in the area, arrived in late summer "when the heads of grass were full" and started "grabbing them [Navajos] off like rabbits, a few here and a few there, . . . anywhere they could be found."[53]

The soldiers freed a few of their captives to go and urge others to surrender. To this offer Hashkeneinni replied, "I was born and have lived in this country and I will die in it. I will not come in, even if I am killed by the Utes." He and his family, seventeen people in all, gathered twenty sheep, three horses, and a muzzle-loading rifle, then set out for Navajo Mountain, traveling mostly at night. They watched the soldiers' and Utes' movements by day and their campfires by night, even after the two groups parted company in search of fresh prey. Hashkeneinni drove his livestock, pushed his people unmercifully (earning the name "Giving Out Anger"), foraged food, and drank water trapped in crevices until they arrived on the east side of

Hoskaninni (Hashkeneinii) Begay, or the Son of Hoskaninni, fled with his father to the Navajo Mountain area while other Navajos surrendered to the military and were exiled at Fort Sumner, New Mexico. (Utah State Historical Society)

Navajo Mountain. His wife feared the Utes more than the soldiers, yet she begged her husband to stop this ceaseless traveling. This he did. The travelers took up residence within the protective confines of the canyons and slopes of the mountain.

At first, Hashkeneinni believed his was the only group to escape, but he later learned that other families and individuals such as Daghaa Sik'aad living in the Kaibeto area, K'aayelii near the Bears Ears, and Spane Shank in the Navajo Mountain region had also found refuge. In fact, a report in October 1864 estimated that

> less than one-half the tribe has surrendered. . . . [I]t is the opinion of those best informed as to their resources that it will take years to entirely subdue and remove them, as those still running at large are well mounted, well armed, have stock to live upon, and are the bravest and most warlike of the tribe.[54]

Hashkeneinni stated that he was aware of at least 100 people in the Black Mesa area who had escaped and that much of the livestock was never rounded up until he collected a herd of sheep that would grow to more than 1,000 by the time the Navajo returned from Fort Sumner to Monument Valley in 1868.

The San Juan Paiutes also played a role in this drama. By the late 1850s many of them had adopted the Navajo language and style of dress, and there was some intermarriage between the groups. Paiute camps were often established near Navajo settlements while trading and mutual support flourished. Though the Navajos looked down on the Paiutes, they considered the Paiutes useful to perform tasks in exchange for food. This symbiotic relationship occurred in a number of locations—in Paiute Canyon, near Paiute Farms, along the San Juan River, by the Bears Ears, on Blue Mountain, and near Monument Valley.[55]

As pressures from the Utes increased during the 1860s, the Navajos intensified their use of the Paiutes. Beyond more mundane cooperation in daily life, the Paiutes provided a lookout service to protect Navajo camps. For instance, K'aayelii lived in the Bears Ears area, where he established a settlement of five or six hogans. To prevent surprise attacks, he posted Paiutes along the various approaches to his camp. This was also done in the Navajo Mountain area, where the Navajos were said to be "hiding behind" the Paiute.[56]

Perhaps the most dramatic proof of Ute, Paiute, and Navajo cooperation occurred in September 1866 when a group of Capote and Weenuche Utes and a few Mexicans met to plan a trap for some Navajos who had evaded capture and were living in northern Arizona. They planned to invite the Navajos to live nearby but then kill the men, enslave the women and children, and capture the livestock. However, upon hearing this plan, Cabeza Blanca, a Weenuche leader, objected, saying that he had friends whom he did not want killed among those Navajos. A fight ensued; the Capotes killed Cabeza Blanca and then fled to Tierra Amarilla for protection. After exacting revenge, the Weenuche "then left, joining as is supposed the Wymin and Pah Utes who had made friends with the Navajos in the meantime. The whole party of Wymin, Pah Utes, and Navajos then left that region and went to the neighborhood of Rio Dolores, Sierra Salir [La Sal Mountains], and Sierra Orejas [Bears Ears]."[57]

In 1868, with the official end of hostilities and the return of the captives from Fort Sumner, a whole new set of problems now confronted the Navajos and Utes residing in the Four Corners area. As Civil War veterans poured into the West, mining strikes became more common and agricultural settlements were established. The whites demanded that Indians be kept on a reservation far from civilization. The Utes refused. They wanted little to do with a way of life primarily concerned with agriculture. They enjoyed their freedom, insisting they had performed a good service for the Americans and so should remain unmolested.

Western Colorado had always been Ute territory, and so the non-Indian people of New Mexico urged they be expelled to this territory and that the Abiquiu agency be closed to the Capote and Weenuche bands. It was thought that the Muache at the Cimarron agency, "with a little management," could also be persuaded to leave. Underlying the Utes' reluctance to leave were their religious beliefs. Diego Archuleta, an unsympathetic agent, explained, "These savages are possessed of the most heathenish superstitions against abandoning those places where the remains of their ancestors lie . . . [and] they consider their reduction to reservations as a species of slavery."[58]

The local Ute agent, W. F. M. Arny, even encouraged the taking of Ute lands by stating in his annual report of 1867 that several thousand white families could homestead in the area north and east of the Animas River. By establishing a reservation, the mining and agricultural resources of the region would be opened for development and could be "done at a comparatively small expense, for it is cheaper to dispose of these Indians in this way than to fight and exterminate them."[59] Arny felt that he could move the Capote and Weenuche onto a reservation on the San Juan for $49,500. Within a year, the paperwork was completed.

On 21 March 1868 the Utes begrudgingly signed a treaty in Washington that removed them to Colorado, though the Abiquiu and Cimarron agencies did not close until 1878 when the two new agencies in Colorado were completed. In 1873 the Utes signed another treaty, the Brunot Agreement, that removed massive chunks of land from their new reservation, so that by 1880 and one more treaty comparatively little remained of their land holdings. In Colorado, for example, from their original holdings of some 56 million acres, the first treaty promised only 18 million acres (about nine million to the Southern Ute and a similar amount to the Ute Mountain Ute, or Weenuche). By 1934 the holdings of both of these groups had been reduced by various means to 553,600 acres.[60] Ironically, on 1 June 1868 the Navajos also signed a treaty, giving them approximately one-fourth of the territory they used to roam. But, unlike the Utes, the Navajos consistently obtained additional lands for their reservation. How this inequity occurred will be discussed in Chapters 6 and 7.

It took a while for old Navajo and Ute wounds to heal. As early as 1866, Navajos told the soldiers at Fort Sumner that "without protection from the Utahs who are our enemies, we would not care to go back."[61] Once returning became a reality, the Navajos indicated that they wanted to make a peace agreement with the Utes similar to the one they had in the past, so that they could trade and "become one people with them." On 28 May 1868, just before the treaty signing, General William T. Sherman warned the Navajos "that if you go to your own country, the Utes will be the nearest Indians to you; you must not trouble the Utes and the Utes must not trouble you. . . . You must not permit any of your young men to go to the Ute or Apache country to steal."[62]

This advice was hardly necessary. Following a few sporadic raids for women and livestock in 1868, the Utes started to become more peaceful. Agent reports indicate that for the next few years, large Navajo populations avoided living too close to the San Juan region. The friction of the previous war had burned an indelible scar into the memories of the Navajo—a scar that has continued to this day through their oral traditions. The Utes had earned their Navajo name of Nooda'i, "The Enemies You Continually Fight With."

ENDNOTES

1. James A. Goss, "Culture-Historical Inference from Utaztekan Linguistic Evidence," paper presented at Plenary Symposium on Utaztekan Prehistory of the Society for American Archaeology and the Great Basin Anthropological Conference, May 1966, 11, 27.

2. Ibid., 28.

3. Alan D. Reed, "Ute Cultural Chronology, in" *An Archaeology of the Eastern Ute: A Symposium*, ed. Paul R. Nickens, Colorado Council of Professional Archaeology Occasional Papers Number 1 (Denver, 1988), 80–81; Winston Hurst conversation with author, 9 September 1992.

4. Robert C. Euler, "Southern Paiute Archaeology," *American Antiquities* 29 (January 1964): 380.

5. Reed, "Ute Cultural Chronology," 82; C. S. Fowler and D. D. Fowler, "The Southern Paiute: A.D. 1400–1776," in *The Protohistoric Period in the North American Southwest, A.D. 1350–1700*, D. R. Wilcox and W. B. Masse, eds., Arizona State University, Archaeological Research Papers Number 24, 129–62.

6. C. Melvin Aikens and Younger T. Witherspoon, "Great Basin Numic Prehistory Linguistics, Archeology, and Environment," in *Anthropology of the Desert West: Essays in Honor of Jesse D. Jennings*, University of Utah Anthropological Papers Number 110 (Salt Lake City: University of Utah Press, 1986), 9–20.

7. Stephen C. Jett, "Testimony of the Sacredness of Rainbow Natural Bridge to Puebloans, Navajos, and Paiutes," *Plateau* 45 (Spring 1973): 54.

8. Goss, "Culture-Historical Inference," 29–30.

9. W. H. Jackson, "Ancient Ruins in Southwestern Colorado," in *The United States Geological and Geographical Survey of the Territories*, Eighth Annual Report (Washington, D.C.: Government Printing Office, 1876), 380.

10. Jesse Walter Fewkes, *Antiquities of the Mesa Verde National Park*, Bureau of Ethnology Bulletin 41 (Washington, D.C.: Government Printing Office, 1909), 2.

11. J. Richard Ambler and Mark Q. Sutton, "The Anasazi Abandonment of the San Juan Drainage and the Numic Expansion," *North American Archaeologist* 10 (Winter 1989), 41–46.

12. Goss, "Culture-Historical Inference," 33–34.

13. S. Lyman Tyler, "The Yuta Indians Before 1680," *Western Humanities Review* 8, no. 2 (Spring 1951): 157, 160.

14. Donald G. Callaway, Joel C. Janetski, Omer C. Stewart, "Ute," in *Handbook of North American Indians* 11 (Washington, D.C.: Smithsonian Institution, 1986), 339.

15. Ibid., 366.

16. Isabel T. Kelly and Catherine S. Fowler, "Southern Paiute," in *Handbook of North American Indians* 11 (Washington, D.C.: Smithsonian Institution, 1986), 368, 396.

17. William R. Palmer, "Utah Indians Past and Present—An Etymological and Historical Study of Tribes and Tribal Names from Original Sources," *Utah Historical Quarterly* 1 (April 1928): 52.

18. Omer C. Stewart, *Culture Element Distributions: Ute-Southern Paiute* (Berkeley: University of California Press, 1942), 236.

19. Harry Hoijier, "The Chronology of the Athapaskan Languages," *International Journal of American Linguistics* 22 (October 1956): 219–32.

20. Florence H. Ellis, *An Anthropological Study of the Navajo Indians* (New York: Garland Publishing, 1974), 3; see also George E. Hyde, *Indians of the High Plains* (Norman: University of Oklahoma Press, 1959); Morris E. Opler, "The Apachean Culture Pattern and its Origins," in *Handbook of North American Indians* 10 (Washington, D.C.: Smithsonian Institution, 1983), 382.

21. Clyde Kluckhohn and Dorothea Leighton, *The Navaho*, revised ed., (Cambridge: Harvard University Press, 1974), 33; David M. Brugge, "Navajo Prehistory and History to 1850," in *Handbook of North American Indians* 10 (Washington, D.C.: Smithsonian Institution, 1983), 490.

22. See Robert S. McPherson, *Sacred Land, Sacred View: Navajo Perceptions of the Four Corners Region*, Charles Redd Center Monograph Series Number 19 (Provo: Brigham Young University, 1992), 77–127.

23. Alan D. Reed and Jonathan C. Horn, "Early Navajo Occupation of the American Southwest: Reexamination of the Dinetah Phase," *Kiva* 55, no. 4 (Fall 1990): 297.

24. J. Lee Correll, *Through White Men's Eyes: A Contribution to Navajo History* 1 (Window Rock: Navajo Heritage Center, 1979), 27, 45.

25. Ellis, *Study of Navajo Indians*, 58–103; see also Paul G. Zolbrod, *Dine Bahane: The Navajo Creation Story* (Albuquerque: University of New Mexico Press, 1984).

26. Tyler, "Yuta Indians," 160; Correll, *Through White Men's Eyes*, 30.

27. Correll, 35.

28. Ibid., 37, 39, and 48.

29. Ibid., 54, 57, 59–60.

30. Fray Angelico Chavez and Ted J. Warner, *The Dominguez-Escalante Journal: Their Expedition through Colorado, Utah, Arizona, and New Mexico in 1776* (Provo: Brigham Young University Press, 1976), 9.

31. Ibid., 27–31.

32. Ibid., 90.

33. Ibid., 101–04.

34. Correll, 141, 147, 149, 154, 179–80.

35. David M. Brugge, "Vizcarra's Navajo Campaign of 1823," *Arizona and the West* 6 (Autumn 1964): 237.

36. Ibid., 237–39.

37. Ibid., 242–44.

38. "Hoskaninni Begay," interview with Charles Kelly, 13 August 1938, unpublished manuscript in Charles Kelly Papers, Special Collections, University of Utah Library, Salt Lake City, Utah, 1, 11.

39. Correll, *Through White Men's Eyes*, 166.

40. Meriwether to George Manypenny, 1 January 1857, Record Group 75, Letters Received by the Office of Indian Affairs, New Mexico Superintendency, 1857, National Archives, Washington, D.C.

41. Henry Kendrick to William Nichols, 11 February 1857, Record Group 98, Records of the United States Army Commander, Department of New Mexico, 1857, National Archives, Washington, D.C.

42. U.S. Congress, Senate, *Report of the Secretary of War*, John Garland to Army Headquarters, 31 January 1858; J. G. Walker to Commander, 20 September 1859, S. Ex. Doc 2, 36th Cong., lst Sess., 339–40.

43. Robert Walker to Commander; Benjamin Bonneville to Nichols, 8 February 1858, Record Group 75, Letters Received by the Office of Indian Affairs, New Mexico Superintendency, 1858, National Archives, Washington, D.C.

44. *Santa Fe Gazette*, 13 March, 27 February, and 10 April 1858, cited in Correll, *Through White Men's Eyes*, 112, 116, 122; William Brooks to

Assistant Adjutant General, 20 March, 4 April, and 30 May 1858, Record Group 98, Records of the United States Army Commander, Department of New Mexico, 1858, National Archives, Washington, D.C.

45. William Brooks to Assistant Adjutant General, 1 and 15 July 1858, Record Group 98, Records of the United States Army Commander, Department of New Mexico, 1858, National Archives, Washington, D.C.

46. See the following books concerning this period of Navajo history: Lynn R. Bailey, *If You Take My Sheep: The Evolution and Conflicts of Navajo Pastoralism, 1630–1868* (Los Angeles: Westernlore Press, 1980); Bailey, *The Long Walk* (Los Angeles: Westernlore Press, 1964); Bailey, *The Navajo Reconnaissance* (Los Angeles: Westernlore Press, 1964); Lawrence C. Kelly, *Navajo Roundup: Selected Correspondence of Kit Carson's Expedition Against the Navajo, 1863–65* (Boulder: Pruett Publishing Company, 1970); Frank McNitt, *Navajo Wars, Military Campaigns, Slave Raids and Reprisals* (Albuquerque: University of New Mexico Press, 1972); and Clifford E. Trafzer, *The Kit Carson Campaign* (Norman: University of Oklahoma Press, 1982).

47. Dixon Miles to Nichols, 3 and 8 September 1858, Record Group 98, Records of the United States Army Commander, Department of New Mexico, National Archives, Washington, D.C.

48. Electus Backus to William Lane, 19 November 1858, Record Group 98, Records of the United States Army Commander, Department of New Mexico, National Archives, Washington, D.C.; "Return of Spies and Guides," *Santa Fe Gazette*, 15 January 1859, cited in Correll, *Through White Men's Eyes*, 239.

49. James L. Collins to James Denver, 20 March 1859; Albert Pfeiffer to Collins, 15 May 1859, Record Group 75, Bureau of Indian Affairs, Letters Received, New Mexico Superintendency, 1859, National Archives, Washington, D.C.

50. Thomas T. Fauntleroy to Winfield Scott, 29 January 1860, Record Group 98, Records of the United States Army Commander, Department of New Mexico, National Archives, Washington, D.C.

51. Collins, "New Mexico Superintendency," 8 October 1861, *Report of the Commissioner of Indian Affairs* (Washington, D.C.: Government Printing Office, 1862):124–25; Andrew Evans to Acting Assistant Adjutant General, 28 October 1861, Record Group 98, Records of the United States Army Commander, Department of New Mexico, 1861, National Archives, Washington, D.C.; William Arny to William Dole, 6 January 1861; Testimony of James H. Carleton, 3 July 1865, Record Group 75, Letters Received by the Office of Indian Affairs, New Mexico Superintendency, National Archives, Washington, D.C.

52. For a more detailed account of this period of San Juan and Navajo history see Robert S. McPherson, *The Northern Navajo Frontier: Expansion through Adversity, 1860–1900* (Albuquerque: University of New Mexico Press, 1988), 5–19.

53. "Hoskaninni Begay," interview with Charles Kelly, 11 April 1939, unpublished manuscript in Charles Kelly Papers, Special Collections, University of Utah Library, Salt Lake City, Utah, 1–2, 8–9.

54. U.S. Congress, House, *Report of the Commissioner of Indian Affairs*, New Mexico Superintendency, 1864, 185.

55. Charlie Begay interview with Aubrey Williams, 6 January 1961, Duke #687; Paul Goodman interview with David Brugge, 6 January 1961, Duke #689; Dave Holiday interview with David Brugge, 7 January 1961, Duke #691; Tall Salt interview with Aubrey Williams, 17 February 1961, Duke #762 in the Doris Duke Oral History Collection, Special Collections, University of Utah Library, Salt Lake City.

56. Paul Jones interview with Aubrey Williams, 19 January 1961, Duke #712; George Martin, Sr., interview with David Brugge, 22 March 1961, Duke #913; Maggie Holgate interview with Gary Shumway, 13 June 1968, Duke #956.

57. Major Albert Pfeiffer to A. K. Graves, 10 December 1866; Felipe Delgado to Office of Indian Affairs, 7 January 1866, Record Group 75, Letters Received by Office of Indian Affairs, New Mexico Superintendency, 1866 and 1868, National Archives, Washington, D.C.

58. "Report of Special Agent J. K. Graves," 1866 *Report of the Secretary of the Interior*, 39th Cong., 2nd. Sess., House Ex. Doc. 1, 132; Archuleta to Graves, 1 January 1866, ibid., 141.

59. W. F. M. Arny to A. B. Norton, "Abiquiu Agency Report," 24 June 1867, *Report of the Commissioner of Indian Affairs*, 206.

60. Calloway et al., "Ute," 355.

61. Navajo Council with Military in February or March 1866, as cited in Correll, *Through White Men's Eyes*, 139.

62. Sherman in council on 28 May 1868, as cited in Correll, *Through White Men's Eyes*, 133.

4

Entradas and Campaigns,
Entrepreneurs and Surveys

EARLY ENTRANTS INTO
THE SAN JUAN COUNTRY

For over a hundred years the San Juan region was a vast blank spot on the maps of New Spain, for a good reason. The Spanish empire in the New World began the day Christopher Columbus set foot on San Salvador; it spread to the mainland of Central America and then mushroomed over the continent. For approximately 300 years the Spanish ruled a vast collection of lands that ranged from the tip of South America through Central America and far into North America. Spanish claims of ownership went as far north as Oregon, with settlements from Florida to California; in addition, numerous islands in the Pacific fueled its Far Eastern trade.

The northern province of New Mexico, with its capital in Santa Fe, sat at the end of the 1500-mile Camino Real, the road that stretched from Mexico City, the administrative center for these borderlands. Santa Fe, founded in 1610, was the control center of both Spanish and Native American activities in New Mexico. This city also served as a jumping-off point for exploration beyond the eastern pueblos along the Rio Grande and the western pueblos of Zuni, Acoma, and Hopi. The actual control this government exerted was

tenuous at best, since long distances, political and ecclesiastical conflicts, Native American rebellion and warfare, and a host of other
problems kept Spanish authorities occupied on a daily basis.[1]

A few men, however, explored the Four Corners region and left
behind scattered reports and a legacy of legends and tales that continue to keep researchers digging and hopeful discoverers dreaming.
San Juan County has its share of early fact and fiction, with a large
body of unsubstantiated claims that are hard to either prove or dis-
prove. This chapter will examine Spanish activities, as well as
Mexican and early Anglo-American exploration of the region, with
the understanding that documentary evidence is slight while conjec-
ture abounds.

Spanish exploration was initially based on the entrada, an expedition into an unconquered area. In 1540 Don Francisco Vasquez de
Coronado led a force of over 1,000 men into the Southwest to search
for the fabled Seven Cities of Cibola and the gold they supposedly
contained. When he arrived at Zuni, one of the "cities" and one of
many disappointments, he dispatched on reconnaissance missions
Don Pedro de Tovar, the first European to enter the Hopi villages, and
Garcia Lopez de Cardenas, the first to see the Grand Canyon.[2] Other
Spanish leaders visited the Hopis, but it was not until 1628 that
Roman Catholic missionaries took up residence on the mesas.[3] Their
involvement there was sporadic and often challenged, but to the
Spaniards, the cross (church) and crown (government) went hand in
hand as part of an effective plan to control territory and its inhabi-
tants. The Spanish presence was now established fewer than eighty
miles below the future boundary of Utah.

The date of the earliest entrance of Spaniards into San Juan
County is highly debatable. Most likely it occurred when a military
expedition pursued a Navajo or Ute raiding party, as discussed in the
previous chapter. Physical corroboration of a Spanish presence is elu-
sive. An inscription reportedly made in 1640 on the walls of Glen
Canyon offers little information.[4] Controversial writing at Inscription
House, twenty-five miles south of Navajo Mountain, furrows even
more brows. Discovery of this signature occurred in 1909 when
archaeologist Byron Cummings and his guide, John Wetherill, were
examining ruins. Their children, Malcom Cummings and Ben and

Ida Wetherill, uncovered a portion of a wall inside an Anasazi dwelling and found scratched into the surface a date with letters. Cummings reported that some of the figures were illegible, but the numbers—1661—left no doubt in his mind. Various decipherings of the writing include "Ghos Annod 1661," "Carlos Arnais 1661," "S—haperio Ano Dom 1661," and "S—hafi an Dom 1661"; however, to some later visitors, the numbers appeared as "1861."[5] Toney Richardson, a trader at nearby Inscription House Trading Post, saw the writing in 1928 and emphatically believed the four-inch-high numbers were clearly a legible "1661." Unfortunately, they have since eroded away.[6]

The first half of the 1700s yields equally vague information. In 1712 Governor Juan Ignacio Flores Mogollon forbade Spanish traders from venturing into Ute lands, which lay generally in northern New Mexico, Colorado, and Utah.[7] Not until June 1765 did Governor Tomas Velez de Cachupin grant special permission for Juan Maria Antonio Rivera to travel into Indian country. How many others had preceded Rivera is unknown, but part of the decision to bend official policy sprang from the governor's wish to find a crossing of the Colorado River, to identify the local Indian groups en route, and to determine their attitude toward the Spanish. They also hoped to discover if there was truth to the rumor that silver deposits existed in the area, which seemed possible after a Ute named Wolfskin from that region appeared in Abiquiu carrying a small silver ingot. More precious metals might be found, and so Rivera, in the guise of a trader, set out with a small expedition in search of mineral wealth and a trail. Following old Indian paths, Rivera and his party arrived at the Los Pinos River in Colorado, where they found an adobe retort used to remove impurities in gold. Rivera took some of the bricks with him as proof and then sent four Spaniards and a Ute guide to locate Wolfskin. The party traveled from the Dolores River to Cross Canyon and then down an old Ute trail in Montezuma Canyon to the San Juan River. There they met a band of "wild Payuchis," living in ten lodges on the bank near present-day Montezuma Creek. One of the Indians waded out to midstream where he used sign language to ascertain the Spaniards' intent. The groups established peaceful relations, and three days later the Ute leader, Chino, accompanied the newcomers back to their main camp on the Dolores. Chino related that Wolfskin had recently left for his home on the La Plata River and warned that the heat and lack of water would make the trip to the Colorado River in July dangerous for the Spaniards. But he promised that if they returned in the fall he would guide them to their destination.[8]

Rivera, happy with his discovery, went back to Santa Fe, received permission and additional instructions to find a ford on the Rio del Tizon (Colorado River), outfitted another group, and returned by a more direct route to the Dolores River. From there, his party crossed into Utah northeast of Monticello on 6 October, proceeded to the base of the La Sal Mountains, and then moved to Spanish Valley and the present site of Moab. The recent discovery of Rivera's journal indicates that the Utes did all they could to discourage and lead astray the expedition. The Ute guide took them into the rough country of Indian Creek, Harts Draw, and part of what is now Canyonlands National Park before another Ute led them on a more direct route. The party eventually took a high trail on the western slopes of the La Sals before dropping down into Castle Creek and a crossing place on the Colorado River.[9]

Once he had found a suitable ford, Rivera carved a cross and the words "Viva Jesus" in a nearby cottonwood tree. His Ute guide warned that the party would now travel through lands inhabited by "child eaters," "strawheads" (so named because of their hair), and "stone people." With the promise of winter and troubles ahead, Rivera returned to Santa Fe in fourteen days' time. He left behind his carved cross to assert Spanish rights to the area and set the stage for the next act in the drama, the Dominguez-Escalante expedition, played out eleven years later.[10]

There undoubtedly were also unofficial expeditions to this area, such as the one of Pedro Mora, Gregorio Sandoval, and Andres Muniz, which reported seeing Rivera's cross in 1775, but most of these excursions are lost to history.[11] Muniz, however, served as a guide the next year for Fray Francisco Atanasio Dominguez, Fray Silvestre Velez de Escalante, and seven other men as they wound their way through western Colorado and Utah in search of a feasible trail to California. They camped in the vicinity of the La Sal Mountains on 23 August before moving north and then west to Utah Lake, which they reached a month later.

By 7 November, the padres had again arrived near San Juan County as they prepared to cross the Colorado River on their return to Santa Fe. Finding an old Ute trail leading to Padre Creek, the men chiseled out shallow steps for their horses, led them to the river, and hiked a quarter-mile downstream to a shallow ford, the Crossing of the Fathers, where they crossed the Colorado. This ford was at the later boundary between Kane and San Juan counties.

The Dominguez-Ecalante journal notes that by this time the group had lost its guides, perhaps by divine intervention, so that God could provide "merciful chastisement for our faults or so that we could acquire some knowledge of the peoples living hereabouts."[12] The padres took time to talk to the "westernmost Payuchis," probably San Juan Band Paiutes, and learned that they called Navajo Mountain "Tucane—Black Mountain," known in Spanish accounts as Sierra Panoche and El Cerro Azul.[13] Then it was time to move on. The fathers followed an Indian trail and spotted other Paiute groups. They arrived at the Hopi mesas on 16 November and at Santa Fe on 2 January 1777. Parts of their 1,700-mile route later served as a portion of the Old Spanish Trail, first traveled in its entirety in 1830.

The religious objectives of Dominguez and Escalante did little for those primarily interested in economic gain. For instance, Muniz, who initially guided the group, smuggled trade goods along, acting expressly against the fathers' wishes. He and his brother had spent time—three to four months in some instances—trading with the Indians of the Four Corners region.[14] These expeditions, in which furs, horses, guns, and slaves were exchanged, caused constant consternation for the government, which was trying to regulate Indian relations. In 1778, officials issued an edict prohibiting unauthorized trading in an attempt to stem the flow of unlicensed trading activity in the borderlands. Ten men and two Indians stood trial in Abiquiu during 1783; two years later, several others were in similar circumstances for trading "in the interior of the country of the Utes in violation of repeated edicts."[15] In 1812, officials passed a law prohibiting the purchase of slaves from the Utes, and, not surprisingly, a year later, seven men including leaders Mauricio Arze and Lagos Garcia

Navajos acquired sheep from the early Hispanic settlers of New Mexico. The fret and diamond design being woven into this blanket is an example of the consummate skill needed to develop the pattern in the mind before executing it on the loom. (San Juan Historical Commission)

stood before a judge; they were accused of slave trading in Utah Valley.[16] No doubt many of these expeditions—either coming or going—passed through the borders of San Juan County.

Traffic into the region increased, built upon prior exploration, creating by 1830 a 1,200-mile route between Santa Fe and Los Angeles known as the Old Spanish Trail. Thanks to the efforts of Rivera, Dominguez-Escalante, and other less-publicized groups, this horse-and-pack-mule trail connected the interior of New Mexico with the Pacific coast, bypassing a section of Arizona noted for its hostile Indians. San Juan County hosted a portion of one branch of the route, which crossed its boundary at Ucolo near Piute Spring, dropped into Dry Valley, and then generally followed the path of today's Highway 163 through La Sal Junction, past Kane Springs, down Spanish Valley into Moab, across the Colorado River, and then northwest to Green River. From there the trail headed generally west through Salina Canyon, to the Sevier River, south to Richfield and

Circleville, and then dipped into extreme northwestern Arizona and on to Nevada and points west.[17]

Hispanic names dot the trail through San Juan County and include Guajalotes (turkeys—designating a pool of bad surface water, perhaps Piute Creek), Ojo de la Cueva (Cave Spring—probably in East Canyon), Casa Colorado (Red House), La Tinaja (The Tank), and Ojo Verde (Green Spring). One researcher suggests that a short-cut called the "Orejas del Oso" (Bears Ears) Trail passed over Elk Ridge by the Bears Ears, followed the ridge to a point opposite Cataract Canyon, dropped into a side canyon, and then crossed the Colorado River to the Henry Mountains beyond. At the crossing, called Spanish Bottom, on the far side of the river is a "switchback trail up the west wall" four feet wide.

> Work had been done on hillside dugways and rocks had been carried out and lined up at a considerable distance on each side of the trail. . . . There were also ruins of something that could have been a furnace for either heating horseshoes or smelting ore. Near one faint spring were inscribed a cross peculiar to the Spaniards, a Spanish name not understandable, and the date 1777. This same date was also found at another location at some distance.[18]

This information, however, could be merely speculative. A definite path exists, but, as historian Gregory Crampton points out, any time there is an unmarked trail, indecipherable writings, or unexplained remains, the Spanish receive credit for them.[19] It is not clear why Spanish or Mexican traders would have selected such an isolated route, although the route does tie in with purported gold and silver mining operations in the Henry Mountains; however, little evidence exists to substantiate this claim.

One of the major functions of the Spanish Trail was to expedite trade. Indeed, slave and horse trading boomed during the Mexican period. Exchange of human captives and other commodities along the trail by the Utes, Navajos, and Paiutes reached its apex during the 1830s and 1840s and then declined in the 1850s. Chief Wakara, a Ute who ranged the length of Utah and into Nevada, Arizona, and Colorado, exemplified the cruelty associated with the slave trade. Believed to have occasionally wintered south of the San Juan River, he sold Paiute women and children, forced others to fight for him, and selectively waged a campaign of terror and retribution against those who refused.[20]

Wakara systematically plied his trade along the Old Spanish Trail as caravans traveled its length. John C. Fremont, while conducting a geographic survey, met Wakara along the Sevier River on 20 May 1844 and recorded a classic description of the Utes' activities on the trail.

> They were well mounted, armed with rifles, and used their rifles well. The chief had a fusee, which he carried slung, in addition to his rifle. They were journeying slowly toward the Spanish trail to levy their usual tribute upon the great California caravans. . . . They conducted their depredations with form, and under the color of trade, and toll for passing through their country. Instead of attacking and killing, they affect to purchase—taking the horses they like, and giving something nominal in return.[21]

Similar scenes were likely enacted in San Juan County.

New Mexican traders were the foundation upon which this slave, gun, and horse trade was built. Entering San Juan in caravans as large as three hundred men and "dressed in every variety of costume, from the embroidered jacket of the wealthy Californian . . . to the scanty habiliments of the skin-clad Indians," they sought out women and children to sell in New Mexico or to exchange for horses and blankets along the trail or in California.[22] As much as $200 might be paid for a young girl who could be trained as a domestic; boys were worth only half that much.[23]

Many of these bands traded heavily in the Great Basin area; however, once the Mormons arrived in 1847, they came in direct conflict with the Saints' views. By 1852, Utah courts had banned the slave trade, making it a criminal action punishable by imprisonment. Interestingly, the incident that brought the problem to a head centered around a group of New Mexicans led by Pedro Leon, who traveled from Santa Fe via Green River, undoubtedly passing through San Juan County as he plied his trade.[24] Brigham Young brought charges against this band of entrepreneurs and did all he could to frustrate continued sales.

Following this legal action, the slave trade continued but remained more confined to the area of New Mexico and Arizona, where strenuous efforts to stop it were not made until the mid-1860s. As for the Spanish Trail, by the early 1850s only parts of it were being used on a more local basis, while the surrounding lands that had once belonged to Mexico were by 1848 under the control of the United States.

The Spanish and Mexican legacy in the San Juan region also involves the alleged remains left behind by these early transients. Colorful stories of Spanish gold and lost mines persist. Residents of Garfield County next door to San Juan tell of an early time when Spaniards forced Indian laborers to dig for gold until the natives rebelled, killed their oppressors, destroyed any trace of the mine, and then cursed anyone who rediscovered it. A handful of people have supposedly found the mine and died or became incapacitated as a result.[25]

Blue Mountain in San Juan also has its stories. One, printed in the *Montezuma Journal* in 1900, tells of a Mr. A. K. Strouse from Dolores, Colorado, who received a visit from the spirit of his deceased ten-year-old daughter. She wrote instructions on a slate giving directions to the Lost Josephine mine which had been worked "300 years ago by the Spaniards until they were driven out by the Indians."[26] Strouse followed the instructions exactly, found a hidden tunnel entrance, and filed a claim on the property. No further information exists about its success, however.

Another version of the Lost Josephine Mine suggests that a Navajo named "Pajamas" knew the history of the Spanish enslavement and subsequent revolt of the Indians and how part of this gold was later found in the midst of some burro's bones. He produced a portion of the metal which assayed at $35,000 per ton.[27] A subsequent search for the treasure was fruitless.

Although there has never been a well-documented find of Spanish equipment or gold in San Juan County, that fact has not prevented speculation. One man claimed, "There's more lost mines in the shadow of Blue Mountain than most any place in the whole blame world."[28] John Young was said to have found a pick and shovel on a ledge, dug up some ore, and years later had it assayed, only to find his samples rich in gold. As is the case in so many stories, he could never locate the spot again. Another tale discloses how a Mexican sheepherder found a vein of ore in a Blue Mountain cave and then retired to Santa Fe, but returned annually to get more gold for the next year's expenses.[29]

Other stories recount how people found Spanish armor near the Goosenecks and in Fry Canyon, how a cave on Grey Mesa holds a map and a cross etched on its walls, how the Spaniards built a house and mining equipment near Mexican Hat rock, and how there are Spanish mines and tools located in White Canyon and in the La Sals.[30] Even the Navajos have their story about "Gray Robe" or "Long Gray Coat," who started appearing after Father Escalante "blessed the region" because he had found food in an abandoned Havasupai camp near Tuba City, Arizona. This ghost helps people during hard times and miraculously protects them from harm. One trader, driving in the Navajo Mountain-Red Lake area at night, claimed that the ghost appeared to him and his Navajo passengers. The apparition stood by the side of the road, warning that danger lay ahead. The trader and companions stopped the car and got out to find a raging flash flood only a few yards away. Gray Robe had saved them from destruction.[31]

What is one to think of these stories that have persisted in San Juan? While they add a great deal to the charm and romance of the region, there is not much concrete evidence to support them. Until documents or verifiable artifacts are produced, one can only conclude that the many stories of lost Spanish mines or ghosts are just part of the rich mythology of Utah.

The real legacy of the Spanish involvement in San Juan rests in a far less dramatic but immeasurably more important sphere. Consider the impact on Utes and Navajos of the horse, which they obtained from the Spanish by 1675, or of sheep (procured through raids during approximately same period) on the lives of the Navajo.[32] Livestock, wool, and blankets have served the Navajos for more than three centuries as a major part of their economy. Today, though prospectors still wander over the desert in search of lost mines, the Navajos continue to reap these more concrete benefits derived from the Spanish.

Soon after the Spanish relinquished control of the Southwest to

Elaize, Tomacita, and Telesfora Garcia in a La Sal sheep corral in 1928. Hispanic families were important in the county's livestock industry. (San Juan Historical Commission)

the Mexicans, a new adventurer, the Euro-American, began to enter the region in numbers. The Mexican government did not share the same reticence towards Anglo involvement on their lands and in their economy as had the Spanish. Instead, they generally welcomed the harbinger of the approaching American influx—the mountain man.

Starting in earnest in 1822, trappers flooded the Rocky Mountains from Wyoming and Idaho to the red sands of Santa Fe and Taos, New Mexico.

The men who trapped in the Southwest faced a far different landscape and accompanying set of problems than their cohorts to the north. Narrow rivers like the San Juan and Colorado offered untouched beaver habitat, but also limited access because of high cliffs and shallow floodplains. Small mountain ranges such as the La Sals, Blues, Henrys, and Navajo Mountain eventually were trapped, but not as readily as the San Juans in Colorado or the Wasatch and Uinta mountains in northern Utah. On a more positive side of the ledger, the Indians that the mountain men faced in the area generally were not as warlike and their tribes not as large or unified as those to the north, allowing trappers to travel in much smaller groups. The Mexican authorities who issued permits from Santa Fe, however, were often capricious in granting licenses, charged high prices to obtain them, or unlawfully seized furs from returning groups.

The southern trappers did not receive the same renown as those in the north. There is less documentation concerning their exploits, and few journals exist revealing where they traveled. As with the early Spanish traders, far more trapping activity occurred within the limits of present-day San Juan County than the written record indicates. The few pieces of evidence that do exist indicate frequent visits to the region by small groups, many of whom traveled the Spanish Trail as they trapped, traded, and moved throughout the area in search of profitable opportunities and goods.

The first Anglos to venture into San Juan County came by mistake. James Workman and Samuel Spencer were part of a trapping expedition wiped out in 1809 by Comanche Indians near the Arkansas River. The two men escaped, making their way towards what they hoped was Santa Fe. Instead of striking the Rio Grande, they mistakenly hooked into part of the Colorado River drainage system and proceeded generally south and west. The men wandered onto a heavily traveled trail covered with tracks from what they called "several thousand" horses and mules, and so started south and east only to meet a caravan of traders headed west. Not tired of their adventure, they did an about-face and joined the caravan, walking to California for the winter.[33]

Others possibly entered the San Juan region as early as 1823. In 1824 William Wolfskill and Ewing Young trapped west along the San Juan River, returning to Santa Fe with furs reported at $10,000 in value. Encouraged, they outfitted a second expedition the next year to go back to the San Juan.[34]

Other trappers followed suit and spread throughout the Colorado basin. That fall, Thomas "Peg Leg" Smith, with a group of eighty men, trapped in the San Juan Mountains and along the Gunnison River. The party was too large for the terrain, and so it split up for greater coverage of territory and profits. Utes stole horses from Smith and his band, who decided to head to safer Navajo country, south of the San Juan River. Here they traded "trinkets for sheep and goat skins, also serapes of superior quality manufactured by the Indians and so closely woven as to be almost impervious to water."[35] The expedition arrived in Taos in mid-December.

Smith may have returned the next year with a party of nine men, determined to "trap the San Juan, Dolores, St. Miguel, and other tributaries of the Grand [Colorado River above the confluence of the Green River]."[36] Expeditions like this piqued the interest of the Mexican government, which reacted in September 1825. The governor of New Mexico, Antonio Narbona, wrote to the government in Mexico City notifying it that "Americans had built a fort on the San Juan River, to the west of New Mexico settlements."[37] Officials directed the governor to destroy this fort, but there is no further record of its existence or destruction.

James Ohio Pattie wrote a detailed yet controversial narrative of his trapping in the Southwest. Scholars have identified a certain amount of exaggeration in what he said, and the chronology and routes traveled are questionable; however, recent research confirms many other elements of his story. In his diary, he tells of a journey up the Colorado River and into southeastern Utah. Because his recordings are vague in relation to identifiable landmarks and inaccurate in estimating distances, a debate continues about his exact route.

At least one anthropologist—A. L. Kroeber—believed that Pattie not only reached but also trapped on the San Juan River and fought either Southern Utes or Paiutes in this area.[38] Pattie described the incident as a sequel to his losing three comrades in a battle with Indians a few days before. "On the 13th [April 1826] we reached another part of the river [San Juan near Navajo Mountain?] emptying into the main river from the north. Up this we all trapped two days. During this excursion we met a band of hostile Indians, who attacked us with an unavailing discharge of arrows, of whom we killed four."[39]

The mountain man later mentions how he reached a large Navajo encampment and while there told the Indians of the fight. They were so elated that they gave the trappers a horse for each man they had killed; ten Navajos also joined the trappers to serve as guides.[40] Such treatment could well have been offered by the Navajos because of their sporadic yet intense confrontations with the Utes. The San Juan River was a recognized border between Navajos (to the south) and Utes (to the north), although both tribes used lands on either side of the river for various activities.

From the many bands of trappers and traders traversing the area of San Juan County came a familiarization with routes and resting places with water. The Spanish Trail, part of which was known as the "Old Trapper's Trail," served the mountain men as they moved into the Great Basin.[41] William Wolfskill and George C. Yount are credited with being the first trappers and traders to travel the entire length of the Spanish Trail from Santa Fe to Los Angeles, which they did in 1830.[42] Other trappers such as Kit Carson, Antoine Robidoux, and Denis Julien also utilized the trail and trapped in the wilds of San Juan. Julien chiseled three different inscriptions in Labyrinth, Stillwater, and Cataract canyons in 1836 as a testament to his activity.[43]

The fur trade petered out in the late 1830s and early 1840s. The men who had traversed the region as trappers were now ready to help the next group of explorers—the surveyors, map-makers, and early settlers. John W. Gunnison led the earliest group of government workers through southeastern Utah in 1853, as he surveyed the 39th Parallel for a possible transcontinental railroad route. He intersected the Spanish Trail approximately twenty miles below Green River and then headed north and away from San Juan County.[44]

A year later, William D. Huntington crossed Gunnison's route as he carried out Brigham Young's wishes to explore southeastern Utah for the Mormons. Huntington provided an interesting account of his travel with eleven whites and an Indian guide on a route that took them from Springville, Utah, to forty miles south of the San Juan River. He mentioned how Wakara with his Utes and twenty "Spaniards" threatened but failed to stop the group, how Gunnison's route was clearly evident, and how the Navajos were at first hostile but soon mellowed at the possibility of establishing trade relations—"the best letter of introduction a white man can take among the Indians."[45]

After effecting an agreement, Huntington traveled along the San Juan River, taking notes on Anasazi ruins, including a detailed description of the Hovenweep ruins. He was the first of a host of interested people—both professionals and amateurs—to come to San Juan County and study the remains of this ancient people.

The tempo of Euro-American activity increased again the next year when forty Mormon settlers established the Elk Mountain Mission at present-day Moab. The story of this short-lived settlement, only four months in duration, has been told elsewhere. Its men explored and utilized resources from the northern part of San Juan County, and launched a trading expedition under the direction of Alfred N. Billings that allowed some of the mission members to travel the county's entire length. A party of Utes had invited a handful of men to accompany them to trade with Navajos to the south. On 30 August 1855 the party toured through Dry Valley and around the base of Blue Mountain and then crossed the San Juan River to peacefully trade with their neighbors.[46] The traders returned to the Moab area by the middle of September, but by the end of that month hostilities with the Utes forced the entire group back to the Wasatch Front. This ended direct Mormon involvement in the area for twenty-five years.

Another four years passed before the next expedition, led by Captain John N. Macomb of the U.S. Army Corps of Engineers, passed through San Juan County. Macomb's entourage included men capable of taking astronomical observations to define the route, cartographers to draw it, weathermen to record temperatures and barometric readings, a geologist—Dr. J. S. Newberry—to study rock formations, and a detachment of infantry for protection. It was a scientific entrada of exploration, conducted for pragmatic purposes.

The group left Santa Fe in July 1859, traveling and mapping the Spanish Trail while incorporating in their journals many of the historic names of campsites and watering holes. Macomb and Newberry were the first to do this with accuracy; they were also the first to call the area east and north of Blue Mountain the "Great Sage Plain," the first to dig and record their findings of dinosaur bones, and the first to enter the present boundaries of Canyonlands National Park. Though an officer and engineer by profession, Macomb could not resist humanizing the landscape he negotiated. To his eyes, the Great Sage Plain was "exceedingly monotonous," but once he reached Canyonlands, his demeanor changed from boredom to awe. He described these wonders:

> These castellated buttes are from one thousand to fifteen hundred feet in height, and no language is adequate to convey a just idea of the strange and impressive scenery formed by their grand and varied outlines. Toward the west the view reached some thirty miles, . . . while in the intervening space the surface was diversified by columns, spires, castles, and battlemented towers of colossal but often beautiful proportions, closely resembling elaborate structures of art, but in effect far surpassing the most imposing monuments of human skill. . . . Their appearance was so strange and beautiful as to call out exclamations of delight from all our party.[47]

That fall Macomb returned to Santa Fe with the first accurate report of the landscape of San Juan County.

A man equally enraptured with the scenery, as seen from a slightly different angle, was John Wesley Powell, who in 1869 and again in 1871 floated the Green and Colorado rivers. He and a dozen subsequent authors have told this tale of river-running along the western boundary of San Juan County. Powell recounts his expeditions' numerous campsites and portages, the killing of two bighorn sheep for dinner, the exploration of Anasazi ruins, his impression of the Crossing of the Fathers, and his bestowal of names—Cataract Canyon, Gypsum Canyon, Labyrinth Canyon, and Music Temple, among them.[48]

Ferdinand V. Hayden, seated second from left in foreground, directed the 1875 government survey of San Juan County. Henry Gannett, seated far left, led a crew to the "region between Abajo and La Sal mountains" but left before completing the work because of an attack by Utes led by Poco Narraguinep. (Colorado State Historical Society)

But all of this was secondary to the time devoted to describing rocks and the river. Powell's fascination and awe mingled with fear and respect of this encounter in the wilderness provide not only a river-runner's guide but a naturalist's appreciation for the Colorado and its tributaries. Powell's stated purpose, repeated many times, was not to have an "adventure" but to provide an accurate scientific report. This he did, culminating in his study *Report on the Lands of the Arid Region of the United States, with a More Detailed Account of the Lands of Utah*, published in 1879. He was far ahead of his time in understanding the give-and-take nature of human relationship to the environment, a lesson that San Juan farmers and stockmen would take years to understand.

Two years after the spray had dried on Powell's jacket, yet another group ventured into San Juan. As with the Macomb and Powell expeditions, the Ferdinand V. Hayden surveys of 1875 and 1876 were composed of scientists. The first year's efforts centered around the La Sal Mountains, as two different parties wandered about on their slopes and over the Great Sage Plain. One of the parties encountered a group of hostile Utes who were frustrated by the recently signed Brunot Agreement. After a two-day fracas, the white men fled, leaving behind their equipment and records. The next year's expedition succeeded in mapping Blue Mountain, recording the area's landscape, and exploring many Anasazi ruins. By the end of the two years' efforts, members of the survey parties had traveled throughout the La Sals and parts of Blue Mountain; passed down McElmo, Recapture, and Montezuma canyons; journeyed down the San Juan River as far as Chinle and Comb washes; moved across the Sage Plain and Dry Valley; and named features including Mount Peale, Mount Tukuhnikivatz, and Casa del Eco.[49]

William Jackson, a photographer who accompanied the surveys both years, recorded the abundance of Anasazi artifacts and ruins as he traveled down Montezuma Canyon. He wrote: "The ruins were so numerous now that frequently one or more were in view as we rode along. Arrow points were so plentiful that there was an active rivalry as to which one of us found the greatest number. Broken pottery of all kinds and beads and other trinkets were also collected."[50] Unfortunately, Jackson's party also encountered a group of Utes who, although friendly, caused the white men to feel uneasy and to flee the depths of the canyon as quickly as they could find a route out. However, the surveyors took with them a lasting impression of the richness of prehistoric life in San Juan County.

In summarizing the roughly three hundred years covered in this chapter, one finds certain patterns emerging. The San Juan region, lying within peripheral control of three different governing bodies—Spanish, Mexican, and American—served mainly as a stopping point on the way to somewhere else. Spanish explorers and traders developed a trail system as part of their search for precious metals, trade, and a route to California. The Mexican period led to a refining of the trail system and a continuation of military forays and slave raiding/trading activities with warring Indians started by the Spanish. Fur trappers used the trails but left the beaten path in search of furs, in

San Juan's first real Anglo-American economic enterprise. Even the government surveys depended heavily upon previously established routes and campsites, many of which carried Hispanic names.

Mormons made the only permanent attempt to settle in the San Juan region, and that lasted for only four months. Isolation, problems with transportation, friction with Indians, and the lack of female companionship created an undesirable situation, which added impetus to the settlers' sudden decision to evacuate when faced with Ute hostility. Some historians have raised the possibility that the Elk Mountain Mission was part of Brigham Young's attempt to establish an "outer cordon" as part of a Mormon empire—in Moab's case to secure part of the Old Spanish Trail.[51] However, as noted Utah historian Eugene Campbell pointed out: "If it were a planned empire, it was conceived on a small scale, executed in a haphazard manner, and abandoned without the usual heroic efforts that characterized Mormon enterprise."[52]

What, then, were the more lasting effects of this era besides place-names, folklore, and a fascinating slice of history? Hundreds of people still daily travel part of the Spanish Trail as they move from Monticello to Moab and points north. The landscape no longer seems "exceedingly monotonous" to thousands of tourists who escape the cities for fresh air and elbow room in Canyonlands, Lake Powell, or on the San Juan River. The Colorado River still offers adventure and insight for serious students of ecology as they attempt to understand and implement Powell's principles of arid-land conservation. Professional and avocational archaeologists still tramp the lands in search of an understanding of the Anasazi. In the late 1870s, however, these interests were nascent, set on the backstage of a greater drama—the settling of San Juan.

ENDNOTES

1. For two excellent treatments of Spanish borderlands history see Edward H. Spicer, *Cycles of Conquest: The Impact of Spain, Mexico, and the United States on the Indians of the Southwest, 1533–1960* (Tucson: University of Arizona Press, 1962); and John Francis Bannon, *The Spanish Borderland Frontier, 1513–1821* (Albuquerque: University of New Mexico Press, 1963).

2. Bannon, *Spanish Borderland*, 18–20.

3. Spicer, *Cycles of Conquest*, 190–191.

4. Richard E. Klinck, *Land of Room Enough and Time Enough* (Salt Lake City: Peregrine Smith Books, 1984), 22.

5. William B. Douglas to Commissioner of General Land Office, 19 November 1909, Navajo Nation Archives, Window Rock, Arizona; Correll, *Through White Men's Eyes*, 36; Hal K. Rothman, *Navajo National Monument: A Place and Its People*, Southwest Cultural Resources Center Professional Papers #40 (Santa Fe, 1991), 21–22.

6. Toney Richardson, "Trail to Inscription House," *The Desert Magazine* 11, no. 7 (May 1948): 16.

7. David J. Weber, *The Taos Trappers: The Fur Trade in the Far Southwest* (Norman: University of Oklahoma Press, 1968), 23.

8. G. Clell Jacobs, "The Phantom Pathfinder: Juan Maria Antonio de Rivera and His Expedition," *Utah Historical Quarterly* 60, no. 3 (Summer 1992): 201–223.

9. Ibid., 214–219.

10. Donald C. Cutter, "Prelude to a Pageant in the Wilderness," *The Western Historical Quarterly* 8 (January 1977): 4–14; F. A. Barnes, "A Journey to the Rio del Tizon," *Canyon Legacy* 9 (Spring 1991): 16–22; F. A. Barnes, "Update—Rivera's 1765 Expedition," *Canyon Legacy* 10 (Summer 1991): 31.

11. Joseph J. Hill, "Spanish and Mexican Exploration and Trade Northwest from New Mexico into the Great Basin, 1765–1853," *Utah Historical Quarterly* 3, no. 1 (January 1930): 5.

12. Fray Angelico Chavez and Ted J. Warner, *The Dominguez-Escalante Journal: Their Expedition through Colorado, Utah, and New Mexico in 1776* (Provo: Brigham Young University Press, 1976), 100–01.

13. Ibid.; Gladwell Richardson, *Navajo Trader* (Tucson: University of Arizona Press, 1986), 83; C. Gregory Crampton, *Standing Up Country: The Canyonlands of Utah and Arizona* (Salt Lake City: Peregrine Smith, 1983), 46.

14. Chavez and Warner, *Dominguez-Escalante Journal*, 33.

15. Weber, *The Taos Trappers*, 27; L. R. Bailey, *Indian Slave Trade in the Southwest* (Los Angeles: Westernlore Press, 1966), 143.

16. Bailey, *Indian Slave Trade*, 144; Hill, "Spanish and Mexican Exploration," 17–18.

17. C. Gregory Crampton, "Utah's Spanish Trail," *Utah Historical Quarterly* 47, no. 4 (Fall 1979): 361–82; Steven K. Madsen, "The Spanish Trail Through Canyon Country," *Canyon Legacy* 9 (Spring 1991): 23–29. For a detailed account of the trail see Leroy R. Hafen and Ann W. Hafen,

The Old Spanish Trail: Santa Fe to Los Angeles (Glendale: Arthur H. Clark Company, 1954).

18. Bert Silliman, "The Orejas del Oso Trail or Bears Ears Trail," unpublished document, n.d., in folder entitled "Writings," Utah State Historical Society, Salt Lake City, Utah, 1–4; also see E. T. Wolverton, "Legends, Traditions and Early History of the Henry Mountains," in Silliman's folder entitled "Writings," 9.

19. Crampton, *Standing Up Country*, 48.

20. Conway B. Sonne, *World of Wakara* (San Antonio: Naylor Company, 1962), 44–45; Carling and A. Arline Malouf, "The Effects of Spanish Slavery on the Indians of the Intermountain West," *Southwestern Journal of Anthropology* 3, no. 1 (Autumn 1945): 282.

21. John Charles Fremont, *Memoirs of My Life*, Volume I (Chicago: Clarke and Company, 1887): 385–86.

22. G. Douglas Brewerton, "A Ride with Kit Carson," *Harpers New Monthly Magazine* 8 (April 1854): 312–13.

23. Sonne, *World of Wakara*, 135.

24. Hill, "Spanish and Mexican Exploration," 20–22; Bailey, *Indian Slave Trade*, 158–60; Sonne, *World of Wakara*, 135–38.

25. Wolverton, "Legends," 2–5.

26. "Famous Josephine Found by A. K. Strouse through Spiritual Guidance," *Montezuma Journal*, 14 December 1900, 3.

27. Austin Fife and Alta Fife, *Saints of Sage and Saddle: Folklore among the Mormons* (Salt Lake City: University of Utah Press, 1980), 291–93.

28. Ibid., 297.

29. Ibid., 297–98.

30. Kelly Laws telephone conversation with author, 27 August 1992; Kay Shumway conversation with author, 28 August 1992; Carl Osborne telephone conversation with author, 2 September 1992; Winston Hurst telephone conversation with Gary Shumway and author, 2 September 1992.

31. Richardson, *Navajo Trader*, 89.

32. Frank R. Secoy, *Changing Military Patterns on the Great Plains*, American Ethnological Society Monograph Number 21 (Seattle: University of Washington Press, 1953), 104.

33. Faun McConkie Tanner, *The Far Country: A Regional History of Moab and La Sal, Utah* (Salt Lake City: Olympus Publishing Company, 1976), 34–36.

34. Robert Glass Cleland, *This Reckless Breed of Men: The Trappers and Fur Traders of the Southwest* (Albuquerque: University of New Mexico Press, 1950), 217; Weber, *The Taos Trappers*, 61–62.

35. Weber, *The Taos Trappers*, 67, 71–72.

36. Ibid., 91.

37. Ibid., 104.

38. Clifton B. Kroeber, "The Route of James O. Pattie on the Colorado in 1826—A Reappraisal by A. L. Kroeber," *Arizona and the West* 6 (Summer 1964): 132.

39. James O. Pattie, *The Personal Narrative of James O. Pattie* (Philadelphia: J. B. Lippincott Company, 1962), 89.

40. Ibid., 90.

41. James H. Knipmeyer, "The Old Trappers Trail through Eastern Utah," *Canyon Legacy* 9 (Spring 1991): 10–15.

42. Some historians claim that it was Wolfskill and Ewing Young, not Yount, who opened the trail. Yount was Wolfskill's partner in a fur-and-trading enterprise in Taos, but he had traveled to California earlier in 1830 by a different route and so was not present at this initial opening of the entire Spanish Trail. See Weber, *The Taos Trappers*, 144.

43. Crampton, *Standing Up Country*, 53.

44. Charles S. Peterson, *Look to the Mountains: Southeastern Utah and the La Sal National Forest* (Provo: Brigham Young University Press, 1975), 16–18.

45. William D. Huntington, "Interesting Account of a Trip to the Navajos and of the Ancient Ruins in that Region," *Deseret News*, 28 December 1854, 1.

46. "Diary of Alfred N. Billings," Special Collections, Brigham Young University Library, Provo, Utah, 14–17. For a good general account see also Charles S. Peterson, *Look to the Mountains*.

47. J. N. Macomb, *Report of the Exploring Expedition . . . in 1859*, (Washington, D.C.: U.S. Government Printing Office, 1876), 94.

48. J. W. Powell, *The Exploration of the Colorado River and Its Canyons* (New York: Dover Publications, 1961), 211–40.

49. Ferdinand V. Hayden, *Ninth Annual Report of the United States Geological and Geographical Survey* (Washington, D.C.: U.S. Government Printing Office, 1876); Ferdinand V. Hayden, *United States Geological and Geographical Survey of Territories* 10 (Washington, D.C.: U.S. Government Printing Office, 1878).

50. William H. Jackson and Howard R. Driggs, *The Pioneer Photographer* (New York: World Book Company, 1929), 266.

51. Eugene E. Campbell, "Brigham Young's Outer Cordon—A Reappraisal," *Utah Historical Quarterly* 41 (Summer 1973): 220–53.

52. Ibid., 221.

5

Civilization Comes to San Juan

HOMESTEADING AND CITY-BUILDING, 1880–1940

Since the beginning of the United States, three terms—civilization, frontier, and wilderness—have been used to label the opposing ideas and forces affiliated with the westward movement. At one end of the spectrum, "civilization," meaning "city-dweller," gives rise to positive associations of education, safety, economic development, western religion, and an advanced technological lifestyle. On the other hand, wilderness, until recently, stood at the opposite end of civilization and was associated with words such as wild, savage, and heathen. Between these two extremes lies the frontier, that gray area where they meet.

Civilization and city-building came to San Juan relatively late in the American experience. Often touted as one of the last frontiers to be settled in the United States, this isolated portion of Utah actually had three trickles of pioneers who arrived at approximately the same time. Parts of this story have been told elsewhere and so only a cursory look will be taken here. For instance, the saga of the Hole-in-the-Rock and the settlement of Bluff has found its way into numerous books and articles.[1] More time is spent here on places and people generally ignored yet important in this homesteading, city-building experience that lasted for more than sixty years.

The earliest group of homesteaders to utilize the resources of San Juan were those of the Elk Mountain Mission, located at what is now Moab in Grand County. Sent by Brigham Young in 1855, this mission lasted four months and succeeded in establishing only a temporary Mormon presence in the midst of various Ute bands. The forty-man contingent built a fort of rocks and timbers, scouted roads to the south where more lumber and grazing lands were available, planted and irrigated crops, and journeyed on at least one trading expedition with the Utes to the Navajos living south of the San Juan River. In September the Utes launched an attack that succeeded in killing three Mormons and driving the rest back to the Wasatch Front.[2] In terms of homesteading, this undertaking was a first attempt to utilize some of the resources in or near San Juan County, with an eye to obtain some of the permanent fruits of civilization. White settlers, however, would not make another attempt until the late 1870s.

The earliest homesteaders in the northern part of the county utilized the ranges and the water at the southern end of the La Sal Mountains. Groups such as the Tom Ray family, the Cornelius Maxwells, the Bill McCartys, and others homesteaded together in the general area of what is known today as the community of La Sal.[3] Rough-hewn cabins, subsistence gardens, and extensive range for livestock were the keys to their survival, while most of their economic ties lay in Moab, a town newly established by people predominantly from Sevier and Sanpete counties.[4] In terms of actual development, these early settlers of San Juan played a more important role in the growth of what would eventually become Grand County, where businesses and transportation facilities lured them.

The settling of the southern part of the county came from two different directions. The earliest influx of homesteaders came from Colorado. The first recorded white settler, Peter Shirts (an excommunicated Mormon), carved his niche in the Montezuma Creek area. Earlier, he had been active in the settling of Paiute County and in claiming land in Dolores, Colorado.[5] By 1877, Shirts, with two burros, crossed the San Juan River at Bluff, ventured south onto Navajo lands, and then headed north and established a home where Montezuma Creek meets the San Juan. He invited his brother Carl and family to leave their home in Michigan and join him. Shortly after the new arrivals took root, rumors reached Peter that his little settlement might come under attack by Utes. Carl and his family fled permanently, Peter only temporarily, until tensions subsided.[6]

In 1878 President John Taylor of the Church of Jesus Christ of Latter-day Saints directed a group of Mormons in southwestern Utah, most of whom were from Cedar City and Parowan, to settle the San Juan region. Taylor charged the group to establish a colony that would cultivate better relations with the Indians, deprive a white out-law element of a refuge from the law, and expand Mormon control into the area. To facilitate matters, local church leadership dispatched a thirty-man exploring party (also accompanied by two women and eight children) to determine the best route into the area. By the end of this journey, the group had traversed almost 1,000 miles on a reconnaissance that took them through northern Arizona to south-eastern Utah and then on a return loop over the Spanish Trail and back to the southwestern part of the state.

When the exploring party reached the midpoint of their trek at Montezuma Creek on the first day of June 1879, Peter Shirts was there to greet them. A group member described him as "a lone her-mit, subsisting on fish and wearing vestiges of clothes which had been."[7] Shirts welcomed two old acquaintances, Robert Bullock and Silas S. Smith, the leader of the group, whom he knew from days spent in southwestern Utah. He sold them forty-eight pounds of flour shipped in from Alamosa, Colorado, made suggestions con-cerning likely places along the river to homestead, and helped the group erect a few buildings. Shortly after, he left the area. Three years later Shirts died and was buried in Fruitland, New Mexico.

The exploring party built Fort Montezuma on the San Juan River about two miles above its junction with Montezuma Creek. The Harrison H. Harriman and James L. Davis families remained—each had a log room in the fort for their protection. They were dependent on food brought in from the markets of Colorado until the main body of settlers arrived a year later.[8] These two families worked hard to grow their own crops but met with little success.

For two months the exploring party, along with a substantial group of non-Mormons from Colorado who had already settled in the area, constructed a dam to channel the river's water into irrigation ditches near today's Aneth. Shirts, Henry L. Mitchell, and others labored strenuously before they abandoned the project. Only a little corn was successfully planted at the mouth of McElmo Creek, and even that burned from lack of water. By the time the explorers left on 13 August 1879, some members of the party were already disgruntled about the prospects of living along the San Juan River.

After the group returned to the Cedar City area and reported the problems associated with both routes, church leaders decided to take another route not yet traveled. The idea came from two sources, the explorations of Charles Hall and those of Reuben Collett and Andrew P. Schow, all of whom apparently searched for a shortcut under the direction of the church. Although the selection of the route was based on a superficial reconnaissance on the near side of the Colorado River, the men still recommended this as a practical course from Escalante to southeastern Utah. In October 1879, elements of the 230-person expedition, under the direction of Silas Smith, got underway and eventually rendezvoused at Forty-mile Spring southeast of Escalante.[9] For three weeks, from 15 November to 5 December, the party's ranks swelled while the leaders sat and wondered where to go from there. Smith left the group under the command of Platte D. Lyman while he returned to Fillmore to ask the territorial legislature for equipment. He did not rejoin the group until after its arrival in Bluff.

Snow had closed the pass in the mountains behind the wagon train; the only way to go was forward. Ahead lay seemingly impassable terrain and the cold winter months that seemed to stretch interminably into the future. Scouts returned with news of a narrow cleft between the red rock cliffs above the Colorado River, and so half of the pioneers moved to that spot. The remainder camped at Fifty-mile Spring, but both groups supplied men for the three different workforces that either widened the passage through the rock wall, developed the road beneath the steep cliff-face that descended the 1,200-foot-deep gorge, or graded a route out of the canyon bottom on the opposite side of the river.

The people set to work with a vengeance. As Elizabeth Decker reported, "It is about a mile from the top down to the river and it is almost straight down, the cliffs on each side are five hundred feet high and there is just room enough for a wagon to go down. It nearly scared me to death."[10] Cornelius Decker, one of the crew members laboring on the far side of the river said, "I don't think I ever seen a lot of men go to work with more of a will to do something than that crowd did. We were all young men; the way we did make dirt and rock fly was a caution."[11]

On 25 January 1880 the workers declared the road completed. Months of labor were put to the test the next day when the first of eighty-three wagons groaned, scraped, and rumbled its way to the bottom to be ferried across. Most were lowered by rough-locking the back wheels and attaching a large rope that ten men could pull back on, while others controlled the front by guiding the wagon tongue. Down the forty-foot drop-off at the top of the crevice, then over a trail built of rock and brush held in place with oak staves, and finally to the riverbed below, the wagons descended. All of the vehicles along with more than a 1,000 head of livestock arrived safely at the bottom. Almost equally difficult terrain, unexplored by any previous group, waited across the 300-foot-wide Colorado River. Cedar forests, Clay Hill Pass, and San Juan Hill each demanded its toll in effort before the main body arrived at the site of Bluff on 6 April 1880, too exhausted to finish the last eighteen miles to their intended destination at Montezuma Creek.[12]

Until the pioneers reached the Colorado River, there was little to differentiate this expedition from dozens of others launched by the LDS Church in the past. At this point, however, an important attitude, called by Jens Nielson in his Scandinavian accent "stickie-ta-tudy," was born as part of the San Juan heritage. Various members distinguished themselves through sacrifice and by maintaining even tempers to make good a bad situation. Take, for instance, Ben Perkins, who hung suspended over the side of the cliff to mark and drill holes for explosive charges; or George Hobbs and three other men who wandered lost in deep snow and blinding storms without food for four or five days in order to find a passable route on the far side of the Colorado; or L. H. Redd, Sr., who later could not recall his

View from the top of the Hole-in-the-Rock looking east. The white dashes record the trek across (A) the Colorado River then up Cottonwood Creek to (B) Register Rock where the men rested their teams and carved initials on the soft sandstone surface. The pioneers camped in (C) Cottonwood Canyon for ten days preparing for an assault on (D) Cottonwood Hill. Part of this ascent included the Little Hole-in-the-Rock, another narrow notch in the canyon wall blasted out to allow the wagons through. (San Juan Historical Commission)

horses' struggles up San Juan Hill outside of Bluff without weeping.[13] It was this type of commitment that allowed the Hole-in-the-Rock party to survive equally unpleasant challenges after they arrived in Bluff.

The real impact of this six-month venture lay not in the valiant struggle to open a new thoroughfare in the wilderness. Indeed, within a year's time the route had been abandoned. Rather, its importance lay in the impact it had on many of the members of the families who remained in San Juan and over the next century played a dominant political and economic role in the county. Their perception then and to this day is that this episode framed the character and grit of those early settlers, enshrined the importance of the San Juan mission in their hearts, and proved their stalwart ability to see a task through to its end. Even though other settlers, such as those Mormons driven from Mexico in the early years of the twentieth century, arrived in San Juan under trying circumstances, there was still a social difference and distance between them and the "Hole-in-the-Rockers." An important aspect of San Juan social beliefs had been established.

Mormons had founded Bluff as a salient of civilization in the wilderness, and subsequently a handful of them gathered strength and moved beyond to Montezuma Creek. Silas S. Smith, Zachariah B. Decker, and Thales Haskell (famous for his work with the Indians in southwestern Utah and northern Arizona) all decided to settle in the Montezuma Creek area. William Hyde, a Mormon trader sent from Salt Lake City by church president John Taylor, soon took up residence with them. He and one of his plural wives plus at least one daughter temporarily moved into the abandoned Shirts home until he was able to fashion one of the most beautiful houses in San Juan.[14]

Noted for their organizational ability, the Mormons lost little time in arranging the newly created San Juan County's government as well as its ecclesiastical structure. A month after the settlers arrived, they had created a county court that divided the region into three precincts and appointed Smith as probate judge, a position he relinquished to Decker three months later when he left Montezuma. District schools soon followed, with the first established in early November 1880 at Fort Montezuma and the second in Bluff a month later.[15]

William Hyde set in motion a large waterwheel, sixteen feet in diameter and twelve feet across, capable of sloshing 2,300 gallons an hour onto the parched soil of the Montezuma Creek settlement. This area was more fortunate than Bluff, because it had rock shelves on which to anchor its waterwheels, while the people downstream had to depend upon riprap dams and backbreaking shovel work to keep water in the fields and sand out of the ditches. Soon Harriman, Davis,

Three members of the Hole-in-the-Rock expedition and builders of San Juan County. Kumen Jones helped maintain friendly relations with the Navajo and Ute people; Jens Nielson was the Mormon Bishop in Bluff for twenty-six years; and Lemuel H. Redd Jr. was the county's first tax assessor and collector. (San Juan Historical Commission)

and John Allen had each built a wheel on different sections of the river. Allen, in his deep Scottish brogue, is quoted as saying of his wheel, "It's aya fine; I'd wish nothing better."[16] By spring, three more families had joined the community.

In the summer of 1882 John Holyoak established a settlement at what became known as Peak City because of a prominent topographical feature nearby, possibly Peter's Nipple. Described by Platte Lyman as twenty-five miles upstream from Bluff, its probable location is near Rockwell Flat, found on today's maps. The "city" included a home and a store that doubled as a post office; the community was soon supplemented by the homes of John Robb and James Dunton. By November of the same year, however, these two had pulled out, Holyoak eventually following suit. A passerby later described the remnants: "Its lonesome cabins and rude chimneys became the doleful abode of rats and chipmunks, until the pestulent [sic] river whittled the sand from under them and scattered their logs along winding banks."[17]

The river that drew the settlers to its waters also proved to be their biggest adversary. Poor crops, sand-filled ditches, and destruction of dams and channels discouraged even the heartiest pioneers. By December 1882, church authorities in Salt Lake City realized that many of these settlers wanted to be released from the San Juan "mission," but they encouraged them to remain. Some took the easy route and left, but many stayed, hoping for a better year. In November and December 1882 "two good sized companies of settlers" from Iron County arrived to shore up the flagging Bluff spirits in their attempt to make the desert bloom.[18] These newcomers, like the veterans, did not then realize that the spring of 1884 would sound the death knell for the Montezuma Creek settlement and encourage those in Bluff to try a more lucrative livelihood.

Starting in March of that year, the San Juan River began to swell from excessive rains. It rose seven feet above normal, tearing out check dams and gutting irrigation ditches. By May, with melting snows from the mountains, the waters swept away the headgate on the Bluff ditch, and, on 8 June, Hyde's and the other waterwheels disappeared under the brown torrent. On 18 June the river peaked and carried the community of Montezuma Creek before it. Raging waters carved a channel close to the cliff, leaving homes and farmlands on an island. Jane Allen and her small children tried ditching to turn the river away, but it soon was a foot deep in their home. Robert Allen, one of her sons, arrived from Fort Montezuma where things looked just as bleak and tried to rescue the women and children with a buckboard. The wagon quickly mired in the mud and sand. He then lassoed a molasses boiler, placed as many people in it as he could safely manage, and pulled them across the torrent with his horse. After a number of trips, the residents sat safely on shore to watch the disappearance of their homes and belongings. The cabins, property, fields, orchards, Fort Montezuma—the entire community—all flushed down the river, with the exception of the Harriman home, built too high on a rock for the river to take.[19] This was too much; members of the Montezuma Creek community either went to Colorado, returned to southwestern Utah, or joined their neighbors downstream.

Bluff fared somewhat better because of the large floodplain that stood between it and the river. Starting in March, the San Juan River and Cottonwood Wash gushed over the land, filling houses with eight to ten inches of mud while burying in sand "cellars, pig pens, chicken coops . . . and corn in the shock . . . doing hundreds of dollars of damage."[20] The river also tore out three-quarters of a mile of riprap dam, the headgate, and much of the irrigation ditch while filling other parts of the canal with mud. The water from Cottonwood Wash covered portions of the farmland with eighteen inches of worthless white sand.

It is little surprise that the Hole-in-the-Rockers were more discouraged than ever before. Platte D. Lyman, who lived through these trying times, recorded that

> the people here have been growing into the conviction that they have very little if any prospect of establishing themselves independently in this place, and today (May 20) they almost unanimously signed a letter to President Taylor . . . asking to be released from this mission unless suitable help is forthcoming at once to enable them to stay.[21]

In almost the same breath, however, Lyman pointed out the salvation of the colony when he wrote, "Our range is better than ever before since we lived here. Stock are doing well, but money is very scarce and times are dull."[22]

Discouraged settlers suggested that the community move from the river and utilize a more placid source of water. They considered moving to Yellow Jacket Canyon, east of Cajon Mesa, until they learned that its owners wanted $30,000 for the land. Newly appointed Mormon stake president Francis A. Hammond, leader of the far-flung ecclesiastical unit in the Four Corners area, decided that the initially anticipated twenty miles of floodplain farmland would never materialize. When he saw only 300 acres being farmed successfully, he turned to the livestock industry and encouraged others to do likewise. Bluff blossomed as attention shifted away from the brown, roiling waters of the San Juan River. Forty years after the start of this farming project, at an estimated cost of $150,000 to $200,000, only

Bluff, about 1900, looking south. Left to right: The Bluff schoolhouse (beyond) and the LDS meetinghouse (in front) appearing as if their roofs were side by side. Lemuel H. Redd's home and haystack dominate the foreground and suggest the prosperity that some people enjoyed during this period. (San Juan Historical Commission)

175 acres were still under cultivation and the ditch no longer existed.[23]

With the Navajo Reservation to the south, the settlers' eyes turned north, where Blue Mountain with its winter snows, spring rains, and summer showers offered the possibility of limited irrigation and extensive dry farming agriculture. Unfortunately for the Mormons, Harold and Edmund Carlisle, English cattle barons and proprietors of the Kansas and New Mexico Cattle and Land Company, were already established on fifteen private ranch claims on the mountain and held approximately sixty square miles of stock range.[24] Conflict over land and water appeared imminent.

Hammond encouraged exploration with an eye for town building and a mixed economy based on livestock and agriculture, the idea challenging established ranchers dependent upon rangelands for the livestock industry. The grand plan called for the Mormons to move far beyond Bluff to utilize the Elk Ridge range, develop the land, and control the water associated with Blue Mountain, thus blocking non-Mormon expansion into the region.[25] A party of explorers investi-

Frederick I. Jones, a founder of Monticello, Mormon bishop, county commissioner, and president of the Blue Mountain Irrigation Company, stands
chest deep in his wheat field, proof of the soil's fertility. (San Juan Historical
Commission)

gated Recapture Canyon, Mustang Mesa, White Mesa, and the south
and north forks of Montezuma Canyon before returning to Bluff
with a favorable report.

In March 1887 Hammond called Frederick I. Jones and four
other men to start planting crops, laying out the future townsite of
Monticello, and surveying a ditch for irrigation. By the first part of
July, the men had their tasks well underway and had joined in a conflict that would continue for approximately the next eight years with
the cowboys of the Carlisle outfit. Warning shots, heated disputes,
and legal wrangling were all part of this struggle as each group tried
to control access to a steady stream of water.

Homesites established on the south fork of Montezuma Creek, now called Verdure, also were not free of conflict, either with cowboys from the Lacy (or LC) ranch or with the Ute Indians. The Mormons claimed all of the water from the south fork and three-fourths of it from the north fork; and they learned from lawyers that the Carlisles had very little legal title to any of it.[26] Since water was more available on the south fork, the men raised an initial crop of wheat, oats, and potatoes and experimented with both irrigation and dry farming.[27] Once the harvest was stored and a guard stationed to protect it, the pioneer families returned to Bluff for the winter. Around Christmas the guard abandoned his post, and when the settlers returned in the spring of 1888 one-third of the grain was gone, probably consumed by cowboys' horses. Undaunted, the settlers undertook the construction of the town of Hammond, whose name was shortly changed to Monticello, in honor of Thomas Jefferson's estate.[28]

To bolster this new colony, Francis Hammond called twenty additional Mormon men from Moab, Bluff, and Mancos, Colorado. Together they fenced 320 acres, established crude homes from wagon boxes and tents until more suitable accommodations could be fashioned, and started the arduous task of hauling wood from the mountains. Private homes as well as a meetinghouse arose from the sagebrush flats at the foot of the mountain, while the irrigation ditch, built by the newly incorporated Blue Mountain Irrigation Company, snaked its way across the flats to water the crops.[29]

A rudimentary economy blossomed. Most of what was not home-grown or self-made either came from the stores of Moab (supplied by the railroad established between 1881 and 1883 that ran through Thompson) or from the Colorado towns of Mancos, Durango, and, later, Cortez. As was the case in Bluff, freighting in wagons to distant markets provided an extra income, but it created a shortage of manpower for the women and children remaining at home. Thus, sharing and cooperation became the keys to survival in a lonely land populated with hostile cowboys and Indians or vagrants drifting through. As a civilizing influence, Monticello was only a speck on the Great Sage Plain of the Colorado Plateau.

Eventually other specks appeared, the most prominent being

Walter C. Lyman, founder of Blanding, helped survey the town, constructed the first ditches bringing water from Blue Mountain, and operated Blanding's first sawmill. (San Juan Historical Commission)

Grayson, now Blanding. Located on White Mesa south of Blue Mountain, the area held the possibility of being a townsite; Hammond's 1886 exploring party recognized its potential to support both agriculture and livestock due to its springs and seeps, the water from the mountain, and the soil left fallow since the Anasazi departed.[30] The Navajos already called the site "Sagebrush," because of that plant's luxuriant growth that swept along the mesa and through the pinyon and juniper groves to the mountain's base.

The establishment of Monticello, however, required all of the energy that the Mormon colonizers could muster. For ten years White Mesa remained the haunt of the diminishing livestock herds of the LC outfit and a favored camping place for Utes, Paiutes, and an occasional Navajo. Not until 1897, when Walter C. Lyman and his brother Joseph loaded a buckboard with supplies and left Bluff for White Mesa, did the idea of a community start to take shape. Walter told of receiving a vision in which a future city, located in this spot, would one day serve as a beacon of civilization, with a Mormon temple and educational facilities for Native Americans. Water was an important key to the fulfillment of this goal, and so the men rode over the mesa to Johnson Creek on the south side of the mountain, where they perceived a suitable course for an irrigation system, and then returned to enthusiastically report what they had found.

A half-dozen individuals believed the project could succeed, though many more scoffed. Undaunted, the believers marked out the route of the canal and undertook its construction until the snow began to fly. Spring found the men back at work, but they were soon called away to serve various missions for their church. For four or five years the ditch lay unfinished, until the men returned. Finally, by the spring of 1903, water was sluicing its way down the canal to the fields below.[31]

The townsite was surveyed and marked with cedar pegs driven amidst the sagebrush, in advance of the ditch's completion. Albert R. Lyman, Walter's nephew, tightened his belt, and on 2 April 1905 settled on White Mesa. His wife, her sister, and his little girl helped pitch the tent by a corner lot peg, then nestled down as the first official residents. He provided a very clear impression of his attitude toward civilization and the wilderness when he wrote:

> There was no water for house use, in spite of the expensive reservoir which had been built for that purpose; and there was no near neighbors, no fences, no ditches, nor houses, not even a respectable clear patch to be fenced. To make permanent camp on the townsite before any improvements were installed, was to go bare-handed against the stern elements of nature which had prevailed there during the ages. . . . O, what a howling wilderness that first little family had to meet! Nothing in the shape of human convenience, yet they had come to stay, they are staying yet.[32]

By July, five other families were established, and the town of Grayson began its uphill population climb.

The dawning of the twentieth century offered new opportunities to homesteaders on arid, less desirable lands. The Homestead Act of 1862 allowed people to obtain up to 160 acres of land from the public domain as long as the individual patent applicant lived on it for five years and made improvements on one-eighth of the staked claim or lived on it for six months and paid $1.25 per acre. In those regions where the carrying capacity of the land can support a large population, this amount of acreage was ample; but in the arid West, these offerings were generally too meager. The Desert Land Act (1877) provided 640 acres to individuals as long as they irrigated their claim within three years of filing. Applicants also had to pay $1.00 an acre to receive title to the tract. The Enlarged Homestead Act (1909) allowed for an individual to obtain 320 acres of nonirrigated lands with one-eighth of this land under cultivation and a seven-month occupancy by the owner. This last act had an important effect in southeastern Utah, attracting dry-land farmers from other parts of the United States in the following years.[33]

The dry lands north and east of Monticello, noted on early topographic maps as the Great Sage Plain, now set the stage for the next advance of civilization. Too far from Blue Mountain to be practical for irrigation, these lands were used to develop dry-farming techniques. Scientific knowledge kept pace with the new interest. The Utah State Agricultural College established one of six experimental stations in Utah at Verdure during 1903. For thirteen years workers tested different types of wheat to determine which were most suitable for dry farming in southeastern Utah. Lofthouse and Turkey Red wheats triumphed, respectively yielding an average of twenty-six and twenty-seven bushels per acre.[34] More importantly, the experimental station proved that the concept of dry land agriculture could be employed on a large scale, not just as a part of subsistence farming. With the Enlarged Homestead Act encouraging settlement on non-irrigated lands, San Juan County could now support a larger influx of settlers.

One harbinger of civilization that promoted the establishment of San Juan was the newspaper. *The San Juan Record*, started in 1915, has never missed a week of reporting county news since it was founded, though it has faced many challenges. Problems confronted the paper at different periods in its history, including obtaining equipment, publishing in cooperation with outside organizations in Moab and Dove Creek, recuperating after a disastrous fire in 1937 that destroyed not only the printing office but also back issues, and surviving economic cycles. This partly explains why the paper changed editors so often in just a fifty-year period. New editors took over in 1917, 1919, 1920, 1921, 1931, 1933, 1934, 1938, 1940, 1949, 1952, 1954, 1955, 1956, 1958, 1960, and 1965.[35] The turnover also illustrates a tongue-in-cheek article on newspaper publishing printed in a neighboring paper, which counseled readers interested in losing weight to either cut down their food intake to a starvation level while at the same time "chopping wood, plowing, pitching hay" or just turn to running a country newspaper.[36]

In spite of these problems, local newspapers helped entice people from far and wide to come to settle and labor in San Juan. Hyperbole ruled the day. Between 1912 and 1924 dozens of articles appeared weekly in the local newspaper and in the papers of Moab and south-western Colorado extolling the future of San Juan County. One example suffices to give the tenor of this boosterism. The author portrayed the county as the "richest in the state in the point of resources," with opportunities that "cannot be duplicated in the West." The lands contained "every natural advantage known to the West," but dry farming led the list. With claims that three-quarters of a million acres of land would yield "20 to 35 bushels [of wheat] an acre," and production doing well even during a drought, it is no wonder the author excitedly pointed out that "there is no possibility of failure in dry farming here." The article continued, claiming that processing the wheat in the Monticello grist mill was inexpensive, sale of the product at a good profit was assured, the county was constructing more roads, and population statistics were swelling.[37]

A brief survey of headlines over the next ten years illustrates the continuing optimism. Articles sported such titles as "San Juan County, Great Inland Empire, Stands on Threshold of Era of Prosperity," "San Juan County, Mecca of Home-Seeker," "Place Chosen for New Town," and "55,000 Acres at La Sal Open to Soldiers."[38] This last entry is instructive. As the demands of World War I increased the consumption of goods at home and abroad, prices favored a seller's market. Agricultural products and livestock across the nation sold at excellent profits, encouraging a farming boom. Hopeful settlers did not have to look far to see dollar signs on the horizon.

The settlement of San Juan skyrocketed between 1910 and the early 1920s, especially in the area "Out East" of Monticello. Small communities of homesteaders fed the economic growth of the larger town, although some, located closer to the Colorado state line, turned to Cortez, Mancos, and Durango. Approximate dates for the establishment of these communities illustrate the pattern: Boulder (1910), Lockerby (1912), Ucolo (1913), Summit Point (1915), Cedar Point (1916), Horsehead (1916), Ginger Hill (1917), Urado (1918), and Torb (1919).[39]

During this same period, Blanding received an infusion of new blood because of political unrest in Mexico. Mormon families that had fled south of the border during the intense antipolygamy activity of the 1870s and 1880s now found that Pancho Villa and other Mexican revolutionaries threatened their havens. Residents of colonias Diaz, Dublan, Juarez, Pacheco, Garcia, and Chuichupa watched the exodus of part of their populations starting in 1910, as Mormons trudged north across the border in search of a sanctuary from a different type of trouble than that which had originally brought them there.[40] Others remained; but for some who left, San Juan County waited with open arms.

The greatest influx of people came between 1912 and 1916. In January 1914 the town of Grayson could claim a population of 500 people; five years later it had risen to 1,100, although Monticello maintained 1,400 residents.[41] Not all of this growth was attributable to events in Mexico, but a sufficient amount occurred to create in the minds of at least some of the early settlers a slight division between them and the newcomers. The refugees settled wherever they could obtain land, some in the north end of town on the edge of the cedars, others in the southeast corner of Blanding. A generally friendly rivalry between the "Hole-in-the-Rockers" and the people from Mexico (collectively called "Pachecoites" regardless of origin) never proved to be a serious disruption to the community.[42]

By the mid-1920s agriculture moved into a slump that would continue through the Great Depression of the 1930s. On a national scale, the boost that World War I had given to farming now lurched to a halt. High tariffs to protect farm products did little to stem foreign competition, while expensive farm machinery absorbed profits and pushed many farmers into a series of extensive loans. Increased production depressed the value of the crops, yet presidents Calvin Coolidge and, to a lesser extent, Herbert Hoover insisted that free enterprise and rugged individualism would correct any economic inequities. They claimed that the economy would naturally adjust itself, in spite of the growing evidence to the contrary.[43]

Farmers on the Great Sage Plain felt the Depression's effects. In 1919 a bushel of wheat commanded $2.10; by 1921 the price had plummeted to $0.82 per bushel, a lowering trend that continued until 1936.[44] The value of local crops peaked in 1919 at $795,000 but by 1929 had declined to $288,000. Mortgages reflected the economy. In 1910 only seven farms in the area reported a debt of $8,300, but by 1930 fifty farms owed $137,020.[45]

Some homesteaders abandoned their claims, looking for greener pastures in a more suitable clime. Sagebrush, symbol of the untamed, crept back into their former fields and again surrounded their old homes. Yet the Depression of the 1930s gave impetus to others, many of whom came from Oklahoma and Texas, to plant new roots through the relatively inexpensive means of homesteading. Despite its drawbacks, San Juan continued as a refuge for those with tenacity. A few figures indicate the county's sustained growth. The number of farms in the county increased 270 percent between 1910 and 1935; total land in farms zoomed 340 percent during the same period though the value of the lands generally decreased.[46] Civilization was in San Juan County to stay, and with the economic boost given by European unrest and the subsequent approach of World War II, economic prosperity returned in the 1940s.

Another indicator of "civilization" is the advance of technology and its accompanying lifestyle. This is a huge topic, parts of which will be touched upon in later chapters dealing with roads, water development, health, education, and government. But one of the single most influential indicators for twentieth-century rural Americans interested in gauging when they had left the "wilderness" was the introduction of electricity with its attendant effects.

Most work and building accomplished during the last half of the nineteenth and the first years of the twentieth century was achieved through hard labor. Electricity would eventually help change that. Take, for instance, food preservation. Root cellars, sun-drying, and canning had been among the most popular means for storing and preserving food. Some people built wooden frame boxes on the north side of their homes, covered them with burlap, and then wet the cloth so that the circulating winds helped cool the boxes' contents.

The family or neighborhood icehouse provided another way to preserve food. Made of wood and insulated with sawdust or dirt, these structures averaged twelve feet square and eight feet high. Townspeople traveled to nearby ponds in winter, cut large blocks of ice with axes or saws, loaded the blocks into a wagon or sleigh, and hauled them home. The men stacked the ice in a bed of sawdust, covered the sides and tops with an additional eight to ten inches, and secured the door to prevent loss of cold. Owners later removed chunks of ice as needed for their domestic iceboxes.[47] These primitive methods were not abandoned until a regular flow of electricity was introduced to the area.

How then, did this boon to civilization—electricity—make its entrance? As with most things in San Juan, the process started on a small scale generated by the energy of a few interested individuals. Monticello, with its growing population, was talking about the possibility of installing this labor-saving miracle in January 1916. The town unanimously passed a resolution to borrow $25,000 from the Deseret National Bank of Salt Lake City to pay for both a water and a

Main Street Monticello, 1918. On the left is Bailey Mercantile, center left the blacksmith shop, and at far right is the George Adams home. (San Juan Historical Commission)

power system. The Blue Mountain Irrigation Company advertised for bids in April, estimating the cost to provide electrical service at an average of $400 per family. This large investment by the monetary standards of the day illustrates the great desire for economic and material progress. Optimism and sacrifice were two of the vaunted values of the pioneering and homesteading heritage; those who became discouraged and quit were soon forgotten.

In 1917 Monticello added to its achievements the installation of a generator that ran twenty-four hours a day to serve the town. Water flowing from a pipe drove this first generator, which featured an enclosed wheel thirty to forty inches in diameter. Lights initially utilized the majority of the power, but as people added other appliances, a diesel generator replaced the water-driven one.[48]

Blanding launched its own electrical program soon after. The White Mesa Company financed and operated the system, installed by the Wilkins Brothers Company from Monticello. Benjamin D. Black delivered 125 poles (cut from timber in Bulldog Canyon) at a price of two dollars each, while the Wilkins Brothers, after installing the main part of the system, emplaced individual hookups during the inclement weather of the winter.[49]

On the evening of 23 April 1918 the *Times Independent* of Moab reported that "Blanding Is Bathed in Flood of Light." Seen as a "brilliant victory over the doubter and the knocker," the newspaper proclaimed the familiar theme associated with so much of the settlement process:

> This [electric system], with the water system, the schools, orchards, farms, homes and industries, which have come so miraculously into existence in so short a time, transforming the sagebrush desert into a green place of habitation, is an infallible prediction of greater things still to come. The resurrecting to active life of an apparently dead country is a first-class miracle, and should lay in the human mind the foundation for unfaltering belief in infinite progress.[50]

With the possible exception of the internal combustion engine, perhaps no other technological advance could have produced such an important series of labor-saving devices. From washing machines and irons, to telephones and lights, to stoves and refrigerators, almost every new convenience hinged upon the availability of electricity. Not surprisingly, the demand for electrical power was usually ahead of the ability to provide service. Once the initial novelty wore off, people began to expect more and more electricity to be made available for both public and private use. The first generator in John Morley Black's flour mill in Blanding had produced an average of only seven to eight kilowatts of power, with a maximum capacity of fifteen. Steam-driven engines, fired by wood, ran the mill during the day and the town lights at night. Payment for the service often came in the form of cords of wood to be burned at the plant. Lighting was available in the evenings until 10:00, with a 9:30 "wink" to warn people that in half an hour it was lights out. For special events such as dances and parties, townspeople provided additional wood or cash to have the lights on until midnight.[51]

On 31 October 1928 Blanding voted to establish a bond that would provide a diesel electrical generating station. Two and a half months later, the station was in operation, providing a maximum output of thirty-five kilowatts. Monday became wash day for those with electric washing machines, but often the task could not be completed by many within the allotted time limit of electrical service, so it soon became extended to Tuesdays. By March, people with refrigerators were demanding more continuous service. Lynn Lyman, operator of the plant, went to Salt Lake City and talked to refrigerator distributors. He found that by providing eight-hour service a day, the refrigerators could maintain fresh foods. By 1935, Blanding leaders decided to provide electricity twenty-four hours a day.[52] An important technological advance of civilization had arrived full-time.

Thus, by 1940, the general city-building, homesteading, civilizing patterns of San Juan County were established. It is true that there would be a large influx of people tied to oil and uranium exploration and mining in the 1950s through to the 1970s; and it is also true that government agencies and the tourist industries have brought thousands of people to San Juan each year for a variety of purposes. But the real settling process, the one that gives San Juan its unique Anglo-American heritage, was now basically over. Much of the toil, discouragement, and abandonment that were a part of earlier everyday life has been forgotten as people point to those who triumphed and set an example of determination for generations to come. However, the bringing of "civilization" to isolated southeastern Utah had exacted a high price; yet, like the native plants of the Colorado Plateau, what had taken root was deeply entrenched and well adapted to survive in this often harsh environment.

ENDNOTES

1. Various accounts of the settlement of San Juan include Cornelia Perkins, Marian Nielson, and Lenora Jones, *Saga of San Juan* (Salt Lake City: Mercury Publishing Company, 1968); Faun McConkie Tanner, *The Far Country: A Regional History of Moab and La Sal, Utah* (Salt Lake City: Olympus Publishing Company, 1976); Charles S. Peterson, *Look to the Mountains—Southeastern Utah and the La Sal National Forest* (Provo: Brigham Young University Press, 1975); Frank Silvey, "History and Settlement of Northern San Juan County," Frank Silvey Collection, Utah State Historical Society, Salt Lake City, Utah; and Albert R. Lyman, "History of San Juan County, 1879–1917," Special Collections, Brigham Young University Library, Provo, Utah. The best study of the trek into San Juan is found in David E. Miller, *Hole-in-the-Rock, an Epic in the Colonization of the Great American West* (Salt Lake City: University of Utah Press, 1959); other accounts include Lee Reay, *Incredible Passage through the Hole-in-the-*

Rock (Salt Lake City: Publishers Press, 1980); C. Gregory Crampton, *Standing Up Country: The Canyon Lands of Utah and Arizona* (Salt Lake City: Peregrine Smith Books, 1983), 101–7; and Albert R. Lyman, "Fort on the Firing Line," *The Improvement Era*, serially, October 1948 to March 1950.

2. Alfred N. Billings, "Memorandum, Account Book and Diary of Alfred N. Billings, 1855," Special Collections, Brigham Young University Library, 1–25.

3. Silvey, "History," 3–5.

4. Peterson, *Look to the Mountains*, 33.

5. Morris A. Shirts (descendant) correspondence with Robert S. McPherson, 24 October 1985, in possession of author.

6. Charles Kelly, "Aneth," Charles Kelly Papers, Special Collections, University of Utah Library.

7. Shirts correspondence; "San Juan Stake History," Special Collections, Brigham Young University Library, 15.

8. Parley Butt, "Life of Parley Butt," Special Collections, University of Utah Library, 4.

9. Miller, *Hole-in-the-Rock*, 45, 142–143.

10. Ibid., 116.

11. Ibid., 104.

12. Ibid., 53, 73, 109, 140.

13. Ibid., 104–105; 83–97; 138–140.

14. Lyman, "History," 15; Kelly papers.

15. "Minutes of County Commission of San Juan County from April 26, 1880, to March 5, 1900," Recorder's Office, San Juan County Courthouse, Monticello, Utah, 8; Platte D. Lyman, "Journal," Special Collections, Brigham Young University Library, 18, 26; Kumen Jones, "Writings," Special Collections, Brigham Young University Library, 213.

16. P. D. Lyman, "Journal," 34, 37; A. R. Lyman, "History," 23, 32.

17. P. D. Lyman, "Journal," 77; A. R. Lyman "History," 32.

18. A. R. Lyman, "History," 33.

19. P. D. Lyman, "Journal," 73, 75–76; A. R. Lyman, "History," 39–40.

20. Platte D. Lyman, "Diary," unpublished manuscript, Special Collections, Brigham Young University Library, 73–75.

21. Ibid., 75.

22. Ibid., 76.

23. A. R. Lyman, "History," 42, 50, 58.

24. F. A. Hammond, "Journal," 24 March 1887, Special Collections, Harold B. Lee Library, Brigham Young University.

25. Kenneth R. Weber, *Cultural Resource Narrative for Class I Cultural Resources Inventory for BLM Lands in South San Juan County, Utah, Part 2, History and Contemporary Cultures*, 15 October 1980, Utah State Historical Society, Salt Lake City, 9.

26. Norma Perkins Young, *Anchored Lariats on the San Juan Frontier* (Provo: Community Press, 1985), 84–85.

27. A. R. Lyman, "History," 54–56.

28. Ibid.

29. Harold George and Fay Lunceford Muhlestein, *Monticello Journal: A History of Monticello Until 1937* (Self-published, 1988), 14–15.

30. A. R. Lyman, "History," 9.

31. Ibid., 91–92.

32. Ibid., 93–94.

33. Melvin J. Frost, "Factors That Influenced Homesteading and Land Abandonment in San Juan County, Utah," M.A. thesis, Brigham Young University, 1960, 46–50.

34. Ibid., 56–58.

35. "San Juan Record Endures Many Hardships; Never Has Missed an Edition," *San Juan Record*, 10 May 1951, 1; "The Saga of San Juan Record," *San Juan Record*, 25 July 1968, 13.

36. *Grand Valley Times*, 18 January 1907, 1.

37. "Prospering San Juan County," *Grand Valley Times*, 12 December 1913, 5.

38. "San Juan County, Great Inland Empire, Stands on Threshold of Era of Prosperity; Demonstration Proves It the Greatest Dry Farm Section," *Grand Valley Times*, 8 January 1913, 5; "San Juan County, Mecca of Home-Seeker," *Grand Valley Times*, 25 December 1914, 7; "Place Chosen for New Town," *San Juan Blade*, 4 January 1918, 1; "55,000 Acres at La Sal to be Opened to Soldiers," *Times-Independent*, 13 March 1924, 1.

39. Perkins et al., *Saga*, 194–211; see also Corinne Roring, "Torb—The Area Forgotten," *Blue Mountain Shadows* 8 (Summer 1991): 5–11.

40. For a good, brief description of life in the Mormon colonies in Mexico see Karl Young, "Brief Sanctuary," *The American West* 4, no. 2 (May 1967): 4–11.

41. "Grayson, Utah," *Montezuma Journal*, January 22, 1914, 1; "San Juan County, Utah," 1920, Special Collections, Brigham Young University Library, Provo, Utah, 1.

42. William Riley Hurst, interviewed by Robert S. McPherson, 23 January 1992, transcript in possession of author.

43. John A. Garraty, *The American Nation: A History of the United States*, 7th ed. (New York: Harper Collins Publishers, 1991), 753–55.

44. Melvin J. Frost, "Homesteading," *Blue Mountain Shadows* 8 (Summer 1991): 3.

45. "Basic Data of Economic Activities and Resources: San Juan County," compiled by the Utah State Planning Board, 1940, on file in Special Collections, Brigham Young University Library, 2–3.

46. Ibid.

47. Brian Eberhard, "Chill Out," *Blue Mountain Shadows* 8 (Summer 1991): 32–33.

48. "Monticello Light Plant," *Grand Valley Times*, 26 May 1916, 1; Muhlesteins, *Monticello Journal*, 136–38.

49. "Electric Lights Are Assured for Blanding," *San Juan Blade*, 31 August 1917, 1; "To Deliver Poles for Lighting System," *San Juan Blade*, 28 September 1917, 1; "Wilkins Brothers to Install Lighting System," *San Juan Blade*, 26 October 1917, 1.

50. "Blanding Is Bathed in Flood of Light," *Times-Independent*, 9 May 1918, 2.

51. Marilyn and Rebecca Lyman, "Electricity in Blanding," *Blue Mountain Shadows* 8 (Summer 1991): 43–44.

52. Ibid.; Lynn Lyman and Chuck Carroll, "Further Comments on Electricity," *Blue Mountain Shadows* 8 (Summer 1991): 47–48.

6

Pushing the Line

NAVAJO CONFLICT AND BOUNDARY EXPANSION, 1880–1933

Following their release from Fort Sumner in 1868, Navajos returned home and then pushed beyond their reservation borders in search of water for agriculture and grass for their livestock. By 1880 they encountered in southeastern Utah the early stages of Mormon and non-Mormon homesteading—white settlers attracted to the area by the waters of the San Juan River. Although only the Utes could justify a strong aboriginal claim to the area, the two most active groups in the region—Navajos and Anglos—were farmers dependent on water for crops and keepers of livestock who were interested in the open ranges. For approximately fifty years both sides competed for land ownership; however, unlike many scenarios acted out elsewhere in the American West, here the Native Americans triumphed. Additions to reservation lands in 1884, 1905, and 1933 were enacted despite political and economic opposition from the white community. The tale of how the Navajos succeeded is the topic of this chapter.

In April 1880 a large contingent of Mormons arrived at Bluff, having endured an arduous six-month journey along the Hole-in-the-Rock Trail. Noted for their organizational ability, these settlers lost little time in implementing a new San Juan County government and ecclesiastical organization. Twenty miles upriver in McElmo Canyon and along the San Juan, eighteen non-Mormon families, consisting of seventy men, women, and children, had been struggling to survive for the past two years.[1]

While the Mormons generally were determined to placate quarrelsome Indian neighbors, some of the people living in the Montezuma-Aneth area followed a policy that led to direct confrontation with the Navajos and Utes along the sparsely settled boundary of the San Juan. The most notable of these was Henry L. Mitchell, whose farm, trading post, irrigation ditches, dam, and pasture sat on the Aneth floodplain. Eking out an existence in this area was challenging, given the fluctuations in the height of the river and the ever-present threat of clashes with Navajos and Utes. Eventually, it all proved too much for Mitchell.

In addition to being a colorful character and a lightning rod for trouble, Mitchell was a prolific writer of letters and recorder of events. He unwittingly has provided information concerning occurrences in San Juan that would otherwise have been lost to history. He also provides an interesting contrast to Mormon settlers in their interaction with Navajos and Utes during a tumultuous time of give-and-take by all four groups. While it is unfortunate that deeds of kindness were not recorded as frequently as those of conflict during this era, Mitchell has contributed to our understanding of just how confusing and troublesome those events could become.

In the latter part of 1879 Mitchell started a trickle of correspondence to government agencies that became a continuous stream of reports of Indian depredations. In all fairness, it must be noted that he was in a difficult position. His ranch bordered the Southern Ute Reservation to the east and the Navajo Reservation to the south, while to the west and north lay lands claimed by small bands of Southern Utes, Paiutes, and Navajos who refused to stay within reservation boundaries and submit to agency control. Government reports often referred to them as "renegades." For the next six years, Mitchell's ranch became a focal point of conflict amongst all these groups as they crisscrossed the area.

Mitchell was a man of contradictions. Although he protested that the Navajos were wandering far from their reservation, he also issued passes, which he had no authority to do, for the Indians to come across to the north side of the river to graze their flocks on Mormon-used public domain. Anything he could do to cause friction between him and his Mormon neighbors seemed to give him delight. No doubt part of this was due to his Missouri background, where he had previously encountered Mormons, part of it was due to the growing political and economic influence of his neighbors, and another part of it was due to a cantankerous disposition. By "opening" the ranges to Native Americans, he frustrated Mormon plans to use the land. One eyewitness noted: "The Navajos and Pah-Utes crossed with their countless herds of sheep and goats, and from the San Juan to the Blue Mountains—north 40 miles—they eat every particle of vegetation. This caused great suffering and loss among stock belonging to the Mormons, who say that remonstrance is useless."[2]

The Mormons, in turn, intimated that Mitchell sold ammunition and whiskey to the Indians. At the same time, Mitchell was trying to convince federal Indian agents that Indian attacks on his establishment were imminent. By filing these complaints, he prepared the way to lodge future claims against the government for failure to control its wards. The claims of loss of property—whether real or imaginary—served as a basis for requesting financial reimbursement. Mitchell constantly insisted that troops be sent to the vicinity to provide protection; these soldiers stayed at his ranch and bought goods at his trading post. Yet he also encouraged Indians to come into the area, thus adding more trading business, irritating the Mormons, depleting their resources, and decreasing their desire to remain.

Mitchell proved to be an opportunist par excellence. At least part of this was not lost on Indian agent D. M. Riordan, who, after explaining why the Navajos felt justified in living outside their boundaries, noted that "the Indians are persistently encouraged to leave the reservation by small traders living around in the country surrounding the reserve. These men generally treat the Indians pleasantly and the Indians listen to them. It is 'business,' pure and simple with the trader."[3]

By the end of 1885, a change occurred. There is no further men-

tion in the historical record of Henry L. Mitchell. Indian depredations continued in 1886, 1887, and 1888—each time resulting in petitions from settlers in McElmo Canyon, but Mitchell's name was
absent.[4] The most important reason for his leaving the area was
undoubtedly the flood of 1884, which wiped out his riverplain homestead, but by this time his credibility had worn thin with the military
and his methods had become predictable. Kumen Jones, a Bluff
settler, provides the only known description of Mitchell's departure
when he wrote that the trader and his family spent "a very few troublesome years" in the area and then "hit the trail back out, much
worse off than when they came in."[5] No doubt this exodus provided
relief to both the local Indians and the Mormons.

In Mitchell, one finds a quarrelsome man who rarely lacked
words. Through prose and deed he was able to involve Navajos, Utes,
Indian agents, Mormons, cavalry, the governor of Utah, and the
Commissioner of Indian Affairs in a series of incidents that encouraged six years of turbulence and indecision. The Navajos and Utes
responded by using intimidation to further their goals when practical. While Mitchell's actions at times seem inconsistent—such as his
encouragement of Navajos to graze their herds north of the river and
then later complaining about it—he was effective in playing one
group against another to his advantage. The frequency and nature of
his complaints laid the foundation for future Navajo agents to claim
new lands north of the San Juan River in order to calm the continuing discontent between white ranchers and Navajo stockmen.

The latter part of the 1880s and 1890s saw more petty and not-
so-petty frays. Livestock, land, and trading posts provided the cata-
lysts for conflict. For example, a man named J. F. Daugherty,
postmaster in Riverview (now Aneth), came center stage in 1893,
when Navajos threatened his trading post. The initial spark was
ignited on 5 April when Navajos commandeered a ferry that ran on a
cable across the river. Daugherty's brother, William, feared the boat
would swamp and called for the two pirate Indians to come back.
They refused. He fired two shots in front of the craft, forcing them to
return, but in a short while they reappeared with a group of thirty
warriors to back up their demand for two hundred dollars in
exchange for not burning the store. Since the five white men at the

Holley's trading post in Aneth about 1900. James M. Holley hired local Navajos as freighters, road construction workers, and as translators for the agent at Shiprock. In 1905 he sold the post and became a government farmer to the people of Aneth. (Western History Department, Denver Public Library)

post were heavily outnumbered, they paid the money and sent for the agent. A few days later, one of the Navajos, encouraged by alcohol, burned the crib that supported the cable on the far bank and then threatened to kill William Daugherty. By the time agent E. H. Plummer arrived, tempers had heated on both sides and were cooled only by the threat of cavalry. Eventually, the two guilty men surrendered and stood trial at Fort Defiance in the tribal Court of Indian Offense.[6]

Petitions continued to flow from the San Juan as J. F. Daugherty, William Hyde, S. J. Berlin, and Peter Guillette, many of whom ran unlicensed trading posts, complained about the actions of their customers. These stores served as magnets to draw Indians off the reservation, creating headaches for agents, settlers, and Indians alike.[7]

Government policy indirectly encouraged Native Americans to take up individual allotments on the public domain. The Dawes Act of 1887 fostered the ideal of the Indian making his living as a farmer. Along the San Juan, Navajos often dug small irrigation canals to water their crops on the floodplain. Now, with ever-increasing herds of sheep and a growing interest in agriculture, competition over resources between white settlers and Indians took on a new intensity. Commissioner of Indian Affairs T. J. Morgan watched the situation fester to a bursting point and claimed that "in the meantime I know of no other way to maintain peace between the non-reservation Navajo Indians who are on the public lands and the white residents except by the aid of the military."[8]

To complicate matters further, the fall of 1892 saw a gold rush along the lower San Juan. Miners found little mineral wealth of value; however, they "staked almost every inch of land along the river between McElmo Creek and the Arizona-Utah border."[9] Within a year, the main rush was over, but not before tensions flared. Later mining strikes in the Carrizo Mountains caused concern, forcing cavalry units to return to the San Juan vicinity to maintain peace.[10]

Navajo unrest can be attributed to what they considered encroachment on their lands as well as having to face what was by then a third year of starvation. Starting in 1892 and peaking in 1895, the Indians living along the San Juan River combatted killer frosts, severe droughts, and cold spring weather that ruined chances for good crops. Citizens from Bluff to Farmington, New Mexico, warned the Navajo agent that his charges were literally starving to death. The once lucrative trade in wool and blankets ceased because of a national depression; all but one of the nine trading posts in San Juan County had closed; and dreams of agricultural self-sufficiency started to evaporate. Still, the agent believed that the San Juan River was the only major reliable source of water in the region and needed to be developed, so he assigned farmers in the area to help teach Indians better agricultural techniques.[11]

As the weather mellowed, a renewed interest grew in establishing some type of agency to help maintain economic and political control in this far-flung corner of the Navajo Reservation. Problems over land, water, trade, hunting, cultural values, and government responsibility underscored the need for the Four Corners region to have someone who could deal with issues before they became inflamed. By the early 1900s, the Shiprock Agency, founded by subagent William T. Shelton, became a reality.

In 1895, however, eight years before Shelton arrived, another one of San Juan's colorful characters settled along the river. Howard Ray Antes, an independent Methodist missionary and self-styled Indian advocate, settled not too far from where Mitchell had pulled up his roots ten years before. Born on 20 October 1850 in Homewood, Illinois, Antes trained for the ministry before moving to Palisade, Colorado, just outside of Grand Junction. Described as an "old fashioned Methodist minister," he was a "holiness preacher" who emphasized a strict interpretation of biblical tenets. Drinking, gambling, and womanizing were sins unacceptable to his beliefs, but many of his parishioners desired a more liberal approach to ethical behavior. He faced the demands of his congregation head on, refused to change his ways, and moved to greener pastures—in this case, the red sands of the San Juan.[12]

In 1895 Antes and his wife, Eva, arrived in the sparsely populated community of Aneth, previously called Riverview, and established the Navajo Faith Mission to bring succor to the Indians during the depths of the 1895 depression. He built his first home of logs but soon started construction on a much larger and more elaborate sandstone structure. How much actual preaching he did to the few white and numerous Indian people in the area is questionable, but the Navajos did name him "Hastiin Damiigo," Sunday Man.

Facilities at the mission continued to grow. By 1904 the site boasted a large house, a smaller school building, and surrounding farmlands and orchards located on the river's flood-plain. Antes, however, never took up homestead rights on this property.[13] Instead, he put all of his energy into dispensing charity, donated from sources in the East, to the destitute Navajos. He and his wife also encouraged the blanket-weaving industry by loaning the wool and dyes necessary for production, while "furnishing people with ton after ton of clothing and flour" to sustain them through long winter months.[14]

After his arrival there really was no other spokesman for the Navajos living along the river as they confronted Anglo livestock owners interested in public grasslands. The government owned a vast amount of territory in San Juan County that was available to use for the asking. The county commissioners helped oversee the activities and obtained revenue from those using the land, but such use was open to any qualified applicant. At the same time, reservation lands

The Navajo Faith Mission, 1901. Founded by Methodist missionary Howard Ray Antes, the boarding school was located near the San Juan River just east of Aneth and averaged twelve to fifteen students. (San Juan Historical Commission)

were under great strain to meet the needs of expanding livestock herds, unclaimed water holes were nonexistent or inadequate, and agents could not effectively patrol the reservation boundaries. These facts, coupled with the belief that Native Americans needed to become more self-sufficient by taking out individual land allotments, encouraged Navajos and agents alike to look for solutions across the San Juan River.

Eventually, Howard Antes assumed the responsibility of writing passes "on the authority of the Commissioner of Indian Affairs and the Secretary of the Interior of the United States" for Navajos wishing to graze livestock on the north side of the river.[15] The San Juan county commission was irate. Kate Perkins, county clerk, fired off letters to the Commissioner of Indian Affairs and the governor of Utah, demanding to know if Antes had the power he claimed and if the Navajos could actually use the lands tax free. The commission cited an ordinance passed in 1897, insisting that all livestock should be licensed, that failure to do so was a misdemeanor, and that the penalty would be double the original cost of the license.[16] Holding true to bureaucratic form, the Commissioner of Indian Affairs stated that as long as the Navajos had paid the proper tax and followed the guidelines of the county and state, they were as free to use the lands as was any white man. If they did not break the law, no action could be taken against them.[17] The Navajos paid no taxes, and the friction continued.

Antes, however, saw another opportunity to end the turbulence over area rangelands. Government surveys conducted through the region in 1899, along with the increased interest in ditch building for agricultural purposes, fostered the idea that perhaps the lands along the north side of the river should become a permanent part of the reservation. As a solution to the problems of self-sufficiency for a burgeoning population, advocates pointed out that "land along the river can be irrigated and put under a state of cultivation far cheaper per acre than any other part of the reservation."[18]

The time was right. William T. Shelton, with his aggressive, straightforward, no-nonsense personality assumed the responsibility to see that this idea came to fruition. The Northern Navajo Agency included Utah lands south of the river, and though peripheral to much of the reservation activity in New Mexico and Arizona, Shelton never lost sight of its potential. The local Navajos petitioned him for surveying help to put in ditches. Antes also heard their wishes and again decided to champion their cause. On 10 April 1904 he wrote a letter to President Theodore Roosevelt, asking for an enlargement of the reservation. Chester A. Arthur had granted the first such extension through executive order in 1884, which had moved the boundary north to the San Juan River. In 1892 mining and homestead interests had forced the return of some of these lands to the public domain, but in 1908 they again returned to reservation status. Lands in the Aneth-Montezuma Creek area were the first that Navajos requested north of the river.

Antes pointed out that a number of white settlers had attempted to farm the region and had given up, there being now only three stores, the Navajo Faith Mission, and the post office which he operated. He anticipated that the extension would lead to less friction between stockmen and Indians and more desirable conditions for the

Navajos.[19] Shelton only partly agreed. He felt that Antes's suggestion of annexing the land was good, but he argued that if the Indians had to obtain it through homesteading, it would take them twenty-five years to clear its title. On the other hand, if Roosevelt issued an executive order, the land would be protected from encroachment by livestock owners, access would be provided to the Navajo, and messy legal entanglements would be avoided.[20]

After some initial revisions due to survey problems, President Roosevelt signed Executive Order 324A on 15 May 1905, creating that portion of the reservation. Known today as the Aneth area, these lands encompass the region beginning at the mouth of Montezuma Creek, east to the Colorado state line, south along the state boundary, then along the San Juan River to Montezuma Creek. Lands previously claimed or settled were excluded from the reservation.[21] Antes had fulfilled his ideas of annexation.

White neighbors near the reservation addition were angry. Some tried to claim mining or homestead rights in the area, and the county commissioners and government officials protested through letters. Local whites continued to discriminate against the Navajos. Yet darker storm clouds loomed on the horizon of 1907. For some time, a Navajo leader named By-a-lil-le had opposed Shelton's plans for improvements in the Aneth area. Using witchcraft, thinly veiled threats, and outright force he and a small group of followers coaxed and coerced a faction of Navajos to refrain from sending their children to school, to refrain from using the government sheep-dip vats located at the mouth of Montezuma and McElmo creeks, and to refuse to follow the orders of Navajo policemen. On 27 October 1907 Shelton and his Indian police led Captain H. O. Williard and two troops of cavalry on a surprise attack of the Navajos' camp. The Indians started shooting. The soldiers returned fire, killing two, wounding another, and capturing By-a-lil-le along with eight men deemed equally troublesome. The agitators were marched to Shiprock, Fort Wingate, and then to the jail at Fort Huachuca, Arizona, where they spent two years at hard labor.[22]

Although the incident ended quickly, and by most accounts was well-handled, Antes seized upon the opportunity to wage another crusade—this time against Shelton. Why their relationship had deteriorated is not entirely clear. Perhaps it was because of a disagreement over building a riprap dam to protect the mission property, perhaps because Shelton had lost interest in purchasing the site, perhaps because of a growing misunderstanding over Antes adopting a Navajo boy, or perhaps because Antes received inaccurate information from biased sources.

Whatever the reason, Antes resorted to the same techniques that had worked so well before. He wrote letters to Colorado Senator H. M. Teller and to the editor of the *Denver Post*. Within six months after the incident, Colonel Hugh L. Scott, superintendent of the United States Military Academy and investigator for the government, received word to proceed to Utah and determine the truthfulness of the charges. On 21 April the investigation started in the local schoolhouse with Captain Williard, Agent Shelton, interpreter Bob Martin, Colonel Scott, and Reverend Antes present. By the end of the investigation, the reverend was defeated. After hearing lengthy testimony, Scott determined that the minister's charges were not proved due to lack of evidence and that his motives were questionable. Rather than struggle further, Antes tried to back out gracefully. Using the guise of protecting his Navajo witnesses from the ravages of an irate Shelton, Antes chose "to suffer the humiliation of falling down on this prosecution personally rather than let any injury come to them [i.e., the witnesses]."[23] The case was closed. By 1909 Antes had abandoned much of his life on the San Juan, selling the Navajo Faith Mission to the government for $1,200 so that it could be converted into a boarding school.[24] By 1919 the river had eroded so much of the bottomlands that the mission-turned-school disappeared in brown, swirling flood waters.[25]

At the same time that Antes first entered the Aneth region, government agents were eyeing the same lands for a different purpose. In the 1890s Constant Williams, as Navajo agent, continued to cry for farming on the San Juan. On 11 December 1894, Williams went to Bluff, where he found the Indians "pitiable" because of crop failures over the past two or three years.[26] Later, another government official looked at lands above Bluff between the Aneth and Mancos Creek (Colorado) area, where farming would be "far cheaper per acre than any other part of the reservation." The Navajos there had repeatedly asked for help in creating ditches. But it was not until the Shiprock Agency brought government help closer in the form of Agent William Shelton that these wishes could become a reality.[27]

Shelton analyzed the situation. He noted that Navajos often constructed ditches that washed out easily at the first high water because the trenches lacked headgates and protective barriers. In 1905, armed with $3,000 for irrigation projects, he appointed a farmer, James M. Holley, to supervise Navajo agriculture and livestock operations. Holley was no stranger to the area; he had come to Aneth in 1899 to open a trading post. During those six years he had been vocal in alerting government officials about the conflict over grazing lands between white and Navajo stockmen, and he had even asked for a position helping the Indians.[28]

Once appointed, Holley worked closely with Shelton; but of more importance was his impact on the Navajo as a government farmer. He built a riprap protective barrier to prevent the river from eating away at the top of the Navajos' irrigation ditches. He started road construction to join Aneth to the Four Corners area and paid his Indian laborers in farm tools, which some found very enticing. Forty-five days of labor could net a worker a wagon, five days a scraper, and one day a shovel, axe, or saw, etc. If a worker organized a group of men and helped feed them, the time needed to earn the wage decreased by half.

As the focal point of the community, the government farmer became increasingly prominent. In most areas of the reservation, the local trading post served as the center of community activity, but where a government farmer lived, assuming that his personality and attitude were acceptable, an even stronger bridge was formed between white and Navajo society, between official policy and Navajo practices.

In 1914 Herbert Redshaw, the new government farmer, arrived in Aneth. To the Navajos, he was "T'aa biichiindii." An exact translation of this name is difficult, but an approximation is "His Own Devil." The Indians did not apply this epithet with rancor or malice. Redshaw moved slowly and swayed slightly as he methodically swung his arms and walked; his Indian name gives a feeling that he moved like a dead man returned to life.

Redshaw hoped to institute a plan for building a dam near Four Corners and eventually another at the mouth of McElmo Creek. The proposed structure would be as high as the surrounding hills, with irrigation ditches paralleling both sides of the river. This would alleviate much of the danger of floodplain agriculture, which by now was becoming increasingly popular, with Navajos farming every available space along the river. Unfortunately, government shortages of funds and enthusiasm precluded the undertaking.[29]

Although Redshaw was not able to realize this dream, he did systematically teach Navajos what he considered to be the proper methods of agriculture. At this same time, he succeeded in having twenty-five families settle around an irrigation canal that supplied water from the mouth of McElmo Creek.[30] He also kept track of the sheep dipping done in the spring and became embroiled in the conflict centering around range rights in the Montezuma Creek-Aneth area.

Cattlemen and sheepherders vied for lands near the northern part of the reservation, with some of the ranchers slipping over the boundaries onto Indian lands. No fence separated property, so Redshaw told the Indians to herd the animals back onto the public domain, an act which did not sit well with the stockmen. Many of the whites thought talk of law and authority a bluff, especially the younger men who lacked "the fair attitude of the old timers." Redshaw pled for immediate government action.[31]

The Indian agent agreed with Redshaw's evaluation and added that some of these stockmen had been involved for years in stealing Indian cattle and making a handsome profit from the sales. Ranchers were also lobbying Congress to open Navajo and Ute lands to white livestock grazing.[32] Tensions increased. The result of the conflict was the 1933 addition to the Navajo Reservation of the lands encompassed by or adjacent to Montezuma Canyon, known as the Aneth Extension.

By the time most of the solutions to these problems were worked out in the early 1930s, Herbert Redshaw had retired from the Indian service. Almost as if the San Juan River knew that he had left and livestock reduction had started, its waters gathered strength to undo what had been accomplished. In 1933 the river once again overflowed

Navajo men visiting Bluff. Interaction with the Mormon community was usually friendly, characterized by trading, sharing food, and horse racing. A boat, manned by employees of the Bluff Co-op, plied the San Juan River during high water to bring the Navajos with their trade goods to the store. (San Juan Historical Commission)

its banks, tore out the irrigation ditches, snatched away the headgates, wiped out Navajo farms, swallowed the government station, and forced abandonment of life on the floodplains. The river also shifted from the south to the north side of the streambed and cut away every vestige of productive land. The Shiprock Agency withdrew its program of maintaining a resident farmer in Aneth and requested that anybody desiring help come to its headquarters. The battle with the San Juan was over.

While livestock and farming conflicts played the central role in disputes with Utah Navajos living on the eastern half of the reservation, the initial problems on the western half were tied to a series of boom-and-bust invasions of miners seeking precious minerals. The rocky shores and canyons of the San Juan, as well as the scenic landscapes of Monument Valley and Navajo Mountain, increasingly came under the scrutiny of individual prospectors, large companies, and the federal government as rumors led to exploration and then discovery of gold and (later) oil deposits. Consequently, the status of a section of land known as the Paiute Strip seesawed back and forth between being public domain and reservation property, depending upon who exerted the greatest pressure for control at a given time.

When President Chester A. Arthur through an executive order in 1884 provided all of the lands in Utah south of the San Juan River to the Navajos, it was hoped that this would quell the competition for territory with settlers. In reality, the action just recognized an accomplished fact, that the Navajos had expanded far beyond the 1868 reservation boundaries. Now there was a clearly defined boundary— the San Juan River—which allowed no room for misunderstanding. Or so it seemed. What President Arthur and some of the local agents had not realized was that the expanding Navajo population, growing herds of livestock, and discovery of precious metals eight years later would drastically change the situation.

By 1892 Navajo Agent D. L. Shipley noted a tendency for Navajos throughout the reservation to leave their confines and move onto the public domain, where they grazed their herds and in some cases homesteaded in accordance with a section of the 1884 executive order. Shipley believed that of the 16,102 Navajos recorded in the census of 1890, 9,241 were off the reservation utilizing public domain water and pasturage for their animals.[33] Although this figure should be treated as a rough estimate, it certainly indicates what was occurring on all of the borders of the reservation: land was at a premium.

White men were eyeing the same land, as well as the rough, sparsely populated reservation area west of the 110th degree longitude. This territory generally encompassed the area of Monument Valley, Navajo Mountain, and the lower part of the San Juan and Colorado rivers before they cross the Utah-Arizona state line. Interest by whites in prospecting this land went back to the early 1880s; by 1892, mining concerns had created sufficient pressure to insure that the government return the lands to the public domain.[34] This action came none too soon. Starting in November 1892, a large influx of miners descended on the banks of the San Juan in search of rumored deposits of flake or flour gold.

News of the rush reverberated from Bluff to Mancos, then Durango, and then throughout the Four Corners region. By the end of January 1893 an estimated 3,000 miners were panning, shoveling, scraping, and burrowing into the banks and bars along the San

Juan.[35] Bluff's infant economy boomed overnight, while rural towns
in Colorado thrilled at their burgeoning business. The *Mancos Times*
boosted the region, claiming that the "gold and silver ore said to be
from that district would be hard to duplicate in any country."[36]

As with most get-rich-quick schemes, the boom in San Juan did
not take long to bust. By March of 1893 most of the miners had left
for richer diggings in western Colorado. A handful of men still clung
to the hope that somehow they could devise a system to retrieve the
fine-grained flakes found in the sands of the San Juan.[37] Men with
wealth introduced different types of machines to dredge the stream
bottoms and separate the precious metals; but it was all to no avail.[38]
The San Juan for the next ten years refused to yield substantial riches.

To the Navajos, this was just another example of the white man's
madness. The loss of this rough country, peripheral to major areas of
livestock industry, was a setback to only a relatively small number of
Indians, yet they still protested the mining on the south side of the
river by destroying claim markers, scattering horses and burros, and
generally intimidating the interlopers.[39] Eventually, interest in the
Paiute Strip faded.

By 1906, Indian agents were again raising the cry for more reservation lands to decrease the tension between settlers and, this time,
Paiutes and Utes. The San Juan Band Paiutes, numbering fewer than
100, had forged strong ties with the Weenuche Utes and some
Navajos of San Juan County. The Paiutes ranged in the region near
the Arizona-Utah line in the vicinity of Navajo Mountain and in the
area between the San Juan and Colorado rivers—a territory, one man
claimed, that was the "most difficult of access of any in the United
States, outside of Alaska."[40]

Members of this Paiute and Ute faction had become so troublesome to the area's white settlers that the Strip was offered as a place
for these Indians to locate on a more permanent basis. Mixing with
Kaibab Paiutes farther to the west, the San Juan Band also maintained
friendly relationships with the Navajos in the area. A government
special investigator suggested the lands west of the 110th degree longitude "be again withdrawn from public entry and set apart as a
reservation for Indian use, specifying particularly the San Juan
Paiutes and including other Paiute Indians of southern Utah who

have not been provided for otherwise."[41] In 1908, when withdrawal of the lands from the public domain became a reality, the Paiutes may have had their name placed on the tract, but it was the Navajos who primarily utilized it.

Approximately a year later, prospectors began filing petitions for access to minerals and oil located on the withdrawn lands. Neither the Northern Navajo Agency in Shiprock nor the Western Navajo Agency in Tuba City, Arizona, was anxious to oversee the use of this area, because it was unsurveyed, extremely isolated, and technically belonged to the Paiutes, whose agency was in distant southwestern Utah. By default, the Western agency took the reins of control, but its agents made visits only when necessary. Justification for this was based on the travels of the Paiute people residing around Navajo Mountain, who frequented Tuba City for help, as did the Navajos living on the Strip.[42]

By 1921, new economic forces called for a new determination on the land's status. Paradise Oil and Refining Company, Monumental Oil Company, and traders such as John Wetherill and Clyde Colville from Kayenta sought the right to locate and pump petroleum from the land, which they believed was vacant. The Bureau of Indian Affairs requested Byron A. Sharp, its agent in Tuba City, to investigate the possibility of opening the territory for exploration.[43]

Within two months, a report lay on the desk of the Commissioner of Indian Affairs. Sharp's investigation had taken him to Monument Valley and surrounding areas, and he determined that the eighty-six Paiutes who had lived there in 1907 were now gone. Some had died during the 1918 influenza epidemic; others had moved to Blue Mountain. Only forty-eight now lived in Paiute Canyon, and even those either frequented Navajo lands or had been absorbed into this neighboring tribe. Navajos used these lands for grazing, but Sharp felt they had "sufficient land within their own reservation to care for their needs," and so the agent could "see no objection to throwing it open to settlement."[44] Indeed, the Monumental Oil Company was already drilling just east of the 110th meridian, and Mormon cattlemen were illegally ranging 500 animals on the Strip. The Bureau of Indian Affairs acquiesced and in 1922 released the 600,000 acres back to the public domain without consulting the Navajos.

That was in July. Three months later, as word of the transaction filtered down to the Navajos, petitions to make the Strip part of the reservation again began to arrive in Washington. Center stage was Elsie Holiday, a twenty-one-year-old, full-blooded Navajo graduate from the Sherman Institute. As a local spokesperson for her people, she drew up four different petitions, attached 134 signatures, and fired them off to the Commissioner of Indian Affairs, the Secretary of the Interior, the Indian Rights Association, and interested agents. Holiday argued that Monument Valley Navajos had lost some of their best rangelands and waterholes with the stroke of a pen, that ancestors and relatives were buried there, that an unclear boundary line would lead to increased range conflicts, and that the Navajos were willing to relinquish any claims to oil and mineral rights in return for grazing privileges. The white men's cattle had already gotten mixed in with Navajo livestock, and some of the owners were masquerading as government men, telling the Navajos to leave and tearing down and burning fences and corrals.[45]

Indian agents now took up the cry. J. E. Jenkins from the Paiute Indian Agency in Reno argued on Elsie Holiday's behalf that the cattlemen were blocking Navajo access to the San Juan River, especially during the dry season. If the river remained a boundary, both groups would have sufficient water for their needs. A. W. Leech, supervisor of the Indian school in Tuba City also came to her aid. During his visit to the area, he noted that seventy-four Navajos lived on the Strip and suggested that each could file for a 160-acre homestead with a spring or water on it, thus denying access to their white neighbors.[46] Yet for the Navajos depending on extensive rangelands and unused to government red tape, this still seemed impractical.

Five years later, the tribal government in Window Rock, Arizona, was still expressing the same sentiments. Council members from the Monument Valley area believed that soon there would be no more lands available for tribal acquisition and that this particular parcel was "by far better grazing or farming land than the average lands of the Western Navajo Reservation."[47] One hundred families now herded sheep in the area, while only three white squatter, trader families lived on the lands, cheating the Indians by purchasing sheep and cattle at

Mrs. H. M. Peabody befriended many Navajo women by teaching basic Anglo homemaking skills while showing great respect for Navajo weavers—a group of whom surrounds her in Bluff in the early 1900s. (Western History Department, Denver Public Library)

low prices when the Navajos were financially desperate. Now was the time to halt this practice.

Between 1930 and 1932, a series of meetings in Blanding drew state and federal government officials, members of the Navajo Tribal Council, Navajo and Ute agents, and stockmen from both sides of the San Juan to the bargaining table. The desire for control of two major ranges—the Aneth Extension and the Paiute Strip—encouraged each side to compromise in an attempt to reach a fair agreement and stop the incessant finger-pointing. On 15 July 1932, committee members reached a final settlement that six months later, on 19 January 1933, became law. Those representing the white interests agreed that the Paiute Strip and the Aneth Extension would become part of the

Navajo Reservation. In return, the Native Americans and their advocates agreed to relinquish their right to establish individual homesteads in San Juan County north of the tribal boundaries, though the
forty-four pending claims would be honored. The Indian Service
would insure that Navajo lands, where appropriate, would be fenced,
that the Indians would abide by state game laws when hunting off the
reservation, and wandering livestock that crossed boundaries would
be handled according to published livestock rules.

Of great future importance was the agreement that as the tribe
allowed oil exploration and leasing of its lands, the State of Utah
would receive 37.5 percent of the royalties, which in turn would be
used for "the tuition of Indian children in white schools and/or in the
building or maintenance of roads across the lands" discussed in the
bill.[48] Time would tell how important this agreement would become
to the Navajos in southeastern Utah.

In summarizing this fifty-year period of Navajo expansion, one
finds three major ingredients that entered into all of the additions
and temporary deletions that occurred in Utah on the northern border of the reservation. The most prominent and best documented
aspect was the expanding population base and increasingly greater
dependence on grass and water to support Navajo lifestyles. This was
true throughout the reservation, where censuses record a dramatic
increase: from 17,204 people in 1890, to 21,009 in 1900, to 38,787 in
1930.[49] While historians may argue about the accuracy of these censuses, especially in the earlier years, no one can question the general
trend they reveal. More people required more land and water to sustain life.

The second factor was the availability of land onto which the
Navajos could expand. Mormons and non-Mormons had settled near
the northern boundaries of the reservation late enough that extensive public domain still existed, while a frontier atmosphere still colored many of their dealings with Native Americans. Though the law
allowed for individual homesteading by all parties, the Navajos were
treated as a group. Consequently, the government cut out large blocks
of land to meet the needs of its charges.

Finally, the Navajos were fortunate enough to have sympathetic
agents and friends who were not afraid to roil the waters on their

behalf. Men like Antes, Redshaw, Shelton, Walker, and others fought through the political red tape, the local cattlemen's associations, oil companies, and government officials to achieve a series of land-acquisition victories that paid both short- and long-term dividends to the Navajos. The Utes, discussed in the next chapter, often failed to have this latter benefit and so suffered from shrinking boundaries on their lands.

In later years there would be another land addition to the reservation, but, for the present, the Navajos sat contentedly on the Paiute Strip and Aneth Extension looking forward to more and better resources for their livestock. Little did they realize that the government was about to destroy their base economy with a livestock reduction program that would devastate them economically and psychologically. A whole new era was about to dawn on the Dine.

ENDNOTES

1. Henry L. Mitchell et al., "Evaluation of Property Destroyed . . . ," 24 December 1879, Letters Received, Consolidated Ute Agency Records, Denver Federal Records Center, Denver, Colorado (hereafter cited as DRC—Ute Agency).

2. Cass Hite to Galen Eastman, 17 April 1883, Record Group 75, Letters Received, Bureau of Indian Affairs, National Archives, Washington, D.C. (hereafter cited as Letters Received—BIA).

3. D. M. Riordan to Commissioner of Indian Affairs, 31 December 1883, Letters Received—BIA.

4. Petition from Citizens of McElmo Canyon, 16 December 1886, DRC—Ute Agency; J. S. Carpenter and B. Gifford to C. F. Stollsteimer, 17 May 1887, DRC—Ute Agency; Petitions of Citizens of McElmo Canyon, 30 January 1888, Letters Received—BIA.

5. Kumen Jones, "Writings," unpublished manuscript, Special Collections, Brigham Young University Library, 203.

6. W. W. Daugherty to Lieutenant E. H. Plummer, 5 April 1893, DRC—Ute Agency; Plummer to Commissioner of Indian Affairs, 20 May 1893, Letters Received—BIA; Plummer to Post Adjutant, 29 June 1893, Letters Received—BIA.

7. For a fuller treatment of this topic see Robert S. McPherson, *The Northern Navajo Frontier, 1860–1900—Expansion through Adversity* (Albuquerque: University of New Mexico Press, 1988), 63–78.

8. U.S. Senate, "Navajo Indians in New Mexico and Arizona," Ex. Doc. 156, 52d Cong., 1st Sess., 4 August 1892, 15.

9. Bryant Jensen, "An Historical Study of Bluff City, Utah, from 1878 to 1906," M.A. thesis, Brigham Young University, 1966, 103; Albert R. Lyman, "History of San Juan County, 1879–1917," unpublished manuscript, Special Collections, Brigham Young University Library, 75.

10. Special Orders dated 24 April 1896, Lt. L. M. Brett, Adjutant, 2d Cavalry, Letters Received—BIA.

11. Constant Williams to Commissioner of Indian Affairs, 26 January 1895, as cited in "Navajo Use and Occupation of Lands North of the San Juan River in Present Day Utah" (hereafter cited as NUOL), an unpublished manuscript by David M. Brugge, on file in the Navajo Documents Collection, Edge of the Cedars Museum, Blanding, Utah. This is an important report, which is used extensively in this paper. Brugge quotes correspondence that is otherwise unavailable. I received approval to use these materials in a telephone conversation with the author on 4 February 1991.

12. Lorena Antes, wife of Howard Antes's adopted son, telephone conversation with Robert S. McPherson, 18 June 1991.

13. Antes to President Theodore Roosevelt, 18 April 1904, NUOL.

14. Antes to Commissioner of Indian Affairs, 2 February 1899, NUOL.

15. Kate Perkins to Commissioner of Indian Affairs, 15 January 1900, NUOL.

16. Ordinance found in Minutes of County Commission of San Juan County, Utah, from 26 April 1880 to March 1900, Court House, Monticello, Utah, 245.

17. W. A. Jones to Heber M. Wells, 1 February 1900, Record Group 75, Letters Received—Navajo Agency.

18. Hayzlett to Commissioner of Indian Affairs, 28 July 1903, NUOL.

19. Antes to Theodore Roosevelt, 18 April 1904, NUOL.

20. Harriet M. Peabody to Commissioner of Indian Affairs, 8 July 1904, NUOL; Shelton to Commissioner of Indian Affairs, 30 July 1904, NUOL.

21. "Navaho Reservation, Utah—Cancellation of Lands Set Apart in Utah," Executive Order 324A, cited in Charles J. Kappler, *Indian Affairs— Laws and Treaties*, 3:690.

22. Earl D. Thomas, "Report Department of Colorado," *War Department Annual Reports, 1908* (Washington, D.C.: Government Printing Office, 1908), 3:151–52.

23. U.S. Congress, Senate. "Testimony Regarding Trouble on Navajo Reservation," S. Doc. 757, 60th Cong., 2d Sess., 3 March 1909, 24–25.

24. Traylor Inspection, 22 January 1917, NUOL.

25. Ray Hunt interview with Robert S. McPherson, 21 January 1991, San Juan County Historical Commission, Blanding, Utah, 2.

26. Constant Williams to Commissioner of Indian Affairs, 11 December 1894, NUOL.

27. Hayzlett to Commissioner of Indian Affairs, 28 July 1903; William T. Shelton to Commissioner of Indian Affairs, 28 December 1903, NUOL.

28. Shelton to Commissioner of Indian Affairs, 24 July 1905; Harriet Peabody to Commissioner of Indian Affairs, 28 February 1905; James M. Holley to Shelton, 20 February 1905, NUOL.

29. Harvey Oliver interview with Robert S. McPherson, 7 May 1991, in possession of author.

30. C. L. Christensen, "Tells of Strange Navajo Ceremonies," Moab *Times-Independent*, 9 February 1922, 3.

31. Herbert Redshaw to Evan W. Estep, 29 January 1921, NUOL.

32. Estep to Commissioner of Indian Affairs, 9 February 1921, NUOL.

33. U.S. Congress, House, *Report of the Secretary of the Interior*, "The Navajoes," H. Ex Doc. 1, Part 5, 52d Cong., 2d Sess., 1892, 576.

34. Ibid., 876.

35. Frank Silvey, "Stampede for Placer Gold," unpublished manuscript, Utah State Historical Society, 10 April 1936, 3–4.

36. *Mancos Times*, 17 January 1893, 4.

37. Silvey, "Stampede," 4.

38. For more information on the gold rush along the San Juan and especially in the Glen Canyon area on the Colorado River see Gregory Crampton, *Standing Up Country: The Canyon Lands of Utah and Arizona* (Salt Lake City: Peregrine-Smith Books, 1983), 120–44.

39. *Salt Lake Tribune*, 17 January 1893, 1.

40. Levi Chubbuck to Secretary of the Interior, 31 December 1906, Record Group 75, Letters Received by Office of Indian Affairs, 1881–1907, Bureau of Indian Affairs, National Archives, Washington D.C., 5.

41. Ibid., 30.

42. Walter Runke to Commissioner of Indian Affairs, 19 September 1909, located in the J. Lee Correll Collection, Tribal Archives, Navajo Tribe, Window Rock, Arizona (hereafter cited as Tribe); Runke to Commissioner, 23 April 1915, Tribe.

43. E. B. Merritt to Paradise Oil Company, 4 June 1921, Tribe; Merritt to Byron A. Sharp, 28 December 1922, Tribe; C. Hauck to Sharp, 24 March 1922, Tribe.

44. Byron A. Sharp to Commissioner of Indian Affairs, 2 June 1922, Western Navajo Agency, Tribe.

45. Elsie Holiday to Secretary of the Interior, 27 November 1922, Tribe; Holiday to Secretary of the Indian Department, 28 November 1922, Tribe; A. W. Leech to Commissioner of Indian Affairs, 18 May 1923, Tribe.

46. J. E. Jenkins to Commissioner of Indian Affairs, 10 December 1922, Tribe; A. W. Leech to Commissioner of Indian Affairs, 18 May 1923, Tribe.

47. C. L. Walker to Commissioner of Indian Affairs, 6 December 1928, Tribe.

48. C. L. Walker to Commissioner of Indian Affairs, 21 March 1930, Tribe; Chester E. Faris to Commissioner of Indian Affairs, 23 September 1930, Tribe; J. M. Stewart to Assistant Commissioner of Indian Affairs, 19 July 1932, Tribe; Mark Radcliffe to Commissioner of Indian Affairs, 29 September 1932, Tribe; J. M. Stewart in Memorandum to John Collier, 31 August 1933, Tribe; U.S. Congress, House, "Bill to Permanently Set Aside Certain Lands in Utah. . . ," H.R. 11735, 72d Cong., 2d Sess., 19 January 1933; "'Piute Strip' Controversy Settled at Last," San Juan Record, 21 July 1932, 1.

49. Garrick Bailey and Roberta Glenn Bailey, A History of the Navajos—The Reservation Years (Santa Fe: School of American Research Press, 1986), 105.

7

Shrinking Lands in a Crucible of Change

THE UTE AND PAIUTE EXPERIENCE, 1880–1933

At the same time that the Navajos received their reservation along the New Mexico–Arizona border and well below the San Juan River, the Southern Ute Tribe also obtained theirs. On 19 August 1868 William F. M. Arny, the Ute agent, met with the Weenuche and Capote leaders at Pagosa Springs in southwestern Colorado. The Indians outlined what they considered desirable reservation boundaries, given the already deteriorating circumstances of their lands to the east. They wanted to be guaranteed the territory encompassed by the Grand (Colorado) and Green rivers to the north and west, the headwaters of the San Juan River on the east, and the Navajo country to the south.[1]

What they received, however, was far different, with all of their territory lying in Colorado. Although this reservation initially included much of the upper San Juan River, the lower San Juan remained a fringe area that no one seemed too excited about in 1868. The Four Corners area was peripheral to the mining and settlement activities of the 1860s; it received some general use by some Navajos and Paiutes but was dominated by the Weenuche Utes.

This relative isolation soon disappeared.[2] By the early 1870s, the estimated 700 to 1,000 Weenuche Utes still lived by "the chase" and came to their Abiquiu agency in New Mexico only for gunpowder and lead. According to their agent, they were "very much attached to the localities" in which they lived and were characterized as "excellent shots . . . great friends of our government . . . and are . . . reasonable and docile."[3] But they also needed to protect what they had. In 1871 the agent noted that prior to that time other groups of Utes had feared entering Weenuche country but now were overcoming this fear and were hunting in Weenuche territory, thus increasing the pressure on available resources.[4]

The Weenuche also faced the problem of Navajo incursion on their lands. Navajo agent James H. Miller set out from Fort Defiance, Arizona, on 4 June 1872 with B. M. Thomas, agency farmer; John Ayers, trader; and Jesus Arviso, interpreter, to locate agricultural lands on the San Juan. A week later, while the men were camped on the river, two Utes stampeded the group's horses and killed Miller. This served as one more reminder to the Navajos of their recent defeats by their enemies, emphasizing again that to venture near Ute lands could mean death. Although the Utes were "disposed to prevent the Navajos from planting there," the acting agent believed that this obstacle could be overcome by stationing a small garrison of troops nearby.[5] Extended control, however, did not become a reality for another thirty years.

In 1873 Southern Utes signed the Brunot Agreement, which was followed by an executive order in 1874; the result was that they relinquished control of the San Juan Mountains to mining interests. The three southern bands, represented by 280 signatures, lost 3,450,000 acres of valuable Colorado lands, which only increased their dependence on a shrinking land base and on government intervention.[6] Anger at the loss of these lands resulted in sporadic outbursts such as that encountered by members of the Ferdinand V. Hayden survey expedition in 1875. As the thirteen-man party crossed through Dry Valley on their way to Blue Mountain, they were attacked by an "outlawed band of Utes, Paiutes and Navajos, who under the lead of Pahghe-nob-i-gant [Poco Narraguinip], infest the canyons of Southeast Utah."[7] The survey crew abandoned its equipment and fled to safety,

but not before the Utes had made a lasting impression on the interlopers.

Of even greater concern to the Native Americans was the influx
of white settlers, who, beginning in 1878, scouted out farms and livestock ranges along the San Juan and in McElmo Canyon, a natural
thoroughfare leading from Colorado into Utah. The Weenuche Utes
and Paiutes of San Juan County became increasingly uneasy about
this invasion from the east, especially in 1880 when Mormons joined
the growing cluster of settlements. Add to this the probing tentacles
of Navajo expansion from the south, and the resulting friction over
resources became inevitable and continuous.

A few examples will suffice. The Utes complained about Navajos
grazing sheep and horses on their lands, destroying ranges, and
monopolizing waterholes. Mexican herders, likewise, used tribal
lands, forcing the Utes onto the public domain in search of fodder.[8]
The Utes traveled and camped in McElmo Canyon on the border of
Colorado and Utah, insisting that it was their land; the Navajos, with
their large flocks of sheep, went wherever they pleased; the whites in
the area watched fences being torn down and gardens trampled by
Indian livestock. The Utes, according to the settlers, "offered . . .
insults, abuse, threatened lives . . . and have driven us from our
houses. . . . We do not want war, but if we fight, we must exterminate."[9]

The day after Christmas in 1886, Captain J. B. Irvine, 22d
Infantry, evaluated the situation in McElmo Canyon. The problem
stemmed from the narrowness of the canyon, which allowed settlers
to place rail or brush fences every mile or two for livestock control.
Whenever the Indians traveled to either end of the canyon or ventured beyond to hunt, they tore down the fences or left the gates
open.

A typical example of the fear and hatred engendered on both
sides involved A. L. Smaed, who homesteaded near Battle Rock,
halfway down the canyon. Ute "squads" of from four to twelve men
showed up at his door regularly, demanding food. One time, while
Smaed's wife cooked, the Indians stole an "ax, pick, grub hoe, shovel,
harness, pair of blankets, a box of cartridges, and numerous small
articles." While Smaed carried a petition to Fort Lewis, Colorado, to

Ute hunters in search of game. Deer played a major role in traditional Ute economy and so Indian migration patterns paralleled those of the animals. Favorite winter camp locations included Montezuma Canyon, Dry Valley, Butler Wash, and Douglas Mesa; summer locations included springs and streams on or near Blue and La Sal mountains—the same areas that attracted white settlers for natural resources. (Western History Department, Denver Public Library)

try to stop this thievery, the Utes liberated his $100 horse, shot and killed cattle, continued to demand food, and ordered other settlers to clear out. After he returned, the Utes went to Smaed's ranch and told him to come out of his house. One of them, called "Billy the Kid," tried to pull him through the doorway by his ear, saying, "White man must go; cowboy must go; . . . you go right now or me heap shoot." Smaed broke loose, exchanged shots, packed some belongings, and fled two miles up the canyon to a nearby rancher's home. The Indians followed, but well-armed settlers scared them off. As far as the local whites were concerned, the Utes needed to be permanently forced back onto their Colorado reservation.[10]

At the mouth of McElmo Canyon, friction was just as evident. The last half of the 1880s and the first half of the 1890s saw a litany of recriminations and protest, as Utes and Navajos descended on the settlements of the San Juan. One man, James F. Daugherty, chronicled the events in frustrated letters. One reported: "Navajos drove off herd of cattle eighteen miles, killed one, the rest on reservation; . . . has had twenty-three head of horses stolen, and gotten none back; . . . Navajos have killed at least six people and nothing done about it."[11] The Indians returned "lost" livestock only after receipt of a five-dollar reward. The Utes added demands that the San Juan should be vacated immediately and threatened that settlements in lower McElmo Canyon would be "cleaned out" and that livestock would continue to disappear. Angry settlers described the Indians as "red devils," "cut throats," and "saucy." They also reported a "rankling in the breast" of some Ute leaders.[12]

Various Ute groups in San Juan County under the leadership of Red Jacket, Narraguinip, Mariano, Bridger Jack, Polk, Johnny Benow, and Posey reacted to the general deterioration of their lifestyle during this and later time periods. Many of these fragmentary bands eventually either moved to their reservation in Colorado or coalesced into what would be recognized by the early 1900s as the Montezuma Canyon and the Allen Canyon Ute groups. Although these two factions were interdependent, the particulars of their experience varied somewhat and so will at times be treated independently.

One of the greatest threats to Ute resources came in the form of cattle companies searching for free-use public lands. By the 1880s four major outfits ranged thousands of cattle on the grass and brush of San Juan canyon country. The two most important were the Kansas and New Mexico Land and Cattle Company of Edmund and Harold Carlisle, and the L. C. outfit, located on Recapture and Verdure Creek at the head of Montezuma Canyon. The herds of these companies were considerable, the L. C. alone selling 22,000 animals between 1891 and 1893.[13] Herds of this magnitude changed the quality of the environment within just a few years' time, increasing the problems between Indians and whites. Although many of the area cattle companies would rise to meteoric heights only to fail, there always was another group to step in to keep the cattle business alive.

For the Weenuche Utes living and ranging throughout San Juan County, the cumulative impact of these events was overwhelming. With Mormon and non-Mormon settlers creating homesteads on critical resource lands and trail networks, livestock companies herding cattle on Blue Mountain and the La Sals, and the government compressing the Muache, Capote, and Weenuche into a strip of Colorado land fifteen miles wide and 110 miles long, there smoldered a growing resentment. Utes, Paiutes, and some Navajo allies reacted violently. Fights at Pinhook Draw (1881), White Canyon (1884), around Bluff, and in the La Sal and Blue mountains erupted when the tension became too intense. Many of these better-known encounters have been written about elsewhere and so do not bear repeating here, but rarely are the reasons for these conflicts or the personalities involved given a fair assessment.[14]

Take, for instance, the Weenuche Johnny Benow, living in Montezuma Canyon. He and his associates made life miserable for area cattlemen. Edmund Carlisle wrote to the Southern Ute Agent saying Benow's people were at Paiute Springs (near present-day Monticello) and in Cross Canyon (which enters into Montezuma Canyon) "killing many cattle and burning the grass and timber. Unless something is done to check them, they will do very serious damage. The citizens talk of organizing and killing off these Utes. . . . Benow is the leader at Cross Canyon and Narraguinip and Mancos Jim appear so out here [Monticello area]."[15]

In July 1884 the government sent a troop of cavalry, augmented by a detachment, to Montezuma Creek to protect the cattlemen whose property was being stolen by Indians. An earlier fracas had ended with the death of a Ute over the ownership of a horse. The Indians retaliated by driving off a herd of horses; the cavalry and cattlemen went in pursuit, the result of which was the fight in White Canyon.[16] Edmund Carlisle identified Benow as a participant in this fray and complained that some cowboys later saw Benow riding one of Carlisle's favorite horses. The rancher then requested "a fair recompense from the government for the heavy losses my company has sustained from depredations of the Ute Indians," estimated at this time as including over 150 head of horses.[17]

Each spring, summer, and fall trouble regularly arose. Agents sought help from the military to move the Utes back to the reservation. Talk was common of secret organizations formed by cattlemen and settlers to rid themselves of the Indians. One of these vigilante groups exterminated a Ute family of six as it camped on the Dolores River in southwestern Colorado. Chiefs on the reservation did not have the power to maintain total control of their charges, and they also occasionally denied Ute involvement in altercations that arose. On 20 July 1887 a company of infantry camped on the North Fork of Montezuma Creek to maintain the peace and stayed there until 9 October.[18] Although no incidents occurred at the time, correspondence indicates the reason for some of these problems. One letter stated that

> a number of Ute Indians under the leadership of Ben-ar [Benow] living in the Blue Mountains in Utah . . . is not on the Agency rolls. . . . The Indians referred to are a band of wild Indians that have never been brought under the influences of civilization. . . . [They] have the appearance of extreme poverty, look half-starved, are nearly naked, and are subsisting upon rations issued to the Southern Utes.[19]

The situation did not improve. A military report of 1894 states that a group of about 95 Utes and 80 Paiutes under Benow refused to come in to the reservation.[20] They realized what was happening on the eastern part of the Southern Ute Agency land: where whites took unalloted lands not filed-on by Indians; where Ute culture deteriorated through the civilizing processes of education, missionary efforts, and agent control; and where agriculture, not hunting, became the only practical lifestyle. Indeed, large deer drives and out-of-season hunting by the Utes put intense pressure on area deer herds. Letters from settlers, game wardens, and government officials to the agents stressed the harm being done to the diminishing wildlife resources.

The Northern Utes in Colorado had just as rocky a history as their relatives in southern Utah and Colorado.[21] In 1879 they killed their abrasive agent Nathan Meeker as well as a military officer and twenty-eight other whites before the fighting ended. This, added to the pressure from farmers, livestock owners, and land developers in Colorado caused the removal of the Northern Utes to the Uintah Reservation in northeastern Utah. Similar white forces wanted to evict the Southern Utes from their strip of land in the Four Corners area. Pressures from mining interests created even more reason to relocate the Utes.

As agents and Washington bureaucrats cast about for an answer, San Juan County, Utah, suddenly looked like a solution. Ignacio, leader of the Southern Utes, agreed to look the land over. He traveled with a party of Utes as far as the Carlisle ranch north of Monticello before giving a final nod of approval. That was in 1887. A year later, the government presented a plan that signed over to the Utes 2,912,000 acres, a promise of $50,000 in ten annual payments, sheep valued at $20,000, an agency, and the right to hunt in the La Sal Mountains.[22] In effect, this gave all of San Juan County, minus Navajo lands south of the San Juan River, to the Utes.

Utah ranchers and settlers were irate. The Mormons, the Carlisles, and members of the Pittsburgh Cattle Company fought back by lobbying state and federal government officials to prevent seizure of their land. The Indian Rights Association, headquartered in Philadelphia, politicked in Washington, fearing that even if the government removed the settlers, nasty friction would still erupt with the whites in Moab. They also said that previous mining claims would still be an issue and that there was insufficient water for large-scale farming projects. The Territory of Utah was even more blunt, insisting that it already had enough Indians.[23]

The wrangling went on; finally, the Utes decided to move. In November 1894 an estimated 1,100 Indians with their agent, David Day, arrived in San Juan County to select new homes. Utah Governor Caleb West, surprised county commissioners, and interested citizens jammed along with Utes into the log school in Monticello. As the deliberations heated, a messenger delivered a note from Washington saying the Indians had five days to go back to Colorado. The threat of cavalry convinced the Utes. They eventually went back to the Southern Ute Reservation, the eastern portion of which was opened to Indian allotments, with the remaining land being sold to white settlers. By 1900 the western half became an unalloted section called the Ute Mountain Ute Reservation, with an agency in Navajo Springs (present-day Towaoc).[24]

There was little to attract San Juan Utes to Towaoc where, according to a government report, "upon this vast tract of land, no water has been provided to even cultivate an acre of land, and during the summer the Indians are compelled to take to the mountains with their stock so as to find a sufficient supply of water to quench their thirst."[25] It was no surprise, therefore, that in 1896 "the great majority" of the Weenuche were "largely in the blanket and divide their time between Colorado and Utah, the latter pilgrims being the Pi-Utes or renegades who inhabit the Blue and La Sal Mountains in Utah and [who] were added to the rolls of this agency in June, 1895."[26]

The turn of the century saw no change in conditions. The Utes living at Navajo Springs as well as those living off the reservation eked out a bare existence: no irrigation ditch existed to water the land, ration issues proved to be a lifeline that extended for only two weeks in a month, springs on Ute lands were dry by the end of summer, and agent turnover was a continuing problem—in 1900 alone there were three such changes.[27] That same year saw a smallpox epidemic that claimed at least fifty-five lives; how many more deaths went unreported is unknown. There were eight births during the same period. A year later their agent prophetically warned that "a clash will eventually occur [as] is demonstrated by the fact that on several instances, serious conflicts have been narrowly averted."[28]

The Utes in San Juan County, however, reacted according to what they considered justifiable reasons to maintain their holdings; interestingly enough, a number of whites agreed. For instance, in September 1908 J. S. Spear, superintendent of the Fort Lewis school in Durango, Colorado, visited Montezuma Canyon and reported his findings. He talked to Johnny Benow, who said that the Indians had lived in the canyon all of their lives and that it was far better than being on the reservation. They grew small crops, had about 1,500 sheep and goats, were prosperous, and were "well spoken of except by those who have filed complaints."[29] Spear suggested these complaints provided a convenient way for whites to remove the Indians in order to obtain rangelands, even though he believed that the members of Benow's band had not given white citizens any trouble.

Although no verbatim transcript exists of Benow's interview, Spear provided a summary. After denying that he had killed cattle or horses, Benow claimed that the Mormons were trying to drive him out of the canyon by fencing the land. The Utes retaliated by doing the same, provoking threats to have them put on the reservation. Benow refused to move. Spear closed by generally agreeing that the Indians had at least as much (and probably more) right to be there than the settlers.[30]

The Utes and Paiutes in Allen Canyon were even more notorious. Ever since the first settler placed his boot in the sands of Bluff or the first cattleman ran a steer on Blue Mountain, this band of "rene-gades" had played a part in each of the conflicts occurring between the 1880s and the early 1900s. In March 1914 an even more serious event took place that assumed headline proportions for six months. The problem began when a Mexican sheepherder named Juan Chacon camped with some Utes and Paiutes from the Montezuma Canyon area. Among them was Tse-Ne-Gat, also known as Everett Hatch, who spent time with both Ute groups. Chacon spent the evening playing cards and visiting around the campfire. A few days later he was found dead, and witnesses claimed Tse-Ne-Gat had killed him.[31]

Ten months later Tse-Ne-Gat had still not surrendered to law enforcement authorities. He feared his life was in danger; but, in the eyes of the law, this was not sufficient justification for not turning himself in. U.S. Marshal Aquila Nebeker, along with local helpers from Cortez, Bluff, Blanding, and Monticello, decided to arrest Tse-Ne-Gat. The newspapers set the stage for the approaching drama by saying that "Hatch has a notorious reputation as a bad man," that he "had defied several attempts to bring him into custody," was "strongly entrenched with fifty braves who will stand by him to the last man," and that this group had been "terrorizing" the people of Bluff.[32] The headlines a week later could almost be predicted.

In Moab, the *Grand Valley Times* headline splashed across the page: "1 White and 3 Piutes are Killed," with a subheading of "Indians Defy U.S. Authority—Entrenched in Cliffs South of Bluff, Renegades under 'Old Polk' Say They Will Never Give Up." *The Mancos Times* followed suit with "Indians Resist Arrest; Joe Aiken Killed." Both papers tried to paint the picture of treacherous Indians, heavily armed waiting in ambush for the whites to approach. The "uprising" occurred when the seventy-five man posse approached the Ute camp in the early light of dawn. A startled early riser gave "whoops of warning" to awaken the others, then opened fire. Initial volleys resulted in two Indians and one white being killed (one "killed" Ute was only wounded), as the posse implemented "Indian strategy of the kind that one is accustomed to read in the histories of early life in the West."[33] Another group of Indians hearing the commotion came up from the San Juan River, approached the cordon from the rear, and started firing. The whites and Indians called a truce, the engagement ended, and the Utes fled for the wide open spaces.

Bluff, at least according to the newspapers, took on the air of a besieged town. Indian agents, state officials, and the military all became involved and no doubt sighed with relief when the newspapers reported that "Brigadier General [Hugh L.] Scott, Chief of Staff of the United States Army" was on his way to "attempt a peaceful settlement with the recalcitrant Piute Indians." The decision to send Scott was made only "after conferences between officials of the war department, department of justice, and the interior department."[34] What greater military dignity could be bestowed upon this small fray than to have Washington leaders conferring over its outcome.

To contrast the opposing sides, the *Grand Valley Times* spoke of the "Blanding volunteers" and the "Monticello boys" "stringing" back to their respective communities, while another article told of how "Old Posey" killed his brother Scotty, who had wished to end the conflict. Posey was "sullen and refused to bow to law," while Scotty was "pleasant . . . and among the last to join with the outlaws."[35]

When General Scott arrived in Bluff, he made it clear that he would try to settle the issue peacefully. Two weeks later, Scott had "captured renegade Indians" by meeting with them, promising all twenty-three of them protection, and by honoring the request that the four captives—Polk, Posey, Tse-Ne-Gat, and Posey's Boy—be brought to Salt Lake City for questioning. As the papers put it, "the redskins . . . had come to smoke a pipe of peace . . . with a representative of the Great White Father," and "he had succeeded."[36]

By April, officials in Salt Lake released all of the prisoners except Tse-Ne-Gat, who went to Denver to stand trial. Before the Ute ever entered the courtroom, *The Mancos Times-Tribune* announced that the charges against him could not be proven; but, when he was

Left to right—Bob Martin (Navajo interpreter), Posey, Jess Posey (son), Tse-Ne-Gat, and Polk enroute to Salt Lake City. (San Juan Historical Commission)

acquitted, the ire of the settlers in the Four Corners area reached meteoric heights.

Yellow journalism continued to vilify the Indians. Articles and news clips informed the public of Tse-Ne-Gat's, Polk's, and Posey's activities, reinforcing their negative images. Brushfire conflicts in 1919, 1921, and 1923 became important news and fanned the coals of disagreement. Even in the "off" years, when nothing newsworthy occurred, newspapers reminded people of the aggravation felt by the two races. A quick perusal of information concerning Utes for the last half of 1917 shows the intensity of feelings.

Starting in August the *San Juan Blade*, a short-lived newspaper published in Blanding, reported that "Ute Threatens Man with Gun . . . When Told to Move on; Utes Becoming Ugly." Another article derided Indians John Soldiercoat, who lost his "superstitious fear" of the "mysterious paper talk," and Posey, who spoke on a phone for the first time with "guttural grunts, inarticulate groans, and 'toow-itchchamooroouppi' . . . [so] that [the] line was put out of commission for three weeks." Other headlines insisted the "Utes Growing Ugly . . . [when they] Helped Themselves to Farmers Feed and Defied

Interference by the Settlers"; that a "Noted Indian Prepares for War . . . [as] Old Posey Stored Up Guns and Ammunition . . . to Oppose Uncle Sam"; that "Indians Again Growing Bold," when three Utes jumped on a lone woman's car four miles south of town and frightened her with their aggressive actions. Other accounts reported that "Ute Indians Hold Up Blanding Boy" and took his watch; that "Ute Trespassers Made to Pay" when confronted with charges of grazing their horses in a settler's field; and that "Old Posey May Stir Up Trouble" because he "had assumed a surly and threatening manner and appeared to be gathering about him a number of renegade redskins."[37]

There were other articles and clips; even those few that attempted to be partly complimentary, such as one that told of hiring Ute labor to clear sagebrush, used such language as "Noble Redman Works Best on Empty Stomach."[38] This tendency became so pronounced that a note in the *San Juan Blade* published on 30 November 1917, criticized the paper for "openly convicting itself of jealousy and ignorance." It went on to say "that the people of San Juan wanted the news instead of knocks."[39]

Yet the really pro-Ute journalism came from outside of the region and was sponsored by the Indian Rights Association (IRA). In November 1915, shortly after the Tse-Ne-Gat incident, M. K. Sniffen, the secretary of the IRA, wrote an article based on his visit with the Polk and Posey bands. His evaluation of the fracas flew in the face of the local accounts. He claimed that two-thirds of the posse that attacked the peacefully camped Indians was composed of "'roughnecks' and 'tinhorns' to whom shooting an Indian would be real sport!" The Utes had only protected themselves and their families who were not living on the reservation because of its undesirable conditions. Cattlemen had seized upon the fight as an opportunity to move the Indians off the rangelands, which was expressly against the government's desire to allot individual tracts of land from the public domain to start the "civilizing" process by stopping the Indians from living as a tribe. Sniffen concluded his remarks by writing, "The progressive Utes . . . are now patiently waiting to see if the United States Government intends to give them 'a white man's chance.' Surely they have proved their right to it."[40]

Local papers went wild. Far from helping the Utes' situation, Sniffen had unwittingly polarized even more whites against the Indians and their advocates. For about a month in the early days of 1916, frontline attacks marched across the pages of the *Cortez Herald*. One maintained that no kick was too low for this "Indian lover," who was "probably being paid a big salary for traveling over the country to fix up fairy tales about the persecuted red men."[41] The papers argued that the members of the posse were really heroes who had risked their lives under "Uncle Sam's command." Writers insisted that if Sniffen wanted a crusade, he should investigate where the Utes got their high-powered rifles and ammunition, or who shot at the builders of the school on the reservation, or why the government had not yet built the promised irrigation ditches for the Indians.[42]

Antagonists accused Sniffen of shoddy investigative techniques, jumping to conclusions, and not understanding the real situation of the local people. Papers refuted all of his charges in one way or another, but, in doing so, laid bare many of the real problems facing the Utes, and revealed how few of these concerns had yet been addressed.

By January 1917 the federal government wanted to find out why there was the continuing unrest. Special investigator Major James McLaughlin arrived in the area on 1 January and remained for eighteen days, interviewing the Indians at Towaoc, Montezuma Canyon, and Bluff. His unbiased findings show clearly the destitute conditions and the fear felt by the Utes and Paiutes of San Juan County.

McLaughlin hoped that the Indians would journey to the agency to meet with him, but James C. Wilson, an assistant of Samuel Rentz, who owned a small trading post and home in Montezuma Canyon, wrote a letter on the Native Americans' behalf saying that the trip would be too great a hardship. These Utes, he insisted, were afraid to go to the agency; many were sick, most were without sufficient clothing, many were walking barefoot in the snow and living in shelters made out of "old rotten canvas full of holes," and their horses were too worn to travel.[43] They were, however, very anxious to talk with Mclaughlin.

The inspector departed the agency and first bumped down McElmo Canyon by auto and then by wagon up Yellowjacket Canyon and across Cahone Mesa to the Rentz trading post, where he arrived on 9 January and stayed for two days. He met with all of the adult male Indians living in the canyon, whose total population he estimated at 160, with another fifty living around Bluff. All of the Utes were enrolled members of the Ute Mountain Ute Agency at Towaoc, but all refused to live on the reservation because they felt the Indians there were unfriendly to them and would not share the land with its insufficient water. Spokesmen from the Montezuma group included Johnny Benow, who assumed the chieftainship; George Brooks, a medicine man; and old Polk. The seven-hour conference was a cordial opportunity to air past grievances. Posey and his Bluff contingent met with McLaughlin a few days later and expressed a similar anxiety about moving to the reservation.[44]

The settlers in Bluff also talked to the inspector and gave him a list of suggestions that included no surprises. The basic message of this correspondence maintained that the Utes were a "law-unto-themselves," that they should be put on the eastern end of their reservation, that their leaders should be moved away from the main body of people, and that this roundup would best be conducted in the winter when the Indians were less mobile.[45]

Although McLaughlin appears to have made a favorable impression on both Benow and the settlers, his later correspondence hints that he viewed the ultimate solution to the problem to be the removal of the Utes to Colorado. Agent A. H. Symons later visited with Benow, who was waiting for the Commissioner of Indian Affairs to visit and insure the Indians' rights to remain. The agent knew that the opposite might happen and so asked that his replacement be given the responsibility of moving the Indians so that the move could be blamed on the military and not him. He explained: "If a new man were in charge here, they [Utes] would not attach the blame to him and would start with a clean slate."[46] The move, however, did not take place for a number of years.

This volatile situation could only be resolved in a "final solution" for both sides, winner take all. It came in the form of what has been called the "Posey War" and the "Last Indian Uprising." Briefly, what occurred followed the same pattern as previous flare-ups, but this time the whites made a conscious effort to prevent the same results

Allen Canyon Utes with government inspector Elfego Baca in Bluff, 1921. The Indians' refusal to live on the Ute Mountain Ute Reservation in Colorado and the inconsistent support by the government in meeting the Utes' needs in San Juan County encouraged them to obtain food and supplies from their white neighbors—an uncomfortable, antagonistic situation for both sides. (Utah State Historical Society)

as the 1915 episode.[47] Local people minimized the influence of outsiders, forces combatting the Utes mobilized quickly, not giving the Indians time to react, and the settlers did not release captive Utes until they had signed an agreement as to what lands they would promise to live on.

All of this was accomplished because of a relatively insignificant affair which started when two young Utes robbed a sheep camp, killed a calf, and burned a bridge. The culprits voluntarily turned themselves in, stood trial, but then escaped from the sheriff's grasp. The townspeople moved quickly to get not only the two boys but Posey as well, who by this time had become synonymous with all of the ill will felt between these factions. To the white people, he was the living symbol of all degraded or troublesome Indians.

The newspapers played a significant role in developing this attitude, making Posey the lightning rod waiting to be struck. His name had appeared, in either direct or indirect accusation, with almost every bothersome incident that occurred. People often cited his band of Utes as the culprits in a misdeed; Posey was said to have been the man who killed Joe Aiken, the white fatality in the 1915 fight; he reportedly murdered his brother Scotty because the latter wanted a peaceful settlement of that conflict; he had also killed his wife by accident, though many settlers refused to believe it was a mishap; he resisted living on the reservation; and he was such a colorful character that his threats, cajoling, and antics often brought a strong reaction to what would normally have been forgiven.[48] Thus, the 1923 "war" served as the means by which this "evil" could be exorcised.

The actual events of the conflict have been documented elsewhere, but in terms of the coverage of the press it was described in the finest tradition of hysterical, World-War-I-era yellow journalism. The prose is too voluminous to recount in detail here, but glimpses of it show its general tenor. On 22 March the *Times-Independent* noted that "Piute Band Declares War on Whites in Blanding" and reported that the county commissioners had sent a note to Utah governor Charles Mabey requesting a scout plane armed with machine guns and bombs. Supposedly, members of the posse had five horses shot out from beneath their riders, the men feared that four of their number had been ambushed, and "the most disquieting feature is the fact that Old Posey, the most dangerous of all the Piutes, is in charge of the band."[49]

In reality, there was little to the situation beyond a massive exodus of Utes and Paiutes fleeing their homes to escape into the rough canyon country of Navajo Mountain. Posey fought a rearguard action to prevent capture, was eventually wounded, and watched his people get carted off to a barbed-wire compound set up in the middle of Blanding. He died a painful death a month later from his gunshot wound.

The newspapers continued to report that the State of Utah had put a $100 reward—dead or alive—on Posey, now charged with insurrection, a crime punishable by death. C. F. Sloane of the *Salt Lake Tribune* stayed in Blanding and fired off press releases with a thin veneer of truth covering a mass of outright lies. He wrote that Blanding had been surrounded during "thirty-six hours of terrorism," with Indians in war paint riding the streets; he claimed that

Charlie Ute, also known as Charlie Ketchum, inside the barbed wire stockade built in the center of Blanding, 1923. Behind him is the San Juan State Bank. Ute prisoners remained within the enclosure until Posey's death had been verified and a firm agreement reached that the Utes would remain on individual allotments in Allen Canyon. (San Juan Historical Commission)

Posey, "the red fox," was forming a "mobile squadron," that there was a well-planned Paiute conspiracy that included robbing the San Juan State Bank, and that there were "sixty men skilled in the art of mountain warfare awaiting the call to service."[50]

The newsmen covering the incident gave the town a military character: "Blanding since the outbreak has become more or less an armed camp. It wears the aspect of a military headquarters. The arrival and departure of couriers from the front is a matter of public interest."[51] However, the citizens of Blanding were not fooled. Many of them kidded the reporters about their coverage of the incident; but this had little effect. When one person asked a correspondent why he was not writing the truth, he gave a very simple answer: "We're not ready to go home yet, and if we don't keep something going, we'll be getting a telegram to come home."[52]

Reporters found Posey's death just as dramatic as had been his life. One newsman said that Posey had been killed in a flash flood that flushed him down a canyon. Another believed he had died of natural causes; some Utes believed that poisoned Mormon flour had done the job.[53] The generally accepted explanation was that he had died from blood poisoning incurred by the gunshot wound. Regardless of the cause, the newsmen could report with finality that Posey had gone to the "happy hunting grounds." They also mentioned that many of the Utes were content that Posey had "gone beyond," while the whites vied to have the best stories to come out of the war.

When Posey's death was certain, some of the Utes took Marshal J. Ray Ward to the body's location in order to certify the death. The law officer buried the corpse and disguised the grave, but to no avail. The body was exhumed at least twice by men who wanted to have their picture taken with the grisly trophy. A forest ranger, Marion Hunt, claimed in the newspaper that he had found the body during a routine range examination a few days before Marshal Ward ever appeared on the scene.[54] It seems as though everyone wanted some type of claim in the matter.

Of greater import was the solution to the question of who controlled the ranges. The Posey incident served as an excuse for officials to force land allotments on the Utes. Hubert Work, Secretary of the Interior, issued an order in April that both Ute groups stop their nomadic life and settle on individual land holdings. Moab's *Times-Independent* reported:

> Old Posey's band, consisting of about 100 Indians will be given parcels of land located on or near Allen Canyon while Old Polk's band, numbering about 85 men, women, and children will be allotted land along Montezuma Creek. The two bands which are not friendly, will be located some distance apart.[55]

The number of allotments in Montezuma Canyon varied. Ira Hatch, who owned and operated a trading post in the area, estimated there were twenty-three Ute camps in Montezuma and Cross canyons.[56] Today there are no Ute allotments in the former and only a few in the latter canyon, the tribe having bought many of the individual holdings. In Allen Canyon, individual Ute families still own thirty allotments.

While the Utes were losing their hold on Montezuma Canyon, the Navajos were successfully tightening theirs. Undoubtedly there had been small groups of Navajos who had lived in the canyon before 1900. One man named Dishface insisted his residency went back to 1888, while others were not far behind in their claims.[57] The general Navajo population influx, however, occurred after 1900, as the Indians with their herds of sheep roamed in search of water and grass. By 1905 the Navajo agent stated that 250 Indians lived in a triangle of land that started at the mouth of Montezuma Creek, extended east to the Colorado border, south to the San Juan River, and then returned to Montezuma Creek. On 15 May 1905 the government added the land to the reservation by Executive Order 324A.[58]

Friction between Navajos, Utes, and cattlemen continued into the 1920s. While the Navajos and Utes appear to have worked out an unofficial boundary at the intersection of Cross Canyon and Montezuma Canyon, with the Navajos remaining to the south, problems with the Bluff cattlemen became increasingly serious.[59] Evan W. Estep, superintendent of the Shiprock Agency, noted that

> the outside stockmen are crowding the Indians just about as hard as it is possible to crowd them and avoid trouble. . . . The present offenders are the younger stockmen and apparently the younger Mormons are not of the same caliber as their fathers were.[60]

The underlying assumption of the cattlemen was that the Indians did not have the same right to the public lands as the white man. The solution to the problem again tied in with the Posey conflict; when A. W. Simington registered allotments for the Utes, he also did so for the Navajo. Of the thirteen family heads who filed for allotments in 1923, the average length of previous occupancy in the area was fifteen years, with a median of fourteen years; the shortest occupancy was two years and the longest thirty-five years.[61]

Conflict over the ranges in the Montezuma Canyon area continued until it was divided in 1933. The Paiute Strip was officially added to the Navajo Reservation. For the Utes, it was a dead issue. They had already lost their ancestral lands ten years before. Fewer than a hundred Utes still remained off the Colorado reservation, sequestered along Allen Canyon and Cottonwood creeks, endeavoring to become twentieth-century farmers.

The Ute and Paiute experience between 1880 and 1933 was traumatic. Squeezed in a vise of Mormon and non-Mormon farming communities, livestock operations—both Anglo and Navajo, and an inadequate reservation, these Native Americans had no choice but to give up their hunting-and-gathering way of life. If they had been as fortunate as the Navajo—who had a number of aggressive agents to work on their behalf, an expanding population base, important economic interests to catapult them beyond a barter system, and a more docile reputation, then perhaps the story would have turned out differently. The Utes had none of these things. Instead, they were forced to fight for what was theirs. As a result, they lost most of what they had as their lands were taken and their way of life melted away in the crucible of the twentieth century.

ENDNOTES

1. W. F. M. Arny to Charles Mix, 3 October 1868, Letters Received, Office of Indian Affairs—New Mexico Superintendency, 1868 (hereafter cited as Letters Received—NM).

2. For a fuller treatment of this period for both the Utes and the Navajos see Robert S. McPherson, *The Northern Navajo Frontier, 1860–1900: Expansion through Adversity* (Albuquerque: University of New Mexico Press, 1988).

3. John Ayers, Abiquiu Agency Annual Report, 16 August 1869, Report of the Commissioner of Indian Affairs (hereafter cited as RCIA), 240–43; Ayers, Abiquiu Agency Annual Report, 3 September 1870, RCIA, 618–20.

4. J. B. Hanson, Abiquiu Agency Annual Report, 11 September 1871, RCIA, 408.

5. Nathaniel Pope, Navajo Agency, 10 October 1872, RCIA, 296–97.

6. Donald G. Callaway, Joel C. Janetski, and Omer C. Stewart, "Ute," in *Handbook of North American Indians* 11 (Washington, D.C.: Smithsonian Institution, 1986), 355.

7. William H. Holmes to Dr. F. V. Hayden, 30 December 1876, *Ninth Annual Report of the United States Geological and Geographical Survey of the Territories . . . 1875* (Washington, D.C.: Government Printing Office, 1877), 239.

8. J. F. Daugherty to Charles Stollsteimer, 5 November and 3 December

1885, Record Group 75, Bureau of Indian Affairs, Ute Agency Records, Denver Record Center, Colorado (hereafter cited as DRC—Ute Agency).

9. Daugherty to Southern Ute Agent, 7 June 1886, DRC—Ute Agency; Petition to Ute Agent, 16 December 1886, DRC—Ute Agency.

10. Captain J. B. Irvine to Col. P. T. Swain, 26 December 1886, DRC—Ute Agency.

11. Daugherty to J. D. C. Atkins, 19 September 1888, National Archives, Record Group 75, 1881–1907, Bureau of Indian Affairs (hereafter cited as BIA—1881–1907).

12. William Davidson to Southern Ute Agent, 11 April 1889; Milton T. Morris to Charles Bartholomew, 25 September and 1 October 1891; petition from Residents of McElmo, Utah, to Commissioner of Indian Affairs, 30 January 1888, DRC—Ute Agency.

13. "Cattle Companies," General File, Monticello Ranger District, Monticello, Utah, 2.

14. For further information see Faun McConkie Tanner, *The Far Country—A Regional History of Moab and La Sal, Utah* (Salt Lake City: Olympus Publishing Company, 1976), 105–46; Don D. Walker, "Cowboys, Indians, and Cavalry—A Cattleman's Account," *Utah Historical Quarterly* 34 (Summer 1966): 255–62; Cornelia Perkins, Marian Nielson, and Lenora Jones, *Saga of San Juan* (Salt Lake City: Mercury Publishing Company, 1957), 234–44; and Albert R. Lyman, "History of San Juan County, 1879–1917," unpublished manuscript, Brigham Young University Library, Provo, Utah, 22–23, 41–42.

15. Edmund S. Carlisle to William M. Clark, 1 October 1884, DRC—Ute Agency.

16. See Don D. Walker, "Cowboys, Indians, and Cavalry," *Utah Historical Quarterly* 34 (Summer 1966): 255–62.

17. Edmund S. Carlisle to William M. Clark, 30 December 1884, DRC—Ute Agency.

18. Larabee to Thomas McCunniff, 17 June 1889, Consolidated Ute Agency; "Report of Brigadier-General Crook," *Report of the Secretary of War*, 1887, 1st Sess., 50th Cong., 133.

19. Ibid.

20. Frank Moss Papers, Special Collections, University of Utah Library, 55.

21. For an excellent summary of the events of this period including the political dealings in Washington see Gregory C. Thompson, "The Unwanted Indians: The Southern Utes in Southeastern Utah," *Utah Historical Quarterly* 49 (Spring 1981): 189–203.

22. Ibid., 198.

23. Ibid., 202.

24. Christian L. Christensen, "When the Utes Invaded Utah," *Times-Independent*, 3 August 1933, 4.

25. Report of Agency in Colorado—Southern Utes, *RCIA*, 1898, 140.

26. Report of Agent in Colorado—Southern Ute Agency, *RCIA*, 1896, 132.

27. Report of Agent for Southern Ute Agency, *RCIA*, 1900, 213–4.

28. Report of Agent for Southern Ute Agency, *Annual Report of Department of the Interior Fiscal Year Ending June 30, 1901*, 205.

29. F. E. Leupp to John C. Cutter, 11 January 1908, cited in *Lemuel Hardison Redd, Jr., 1856–1923, Pioneer-Leader-Builder*, compiled and edited by Amasa Jay Redd (Salt Lake City: published privately, 1967), n.p.

30. Ibid., statement by Johnny Benow, n.p.

31. For a detailed explanation of this event and others surrounding it see Forbes Parkhill, *The Last of the Indian Wars* (n.p.: Crowell-Collier Publishing Company, 1961).

32. "Armed Posse Is After Renegade," *Grand Valley Times*, 19 February 1915, 1.

33. "1 White and 3 Piutes Are Killed," *Grand Valley Times*, 26 February 1915, 1.

34. "Blanding News" and "Piute Indian Chief Slays His Brother," *Grand Valley Times*, 5 March 1915, 7–8.

35. Ibid.

36. "Scott Captures Renegade Indians," *Grand Valley Times*, 26 March 1915, 2.

37. "Ute Threatens Man with Gun," *San Juan Blade* (hereafter cited as *SJB*), 24 August 1917, 1; "Ute All-Same-White-Man with Telephone," and "Noted Indian Prepares for War," *SJB*, 5 October 1917, 1 and ibid.; "Indians Again Growing Bold," *SJB*, 24 October 1917, 4; "Ute Indians Hold Up Blanding Boy," 1, and "Ute Trespassers Made to Pay," *SJB*, 2 November 1917, 5; "Old Posey May Stir Up Trouble," *SJB*, 21 December 1917, 1.

38. "Indians Help on White Mesa," *SJB*, 12 October 1917, 1.

39. "Note," *SJB*, 30 November 1917, 4.

40. M. K. Sniffen, "The Meaning of the Ute 'War,'" 15 November 1915, (Philadelphia: Indian Rights Association), Special Collections, University of Utah Library, 1–7.

41. "Hot Air About Neglected Utes," *Cortez Herald*, 13 January 1916, 1.

42. "The Poor Innocent Indian," *Cortez Herald*, 27 January 1916, 1.

43. James C. Wilson to Agent A. H. Symons, 5 January 1917, James McLaughlin Papers, Microfilm #8, Denver Public Library, Denver, Colorado (hereafter cited as McLaughlin Papers).

44. James McLaughlin to Indian Commissioner Cato Sells, 18 and 20 January 1917, McLaughlin Papers.

45. Undersigned of Bluff to Major James McLaughlin, 12 January 1917, McLaughlin Papers.

46. A. H. Symons to Major James McLaughlin, 3 February 1917, McLaughlin Papers.

47. For a more complete treatment of the Posey incident see Robert S. McPherson, "Paiute Posey and the Last White Uprising," *Utah Historical Quarterly* 53 (Summer 1985): 248–67; and Albert R. Lyman, *The Outlaw of Navaho Mountain* (Salt Lake City: Publishers Press, 1986).

48. "Piute Indian Chief Slays His Brother," *Grand Valley Times*, 5 March 1915, 7; "Indians Refuse to Go to Reservation, Is Report," *Grand Valley Times*, 4 June 1915, 1; "Posey at Bluff," *Grand Valley Times*, 11 June 1915, 1.

49. "Piute Band Declares War on Whites at Blanding," Moab *Times Independent*, 22 March 1923, 1.

50. *Salt Lake Tribune*, 21 March to 5 April 1923.

51. *Salt Lake Tribune* 24 March 1923, 1.

52. John D. Rogers, "Piute Posey and the Last Indian Uprising," Charles Redd Center for Western Studies, Brigham Young University Library, 22.

53. "Marshal Gives Up Chase for Posey," *Times Independent*, 5 April 1923, 1; "Old Posey Is Dead, but Details of His Passing Will Remain a Mystery," *Times-Independent*, 26 April 1923, 1; Chester Cantsee, Sr., interview with Aldean Ketchum and Robert S. McPherson, 6 September 1994, transcript in possession of author.

54. "Forest Ranger First to Find Posey's Body," *Grand Valley Times*, 17 May 1923, 1.

55. "Government Allots Farms and Livestock to San Juan Paiutes," *Times-Independent*, 19 April 1923, 1.

56. Mr. and Mrs. Ira Hatch, interviewed by Floyd A. O'Neil and Gregory C. Thompson, 10 September 1970, Doris Duke Oral History Project, Special Collections, University of Utah Library, 9.

57. A. W. Simington to Commissioner of Indian Affairs, 23 July 1923, as cited in unpublished manuscript by David Brugge, "Navajo Use and Occupation of Lands North of the San Juan River in Present-day Utah to 1935" (hereafter cited as NUOL), in possession of author.

58. William Shelton to Commissioner of Indian Affairs, 1 March 1905; Harriet Peabody to Commissioner of Indian Affairs, 28 February 1905, NUOL.

59. McLaughlin to Commissioner of Indian Affairs, 20 March 1917, NUOL.

60. Evan W. Estep to Commissioner of Indian Affairs, 9 February 1921, NUOL.

61. Brugge, "Navajo Use," NUOL, 170–76.

8

Beef, Wheat, and Biology

LIVESTOCK AND FARMING INDUSTRIES IN SAN JUAN, 1880–1990

During the course of San Juan history, three events emerge as perhaps the most colorful and best-known symbols of the county's heritage. The first two—the Hole-in-the-Rock expedition and the Posey "War"—are fabled. This is not to deny that they happened but only to suggest that the events have become a standardized, mythologized cover that is sometimes difficult to peek under. They are important in explaining what it means to be from this area and in understanding what historian Charles Peterson has recognized as a conscious effort to foster a "San Juan mystique."[1]

The third of this mythic triad involves the early cattle industry and the rough-and-tumble cowboys associated with it. Although they were controlled by such wealthy entrepreneurs as Edmund and Harold Carlisle of the Kansas and New Mexico Land and Cattle Company, most of the emphasis placed on this period focuses on their antics and rough-shod ways. In a broader sense, this period of San Juan history—though very different in some particulars—may also be considered representative of general patterns that occurred throughout the West. Indeed, American popular culture has insisted on romanticizing the lonesome cowboy on the trail, the wild sprees in town after the long drive, and the conflict over rangelands. These same dramatic events, on a diminished scale, are also part of San Juan's heritage.

The focus of this chapter will take a different perspective on both livestock ranching and farming. A great deal has already been written about the former topic, some of which is very good, some of which emphasizes only the dramatic.[2] No one will deny the excitement associated with tales about the early conflicts between settlers and cowboys over range and water; the Carlisle men's fights with the Utes during the 1880s; the raid by mounted hooligans on Mons Peterson's store; the shooting of the school bell and the story of townspeople who "danced" to blazing sixguns after cowboys imbibed some "red eye" from the Blue Goose Saloon; or the colorful image of such cowboys as Latigo (William E.) Gordon, foreman of the Carlisle spread.

Indeed, the song "Blue Mountain," composed by Fred W. Keller and accepted by many as the county anthem, centers on this unsettled epoch of cowboy activity. Keller borrowed the tune from an old Texas cowboy song and added local events and color from San Juan's history. Briefly, the song tells of a man from Texas who is hiding from the law by working for the L.C Company. He hopes to eventually own the Carlisle outfit, a symbol of successful ranching. In the meantime, he spends his life at the Blue Goose Saloon, at Mormon dances, trading at Mons Peterson's store "with bullet holes in the door," or visiting "Ev" (Evelyn Adams), whose home at Verdure provided food and refuge for tired, hungry cowboys.[3] In these few lines, Keller not only sings of real personalities like "Doc Few Clothes," "Yarn Gallus," and "Slick" but also encapsulates the feelings of the era—an era that has since become enshrined in the hearts of county residents.

Yet this period was relatively brief, its stories tending to draw the listener away from the more significant and enduring impact of livestock and farming on the lands of San Juan County. The siren's song that lured large cattle outfits to the area's mountains and mesas harmonized with the government's policy of the open range and with the native grasses that had hitherto not been heavily utilized. Starting in 1877 a number of relatively small cattle and homesteading outfits exploited the resources on the slopes or at the foot of the La Sal Mountains. The families of Tom Ray, Cornelius Maxwell, Billy McCarty, and others brought in milk cows and beef cattle, some of these herds numbering as high as 2,000 head.[4] Two years later, Joshua B. (Spud) Hudson started his herd at the foot of Blue Mountain and watched it swell to 6,000.[5]

But in 1880 the truly large cattle companies arrived, buying out many of the smaller herds and dominating the grass and water resources. Many of these big companies trailed in cattle from out of state—Texas, New Mexico, and Colorado—as well as herds from within Utah. The Lacy Cattle Company (L. C.) ranged its animals on Recapture, Cottonwood, Johnson, and South Montezuma creeks, with an estimated 17,000 animals grazing on the lush canyon and mountain grasses.[6] The Carlisle brothers extended their operations from New Mexico with 7,000 head that eventually mushroomed to an estimated 30,000 before they finally sold their holdings in about 1896.[7] The Pittsburgh Cattle Company, after buying out the herds belonging to the earlier ranchers on the La Sals, ran thousands of cattle on the mountain and in Dry Valley, a favored winter range. Although the number given to this herd varies, one figure reaches as high as 20,000 animals spread over the company's range in Colorado and Utah.[8] Despite the difficulty in ascertaining exact numbers due to the ebb and flow of the business, most historians agree that there was a sudden, overwhelming infusion of livestock, on a scale never before seen in San Juan.

Besides the rich grasslands made available by the government, there were other reasons for this great interest. The county's isolation encouraged tax rates thought to be generally lower than those of neighboring states and territories. Also, accurate counts were difficult to assess. Shortly after the Mormons arrived in Bluff, they established a county government with tax-collecting powers. A 7 June 1880 meeting of the San Juan County Court provided for a tax rate of six mills on every dollar of assessed property value, and Lemuel H. Redd, Jr., was given the job of collecting the revenue. He did this to the best of his ability, in spite of the emotional issues arising between Mormon farmers and non-Mormon stockmen. How many cattle he missed as they grazed throughout the canyons and over the plateaus and mountains will never be known, but Colorado livestock owners continued to winter their herds in southeastern Utah because of the comparatively inexpensive pasturage.[9]

Other favorable factors conducive to the development of the cattle industry included a low population base, with only a handful of settlements like La Sal, Bluff, and Monticello springing up in the midst of livestock country; unfenced lands for general use; good winter and summer ranges at various elevations that nurtured different types of forage that could be utilized during different seasons of the year; a growing railroad feeder system that made towns like Dolores, Durango, Mancos, and Montrose, Colorado, as well as Thompson, Utah, natural starting points for the cattle to be moved to eastern markets; and favorable prices at the stockyards. At its zenith around 1886, cattle could be sold for between $30 and $75 apiece, creating a substantial profit margin to facilitate restocking of the ranges.[10]

Competitors soon arose. Realizing that their riparian agricultural efforts had failed, county Mormon farmers turned to their leader, Francis A. Hammond, for guidance in reaping profits from the livestock industry. Hammond estimated in 1885 that there were 100,000 cattle on county ranges. Success in the industry required that the settlers obtain control of the land, thereby removing the competition and making the area livestock industry a Mormon-dominated business.

The settlers accomplished this by what one historian characterized as the "Bluff Tigers' [cattle company] . . . vigorous and almost ruthless self-interest," in taking over use of the land.[11] This resulted in the Carlisle outfit beginning to abandon its ranges in 1892; by 1910 their Utah cattle holdings were sold. By 1896 the Pittsburgh Company was close to being finished, as was also the L. C. Company.[12] The only important remaining competition was Native American livestock holders. This controversy and conflict lasted well into the twentieth century and has been discussed in Chapter 6.

Other factors in the decline of area cattle ranching need to be considered. What had been a seller's market, with cattle averaging around $35, suddenly plummeted in the late 1880s. The boom went bust for a number of reasons. First, sales throughout the nation dropped off due to a flood of animals, many of which came from overseas markets. By 1889 Bluff cattle could be purchased for sixteen dollars, half of what they had commanded two years before; in 1894, assessors valued cattle at only eight dollars a head.[13] There was also a growing demand for better breeds of cattle to provide more palatable cuts of beef. Range stock, after being interbred with more domestic, expensive types of cattle, became increasingly dependent on being fed and cared for by their owners. And after the disastrous losses of livestock in other parts of the West during the summer and winter of 1886–87, a shift away from the old open-range philosophy started to reshape the industry. Sheep appeared to many to be a better solution because wool crops were a continuing source of income compared to a steer that must be killed to provide its products.

Yet one of the most disturbing elements of this era of bonanza profits before it collapsed was the overstocking of the range. If Hammond's estimate of 100,000 cattle grazing upon county lands is close to correct, and one adds another estimate of the same number of sheep coming in from Colorado at approximately the same time for winter grazing, plus 12,000 Bluff Co-op sheep, then adds a large, untallied number of off-reservation Navajo livestock, it can be understood why the carrying capacity of the lands deteriorated so rapidly. By the early 1900s J. W. Humphrey, an early supervisor of the La Sal National Forest, believed the ranges had been "so closely grazed that they did not appear to have any forage on them other than the browse which was closely cropped."[14]

Range managers know that many factors help determine how quickly vegetation will spring back once it is overgrazed. In San Juan during the initial explosion of livestock into the area, southeastern Utah was enjoying an uncommonly heavy amount of moisture. The most dramatic evidence of this was the flooding of the San Juan River in 1884, with the subsequent abandonment of Montezuma Creek and other settlements along the river.

Beginning in 1886, however, the ranges of San Juan started to suffer the effects of what would become a decade of drought. By 1896 Hammond declared, "We have just passed through the driest winter in the history of the county. . . . As a result, streams that were formerly large and springs that gave forth abundantly are now almost devoid

Al Scorup, about eighty years old, sitting on his favorite horse, "Ol Booger," at his Indian Creek Ranch. (Utah State Historical Society)

of moisture as a tinder box."[15] Navajo and Anglo crops alike suffered from the lack of moisture and from late and early frosts. Range grasses that were not eaten or trampled withered under the heat and drought. Frank Silvey, who lived through these times, tells of losing half his cattle to starvation.[16] The days of large-scale, open-range cattle operations appeared to be coming to a close.

Ironically, as most large cattle companies suffered, John Albert (Al) Scorup, a Mormon cowboy from Salina, Utah, started his own livestock operations in the county. Hard work and good investments made his rags-to-riches story a lasting tribute to and symbol of the dedication of members of the livestock industry in San Juan. It was anything but easy. Scorup labored throughout the canyons and mesas, rounding up cattle for the Bluff Pool, saving his money, holding out in the economic slumps of the 1890s and post–World War I eras, and always taking advantage of less accessible rangelands.

At one point, he sold his Wooden Shoe–White Canyon herd and was thinking about returning home to Salina with his partner-brother Jim when, in 1918, he formed a partnership with William and Andrew Somerville from Moab. Together they formed the Scorup-Somerville (S. S.) Cattle Company. Even after Jim died, Al remained in the business. The company grazed from 7,000 to 10,000 cattle each year on a two-million-acre range that extended from Blue Mountain to the confluence of the San Juan and Colorado rivers. In 1927 the company held a grazing permit for 6,780 cattle on Forest Service lands, the largest ever granted by the federal government.[17] Al continued to supervise the operation until his death in 1959.

Another part of the livestock equation included sheep. In addition to the burgeoning Navajo flocks, significant Anglo herds were in San Juan County by the mid-1880s. Changes in range conditions caused by drought and overgrazing had placed the cattle companies in trouble and, as a result, many ranchers either completely switched to or integrated sheep as a part of their operation.[18] Thus, much of the friction experienced in other parts of the West was avoided between these two livestock factions.

Along with the sheep came skilled Hispanic herders. These low-paid but highly experienced workers often left Colorado and New Mexico and came to San Juan, where they wandered the rangelands caring for large flocks of sheep and cattle. Monticello became the central community for the Hispanic population in the county, where they were generally accepted by local residents. One rancher, Joe Redd, for example, noted that if by chance they lost a sheep, "they would feel worse than the fellow who owned them." Speaking of a worker named Lopez, Redd explained that no one could have been more "loyal or better. . . . Lopez knew cattle . . . horses . . . could build a house . . . [or] corral. That fellow could do anything."[19]

There were many other Hispanics who came to San Juan as herders but eventually branched out into different occupations. Take, for example, the experience of José Prudencio Gonzales, who celebrated his 100th birthday in Monticello in 1984. He was born in New Mexico into a family already employed as herders. In 1890 the family moved to Colorado to work with livestock; they then relocated to Monticello in 1900. They homesteaded on Indian Creek, but after his father's death Jose followed tradition, herding cattle and sheep to support his family. He gained a reputation as an outstanding cowboy. As problems in the livestock industry arose and his personal circumstances changed, he secured other types of employment, including work with the Works Progress Administration, in the uranium mills in Dry Valley and Monticello, and as deputy sheriff for the county. But he never lost his skill in working with animals, something he enjoyed throughout his life.[20]

With men like Gonzales providing a good pool of labor to draw from, and with the livestock ranges and transportation networks already in place, the decreased feed requirements per head, and the ability to obtain both wool and meat on a regular basis, sheep appeared to some ranchers to provide an answer for hard times in the cattle industry. The Bluff Pool, the Carlisle outfit, and the Cunningham-Carpenter Company (which had replaced the Pittsburgh Cattle Company in La Sal) all tried their hand at herding woolies. Eventually, much of the livestock industry became more individualized, with the large, cooperative efforts like the Bluff Pool (dissolved in the late 1890s) being abandoned. By 1904 many livestock owners ran a combination of cattle and sheep on their lands, hoping thus to minimize the possibility of failure.[21]

The twentieth-century livestock industry was characterized by increasing government control of resources. A growing complex of regulations, complicated by national events such as world wars I and II and the Great Depression, moved the San Juan sheep and cattle operations from an Old West open-range mentality of "use it or lose it" to one of enforced, responsible husbandry. This is not to suggest that livestock owners were in constant conflict with government officials, though friction did exist. Many ranchers became increasingly aware that scientific range management could yield greater profits as well as improve the land. Gradually, both government and individual businesspeople moved toward a more enlightened approach to the task at hand.

The availability of government-controlled public lands became the central issue of ranching in the twentieth century— with good reason. For instance, in 1903 the *Montezuma Journal* pointed out that if a sheepman used public lands without paying rental or taxes and

Sheep traversing the old cable bridge at Mexican Hat. (San Juan Historical Commission)

did not have to provide winter feed for his stock, the cost per head per year was about forty cents. If these conditions were not present, the cost jumped to between $0.75 and $1.25. Wool at this time sold for $1.00 to $1.50 per animal, while a lamb in the fall brought $2.00 to $3.00. Thus, the amount of profit was intimately connected to costs associated with the land.[22]

There was a great impact on county grazing operations in 1906 when President Theodore Roosevelt created the 158,000-acre National Forest Reserve on the La Sal Mountains and the next year added the Monticello Forest Reserve on Blue Mountain.[23] The government soon began to dictate the number and type of stock to be grazed, the range division and distribution of animals, the amount of grazing fees, protective limits for small stock owners, and proposed forest additions.

Forest supervisor Orrin C. Snow presided over one of the first meetings with livestock owners after the formation of the southern division (Monticello) reserve. On 20–21 August 1907 livestock owners and Snow thoroughly "cussed and discussed" the proposed reduction of twenty-five percent of the sheep and ten percent of the cattle then foraging on the mountain. Complaints regarding the Forest Service, various livestock owners, and animals grazing in Blanding's watershed were "thrashed out," with the men finally reaching an amicable agreement.[24]

Feelings were anything but amicable in the months and years that followed, however. With the establishment of new range regulations, the government became an enforcement agency. Numerous meetings, both public and private, between livestock owners and officials fostered the growing attitude of a power struggle instead of cooperation. A meeting held at the Indian Creek Cattle Company's ranch on 24 January 1910, found the two sides involved in open dispute. According to one witness, "Everybody said exactly what he pleased about everybody else. . . . Many of the sentiments contravened the third commandment."[25]

Forest supervisor John Riis stated that he did not trust the owners' count of livestock even though the government had appointed them to do the job. He believed that the five-cents-per-head increase was in line with fees charged in other forests, that the range could support a rate of only five, not eight, sheep for each cow; and that the land was in such poor condition that the current allowable number of animals should be reduced. The livestock owners countered that other cattle had drifted in from the winter ranges, that nobody actually knew how many animals they had in their herd, that no general count had been made "for years," and that possibly the figure of twenty percent over the limit was fair and should not be a concern. Riis, with the approval of his superior, stated that henceforth an officer would be appointed to count the animals onto the forest lands. The government held the upper hand.

This is perhaps one reason why the era saw such a proliferation of grazing associations; with the government wielding such power, through collective strength local organizations might also make themselves heard. The Forest Service initially encouraged the formation of these groups as a democratic voice in helping develop policy, but, as the associations grew in number and membership, they took on a more politicized role. The rapidity and frequency with which they were formed certainly indicates their importance: the Southeastern Utah Stock Growers' Association (1907), Elk Mountain Stock Growers' Association (1909), La Sal Wool Growers' Association (1912), Camp Jackson Livestock Association (1917), Monticello Stock Growers' Association (1918), Paradox Cattle Association (1919), La Sal Cattlemen's Association (1921), San Juan Cattle and Horse Growers' Association (1925), San Juan Wool Growers' (1928), and the La Sal National Stock Permittees (1937).[26] Although there were many different concerns facing these associations, in one way or another every issue came back to the land.

Even the most skeptical rancher could not return to the days of free-for-all open grazing. The extremely cold winter of 1912–13 saw "hundreds of cattle die on the range for lack of feed," encouraging the Indian Creek Company to plant 1,500 acres of range in alfalfa to prevent winter loss.[27] A drought in 1917–18 burned the grass, leaving only those stockmen with hay lands on the mountain a good chance of keeping their herds intact. Those with cattle and sheep in the Bluff area lost heavily due to scarcity of feed and water, while the weather forced others to sell as much as half their herds.[28]

Yet the effects of the drought eventually ended, and the county continued to receive some healthy benefits from the industry's presence. In 1924, owners reported 18,000 cattle and 30,000 sheep grazing on the forest lands of the La Sal and Blue mountains, though this figure was believed by many to be well below the actual count. More than $3,000 in permit fees for these animals was used to improve county schools and roads.[29]

Such profits and upswings in the market, however, were crushed by the Great Depression of the 1930s. By 1934 the Taylor Grazing Act became a reality, withdrawing federal lands from unrestricted public entry and placing them under the control of the Grazing Service. In anticipation of this move, major San Juan livestock owners applied for permits for 3,750,000 acres of land when the county had only 5,100,000 acres—a good part of which was already controlled as forest reserves, Navajo Reservation, and public school lands.[30] Many of the small livestock owners felt deeply threatened.

At the same time, the government began to supervise a general livestock reduction, brought on in part by a severe, prolonged drought and close-cropped ranges. The Grazing Service offered to buy all stock above the number that it felt could survive on the ranges, offering scaled prices for cattle: two years and older, $6–14; one to two years, $5–10; under one year, $1–5. No one got rich on this government-mandated plan.[31] Sheep reduction soon followed.

Initial concerns about the effects of the Taylor Act gave way by 1938 to general compliance. Grand and San Juan counties formed District Six, one of eight in the state of Utah. They agreed with their neighbors that it was "not only feasible but advisable for all interests concerned to group all public lands . . . as a unit on a carrying capacity basis, keeping in mind the elimination of overgrazing and carrying out a joint program of range improvement such as water development, road and trail construction, and extermination of rodents."[32] What this meant in real terms to District Six was that the 285 licenses issued for the district's 193,024 sheep and 24,992 cattle were now part of a highly regulated program. Forthcoming benefits in 1939 included the construction of ten reservoirs, development of five springs, reseeding of 15,000 acres in grass, completion of 2,817 rods of fencing, treatment of 101,504 acres for rodent control, building of a 4,300-foot diversion dam, among other improvements to the range.[33] The carrot extended for government compliance proved far more successful than the stick.

World War II saw a rising demand for livestock, followed by escalating prices. Even in the war's darkest hour, when needs were greatest, the government counseled stockmen that range condition was the most important factor in determining when to sell. Since ninety percent of the forage was produced in the Southwest between July and September, "any rancher who gambles on holding excess stock on a poor range until next spring has the deck stacked against him."[34] The government reasoned through science and range management that fall was the preferred time to market the animals.

One way to understand the effect of these trends is to take a brief glimpse at Charlie Redd, whose life spanned both early and contemporary forms of livestock management. Born in a log cabin in Bluff, he grew under the tutelage of his father, Lemuel H. Redd, Jr., who had worked as a moving force in San Juan cattle operations since their inception. In 1914 Lemuel had become the largest stockholder in a group of ten to twelve men who bought the (J. M.) Cunningham and (T. B.) Carpenter spread and renamed it the La Sal Livestock Company. The group appointed his son Charlie to be manager of the $220,000 ranch. A couple of months later, the Somervilles also sold their outfit to the same group, bringing the partners' total debt to $311,000. At a time when every rancher was struggling to survive, this sum represented a huge investment in money and faith.

Charlie faced this problem head on. Since he grazed both sheep and cattle, he enjoyed a certain flexibility in sales. He also diversified into other businesses, including a store, shipment of supplies, hay sales, and automobile and farm-machinery dealerships; but it was ranching that paid most of the bills. One time a banker in Salt Lake gave him some blunt advice. He started by telling Charlie, "You don't know when you are broke, and you won't let anyone tell you you are." Charlie summarized the rest of the advice and then outlined the reason for his success at a time when other ranchers were failing. He believed that although there might be a drought today, it would not last forever. He then continued, "But most ranchers don't realize that they should be like the packrat or the squirrel and lay in a supply for the years of drought and low prices."[35] Like other successful entrepreneurs during the Depression, Redd bought when the prices were low and sold when they were high.

Charlie eventually obtained all the property and stock from those within the investing group outside of his family, and, most importantly according to his account, made his word his bond in his continuous dealings with various banks. Fortunately, he was able to obtain credit or prevent foreclosure on his property when others less dependable or with fewer assets lost what they had. This economic buffer allowed the La Sal Livestock Company, now Redd Ranches, to weather the economic turmoil and the decreasing number of livestock allowed on the range, until prices rose.

During the Depression, as his debts accumulated and the outlook darkened, a business associate asked why he did not just quit. Charlie replied, "I don't know whether the drought is going to break or whether prices are going to improve or not. The whole country is in terrible condition. Of all the things the government has done, there seems little hope of finding a solution. . . . If it doesn't improve. . . . I can say, 'Well, I did my damnest [sic].'"[36] He did do his damnedest, and he survived. Charlie left a legacy in the Redd Ranches of today, which continues to flourish. Many other cattlemen were not nearly as fortunate.

Starting in the 1940s, generally positive trends began to characterize the economic roller coaster of the livestock industry. For instance, in 1955, as uranium grabbed the spotlight of attention, local ranchers reminded citizens of their contribution to the county. Twenty-five sheepmen had a total of 72,000 head, which had yielded 720,000 pounds of wool the previous season.[37] Ten years later as uranium started into its decline, 146 stockmen were running 24,841 cattle and 165,231 sheep.[38] The livestock industry, though regulated, paid positive dividends. But more than merely moving from free-use to government control, a greater feeling of stewardship, responsibility, and scientific understanding about the land now characterized range operations. The early cattlemen may have felt they were economically taming the Wild West, but now it was the government that dictated the use of the land.

The same pattern of boom to bust to control that characterized the ranching industry also exhibited itself in agriculture, though at a somewhat later date. Following the agrarian fizzle in Bluff, but simultaneous with the irrigation projects of the nascent towns of Monticello and Blanding, the produce of dry farming arrived in a rush. Its precepts were simple to apply, but its impact, by allowing homes and communities to move away from sources of mountain water, was tremendous. Now, people could venture onto the Great Sage Plain, stake out a 320-acre homestead and begin a new life at minimal expense except hard manual labor. Personal accounts abound that relate how these farmers grubbed out acres of sagebrush, put up fence with blistered hands, hauled water from springs or dug a shallow well for culinary use, lived in a tent amidst the junipers while raising a log cabin, protected their chickens and milk cow from predators, planted a subsistence garden for family use, prayed their cash crop would provide necessities, and socialized locally or in the "big" town when practical.[39]

A few significant differences characterized this movement to the land compared with the early stages of the cattle industry. The first was the lack of significant capital investment necessary to get started. Those who came to San Juan were generally poor folks seeking a new start. Although people came to the area from all over the United States, proportionally significant numbers either were refugees from the Mormon colonies in Mexico, World War I veterans, or impoverished farmers from Oklahoma and Texas.

Starting around 1910 and lasting for thirty years, a steady ebb and flow of homesteaders cast their lot in San Juan, the numbers peaking between 1911 and 1920, with 346 land patents recorded at the county courthouse during this time.[40] Each of these waves of people brought families and friends, further increasing the county's population. A 1912 newspaper article noted that in the previous ten years San Juan had jumped from being the least populated county in Utah, with an increase of 130 percent, it now ranked above six other counties.[41] By 1920 the population hovered around 4,000 non-Indian residents; and within the past two years, new residents had entered on 200,000 acres of homestead lands.[42]

Another difference between the livestock and dry-farming experience was the amount of encouragement and technical advice given to those who farmed. The Utah State Agricultural College (now Utah State University) had an experimental station at Verdure that played an important role in dispensing information about the latest farming techniques and most successful crops for the area. The college also offered six-week courses during the winter so that farmers could attend during the slow time of the year. But perhaps its most important contribution was the credibility and "official tone" it lent to sweeping claims of the county's potential. P. A. Yoder, director of the experiment station, wrote letters published in newspapers in which he described the crops at Verdure as "exceptionally good, being among the best of those on our six experimental arid farms . . . strongly urg[ing] citizens to visit this experimental farm"; but he cautioned that he "feared that those people will not realize their opportunities until outsiders come in and take up the choice land."[43]

Haystacks like these found at Indian Creek required hundreds of man-hours in watering, harvesting, and distributing as feed to widespread cattle herds. Mechanized production started in the early 1900s, speeding agricultural pursuits while pushing groups of individuals together to purchase the expensive machinery. (San Juan Historical Commission)

The statistics from the experiment station encouraged farmers. Crops of wheat, oats, beans, corn, and alfalfa provided scientific proof of what the land could provide, and neighbors watched with interest. In 1909, 200 acres of fall wheat yielded an average of 33 bushels per acre. That same year, farmers staked out more than 38,000 acres of public lands around Blue Mountain and cleared 1,100 acres of it for planting.[44] Two years later, local dry farmers harvested 1,200 acres, while the newspapers advertised as a "conservative estimate" that San Juan County contained "1,500,000 acres susceptible to dry farming." Professors from the college gave glowing grades to San Juan as the "very best dry farming county in the state of Utah and . . . in . . the West."[45]

Thus when the Nielson brothers averaged forty-seven bushels of wheat on their 100-acre dry farm, and D. B. Perkins averaged 64 bushels per acre on his twenty-seven-acre spread in Bulldog, they only foreshadowed the possibilities. In 1920 Jesse Bailey from Monticello showed what really could be done. He received a gold medal and a $1,000 first prize cash award from the national *Farm Journal* "for the largest per acre crop of oats raised in the country last year without irrigation"—a whopping 111 bushels per acre on five acres of land.[46]

Other inducements that encouraged farming included the government's role in fostering massive production, especially during world wars. President Woodrow Wilson guaranteed wheat growers would profit when he set a fixed price of two dollars per bushel. The federal Farm Loan Act, passed on 17 July 1916, helped decrease rates of interest on mortgaged farms, increased the amount of acreage owned and planted, and created more loan associations in the United States than there were counties. For San Juan County, this allowed loan associations to make a total of $107,500 in loans to farmers in or near Monticello in 1918 alone. At the same time, local production of wheat rose, alleviating the necessity of shipping it in from Thompson and Moab.[47]

A final inducement for farmers was the introduction of machinery capable of tearing out sagebrush on large tracts of land and plowing the fields for seeding. This newfound necessity caused members of a community to band together to purchase such a labor-saving device. For instance, in 1908 five farmers from Blanding formed the "San Juan Arid Farms" organization (commonly known as the Grayson Dry Farm, located twelve miles east of Monticello). Four years later they purchased the first tractor in the county, had it shipped by rail to Thompson, and then tried unsuccessfully to drive it to their homesteads. Sand in the bearings threatened to destroy the machine, so the men disassembled it, shipped the parts by wagon, and reassembled it, only to learn that the tractor was inadequate for its task.

The next year, three other men joined the organization and pooled their money with the group, which bought a second tractor for $4,000. This machine, called "The Big Four," had four eight-foot-high wheels and a fifth wheel that extended fifteen feet in advance of the body to serve as a self-steering device.[48] The San Juan Farm Lands

Company, a similar organization, purchased a tractor for its 5,120-acre farm on Mustang Mesa near Blanding. The machine allowed two men to clear ten acres of land a day, a far cry from the poor man's backbreaking labor with a grubbing hoe.[49] Community or partner-owned reapers, headers, and (later) combines followed.

Yet all of this farming activity, like the livestock industry, was dependent on weather and exacted a heavy toll upon the land. Dry farming is based on the principle of trapping sufficient winter and early spring moisture in the soil long enough to germinate the seeds that will then be nourished by spring and summer rains. An average of sixteen inches of water fell each year between 1911 and 1933 near Blanding and Monticello, an amount sufficient to maintain the crops.[50] During that time, headlines often boasted that the "Season Was Dry: Crops Are Good," or "Conditions Good at La Sal Despite Drouth."[51]

There were years, however, when precipitation was marginal, insufficient, or came at the wrong time. Unpredictable weather coupled with the ravages of rodents and fluctuating market prices could discourage the heartiest of farmers. In 1925 an agronomist from the agricultural college wrote about the "pessimistic spirit" he encountered on tour, noting that he had "never witnessed such a psychological depression as exists at present among the farmers in the eastern part of San Juan County."[52] A lack of moisture or its erratic arrival was the cause, as would be the case in many other years.

A good example of how weather and economics combined to make continued life on a homestead tenuous occurred during the Great Depression of the 1930s. The government, in an attempt to get as many people working as possible, encouraged a "back to the farm" movement. The national census showed an increase of 200,000 homesteads over the past twenty years. One writer claimed that "more log cabins are being built now than at any time since Lincoln's day."[53]

To spur this movement on, President Franklin D. Roosevelt's New Deal provided loans for summer fallowing, seed purchase, and plowing. Twenty-five million dollars went to subsistence homesteads to "reduce congestion and relieve suffering," thus pushing more farmers onto the land. In San Juan there were a total of 880 homesteads, on 1,368 parcels of land, valued at $442,244.[54] In 1934, however, the county suffered through its worst recorded drought, receiving only half the normal moisture. The wheat crop was a total failure despite emergency relief money earmarked solely for aid for crops.[55] Great discouragement and the abandonment of many homesteads followed.

The government, having witnessed the terrible mismanagement of lands throughout the nation, became increasingly involved in salvaging and controlling their condition. The Soil Conservation Service (SCS) arrived in San Juan in 1939 in the guise of the already existing Civilian Conservation Corps (CCC): its primary mission was saving soil and water. Early on, the SCS noted that dry-land farms suffered from a loss of fertility due to constant cropping and lack of crop rotation, as well as loss of topsoil through wind erosion and torrential rainstorms, and from plowing ground on too steep a slope.[56]

Part of the solution lay in withdrawing vast tracts of land—3,000,000 acres in Grand and San Juan counties—from settlement by mining and homesteading claims. Another part of the solution lay in the 14,000 man-days provided in one year alone by the CCC workers who planted 21,800 trees and shrubs, seeded 962 acres of rangeland, and contour-plowed 270 acres. This last technique—contour plowing—became important in decreasing erosion as well as augmenting production.[57] For instance, William King, a Monticello farmer skeptical of SCS suggestions, put the agency's word to the test. He planted twenty acres in beans on contour-plowed land and thirty acres using his standard method. His harvest showed an increase of one and a half sacks of beans more from the contour-plowed land, with the added benefit of rainwater tending to remain where it fell rather than running in rivulets off the land. King slowly became a believer, probably echoing the sentiments found in a newspaper at the time: "Nature will always pay dividends to the man who uses his intelligence to protect the soil from misuse. . . . Man and nature make a powerful team when they work together."[58]

By 1946, ninety-five farmers and ranchers in San Juan were at various stages of the implementation of good land practices as outlined by the government. This represented only 87,288 of 300,000 acres of privately owned land, but it was a good start. Increased crop yields, at times as high as thirty-four percent, made believers of some. Care for the land motivated others, as officials reported 1,078 acres of contour-plowed land and 6,255 acres cleared of sagebrush and planted in grass. Eight years later, the trend continued, with 1,979 acres contour-plowed, 1,407 acres strip cropped, and 432 acres stubble-mulched.[59]

What then do these facts and figures indicate? Like the cattle industry in an earlier era, farming in San Juan had moved beyond the time when nature could absorb man's mistakes and mistreatment. Government-controlled lands now followed dictated scientific-management policies reflecting the prevailing understanding of the times. Owners of private homesteaded lands, on the other hand, often needed to be helped financially and encouraged to abandon older techniques surviving from a less restrictive past. Long-term benefits, not short-term profits, became an important goal for government and husbandman alike.

As farms became increasingly expensive for individuals to run, many were abandoned, the land receiving a much needed rest after the feverish activity of the first four decades of the twentieth century. The 1990 census indicates that fewer than fifty people in San Juan County still claim agriculture as their self-supporting livelihood; and, though a number of land owners maintain substantial tracts of ground in the soil bank, a program initiated during the Depression years, few appear to want to do much more than let the land lie fallow. Entire homestead communities have been abandoned, leaving little evidence of what once existed, while only a handful of cattle companies or individual stockmen still graze their animals on mountain slopes or canyon floors.

Yet today, even with all of its restrictions, the livestock industry is second only to the federal government in bringing money to the county. Approximately $12,000,000 each year comes into San Juan, while the average rancher adds $9,108 annually to tax revenues.[60] The days of the open range and individual homesteading have come to a close and left a colorful legacy from the past, but the county is still dependent on the land for its economic survival.

Endnotes

1. Charles S. Peterson, "Cowboys and Cattle Trails: A Centennial View of Emery County," *Emery County: Reflections on Its Past and Future*, ed. Allan Kent Powell (Salt Lake City: Utah State Historical Society, 1979), 83.

2. For some of the best work published on the cattle industry of San Juan see Charles S. Peterson, *Look to the Mountains: Southeastern Utah and the La Sal National Forest* (Provo: Brigham Young University Press, 1975) and Peterson's "San Juan: A Hundred Years of Cattle, Sheep, and Dry Farms," in *San Juan County, Utah: People, Resources, and History*, ed. Allan Kent Powell (Salt Lake City: Utah State Historical Society, 1983), 171–203; David Lavender, *Colorado River Country* (New York: E. P. Dutton, 1982), 143–50; and the unembellished "clips" found in Harold G. and Fay L. Muhlestein, *Monticello Journal: A History of Monticello Until 1937* (Self-published, 1988). More dramatic and less scholarly accounts are found in Cornelia Perkins, Marian Nielson, and Lenora Jones, *Saga of San Juan* (Salt Lake City: Mercury Publishing Company, 1957); Faun McConkie Tanner, *The Far Country: A Regional History of Moab and La Sal, Utah* (Salt Lake City: Olympus Publishing Company, 1976); Albert R. Lyman, *Indians and Outlaws: Settling the San Juan Frontier* (Salt Lake City: Publishers Press, 1962); and parts of James H. Beckstead, *Cowboying: A Tough Job in a Hard Land* (Salt Lake City: University of Utah Press, 1991). There are also a number of good unpublished works which will be cited in notes throughout this chapter.

3. Fred W. Keller, "Blue Mountain," A. J. Redd Files, Utah State Historical Society, Salt Lake City, Utah; "Blue Mountain Song," *San Juan Record* (hereafter cited as *SJR*), 22 December 1955, 34.

4. Frank Silvey, "History of Northern San Juan County and Paradox Valley," Silvey Collection, Utah State Historical Society, Salt Lake City, Utah, 2–5.

5. Tanner, *The Far Country*, 80.

6. Kate B. Carter, ed., *Heart Throbs of the West*, vol. 12 (Salt Lake City: Daughters of Utah Pioneers, 1951), 341.

7. Don D. Walker, "The Carlisles: Cattle Barons of the Upper Basin," *Utah Historical Quarterly* 32, no. 3 (Summer 1964): 270–272.

8. Charles S. Peterson, "San Juan in Controversy: American Livestock Frontier vs. Mormon Cattle Pool," *Charles Redd Monographs in Western History: Essays on the American West, 1972–73* (Provo: Brigham Young University, 1974), 3:52.

9. Thomas E. Austin and Robert S. McPherson, "Murder, Mayhem, and Mormons: The Evolution of Law Enforcement on the San Juan

Frontier, 1880–1900," *Utah Historical Quarterly* 55, no. 1 (Winter 1987), 38–39.

10. Franklin D. Day, "The Cattle Industry of San Juan County, Utah, 1875–1900," M.A. thesis, Brigham Young University, 1958, 47–49.

11. Peterson, "San Juan in Controversy," 59.

12. See Peterson, "San Juan in Controversy."

13. Daniel K. Muhlestein, "The Rise and Fall of the Cattle Companies in San Juan, 1880–1900," unpublished manuscript, n.d., Utah State Historical Society, Salt Lake City, Utah, 24–25.

14. Ibid., 34–35; 39.

15. F. A. Hammond as cited in Daniel Muhlestein, 43.

16. Silvey, "History," 55.

17. Neal Lambert, "Al Scorup: Cattleman of the Canyons," *Utah Historical Quarterly* 32, no. 3 (Summer 1964): 301–20.

18. Peterson, *Look to the Mountains*, 100–104.

19. Joe Redd, interview with Charles Peterson 26 July 1973, Charles Redd Center for Western Studies, Brigham Young University, 9.

20. "100th Birthday" *SJR*, 17 October 1984, 7.

21. Peterson, *Look to the Mountains*, 104.

22. "The Costs of Running Sheep," *Montezuma Journal*, 10 December 1903, 4.

23. Peterson, *Look to the Mountains*, 124.

24. "Stock Men Meet at Monticello," *Grand Valley Times* (hereafter cited as *GVT*), 30 August 1907, 1.

25. "Proceed with the Case," *GVT*, 28 January 1910, 1.

26. "Highlights from Inspection and Accomplishment Reports," found in La Sal National Forest folder, Manuscript A 326b, Utah State Historical Society, 1–3.

27. "Cattlemen Will Prevent Heavy Winter Loss," *GVT*, 25 April 1913, 1.

28. "San Juan Range Stock Will Suffer," *San Juan Blade*, 28 September 1917, 1; "Our Neighbors," *Montezuma Journal*, 4 July 1918, 3, and 5 September 1918, 5.

29. "18,000 Cattle, 30,000 Sheep to Be Grazed on Forest," and "Interesting Notes of Livestock Industry in Southeast Utah," *Times-Independent*, 28 February 1924 and 30 October 1924, 1.

30. "San Juan Livestock Men Apply for 3,750,000 Acres of Land," *SJR*, 22 February 1934, 1.

31. Cattle Buying Starts as Relief Measure," *SJR*, 19 July 1934, 1; "Cattlemen Hear Plan of Govt. Purchase," *SJR*, 5 July 1934, 1.

32. "Vital Changes Affecting State Land Negotiated," *SJR*, 9 September 1938, 1.

33. "Grazing Report for Fiscal Year," *SJR*, 20 July 1939, 9.

34. "Heavier Marketing of Cattle Urged," *SJR*, 30 September 1943, 1.

35. "Memo" to Hardy, Robert, and Paul [his sons] from Charles H. Redd, July 1965 in *La Sal Reflections: A Redd Family Journal*, ed. Jessie L. Embry (Charles Redd Foundation, 1984): 146.

36. Ibid., 150.

37. "San Juan County Economy Strongly Stabilized by Sheep," *SJR*, 22 December 1955, 23.

38. "Monticello BLM District Covers 5.4 Million Acres," *SJR*, 12 August 1965, 2.

39. For personalized accounts of the lifestyle of a homesteader see *Blue Mountain Shadows* 8 (Summer 1991); see also Norma Perkins Young, *Anchored Lariats on the San Juan Frontier* (Provo: Community Press, 1985). For more formal discussion of the patterns associated with homesteading see Peterson in *San Juan County*, 183–201; see also Stanford J. Layton, *To No Privileged Class: The Rationalization of Homesteading and Rural Life in the Early Twentieth-Century American West*, Charles Redd Monographs in Western History, no. 17 (Provo: Brigham Young University Press, 1988).

40. Melvin J. Frost, "Factors That Influenced Homesteading and Land Abandonment in San Juan County, Utah," M.A. thesis, Brigham Young University, 1960, 66–67.

41. "The Empire of San Juan," *GVT*, 8 January 1912, 4.

42. Anonymous, "San Juan County, Utah," unpublished manuscript, Utah State Historical Society, Salt Lake City, 1920, 12.

43. "The Trip of the Dry Farmers," *GVT*, 24 August 1906, 1.

44. "Growing San Juan," *GVT*, 9 December 1910, 4.

45. "Dry Farming, the Absorbing Topic," *GVT*, 22 October 1911, 1; "The Empire of San Juan," *GVT*, 8 January 1912, 4; "San Juan Ranks above Them All," *GVT*, 2 August 1912, 1.

46. "San Juan Dry Farming," *GVT*, 15 January 1915, 1; "64 Bushels of Wheat to Acre," *GVT*, 23 October 1914, 4; "52 Bushels of Oats per Acre on Dry Farm," *San Juan Blade*, 28 September 1917, 1; "Monticello Man Wins Gold Medal," *Mancos Times-Tribune*, 12 March 1920, 1.

47. "President Guarantees Wheat Growers Profit," *San Juan Blade*, 7 September 1917, 1; "Farm Loans—A Wonderful Year's Record," *San Juan Blade*, 20 June 1918, 2; "San Juan Farmers Get Loans from Government,"

GVT, 26 July 1918, 1; "Monticello Flour in Big Demand Here," *Times-Independent*, 17 February 1921, 1.

48. Wes McDonald, "San Juan's Early Day Tractors," *SJR*, 24 May 1962, 6.

49. "Dry Farming on Extensive Scale," *San Juan Blade*, 17 August 1917, 1.

50. Herbert E. Gregory, *The San Juan Country: A Geographic and Geologic Reconnaissance of Southeastern Utah*, Professional Paper Number 188, U.S. Department of the Interior (Washington, D.C.: Government Printing Office, 1938), 18.

51. "Season Was Dry: Crops Are Good," *GVT*, 21 November 1913, 1; "Conditions Good at La Sal Despite Drouth," *GVT*, 14 June 1918, 1.

52. "Peterson Deplores Pessimistic Spirit," *Times-Independent*, 11 June 1925, 1.

53. "Back to the Farmland: The Big Migration," *SJR*, 1 June 1933, 1.

54. "Dry Farmers May Secure Help From the Government Now," *SJR*, 18 May 1933, 1; "Land Officials Ask for Aid in Using Idle Farms," *SJR*, 2 November 1933, 1; "What Homestead Survey Shows," *SJR*, 20 February 1936, 1.

55. "Emergency Drouth Relief Money Ready," *SJR*, 24 May 1934, 1; "Nearly All the Wheat Crop Is Ruined by Worst Drouth on Record in Utah," *SJR*, 14 June 1934, 1.

56. "Soil Conservation Service Moves to San Juan County," *SJR*, 11 May 1939, 1; "Soil Conservation Story Continued," *SJR*, 12 September 1946, 1.

57. "Vast Acreage of Land Withdrawn," *SJR*, 2 September 1943, 1; "Soil Conservation Service Report," *SJR*, 19 March 1942, 5.

58. "Contour Farming Pays Dividends," *SJR*, 25 October 1945, 1; "What Is an Acre of Land Worth?" *SJR*, 22 June 1944, 1.

59. "Soil Conservation Work Progressing," *SJR*, 11 July 1946, 1; "Soil Conservation Story Continued," *SJR*, 17 October 1946, 1; "Soil Conservation Report for 1953," *SJR*, 11 February 1954, 8.

60. Jim Keyes, "Cattle by the Wayside First . . . Then the Communities?" *SJR*, 18 May 1994, 1.

9

From Beads and Blankets to Dollars

UTE AND NAVAJO ECONOMIC
DEVELOPMENT, 1900–1990

*P*rogress, defined in the dictionary as "movement toward a goal" or "steady improvement," is a word laden with cultural assumptions. To an outsider, what has occurred economically to the Navajos and Utes of San Juan County over the past century appears to fit well within this definition. However, many tribal elders who have lived through this era cling to a desire to return to a simpler life, when they had far greater control of how they lived and what they did. Thus economic progress, one of the most important concepts fostered in Anglo society, was actually a two-edged sword for Native American communities as it sundered centuries-old traditions while enticing individuals and groups to acquire new products and a different lifestyle. The uncharted course these changes took often created more problems than it solved.

By the turn of the century, the Navajos had survived the drought of the 1890s, the subsequent closing of many off-reservation posts, and the unsettling stream of miners in quest of precious metals in the Four Corners region. The 1900s offered a new hope physically tied to the core of life—water, sheep, and corn. All else was peripheral.

194

Interior of the Aneth trading post (trader unidentified) in the 1930s. The men standing and sitting in the foreground are in an area called the "bullpen," a space surrounded on three sides by high, wide counters which prevented easy access to the shelves by the customers. (William Snow Collection, Navajo Nation Archives)

Sufficient grazing lands and agricultural plots, as well as the ceremonies that insured health and fruition, provided focus for a set of values that had existed in one form or another at least since the Spanish arrived in the Southwest. Though far different in their basic perception from their Anglo neighbors, the expanding Navajo population did share a number of economic interests where the two societies met, exchanged, and improved upon their own cultural lifestyles.

Perhaps the most colorful of these meeting places was the trading post, an institution that flourished between 1900 and 1930. Trading participants overlooked cultural diversity in favor of economic growth and development, as each group offered products and forged bonds of cooperation despite their differences. There is perhaps no better symbol of the bridge formed to span the cultural gap between the two societies than the men and women who lived and worked in the trading posts of the Four Corners region.[1] Many spent their lives fostering an appreciation of Navajo culture while gently moving their Native American customers into the mainstream of twentieth-century economic life.

In southeastern Utah, these traders located their posts on the San Juan River or at strategic points along road networks in the interior of the reservation. The Aneth post, for instance, was built in 1885 on 160 acres of school-section property, which later insured its immunity from the reservation boundary change in 1905 that swallowed the surrounding land. Nearby McElmo Canyon provided a natural thoroughfare through the red rock country of southwestern Colorado and southeastern Utah, while McElmo Creek twisted its way to the San Juan, serving the store as a source of water for both agriculture and livestock. The Aneth trading post also lays claim to being the oldest continuing business in the county.

Other posts along the San Juan that enjoyed Navajo trade in the twentieth century include Owen E. Noland's Four Corners trading post, as well as posts at Montezuma Creek, Mexican Hat, and Bluff. Stores situated on routes of travel or in central locations included Hatch, Ismay, Oljato, Gouldings, and Navajo Mountain, as well as other more temporary stores in Montezuma Canyon, Marble Wash, McElmo Canyon, and the northern entrance to Monument Valley. Still other posts lay just beyond the boundaries of the county, drawing Navajo trade to Inscription House, Shonto, Kayenta, Chinle, Red Mesa, Mancos Creek, Teec Nos Pos, and Mexican Water.

Over this thirty-year period, the number of posts fluctuated. A military expedition led by Lieutenant Colonel George Hunter in 1908 provides some educated estimates concerning the amount of traffic generated by these businesses.[2] He identified posts at Oljato, Round Rock, Bluff, Tuba City, Teec Nos Pos, and Red Lake as those visited by the Navajos from the Monument Valley-Navajo Mountain region. There were also stores in the Farmington/Shiprock area, though Hunter did not mention them. One of Hunter's captains visited the San Juan Co-op in Bluff and reported that 950 adult Navajos had traded there within the past year but that only half of them had homes within a sixty-mile radius. Hunter, basing his population figures on traders' statements, concluded that from Navajo Mountain to the Carrizo Mountains, there was a total population of 1,512

Native Americans. Even as a rough estimate, these figures are a strong indicator of Navajo mobility in regard to trade.

Although the actual may be far from the ideal, the general impression of the traders who manned these stores was that they were basically honest, moral people who worked hard. Those who were not, did not last long, forced out of the market by competitors who were. Most of the traders were white men, though a handful were Navajo. An Indian had an advantage in that he could establish a post at any place, whereas an Anglo went to a location specified by the government. For example, John Wetherill opened a store in Oljato in 1906 only after receiving approval to locate on an abandoned mining claim that was surrounded by, but not part of, reservation lands. By 1910 he, his wife Louisa, and his partner Clyde Colville decided that Kayenta, twenty-six miles away, would be a better site because of the traffic that flowed through Marsh Pass.[3] It then became necessary for the Wetherills to again submit an application with accompanying character references for approval.

One important commodity to come from these posts was ten-foot-long sacks of wool, shipped to Kansas City or other markets in the East. Local white entrepreneurs quickly seized upon this important product, augmenting their own shipments with Navajo wool. Yet the most colorful aspect of the Navajo livestock industry centered on the rugs and saddle blankets woven in the hogans of the people. Starting in the late 1890s, real commercialization of the craft began, as Navajo weavers grew desirous of entering the Anglo-American marketplace. Part of this shift occurred because of a recent economic depression, part because of the abandonment of older, heavier blankets for lighter, machine-woven blankets for personal use, and a third part because of a developing craze for Indian decorations in Anglo homes.

Traders welcomed the demand, encouraging Navajos to weave for the tourist industry and for export to outlets as far away as New York and Los Angeles. Their impact was obvious. In 1899 the weaving trade amounted to only $50,000 reservationwide; fifteen years later it had skyrocketed to $700,000, and by the 1920s a person could order a variety of Indian-made blankets from the Sears and Roebuck catalog.[4]

Weaving varied from region to region, family to family, and person to person, some individuals' work commanding better prices at the post than that of others. Blankets called "quickies" or "bread and coffee rugs" were loosely woven, poorly designed, and bought according to weight, varying anywhere from fifty cents to a dollar a pound. A well-woven 3-by-5-foot rug, on the other hand, might command up to eight dollars and a 9-by-12-foot rug twenty dollars.[5]

To develop higher quality products, agents introduced different types of sheep and wool, and, as one newspaper reported, the Navajos, "stalwart nomads of the Painted Desert, have gone far afield to improve the strain of sheep which provide wool for the famous Navajo blanket."[6] The federal government submitted short clips to newspapers announcing its desire "To Stimulate Trade in Navajo Blankets."[7] In 1914 local people from southeastern Utah urged Senator George Sutherland to take action to protect the Navajos from being cheated because of imitation rugs. Under a new Bureau of Indian Affairs plan, the traders who accepted the rug, as well as the superintendent from the part of the reservation in which the rug was produced, needed to verify its authenticity.[8]

Newspapers also boosted the trade. When Addie Hammond from Moab got into the blanket business, she provided news releases telling of how she had obtained "the most remarkable line of Navajo rugs and curios ever seen in Moab," and that "in spite of the scarcity of blankets," hers were of "superior quality and quantity."[9] Another advertisement caught the eye with bold letters asking, "Why a Navajo?" with smaller print saying, "Because the Indians are not all dead," that their blankets would be hard to find, but that there were a few left.[10] Yet another argued that "even the Navajos have 'caught on' to the mild craze . . . for blankets, pottery, silversmith work, etc. . . . getting double the worth of their wares from awe-inspired young ladies and classical-browed professors."[11] To add to this good press, some Navajos from San Juan County donated six beautiful blankets to the Red Cross in 1919 and had them presented in Monticello and then in Salt Lake City. The Red Cross put the handicraft up for bid and received fifty-three dollars for one rug that contained only six dollars worth of materials.[12]

The results of this burgeoning trade were salubrious. As early as

1896, Colorado papers touted the beneficial effects of the San Juan trading posts on the economy, claiming that freighting outfits "loaded out from Bauer Store [in Mancos] often $1,000 worth of goods a day."[13] By 1913 *The Mancos Times-Tribune* felt that trade "naturally gravitated to this area," with sometimes as many as six or seven heavily laden wagons groaning their way to the river. This economic boon made Mancos the "recognized commercial and financial center" of Montezuma County, Colorado.[14]

The trade had its ups and downs as demand fluctuated. For instance, a decline in weaving occurred as World War I markets gobbled up wool for military purposes. The general pattern existing through the early 1930s, however, was that when wool was available and cheap the rug industry prospered, but when wool became scarce, weaving slowed down appreciably. Before and after World War I when wool was plentiful and its price low, the rug industry reached its greatest height.[15]

While the Navajos were relatively prosperous, the Utes had little to offer would-be consumers along these same lines. During the late 1800s, they had been heavily involved in the hide trade; however, the newspapers began to report any hunting trips off the reservation as "slaughter" and decimation of the already diminishing deer herds.[16] Hunting as a way of life became totally impractical. Beadwork and baskets, famous crafts of the Utes, were not as useful or as stylish in appearance as Navajo rugs and produced little revenue, so they rarely moved beyond a very local economy.

Agriculture fared just as badly. Ute farming efforts generally were on a subsistence level, failing to compete in the twentieth-century market economy with Anglos who had better land, equipment, and techniques. In Allen Canyon, for instance, the government farmer, E. Z. Black, plowed allotted lands that averaged only around ten acres per family. He was also totally dependent upon the agents at Towaoc for teams, plows, seeds, and general financial backing.[17] As soon as the funds dried up, so did the work on projects. Part of this problem arose because the Allen Canyon Utes in 1929 comprised only fourteen families, whose activities were so peripheral to those on the main reservation in Colorado that few people could muster sufficient funds or support for any sustained, large-scale local farming project.[18]

Ute families and Edwin Z. Black planting a garden at the Allen Canyon allotments in the 1920s. Spring runoff from Blue Mountain watered the garden, alfalfa, and orchard. The house in the background served as Black's home and local agency for the Utes who lived in tents and summerhouses up and down the canyon. (Courtesy Helen Shumway)

How much this bothered the people of Allen Canyon is difficult to determine, but they continued to wrestle with dire poverty, living in tents while depending on rations and other government subsidies.

Sheep, cattle, and horses presented Utes a more culturally acceptable opportunity, but the battle for the ranges that took place during the first quarter of the twentieth century put a stop to free use of Montezuma Canyon, McCracken Mesa, and the plateaus surrounding Blue Mountain. Between the Forest Service, Bureau of Land Management, and private livestock companies, the lands encircling Allen Canyon were heavily controlled, forcing the Utes to keep their herds small and within certain limits. Thus, physical and cultural restraints stifled the Ute economy. Clearing land for white farmers, chopping wood for townspeople, and doing odd jobs for individual families served as only temporary employment in their hand-to-mouth existence.

Soon the government unwittingly enforced similar restraints on the Navajo, in what became to the Indians a traumatic show of force. As already suggested, livestock was one of the most important foundations of the traditional Navajo economy during the first quarter of the twentieth century. Horses provided transportation and food for the winter months, while goats and sheep served as a continuing source of sustenance, blankets, clothing, and the means for entering the barter economy of the trading post. Livestock also became synonymous with social status and emotional satisfaction, as Navajos watched their herds multiply and prosper.

But starting in the late 1920s much of this came to an end. The events that set the livestock reduction program in motion were rooted in the past, long before the slaughter started. Although the Navajo reservation expanded at a sporadic but significant rate during the late nineteenth and early twentieth centuries, land acquisition did not keep pace with the growing number of Navajos. In Utah, the land additions of 1905 and 1933 only recognized what was already occurring on the public domain. Ironically, the year after the government added the Aneth Extension, the Bureau of Indian Affairs (BIA) reported that "these Indians will be willing to dispose of all of their range stock in exchange for a farm of adequate size to support their families."[19]

It appears that the Northern Navajo agent, B. P. Six, little understood the role of livestock in Navajo culture. He did, however, watch the herds expand. During 1930 in the Montezuma Creek and Aneth area 19,514 sheep and goats passed through dip vats to prevent scabies. The Oljato and Shonto areas that year produced 43,623 animals, while some Utah Navajos undoubtedly went to vats located at Kayenta, Shiprock, Dennehotso, and Teec Nos Pos. Still others probably skipped the process entirely; but, if the totals from the Aneth and Oljato areas are combined, at least 63,137 sheep and goats ranged over the reservation lands of southeastern Utah.[20] The Soil Conservation Service and other government agencies tried to stem the growth of what some considered the "hoofed locust" destroying the ranges.

By 1934 the entire Northern Navajo Agency reported that government officials had killed or sold 70,000 animals, and that the Utah Navajos' herds were now down to an estimated 36,000 animals.[21] With the nation's economy wallowing in the depths of the Great Depression, Indian agents could price a sheep at only two dollars and a goat at one dollar. The annual report went on to say that "an excessive number of goats and sheep were slaughtered for food. There is every reason to believe that the next dipping record will show even a greater reduction than indicated by the number sold."[22] Many horses and cattle suffered a similar fate.

The cold, hard statistics of livestock loss reflected the scientific logic employed to save the range. Depleted vegetation, soil erosion, silt accumulation at Hoover Dam, expanding herds, restrictions on off-reservation grazing, poor animal quality, and the faltering national economy were all part of the motivation to reduce livestock, modernize the Navajos' lifestyle, and improve the management of resources.[23] In Utah, as in other parts of the reservation, logical scientific methods proved to be an economic and emotional disaster for the Navajos who depended on their herds for survival.

Starting in 1933, the goat herds were the first to be selected, gathered, and killed. A year later, sheep came under the knife, followed by horses and cattle. The reduction that had started out voluntarily, as just one more incomprehensible government program, soon became a major threat to the Navajos' subsistence economy. Richer Navajos were more powerful and harder to entrap, so often the poorer people, those who could least afford the losses and still maintain self-sufficiency, were the first to suffer. Further impoverishment and dependency on the government became a part of reservation life.

The Navajos reacted to all of this with stunned disbelief and shock. What had at first seemed like only one more requirement of the government turned into an economic war of attrition and destruction, symbolically comparable in the tribal memory to events seventy years before—the roundup of Navajos for the Long Walk to Fort Sumner. This time, instead of the U.S. cavalry, the "soldiers" were government agents, range riders (known in Navajo as the One-Who-Leads-His-Horse-Around), and tribal government officials sympathetic to Washington's plans. As was the case during the 1860s, those who resisted were removed and incarcerated.[24]

But it was the responsibility of these white "troops" to administer the program. Many of these public servants were endangered, facing the possibility of physical confrontation. In some cases, Navajos beat these hated enforcers of stock reduction, and in a few instances, the government men were killed. The loathing and fear engendered by this program, however, usually focused on a living symbol, the head of the Bureau of Indian Affairs, John Collier. Some Navajos believed that he hated them and that he looked at them with "hungry eyes" because they were "getting rich by having too many sheep." To others, he was a "white cowboy" who brought in his friends to kill the goats. Still others thought he was "crazy" because he liked to "steal, cheat, and lie." As one white rancher explained, he never had a conversation with Navajos about livestock reduction that did not end with "John Collier heap son-of-a-bitch."[25]

By the time reduction had run its course between 1933 and 1946, the Navajos' economy was devastated. Tribal figures indicate that the Indians' dependence on agriculture and livestock had decreased by fifty-seven percent in a little more than a decade, though this figure varied by region, by outfit, and by individual.[26] For example, John Holiday from Monument Valley drove thirty-seven horses into the stock corrals and came out with only thirteen. Of his six hundred plus sheep, he kept three hundred and fifty-four.[27]

While livestock ceased to be a major part of the Navajo economy, another element—large scale agriculture—also ceased to hold much promise. As early as 1901, government irrigation inspectors estimated that one-third of the Navajo tribe could prosper along the San Juan River if they just had enough ditches.[28] In 1902 Samuel Shoemaker, supervisor of ditch construction near Fruitland, received orders from agent George Hayzlett to start a major ditch in the vicinity of Bluff. Shoemaker paid Navajo laborers a dollar a day and hoped they would "soon make a mile of ditch in that part of the country"; however, no long-term benefit arose from this project.[29]

A few years later, agent William Shelton appointed James Holley as the government farmer in Aneth and started a thirty-year battle to harness the San Juan for Navajo crops. The success and then eventual abandonment of this project is discussed in Chapter 6, but the temporary accomplishments of men like James Holley and Herbert Redshaw were still important in the attempt to move the Navajo through agriculture into a more economically stable lifestyle.

One important impetus to improvement started in 1909 when Shelton and Aneth government farmer W. O. Hodgson instituted an event that continues to this day—the annual Shiprock Fair. Heralded by the *Farmington Enterprise* as marking a "new era of progress of the Southwest," many people viewed the fair as the peak of Shelton's six years of activity to remove the "ignorance and superstition of a barbarous people." [30]

In spite of their supposed "barbarity," the Navajos made a "creditable" showing with 290 exhibits, each containing from five to sixty articles. Categories included blankets, silver jewelry, buffalo robes, beadwork, horses, cows, sheep, goats, and a wide array of farm produce.[31] The fair drew contestants from more than seventy miles away, and for years to come it grew in importance as a place of social exchange and as a tool to encourage the development of quality agricultural produce.

With the collapse of the large-scale Aneth farming project and the devastation of the livestock-reduction program, the Utah Navajos were rudely pushed into the wage economy of twentieth century America. While the women often stayed at home and tried to eke out a bare existence, the men hired out for work in various government programs such as the CCC and WPA during the Depression and for work in the defense industry in cities throughout the West during World War II. In the private sector, large groups of Navajos harvested crops as migrant laborers, laid track for railroads, herded livestock for white ranchers, worked in sawmills, cut wood or cleared brush, and generally tried to keep their families together when they returned home. Others relocated their families to their job sites, creating small communities like Westwater on the outskirts of Blanding.[32]

One aspect associated with the Navajos' search for employment and mobility was the introduction of cars and trucks. Starting around 1915, parts of the northern Navajo reservation became increasingly exposed to the automobile. John and Louisa Wetherill in Kayenta attracted a group of daredevil tourists from Los Angeles who wanted to see if they could conquer sand dunes, washes, and canyons to reach the Wetherill trading post. On 26 October 1915, these "pioneers" arrived at their farthest point of travel and camped on the San Juan River near Navajo Mountain, having mystified many Navajos with their vehicle.[33] Cars setting out from Shiprock around this same time went to Aneth, while others traveled from Monticello and Blanding to Bluff, a place that would eventually become only a stopping point for motor tourists on their way to Mexican Hat and Monument Valley beyond.

Early glimpses of these first metal monsters were disturbing to some. One man went with a friend to the Aneth Trading Post to chop wood. When he got there, a crowd had surrounded something unusual, so he decided to investigate. "Everyone was excited and talking. This 'something' had small wheels similar to a wagon. One person stared in amazement and kept circling it. He was asked to turn the crank in front so he did. Then, with a loud noise it started up," much to everyone's amazement.[34]

Around 1924 Jack Lameman, a respected Navajo from Aneth, bought a Ford in Farmington and drove home in low gear, a journey of approximately 100 miles. The next day, he started for the trading post but went only a short distance before the vehicle died. He sought out Herbert Redshaw, who looked in the gas tank and found it empty. Lameman was amazed. He swore that it could not be, because he had looked in it the day before and it was full. When he learned that it was necessary for a person to put gas in the vehicle on a regular basis, he vowed to go back to Farmington and return it, but Redshaw pointed out the problem of depreciation, so Lameman decided to "make the most of a very bad bargain."[35]

Many years have passed, and many changes have occurred on the reservation since the first auto appeared. The trauma of livestock reduction and subsequent events have encouraged Navajos to become increasingly dependent on automobiles. Now almost every family has at least one vehicle—often a pickup truck—to do the chores once done with a wagon. A study completed in 1975 indicated that the largest expenditure of funds by Navajo families went for transportation, followed closely by food; over half of the average income went to these two items.[36]

As cars and trucks appeared on the reservation, Navajos were able to move in widening circles, while, at the same time, there was increased access to their homelands by non-Indians. In 1944, the Office of Indian Affairs leased its first uranium claim in Monument Valley. The mine, located on the eastern tip of Oljato Mesa, yielded fifty-two tons of uranium and vanadium the first year. The tribe was anxious to receive its ten-percent royalty, so when a group of miners led by Wayne Carroll and Lee Shumway bid $505 for the forty-acre claim, the tribal government at Window Rock agreed.[37] The men set to work with relatively crude equipment and Navajo labor to gouge out the minerals located on the cliffs above. This mine, called Utah One, should not be confused with Monument One, owned and operated by the Vanadium Corporation of America (VCA), started shortly afterward on the valley floor near Oljato. After a few years, Shumway and Carroll canceled their lease, closing the first mine to yield payments for uranium on the Utah portion of the reservation.[38]

As atomic bombs exploded over Hiroshima and Nagasaki, the world suddenly awoke to the mushroomlike fruits of the Manhattan Project and the possibilities of nuclear fission. What had transpired in secret now became public, and Americans learned that the government had been advertising for vanadium but really wanted its companion, uranium. VCA notified the Navajo tribe that it was seeking rich deposits of uranium to mine and that a government-established royalty was available for those who provided the resources.[39] Although prospectors found many of the major uranium mines farther north on the Colorado Plateau in the vicinity of Moab or southeast in Grants, New Mexico, the news generated tremors on the Utah portion of the reservation. Harry Goulding at his Monument Valley trading post took a growing interest in the possibility of having mines in his own backyard. By June 1950 he had located seven deposits of uranium with the help of Navajos who brought in samples.[40] A nineteen-year-old, Luke Yazzie, discovered the largest concentration found by a Navajo.[41] Yazzie had studied the ore samples that Goulding left on his countertop. When Yazzie found some heavy rocks with a yellow stripe through them, he hid them away, thinking that they might be gold. Eventually, he showed the trader a sample and received a free soda pop, lunch, and the impression that he could become rich.

Goulding invited Denny Viles, field manager of VCA, to visit the site. The trader realized that he could not receive the royalties from this discovery, but he was anxious to improve the Navajos' standard of living, which in turn would benefit his own operation.[42] Viles took samples from the site; two years later Monument Two was in operation. All that Luke Yazzie received was a pick, a shovel, and a promise of continuous employment until the mine closed. He worked for fifteen years at a monthly salary of $130.[43]

Soon others started their own searches—a quest for riches that continued throughout the 1950s. Geiger counters issued to Navajos served as one of the primary tools of discovery. Eventually thirty-one mines of varying sizes were established on the reservation in southeastern Utah and northeastern Arizona.[44] Small deposits throughout the Monument Valley region gave rise to mines with the names Daylight, Sunlight, Starlight, and Moonlight. But the biggest, Monument Two in Cane Valley south of Mexican Hat, was by far the most important. John Meadows, foreman of the Navajo crews that worked there, described the mine as having excellent-grade ore close to the surface. Originally this site had been an old river-bed that had become dammed by wood that eventually petrified. The uranium extended for a mile, was 500 to 600 feet wide, and approximately forty feet deep. Black pitchblende and yellow carnotite composed the two most prevalent forms of ore extracted from the mine and sent to different VCA mills in the Four Corners region.[45]

Workers flocked to the mines for the new employment opportunities. At any given time, approximately 140 Navajos drilled, blasted, dug, and shoveled their way to a steady paycheck at Monument Two. Only 10 percent of the mine's employees were white workers, men who were involved primarily in the more technical or managerial aspects of the operation. Experienced laborers teamed up with new men and taught them how to operate a loader, set a fuse, or run a mucking machine. Once employed and trained, however, a skilled miner could stay at work by moving from one mine to another, as the old ones petered out. Those who did not stay in the Monument Valley area could move to other sites in the Four Corners region.[46]

Navajo miners often worked under hazardous conditions in uranium mines of the Monument Valley area. Some Navajos offered traditional prayers and ceremonies before and after entering the mines. The People received protection from harm and appeased the spirit of the earth, which they believed to be an animate being. (William Snow Collection, Navajo Nation Archives)

Mining brought to the reservation a boom-and-bust economy that served as an "exciter" for other development. Navajos and Anglos worked side by side to build new roads stretching over miles of desert where none existed a few years previously. The roads to Mexican Water, through Comb Ridge, down the Moki Dugway, over the new steel bridge at Mexican Hat, and those branching out through the Oljato and Mexican Hat areas are all examples of improvements made in the transportation network of southeastern Utah because of the uranium industry. Texas Zinc, for instance, paid about three million dollars in 1956 for thirty-three miles of road that stretched from the Natural Bridges area to four miles north of Mexican Hat so that their newly established mill could process off-reservation uranium.[47]

With between one-third and one-half of all of the nation's uranium reserves located in the Four Corners region, it is not surprising that the Navajo Tribe worked closely with the Atomic Energy Commission, which purchased all the high-grade uranium produced until 1970.[48] The type of economic boom that arose from the uranium mining is illustrated in tribalwide figures over a four-year period. In 1950 the Navajo Nation garnered $65,755 from the industry, but in 1954 the sum jumped to $650,000.[49] This was a significant amount added to the tribal coffers; Utah Navajos, however, felt that they received few direct benefits. And even though Texas Zinc completed its processing mill at Halchita near Mexican Hat in 1957, an estimated ninety percent of its ore came from off-reservation mines. The mill, with its 775-ton-per-day capacity, did not cease operation until 1970, but by the mid-1960s the relative prosperity associated with Navajo mining had started a downward spiral.[50]

At the same time that the uranium industry in Monument Valley was booming, a second industry, oil, became increasingly prominent in the Aneth-Montezuma Creek area. Starting in 1953, Humble Oil and Shell Oil initiated agreements with the Navajo Tribe and the State of Utah to exploit the rich petroleum reserves locked beneath the Aneth lands. The Texas Company drilled its first well on 16 February 1956 and welcomed a rapid flow of 1,704 barrels per day.[51] Other companies responded immediately; suddenly the tribe found itself administering leases and rentals throughout the northern part of the reservation, known generally as the Four Corners Oil Field.

In 1956 alone the Aneth oil field yielded $34.5 million in royalties to the tribe.[52] With a population of more than 80,000 members, the Navajo Nation decided against making a per capita distribution of the money, which would have amounted to only $425. Instead, the leaders invested the royalties in services such as education and economic development. Much of this money, however, was used in the central part of the reservation and not on the periphery where the oil wells producing this wealth were located.

When the federal government agreed to the Aneth Extension in 1933, the law that removed the land from the public domain specified that 37.5 percent of the revenues coming from oil and gas in the Extension would be used for "Navajos and such other Indians" living on this section.[53] The money could be spent on health, education, and general welfare of the Navajos. The law expanded in 1968 to include all Navajos living on the Utah portion of the reservation.

The Utah State Legislature established a three-member Indian commission in 1959 to return royalties of $632,000 to the Navajo people. On 27 July Governor George D. Clyde attended the first meeting and charged the group to carry out the law. The commission, composed of a chairman who was a member at large, an Indian member, and a citizen from San Juan County, undertook the awesome task of helping improve living conditions across the Utah reservation, from Aneth to Navajo Mountain.[54]

In 1968 the government amended the 1933 act to include other services to be considered general welfare; it also extended the number of beneficiaries to include all of the Navajo people in San Juan County. Road development, establishment of health clinics, economic endeavors, and education filled the agendas of the committee. Different areas had their own requirements, which became so numerous and widespread that a full-time administrative organization was needed. The Utah Navajo Development Council (UNDC) was established in 1971 with an all-Navajo board to meet the growing urgency to deliver necessary services. From a fledgling organization, UNDC expanded rapidly. Take health care, for instance. During its first fiscal year, 1971–72, Navajos totaled 8,421 visits to the two clinics located at Navajo Mountain and Montezuma Creek; by 1983 another clinic had been added at Halchita (1975) and visits had doubled to 16,845.[55] Figures relating to education, housing, livestock assistance, and other programs show a similar rise, indicating that the organization was meeting the needs of many Utah Navajos.

By 1978, however, there was rising discontent in the oil fields. On 30 March 1978, Navajos from the Aneth-Montezuma Creek area physically took over the main Texaco pump station in Aneth and eventually stopped all production throughout the entire region. With an activist spirit common to the late 1960s and early 1970s, the group, known as the Utah Chapter of the Council for Navajo Liberation, or the Coalition, attracted more than a thousand people sympathetic to its cause. On 3 April the group listed thirteen demands that included the need to renegotiate leases, more sensitive treatment of Navajos living in the oil fields, greater environmental

Participants of the "Aneth Takeover" listen to negotiations in 1978. Perceived injustices included abuse of the land, lack of decision-making power by the local people, and Texaco's treatment of the Navajos. (Courtesy Utah Navajo Development Council)

concern, and more benefits for those directly affected by the oil pumps in their backyard. The four oil companies—Texaco, Superior, Continental, and Phillips—that owned the 200 wells in the area, generally acquiesced to the demands, except in regard to changing the lease agreements.[56] This settlement ended almost three weeks of occupation by Navajo protesters.

Today, however, many of the problems of the Aneth oil field continue. Mobil purchased Superior's wells, controlling those on both the north and south sides of the river in the Aneth region. Phillips and Texaco still pump oil in the Montezuma Creek area, but the Utah Navajo Development Council no longer provides services in the Utah strip. The Council and its subsidiary, Utah Navajo Industries, because of problems with mismanagement of funds, lost their economic power until legal action could be taken against those misusing the money.

Along with a diminishing number of barrels of oil and royalties, there is also diminishing enthusiasm for the oil fields among the

older Navajo people, who complain of great environmental destruction. Younger Navajos often do not feel that complaint as strongly,
welcoming the jobs, the royalties that pay for education and health
benefits, and the other businesses attracted to the area. But, as with
many other events, personalities, and technologies that have had an
impact on the Aneth region, oil's long-term effects will more truly
determine whether it has been beneficial or harmful.

The same is true of uranium. Miners of the 1950s and 1960s
risked life, limbs, and lungs to remove uranium from the earth. A
series of claims against the mines and the Atomic Energy
Commission that regulated them led to little satisfaction. No group
would accept responsibility for the deteriorating health of those who
worked in the mines. In 1990 the U.S. Supreme Court determined
that it could not hear these cases because the uranium industry from
the 1940s to the 1970s was immune from lawsuit because of its gov-
ernmental status. However, Congress did pass the Radiation
Exposure Compensation Act, which includes a possible award of up
to $100,000 to deserving miners, widows, or children of deceased
parents. President George Bush signed the law, but only recently has
Congress appropriated funds for compensation.[57] Money has also
been allocated for the removal and burial of the tailings at the
Mexican Hat mill, as well as those in Shiprock, Tuba City, and elsewhere.

The story of the Utes, though not as dramatic or economically
significant as that of the Navajos, has also shown some progress. In
the 1950s, with help from a Salt Lake law firm under the leadership
of Ernest L. Wilkinson, the Utes of Colorado and Utah received
approximately $31.5 million in compensation for lands lost to white
settlers since the treaty of 1868. The government paid part of this
money in a per capita settlement spread over a number of years,
while the rest was set aside for a long-range program for improvement of tribal facilities and projects.[58]

To the 148 Utes living near Blanding, the initial compensation
amounted to $1,025 per person over a two-year period, from an
aggregate sum of $151,700—an unheard of amount to many, when
most family incomes were well below $800 per year. Additional funds
followed on a fairly regular basis, eventually averaging a total pay-

Monument Valley and the Navajos played important roles in the film industry. (William Snow Collection, Navajo Nation Archives)

ment of $8,000 to each man, woman, and child. The initial reaction, reported in area newspapers with an obvious tinge of jealousy, indicated the Indians' desire to own all those things their white neighbors had, such as cars, nice clothes, and high-priced food. Of greater import, however, were the funds allocated to improve housing, roads, and services.[59]

The Utes in Allen Canyon realized their isolation was counterproductive, and others living on the outskirts of Blanding wanted to have better lands for farming and to use their compensation money to build their livestock industry. Starting in the mid-1950s, the Ute Mountain Rehabilitation Program, headquartered in Towaoc, provided funds for the construction of frame houses on White Mesa, eleven miles south of Blanding.[60] Electricity arrived in 1964, and bus service delivered Ute children to the schools in town.

Today the community boasts a population of about 350 people.

It has about 100 modern homes with electricity and running water, and is governed by the White Mesa Ute Council, established in 1978. Many of the Ute people are employed in service industries such as schools and motels; some work for the Council; others help operate a cattle company and a store on White Mesa; still others are employed at Towaoc in farming projects and in the reservation's casino. Many are working towards economic self-sufficiency by obtaining job skills marketable in the twenty-first century.

In summarizing the different economic experiences of the Navajos and Utes over a century of change, one finds common threads woven throughout the fabric of their experiences. Both groups started out with land-based economic systems imbued with cultural values. The Navajo were fortunate enough to develop agricultural and livestock industries that would mesh with mainstream American systems. They also had sufficiently large land holdings and were isolated enough that they could selectively adopt or reject elements of white culture as they saw fit. However, when livestock reduction removed this flexibility, the Navajos had to scramble for economic survival, as had the Utes in an earlier period.

Once these Native American groups obtained a substantial amount of money from uranium and oil, or from treaty violations, they were able to develop and maintain collective tribal programs to improve their way of life. Today, each group faces its problems squarely, entrenched in the mainstream American economic system. Though proudly rooted in their heritage from the past, future generations promise to be heavily invested in the technological, highly educated world of the twenty-first century.

ENDNOTES

1. See Robert S. McPherson, "Naalye'he 'Ba Hooghan—House of Merchandise: Navajo Trading Posts as an Institution of Cultural Change, 1900–1930," *American Indian Culture and Research Journal* 16, no. 1 (Winter 1992): 23–43.

2. LTC George Hunter to Adjutant General—Colorado, 26 August 1908, Record Group 393, U.S. Army Continental Command, 1821–1920, National Archives, Washington, D.C.

3. See Frances Gillmor and Louisa Wade Wetherill, *Traders to the*

Navajo (Albuquerque: University of New Mexico Press, 1934) for further discussion of their lives as traders in Oljato and Kayenta.

4. Garrick Bailey and Roberta Bailey, *A History of the Navajos—The Reservation Years* (Santa Fe: School of American Research, 1986), 150–52.

5. Elizabeth Compton Hegemann, *Navajo Trading Days* (Albuquerque: University of New Mexico Press, 1963), 299.

6. "Navajo Indians Improve Sheep," *Times-Independent*, 21 January 1926, 3.

7. "To Stimulate Trade in Navajo Blankets," *Grand Valley Times*, 25 August 1911, 1.

8. "Government Protects Blanket Weavers," *Grand Valley Times*, 20 March 1914, 1.

9. "Brings Back Remarkable Line of Navajo Rugs," *Times-Independent*, 23 October 1919, 8.

10. "Why Is a Navajo," *Grand Valley Times*, 11 February 1910, 4.

11. *Mancos Times Tribune*, 28 August 1903, 4.

12. "Indians Give Fine Blankets to Red Cross," *Times-Independent*, 25 September 1919, 3.

13. Ira Freeman, *A History of Montezuma County, Colorado* (Boulder: Johnson Publishing Company, 1958), 209.

14. "Trade Relations," *Mancos Times Tribune*, 25 April 1913, 7; "Mancos Best Trading Point, *Mancos Times Tribune*, 9 July 1915, 1.

15. Bailey and Bailey, *A History*, 150–52.

16. "Note," *Grand Valley Times*, 7 September 1906, 1; see also Robert S. McPherson, *The Northern Navajo Frontier* (Albuquerque: University of New Mexico Press, 1988), 51–62.

17. See "Farmers Reports: Allen Canyon, 1925–27," Record Group 75, Consolidated Ute Agency, National Archives, Denver, Colorado.

18. Agent E. J. Peacore to Commissioner of Indian Affairs, 12 March 1929, Record Group 75, Letters Received, Bureau of Indian Affairs, National Archives, Denver, Colorado.

19. Annual Report, 1934, Bureau of Indian Affairs, Navajo Archives, Edge of the Cedars Museum, Blanding, Utah, 4.

20. Annual Report, 1930, Bureau of Indian Affairs, Navajo Archives, n.p.

21. Annual Report, 1934.

22. Ibid.

23. For an excellent explanation of the ecological and economic impact of livestock reduction see Richard White, *Roots of Dependency: Subsistence,*

Environment and Social Change Among Choctaws, Pawnees and Navajos
(Lincoln: University of Nebraska Press, 1983): 212–323.

24. Margaret Weston interview with author, 13 February 1991, manuscript in possession of author.

25. Katso interview with S. Moon, 15 August 1974, manuscript available in California State University–Fullerton Oral History Program, Southeastern Utah Project; Cecil Parrish, interview with author, 10 October 1991, manuscript in possession of author; John Joe Begay interview with author, 18 September 1990, manuscript in possession of author; Norman Nielson interview with author, 1 May 1991, manuscript in possession of author.

26. White, *Roots of Dependency*, 312.

27. John Holiday interview with author, 9 September 1991, manuscript in possession of author.

28. "Annual Report of the Department of Indian Affairs," 30 June 1901, *Report of the Commissioner of Indian Affairs*, 65–66.

29. George W. Hayzlett to Commissioner of Indian Affairs, 16 January 1903, as cited in David M. Brugge, "Navajo Use and Occupation of the Area North of the San Juan River in Present-day Utah," unpublished manuscript in author's possession.

30. "Shiprock Has First Navajo Indian Fair," *Farmington Enterprise*, 29 October 1909, 1.

31. Ibid.

32. See Winston Hurst, "A Brief History of Navajo Settlement at Blanding, Utah," *Blue Mountain Shadows* 11 (Winter 1992): 21–31.

33. Curtis Zahn, "The Automobile Is Here to Stay," *Arizona Highways*, 28, no. 6 (June 1946): 22–23.

34. John Knot Begay interview with author, 7 May 1991, transcript in possession of author.

35. Albert H. Kneale, *Indian Agent* (Caldwell, Idaho: Caxton Printers, Ltd., 1950), 368–69.

36. David C. Williams, "Spending Patterns of Navajo Families," *New Mexico Business* 28, no. 2 (March 1975): 3–10.

37. William Chenoweth, "Early Uranium-Vanadium Mining in Monument Valley, San Juan County, Utah," *Survey Notes* 18, no. 2 (Summer 1984): 3, 19.

38. Ibid., 19.

39. Ibid.

40. Harry Goulding, "The Navajos Hunt Big Game . . . Uranium," *Popular Mechanics* (June 1950): 89–92.

41. There are conflicting accounts of who should actually be credited with Monument Two's discovery. Gary Shumway, who has extensively studied uranium mining in southeastern Utah, believes there were several people who had visited the deposit by the end of 1944. Among them were John Wetherill, Jim Hunt, Preston Redd, and Arah Shumway, who as a Vanadium Corporation of America employee made the first company visit to the site and personally reported it to Denny Viles as a major discovery. Gary Shumway, conversation with author, 10 January 1995.

42. Samuel Moon, *Tall Sheep: Harry Goulding, Monument Valley Trader* (Norman: University of Oklahoma Press, 1992), 175–81.

43. John Meadows interview with author, 30 May 1991, transcript in possession of author.

44. William L. Chenoweth and Roger C. Malan, *Uranium Deposits of Northeastern Arizona* (Grand Junction, Colo.: U. S. Atomic Energy Commission, 1973), 7.

45. Meadows interview.

46. Ibid.; Bud Haycock interview with author, 10 October 1991; Guy Cly interview with author, 7 August 1991; Cecil Parrish, interview with author, 10 October 1991, transcripts in possession of author.

47. Doris Valle, *Looking Back around the Hat: A History of Mexican Hat* (Mexican Hat: n.p., 1986), 49.

48. Philip Reno, *Mother Earth, Father Sky and Economic Development* (Albuquerque: University of New Mexico Press, 1981), 133–34.

49. Peter Iverson, *The Navajo Nation* (Albuquerque: University of New Mexico Press, 1981), 78.

50. Valle, *Looking Back*, 47–49; Jack Pehrson, foreman at Halchita, stated that the mill did not close until 1969, which differs from Valle's date of 1965 (conversation with author, 20 June 1992).

51. Robert W. Young, *The Role of the Navajo in the Southwestern Drama* (Gallup: The Gallup *Independent* and Robert W. Young, 1968), 83–84.

52. Iverson, *Navajo Nation*, 68.

53. U.S. Congress, House, "Amending the Act of March 1, 1933 . . . as an Addition to the Navajo Indian Reservation," S. Report 1324, 90th Cong., 2d Sess., 1968, 1–6.

54. "Minutes of Commission of State Indian Affairs," 27 July 1959, Navajo Files, Edge of Cedar Museum, Blanding, Utah.

55. "Annual Reports of the Utah Navajo Development Council—1978–1983," in possession of author.

56. Iverson, *Navajo Nation*, 188; Reno, *Mother Earth*, 124–25.

57. "Zah Vows to Battle for Due Payment," *Navajo Times*, 22 August 1991, 1.

58. "Ute Indians Awarded $31,000,000 Settlement," *San Juan Record*, 20 July 1950, 1; "Ute Indians to Receive Payment," *San Juan Record*, 6 September 1951, 5.

59. "San Juan Piutes Have Pay Day," *San Juan Record*, 24 April 1952, 3; "Ute Land Settlement Fund Allocation Set by Council," *San Juan Record*, 26 June 1952, 1.

60. "Ute Indian Tribe Building New Homes," *San Juan Record*, 14 October 1954, 6.

10

Tall Timbers, Mountain Streams,
and Desert Rivers

THE DEVELOPMENT OF FOREST AND WATER RESOURCES IN SAN JUAN COUNTY

From any point above the canyons of San Juan County, one can spy a large mountain poking its peaks aloft, standing in sharp contrast to the red rock, high plateau desert below. Strikingly beautiful, the Abajos, or Blue Mountain, as well as the La Sals and Navajo Mountain have reaped praise through song, prose, and poetry forged by the pens of skillful wordsmiths. But for the pragmatic residents who live at their bases, these heights figure significantly in the daily economic issues that concern survival. The mountains, and the streams and rivers fed by them, are directly tied to the land's inhabitants' struggle to wrest a living in an austere, sometimes harsh environment.

From the beginning, wood, water, and grass, found in abundance on the mountains and near the rivers, have dominated the economic and social life of the people. They still play an important part today. Forest and water management are two complex and broad topics that encapsulate some of the county's major past and present issues. A recent book, *Look to the Mountains* by Charles S. Peterson, discusses the importance of the mountains' resources and how local views, economic conditions, and federal policy have sometimes diverged before eventually converging on a desired path.[1] This chapter continues the theme of resource development, as the importance of the county's mountains, forests, streams, and rivers is examined in light of more than a hundred years of utilization and control.

On 6 April 1880, a group of Mormons tethered their tired horses at the future site of Bluff along the banks of the San Juan River. Nearby, they found only cottonwoods for construction; these trees, with their twists and knots, proved as unruly as the river that gave them life. The Mormons improvised as best they could, fashioning crooked "bullfences" for their livestock and using "that same rams-horn breed of trees to . . . build houses, whose walls bowed in and out with wonderful irregularity, [requiring] chinks from nothing to a foot wide." The boards "were so determined to warp and twist like a thing in convulsion, they wouldn't lie still after being nailed down."[2]

There was, however, an alternative source, and it did not take long to find it. Thirty to forty miles to the north on Blue Mountain and in the canyons that led from it grew Douglas fir and white fir, Engelmann spruce, and western yellow (ponderosa) pine. The latter was economically most important, but all of these trees, with their long straight trunks, were ideal for construction. Although the settlers traveled to the mountain within weeks of their arrival, it was not until 1882 that the county government established an official road for the express purpose of obtaining lumber.[3] Shortly after, Willard Butt and George Ipson whipsawed the first boards from timber at the head of Devil's Canyon. With this type of system, two good men at the handles could saw an average of 150 board feet of lumber a day. Still, demand outweighed the ability to supply it. Sawmill replaced saw pit, providing more wood, greater community service, and more cash, "though no one became jealous of the dividends it brought in, according to reports."[4]

From these humble beginnings sprang more and larger itinerant logging camps on both the Blue/Elk Ridge complex and the La Sal mountains. It is conservatively estimated that at least twenty-eight mills had been at work on the two mountain ranges by 1940; in 1925 alone, seven had processed lumber simultaneously.[5] As towns, farms, ranches, and business ventures spread over the lands below, and

The Charles Burr Sawmill, located on Verdure Creek, cut ponderosa pine for nearly twenty years until it was moved to Blanding in 1931. (San Juan Historical Commission)

mines, camps and water-control projects sprang from the mountains' sides, an increasing demand for wood arose. In 1911 the residents and businesses in Monticello, Bluff, and Grayson required so much wood that the Grayson Co-op mill, sawing an average of 10,000 board feet per day, could not keep up, even with two other area mills in operation. Fourteen years later, 513,000 board feet came from the La Sal National Forest. In 1962 the San Juan Lumber Company in Recapture Canyon cut 13,000,000 board feet of timber, some of which was shipped as far east as Chicago and as far north as Toronto, Canada.[6]

The history of early sawmills is difficult to trace. They have been located as far south as Blanding and as far north as the San Juan-Grand County line. Usually, logging and milling were an individual or family operation affected by economic fluctuations, dependent on local sales, plagued by equipment failure, prone to destruction by fire, subject to dangerous working conditions, and relatively short-lived.

Though each operation was different, a typical mill during the old days when powerful labor-saving machinery was not available was located on the side of a gently sloping hill in order to more easily move the logs. Men cut the timber into fourteen-foot lengths, hauled or skidded them to the site, and then mounted them on a carrier that moved the wood back and forth beside the steam- (later gasoline-)

powered circular saw blade. From there the board went to the edger
to be trimmed and cut into standard widths, to the planer to smooth
its sides, and to the stacking yard, where it cured in the sun. Mills
made a point of getting rid of their refuse and scrap to keep the fire
hazard down, but the fate of many companies rested on a spark near
a pile of slabs, edgings, or sawdust.[7]

Control of the early lumber industry was one of a number of reasons why the federal government desired increasing supervision of
access to and use of the mountains. The livestock industry with its
large herds of cattle and flocks of sheep, a growing awareness of natural resource conservation during the progressive administration of
President Theodore Roosevelt, concern over use of watershed lands,
and regulation of the mining industry with its potential for exploding
populations and resource utilization, all suggested federal regulation.
The government began to meet this need in 1906 when it created the
La Sal Forest Reserve (128,960 acres in Utah and 25,502 acres in
Colorado), then again in 1907 with the establishment of the
Monticello Forest (315,668 acres), and again with the consolidation
of the two (474,130 acres) in 1908 under the title of the La Sal
National Forest.[8]

The next step was to find people to supervise this vast area. Orrin
C. Snow, headquartered in Moab, assumed responsibilities as the first
forest supervisor over the northern division, which encompassed two
grazing districts in the La Sals, and the southern division, with three
districts on Blue Mountain and Elk Ridge. The Forest Service established three ranger stations—Baker, west of Monticello; Grayson,
located in Bulldog Canyon; and Cottonwood, in North Cottonwood
Canyon. By 1943, automobiles, improved roads, and established control of water sources encouraged the consolidation of these three districts into one managerial unit, with overnight stations at
Gooseberry, Kigalia, and Indian Creek.[9]

The forest rangers living in these stations were not unskilled
backwoodsmen who fortunately fell into a position. Just the opposite
was true. Supervisor John Riis, the first ranger to work on Blue
Mountain, provides a good example of the quality of men who
served in these positions. He was born in Brooklyn, New York, educated in Pennsylvania, and had practical experience as a rancher,

farmer, and cowboy before passing his entrance exam into the Forest Service. He worked faithfully in this position and was promoted to supervisor, but eventually left the Forest Service and returned to the East.

While in San Juan, Riis had the difficult task of gaining acceptance in the tightly-knit Mormon community of Monticello and working with the stockmen to control their use of rangelands. As a "government man" and a "gentile," his presence reminded the townspeople of past conflicts between federal marshals and polygamists. In Riis's words, "Gentile and government man; there could be no worse combination in the eyes of the rural Mormon. . . . Though respectful and courteous, the Mormons made me feel keenly that I was an alien in the land and my presence was on sufferance only." He later commented that once their friendship had been won, it was "well worth the price."[10]

The early forest rangers had a multitude of duties to perform in this isolated setting. In addition to the primary responsibility of working with the stockmen to control the number of animals on the range, these men also participated in livestock associations, improved water sources, built fences, strung telephone wire, fought forest fires, blazed trails, improved roads, served as game wardens, inspected mining claims, evaluated marketable timber, monitored sawmill activities, and transacted local financial business for the government.

Thus, it is not surprising that the government placed a high premium on obtaining capable, intelligent men skilled in many areas. For example, in 1909 Riis administered a six-hour written exam designed by the Civil Service Commission to ten forest ranger applicants. On it were such questions as: "How many men are employed in a sawmill which cuts ten thousand feet of lumber a day and what does each man do?" "What is the most practical grade to build a trail on?" "How many pounds can a horse pack for six consecutive days traveling 15 miles a day? How much can a man pack?" and "If you were going to build a cabin 14x18 feet, how much and what kind of material would you need? What would be the cost of the building? State in detail." The hands-on portion of the test included marksmanship, horsemanship, surveying, mapping, securing gear on pack animals, and keeping a diary.[11] One of the ten applicants, Rudolph

Mellenthin, passed. He served as a ranger and eventually died in the line of duty. A peak in the La Sal Mountains was named after him.

Of continuing interest to lumbermen, miners, cattlemen, and watershed developers was improved access to the mountains through an expanding network of roads. The Forest Service, in conjunction with other government and private agencies, shouldered the responsibility of surveying, mapping, and constructing the transportation system. In terms of cash expenditures, road and trail construction ranked among the top priorities.[12] The interest in road development varied with the times, but a 1925 report indicates the extent of some of these improvements and the cooperative efforts of civilian and government forces. The Grand County commissioners shared the responsibility of maintaining the road on the La Sals in the Pack Creek to Castleton area, fifteen men from Blanding donated labor to the Forest Service in building the road from the Bears Ears to Natural Bridges, another crew worked on the wilderness trail from Cottonwood to Mormon Pasture, while a fourth group improved the trail in Dark Canyon. Even with all of this activity, as one newspaper reported, the end product of these labors "cannot be considered a boulevard" and "speed cops are not needed."[13]

From 1933 to 1942 San Juan County enjoyed the benefits of the Civilian Conservation Corps (CCC) as part of President Franklin Delano Roosevelt's New Deal policy. Designed to employ young men between the ages of eighteen and twenty-six in a rural setting, the program brought hundreds of people, many of whom were from the East, and placed them in the forests and on the mountains to do construction work in the county. Building roads, fences, corrals, flood-control projects, and emplacing culverts, telephone lines, and campgrounds were just some of the tasks performed by the men stationed in Dry Valley, Indian Creek, Blanding, and Monticello and on the La Sals.

A summary of what the Blanding camp, DG-34, accomplished over a six-year period is indicative of what these groups achieved. The CCC established the camp in 1935, at a time of serious drought. The corpsmen's first project was a long-range water and conservation program. The men constructed a series of reservoirs and wells and improved springs that served thousands of cattle and sheep. They eradicated noxious weeds, thinned timber, removed diseased trees, and virtually wiped out the Zuni prairie dog, whose presence had become "almost as serious as the drouth." The CCC men built miles of truck trails, the most notable being the main road that passes over Blue Mountain from Blanding to Monticello. In so doing, these young men were instrumental in opening large tracts of timber that had hitherto been inaccessible. Revegetation to restore rangelands was another positive contribution. But, as one article quipped, the "biggest thing accomplished by the CCC is the reclamation of the American boy" in a structured environment where the work ethic was enshrined as a way of life.[14]

The government abandoned the CCC program as World War II assumed enormous proportions. At the same time, the nation placed greater demands for the products that came from its national forests to meet the requirements of the administration's "arsenal of democracy" economy. With the end of the war and entrance into the 1950s, there arose hitherto unknown affluence, a growing population, an increased interest in recreation, and a philosophy that the government should be involved to help sustain all three. By 1960 Congress reacted to these forces by adopting the Multiple Use Act whereby the national forests—including the La Sal National Forest—became more closely managed areas for use as outdoor recreation, as well as range, timber, watershed, and fish and wildlife development.[15]

A few figures from 1979 illustrate what this development has meant to San Juan County. Approximately 2,000,000 board feet were harvested that year from the Blue and La Sal mountains; 3,685 cows with calves grazed on forest land; stockmen paid $28,000 in grazing fees, half of which returned in the form of range improvement and another quarter of which went into school and road development; a report sponsored by the San Juan Water Conservancy District in Monticello estimated that 4,400 acre-feet of water each year poured down through North and South creeks, giving rise to a discussion of future water appropriations; on the southern side of the mountain, the conservancy district formulated plans for the future Recapture Dam project.[16] No one should doubt the economic importance of the mountains in San Juan County.

However, all of the products that come from the mountains are

dwarfed in significance by the one element upon which most rely—
water. Indeed, a large part of the history of San Juan illustrates the
dependence on this vital resource. Returning for a moment to the
early Mormon experience, it is useful to examine why their attempts
to harness the San Juan River faltered and failed and why many
settlers moved from Bluff, seeking a more stable source of water at
the foot of Blue Mountain. Their courageous struggle against the
river illustrates what others faced into the 1970s in their attempts to
control the floodwaters of the San Juan and its tributaries.

When the large Mormon contingent settled in Bluff, its members
started immediately to dig ditches and prepare for spring planting.
Community cooperation and organization characterized this first
year, but the ditches proved unsatisfactory for a group of people who
wanted to move beyond a subsistence level of agriculture. By 1881 a
new canal, costing from 12 to 50 dollars a rod, was necessary.[17] The
headgate of this ditch was located four miles above the town on a
long stretch of slick rock. The builders hauled logs, brush, rocks, and
earth to construct the riprap channel extending out into the river to
divert the water. Three such walls allowed the water to be turned onto
individual fields. Men cut cottonwood logs from the river's bank,
using an estimated 1,000 trees which were woven into a framework
to hold tons of rocks and dirt. To encourage cooperation, the leaders
sold stock in the new ditch and Mormon church officials allowed
some people to be rebaptized as part of their commitment to this
new undertaking.

All winter long the men toiled. When April arrived and thoughts
of spring planting arose, the workers turned the water down the ditch
and watched it disappear through the porous walls of riprap. As the
gaps filled with sediment, the water began to inch its way to the fields
close to town. In May, the river gnawed away at the top of the ditch.
The water started to recede, and shovels deepened a course for it to
follow. The crops succeeded.

The next year problems intensified. Banks broke, ditches filled
with sand, crops withered, taxes to support the effort increased, and
stockholders appointed new leaders in an attempt to save the project.
During the flood of 1884, the river carved up the canal, tore out the
headgate, and covered what remained with sand.[18] Francis Hammond

Flood control on the San Juan River was a perpetual problem until the Navajo Dam regulated stream flow beginning in 1962. This 1,000 foot riprap dam, photographed in May 1910, provided partial protection for Bluff but did not influence the runoff coming down Cottonwood Wash, which also could flood the city. (San Juan Historical Commission)

later sent exploring parties to Blue Mountain in search of more easily controlled water and farm acreage. They returned with favorable reports that launched a party of Bluff residents to the mountain's base where they set to work digging ditches.

Monticello, in its early years, faced a different set of water problems. The Carlisle cattle outfit was angered that a group of settlers were assuming control of the range and water, even if the Mormons' irrigation ditch was on public land. Hammond consulted a lawyer in Durango who assured him that the Carlisles had no legitimate claim to the water, but it was a disenchanted ranch-hand, a man named Fritz, who provided the best case for Mormon claims. Earlier, Fritz had filed on the land in question and had planned to deed it to the Carlisles; after a disagreement, he deeded it to Hammond with the assuring words, "Tell Carlisle that if he makes trouble, I'll appear against him for defrauding the government."[19] Although the cowboys threatened and periodically diverted the water from the irrigation ditches, the town eventually triumphed.

Four main streams of water—North, South, Pole and Spring

creeks—flow east and north from the mountain and onto the plain near Monticello. The Blue Mountain Irrigation Company, founded in 1887 and still in operation today, assumed the responsibility for water development by first digging and then improving ditches and reservoirs to supply the town.

As early as 1904, the water company investigated the possibility of piping the water into town from springs above so that livestock and other sources of pollution would not contaminate the water running down the open ditch. Lack of money allowed only part of this system to develop. But when a water-borne typhoid epidemic broke out in the fall of 1910, the Blue Mountain Irrigation Company sprang into action. A committee soon learned that the tax base and bonding ability of Monticello's 375 residents was so small that it was financially improbable the project could be completed. Yet there really was no other choice. Both men and women canvassed members in the community to mortgage their land and water to the Federal Land Bank of Berkeley, California, and banks in Salt Lake City in exchange for $45,000 dollars cash, to be supplemented by $15,000 worth of donated labor. By 1917 clean, piped water flowed from Pole Canyon into Monticello. Until 1930 the water also helped provide electricity for the town.[20]

The system, under the care of the Blue Mountain Irrigation Company until 1936, required continuous maintenance and improvement as the economy and population of Monticello changed. By the time the Vanadium Corporation of America started its mill as part of the war industries, the town had assumed responsibility for water management and qualified as a defense area eligible for federal and VCA funding to improve the water system. In 1942 an engineering firm replaced the old leaking pipes with a new reservoir, fire hydrants on the main streets, and larger conduits capable of providing each resident with 150 gallons of water a day—a big improvement from what it had been forty years before.[21]

But if the story of water development on the northeast side of Blue Mountain was one of trial and sacrifice, it was even more so on the southern end, as Blanding matured and grew. Drought, unproductive artesian wells, lack of capital, and interruption of labor for various reasons impeded the development of an adequate water sys-

A portion of the ditch surveyed by Walter C. Lyman at the north end of White Mesa. Some laughed at the primitive measuring equipment and construction techniques, but by 1903 water from Johnson Creek was "flowing uphill" much to the chagrin of the doubters. (San Juan Historical Commission)

tem. The spring in Westwater Canyon served as the town's main source of water, even after a ditch surveyed by Walter C. Lyman in 1897 was completed. As Blanding's population started to grow, more water from Johnson and Recapture creeks became a necessity. Mormon families seeking refuge from their experience in Mexico provided much of the labor for this lower part of the ditch. By 1916, two-thirds of White Mesa was receiving water.[22]

Problems still remained once the water arrived in town. People dug cisterns or used abandoned wells to store the ditch water on their property. The first community reservoir, completed in 1916, cost the residents $45,000 and was soon followed by two more reservoirs. A system of wooden pipes coated with tar and wrapped with wire delivered the water to homes, but what poured out of the tap was often undesirable, being brackish, at times flavored by dead animals, and insufficient in quantity. The wooden pipes also started to rot, and the reservoirs smelled terrible. In 1934 a new pipeline and an electric pump helped provide more water to the town, but it was not until 1947 that Blanding took out a bond for a new pipeline to extend all the way from the mountain.[23]

One of the most dramatic aspects of water development (and characteristic of the dedication of the people) was the building of a mile-long tunnel. As early as 1914, a few individuals started to think about diverting the underutilized water of Indian Creek to the north into the Johnson and Recapture creeks water system supporting Blanding's growing population. By 1921 the White Mesa Irrigation Company had assumed responsibility for drilling, blasting, digging, and hauling the refuse from a tunnel that was to be constructed from both sides of the mountain. Personal sacrifice and the visionary faith of a few individuals kept the project alive for thirty years. Depression, war, a flagging rural economy, seasonal abandonment, and the skepticism of many people combined to make the effort slow and sporadic. Finally, on 27 December 1951, the two construction crews broke through, joining their respective sections of tunnel, and by June of the next year Indian Creek water was cascading through the tunnel, down the ditch, and into the pipes of Blanding. The estimated cost for the project was approximately $125,000.[24]

Beyond the statistics, the tunnel represents tremendous personal sacrifice for those involved in its construction. Sylvester (Vet) Bradford and Marvin Lyman held the contract for its development at twenty-two dollars a foot, but the tunnel required much more. Imagine the discouragement when an engineer had to resurvey a new southern entrance in 1939 because of cave-ins and washouts of the

North end of the 5,400 foot tunnel used to divert water from Indian Creek to the south side of Blue Mountain and the town of Blanding on White Mesa in 1951. Left to right—a state mining engineer; Nancy and Cleal Bradford; and Thora and Vet Bradford. (Courtesy Cleal Bradford)

first portal. Add to this the fact that shortly after Lyman and Bradford signed the contract, "wages, materials, powder, fuse and everything doubled in price."[25]

Nature also did its best to discourage the workers. Lyman tells of being 4,000 feet into the project when the miners hit a particularly stubborn streak of rock. He quotes Vet Bradford as saying, "We're just about to the end of our rope. We've had this hard rock here for about two weeks now. . . . It's taken three or four times as much powder and as much drilling and three or four times as many rock bits to drill this hole and it only shoots out about half as much in a round and it was getting pretty heavy to bear."[26] Lyman testified that it was one of the most difficult things he had ever done in his life.

So it is surprising that on that June day in 1952 more people did not attend the ceremonious turning of Indian Creek water into the tunnel and ditches that fed Blanding with its 2,000 people. Only two men—Marvin Lyman and Douglas Galbraith—had been present in

1921 when workers removed the first wheelbarrow of dirt.[27] Now they and the many other laborers could rest, secure in the knowledge that they were leaving a legacy to sustain growth of their community for generations to come.

Increasing the waterflow to town also escalated the pressure on the Forest Service to insure its quality. Random livestock grazing presented the greatest concern, as animals contaminated drainage fields high on the mountain. As early as 1925, citizens from Monticello requested that the Forest Service fence specific areas to keep sheep and cattle out of crucial watershed areas. The groups cooperated without a fuss; government personnel and ranchers fenced the land and Forest Service crews patrolled for stray livestock. Today, 4,000 acres encompassing drainages from North and South creeks comprise the Monticello watershed, while Blanding draws upon the drainages of Johnson, Recapture, and Indian creeks as well as Dry Wash in its 6,875 acre watershed.[28]

Starting in the 1950s, the growing population of San Juan County increased demand on the water systems. Wells dug to varying depths secured water for people living outside of city limits, but the needs of those living within the towns and those earning a livelihood in agriculture depended heavily on the flow from the mountains. There was still a large amount of water being wasted as spring run-off, so the San Juan Water Conservancy Council set out to impound as much of it as possible. Starting in 1972, the people of Blanding began to dream about blocking the waters rushing down Recapture Canyon by creating a dam half a mile below Highway 163. Although this required flooding the road and the abandoned San Juan Lumber Company sawmill, the State Division of Water Resources believed this to be the most promising of the possible sites. The need for the dam was underscored in 1977, when the snowpack on Blue Mountain remained well below normal, the pumps in the two city wells broke, and only two feet of water rested in the Blanding reservoirs, whose level declined at the rate of three-quarters of an inch a day. A newspaper article, after giving helpful hints as to how to conserve water, ended with a plea that could have been echoed by the pioneers a hundred years before: "watch every drop—curtail, pray, and hope we get some moisture."[29] Even after all the efforts and expense of the past, mountain waters still held the key to survival in the area.

Ironically, it was this same water and drainage that had attracted the Anasazi a thousand years before to establish their homes, some of the remains of which would soon be flooded with water. The estimated $6,000,000 to build the dam and realign the road did not include the expense of excavating twelve of the forty-eight known Anasazi ruins, the cost of which the county would have to bear. Archaeological site mitigation entailed expenses that many local people felt unnecessary. As one Blanding resident explained, "I wish we'd done this thirty years ago when all we needed was a license."[30] In spite of the cost and delays, workers completed the dam in 1984, creating a 9,000-acre-foot capacity reservoir capable of supporting irrigation for 1,300 acres of farmland and recreation facilities for the people of San Juan County.[31] Blanding now has six and Monticello four reservoirs to meet the culinary and irrigation needs of the towns, utilizing as much of the water that comes from the mountain as possible.

While these cities were striving to obtain every drop of water, the opposite problem persisted at Bluff. A common thread running through this town's history is the sporadic yet intense battle waged against the flooding San Juan River. For instance, in 1905 the *Mancos Times* reported that the city was "washing away." In 1911, the river overflowed its banks, wreaking havoc from Shiprock, New Mexico, all along its course to Bluff; three years later, newspapers spoke of a government survey to determine if a dam should be established at Comb Ridge to control the release of water for agricultural purposes. In 1933 the river again overflowed, wiping out the government station in Aneth and flowing across the floodplain of Bluff.[32] Even in 1941, after the Soil Conservation Service had been active in the county for a number of years, there was still an uphill fight with the river. That June, the river peaked at 17,000 cubic feet per second for three days, tearing out the cottonwood trees, "melting the banks like sugar until 96 acres of irrigable pasture had disappeared . . . two days later an additional 18 acres of alfalfa were sluiced away through this merciless trough while five-foot high waves seemingly played at leapfrog as the stream continued to swing from the Navajo side to

advance upon the townsite."[33] Nothing could stop the rampaging of
the river until the waters abated.

Finally, by 1962, there was hope. The federal government completed the Navajo Dam thirty-nine miles outside of Farmington, New
Mexico, thus creating a water-storage and flood-control system to
regulate the amount of water flowing down the San Juan River. This
solution, however, could not account for excess run-off that had to
be released from the dam, nor how the waters coming down
Cottonwood Wash next to Bluff created an even greater threat. In
1968 and in the 1970s flood waters again imperiled the city. One resident recalled how the fill and bridge abutments in the wash were
undermined, how large cottonwood trees floated about battering the
bridge and anything in their way, how her family turned their livestock loose so the animals could swim to safety, and how one family
hung a sign in its flooded front yard that said "No Fishing."[34] The
river and its tributaries continued to have a will of their own.

Another type of turbulence, this time in the courtroom starting
in 1929, involved the San Juan, Green, and Colorado rivers. The State
of Utah and the federal government joined in a lawsuit to determine
the navigability of these bodies of water in order to determine ownership. If Utah could prove that they were navigable, a term defined
by very loose standards, then it would own the streambed and control how the rivers could be used. Legal counsel on both sides generated 3,000,000 words of expert testimony coming from 170 witnesses
in four different courtrooms in the West. The concluding session was
held in Salt Lake City before the evidence went to the Supreme
Court. A final determination stated that the federal government
maintained control of the rivers' use because all three rivers passed
through more than one state, making the government responsible for
"interstate commerce" as well as "flood protection, watershed development, and recovery of the costs of improvements through utilization of power."[35] Later attempts to change this ruling failed.

For the San Juan River, this means that the Bureau of Land
Management controls access from Montezuma Creek to the vicinity
of Slickhorn Canyon, though the southern bank belongs to the
Navajo Tribe. The area below Slickhorn Canyon is part of the Glen
Canyon National Recreation Area. As the river becomes increasingly

important for agriculture and recreation, control of water rights and access has taken the routine management forms of litigation and active patrolling. Today, 12,000 boaters annually float the San Juan under the watchful eye of BLM rangers.[36]

Similarly, the Colorado River has had its resources oversubscribed. Although this river serves as the western boundary between San Juan and Kane counties, until recently it has had only a tangential impact on the economy of San Juan County. Draining watersheds from seven western states, it is divided into two major districts, the Upper Basin (composed of Wyoming, Colorado, Utah, and New Mexico) and the Lower Basin (formed by Nevada, Arizona, and California). The Colorado courses through Utah in a general southwesterly direction and has two major tributaries—the Green River, which it meets at Canyonlands National Park, and the San Juan River, which it used to meet near Navajo Mountain before the waters of Lake Powell rose.

The Utah portion of the Colorado River, with its high canyon walls and desolate surroundings, did not start to reach the public's attention until after John Wesley Powell floated it. In 1869 and again in 1871–72, he mapped the river below its confluence with the Green River (which he also mapped) in expeditions sponsored by the Smithsonian Institution and Congress, respectively. His ten- and eleven-man crews collected information and navigated their wooden boats down one of the most geographically dramatic and roughest waterways in the United States.[37]

Miners, oil-field workers, and other transients had a passing acquaintance with the Colorado in the late 1800s and early 1900s, but, starting in the 1930s and 1940s, tourism on the river began to attract substantial attention. Norman Nevills, headquartered at Mexican Hat, for example, turned the red waters of the San Juan and Colorado into green cash with his tour guide business as recreation became increasingly important.

Yet the most dramatic change in the history of the river in Utah was yet to come. On 15 October 1956 President Dwight D. Eisenhower pushed a button at his White House desk, initiating the blast that started construction of the Glen Canyon Dam in Arizona, eight miles below the Utah border. Not only did this put in motion a mammoth building project by the Bureau of Reclamation but it was also one more effort to end the free-rolling life of the Colorado River in exchange for a hydroelectric plant and a massive recreational facility.[38]

In 1957 the Navajo Tribe agreed to make this building project possible by swapping 53,000 acres of land bordering the south bank of the Colorado River for a similar amount of land on McCracken Mesa near Montezuma Creek. This transfer provided the necessary land for the dam, located at newly created Page, Arizona—named after John C. Page, Commissioner of Reclamation (1937–43). The town soon became a city of service industries, catering to tourist needs and electric-power-generation requirements. The Navajos, as part of this and later agreements, waived rights to 43,000-acre-feet of Colorado River water. In return, Page was built on leased reservation lands, money was funneled into tribal coffers, and Navajo preference in employment was promised. Glen Canyon Dam was completed in 1963. Today, the 800-megawatt hydroelectric dam is operated by the Bureau of Reclamation, which sends its electrical power to large cities throughout the West.

The dammed waters of Lake Powell also backed up the flows of the Colorado and San Juan rivers 186 miles and 72 miles respectively, creating 1,960 miles of shoreline in the process. It is one of the largest man-made lakes in the United States. Forecasters estimated during the 1950s that the lake would have as many as half a million visitors a year; it now boasts that number on a Labor Day weekend alone. In 1962 the total visitation to the entire Glen Canyon National Recreation Area was 9,282; thirty years later, the annual visitation was 3,620,558 people.[39] Marinas located at Wahweap, Bullfrog, Hall's Crossing, and Hite serve the tourists who come to boat, swim, fish, and generally enjoy the red rock, sand, and sun for which the lake is famous. Thus, San Juan County has enjoyed an increasing number of tourist dollars as vacationers shop in its towns and utilize the marinas within or on its borders.

The history of water development in San Juan County has been filled with trial and error, but it illustrates a pattern of ever-increasing control and utilization. Whether considering Navajo and Glen Canyon dams; the reservoirs, ditches, pipelines, watershed, and tunnel on or near Blue Mountain; or the changes made to improve the quality and quantity of water delivered within city limits, one cannot deny that it appears that no cost was too great, no sacrifice too large, and no possibility left unexplored to obtain water. Residents even attempted to influence moisture-producing weather for their benefit.

In 1951 a rain-making organization from California advertised in the Four Corners region its ability to increase precipitation. The company conducted a weather survey that included analyses of historical patterns of precipitation and the geographical lay of the land, and even a forecast of future weather. The local newspaper applauded the "progressive attitude of the majority of the men in the county" for the support the project appeared to be receiving.[40] Few people in San Juan County did not want the 50–150 percent increase in rain promised by the company at a cost of $50,000 to the seven counties in Utah and Colorado which undertook the project. However, a later analysis by professors from the University of Utah indicated that there was no substantial benefit realized from the undertaking.[41]

In 1976 another rain-making project sent silver iodide into the clouds over thirteen counties in southern Utah. In San Juan, workers located generators for the project at Fry Canyon, La Sal Junction, Monticello, Blanding, Bluff, Mexican Hat, and Monument Valley in the hope that more moisture would make its way to the land. This and similar projects lasted into the early 1990s before they were canceled because of questionable results.[42] This attempt to wring additional moisture onto the high desert country of southeastern Utah had, at least for the time being, come to a close.

In summarizing more than 100 years of forest and water development in San Juan County, one finds increasing government control of these resources. With the exception of a few minor timber sales on Blue Mountain, Elk Ridge, and the La Sals, the logging industry has ground to a halt. The watersheds are protected from livestock and human pollution, but what comes to the cities in the form of culinary and irrigation water still depends upon what falls from the sky. The San Juan River is controlled at each end by dams that affect its flow. Even the groundwater pumped from its subsurface aquifer is controlled by a state regulated permit system. Thus, the pattern is obvious. The days of the rampaging river, water rights demanded at the point of a gun, and backbreaking labor to develop ditch and tunnel have given way to a life of greater ease circumscribed by government regulation and courtroom litigation. Resource control in San Juan has entered a new era.

ENDNOTES

1. Charles S. Peterson, *Look to the Mountains—Southeastern Utah and the La Sal National Forest* (Provo: Brigham Young University Press, 1975).

2. Andrew Jenson, "San Juan Stake History," unpublished manuscript, n.d., Special Collections, Brigham Young University Library, 90–91, 93.

3. "Minutes of County Commissioners of San Juan County, Utah From April 26th, 1880 to March 5th, 1900 ," Recorders Office, San Juan County Court House, Monticello, Utah, 14.

4. Ibid., 94; cited from *San Juan Blade*, 24 December 1917, 13, in "Water Records Index," Church of Jesus Christ of Latter-day Saints Archives, Salt Lake City, Utah; Richard L. Williams, *The Loggers* (Alexandria: Time-Life Books, 1976), 37.

5. Peterson, *Look to the Mountains* 212; "La Sal Forest Notes," *Times-Independent*, 16 July 1925, 1.

6. "San Juan Is Prosperous," *Grand Valley Times*, 23 June 1911, 1; Orange A. Olsen, "La Sal National Forest," *Times-Independent*, 2 April 1925, 1; "Local Sawmill Cuts over 13 Million Feet of Timber," *San Juan Record* (hereafter cited as *SJR*), 10 January 1963, 1.

7. For a good overview of the local logging industry based on personal accounts see Steven R. Meyer, "Sawmills: A Forgotten Industry," *Blue Mountain Shadows* 2, no. 1 (Fall 1988): 51–62.

8. Peterson, *Look to the Mountains*, 125–28.

9. "Forest Service History Dates Back to February 1905," *SJR*, 29 December 1958, 6.

10. John Riis, *Ranger Trails* (Richmond, Va.: Dietz Press, 1937): 32–33.

11. "Tough Bunch of Questions," *Grand Valley Times*, 29 October 1909, 1; see also J. W. Palmer: The Banty Forest Ranger," *Blue Mountain Shadows* 10 (Summer 1992): 46–53.

12. Peterson, *Look to the Mountains*, 223–24.

13. "La Sal Forest Notes," *Times-Independent*, 16 July 1925, 1; "News Notes from Over La Sal Forest," *Times-Independent*, 4 June 1925, 1.

14. "Sixth Anniversary of the Civilian Conservation Corps," *SJR*, 6 April 1939, 1.

15. Albert C. Worrell, *Principles of Forest Policy* (New York: McGraw-Hill Book Company, 1970), 14, 29.

16. "Rest-rotation System on Forest," *SJR*, 21 June 1979, 16; "Water Flow Study Planned," *SJR*, 20 December 1979, 15; "Recapture Dam Report," *SJR*, 2 October 1980, 17.

17. Albert R. Lyman, "History of San Juan County 1879–1917," Special Collections, Brigham Young University Library, 28.

18. Ibid., 28, 31, 34.

19. Ibid., 54–55, 59.

20. Cornelia Perkins, Marian Nielson, Lenora Jones, *Saga of San Juan* (Salt Lake: Mercury Publishing Company, 1957), 123; Harold Muhlestein and Fay Muhlestein, *Monticello Journal: A History of Monticello Until 1937* (n.p., 1988); 67, 83, 103, 115–16, 137–38.

21. "Improved Water System for Monticello thru Federal Aid and VCA Co-operation," *SJR*, 26 November 1942, 1.

22. Albert R. Lyman, *History of Blanding, 1905–1955* (n.p., 1955), 39–46.

23. Ibid., 47–50.

24. Ibid., 50–57; "Water from New Blanding Tunnel Cut into Johnson Creek and Irrigation Ditch," *SJR*, 19 June 1952, 1.

25. Janet Wilcox, "More about the Blanding Tunnel," *SJR*, 27 November 1975, 2.

26. Marvin Lyman interview with Sandy McFadden, "Pages from the Lives of Marvin and Margie Lyman," 1 July 1971, Southeastern Utah Oral History Project, California State University–Fullerton, Oral History Program, 7.

27. "Water from New Blanding Tunnel Cut into Johnson Creek and Irrigation Ditch," *SJR*, 19 June 1952, 1.

28. Willard J. Guymon, "History of Blanding Culinary Watershed," (n.d.), National Forest Service Historical Files, Monticello, 2–3.

29. Janet Wilcox, "Studies Funded for Two Vital Water Projects," *SJR*, 5 October 1972, 1; Janet Wilcox, "Talk Recapture's Future," *SJR*, 27 March 1975, 1; Janet Wilcox, "Recapture Dam Project Subject of Recent Meeting," *SJR*, 29 July 1976, 8; Janet Wilcox, "Blanding Warned to Go Easy on Water," *SJR*, 3 February 1977, 1.

30. "Cost of Recapture Dam and Road Estimated at $6 Million," *SJR*, 30 October 1980, 1.

31. "Recapture Project Phase I Nearing Completion," *SJR*, 22 April 1982, 1.

32. "Locals and Personals," *Grand Valley Times*, 11 March 1905, 4; "Flood Waters at Bluff to Be Impounded," *SJR*, 15 October 1914, 1.

33. "Bluff Farmers Fight with S.C.S. Aid to Avert Disaster," *SJR*, 7 August 1941, 1.

34. Donna Gaines Anderson, "Trials and Triumphs: Bluff's Struggle with Water," *Blue Mountain Shadows* 2, no. 1 (Fall 1988): 18–26.

35. "Hearings End in River Bed Case," *Grand Valley Times*, 19 December 1929, 1; "Navigable Streams in State of Utah," *SJR*, 16 January 1941, 5.

36. Linda Richmond, San Juan River ranger, telephone conversation with author, 10 June 1994.

37. See John Wesley Powell, *The Exploration of the Colorado River and Its Canyons* (New York: Dover Publications, 1961).

38. For a good contemporary history of the Colorado River see Philip L. Fradkin, *A River No More—The Colorado River and the West* (Tucson: University of Arizona Press, 1984).

39. "Glen Canyon National Recreation Area Visitation," statistics on file in the San Juan County Visitors Center, San Juan County Courthouse, Monticello, Utah.

40. "Weather Survey Begins Prior to Rainmaking," *SJR*, 7 January 1951, 1.

41. "Survey Indicates Favorable Rain Making Set-up Dr. Kirk Reports," *SJR*, 5 February 1951, 1; "Rain Making Movement Makes Rapid Progress," and "Contract Signed for Rainmaking," *SJR*, 15 March 1951, 1; "Cloud Seeding No Value Says Scientists; Water Resources Group Defend Program," *SJR*, 7 July 1955, 1.

42. "Cloud Seed Project Start," *SJR*, 1 January 1976, 1.

11

Mines and Roads

A HUNDRED YEARS
OF BOOM AND BUST

Gold. Nothing made the hearts of many nineteenth-century Americans beat faster than the possibility of finding it and becoming independently wealthy overnight. Stories of feverish activity abound from the placer claims of California to the Comstock Lode in Nevada, and from Cripple Creek and Leadville in Colorado to the Black Hills of South Dakota. The reward for most of the large number of people who flooded to these areas were claims that did not pan out, debts that remained for years, and an experience that was better left forgotten. When the boom went bust there was little reason to remain, and so the miners packed their essentials and left for the next strike, where conditions would undoubtedly be better.

San Juan County has seen its own rushes—first for silver and gold, then oil, and finally uranium—each with its own get-rich-quick pattern, ebb and flow of men and machines, and frenzied quest for wealth. Strikes have occurred all around the county, in the Carrizo, Henry, Sleeping Ute, and La Sal mountains.

Even before the area became a county, there were miners on the prowl, trying to find that Eldorado that was going to make them rich.

Earliest mining attempts involved individuals or small groups of prospectors searching in a rugged country where few had previously ventured. Ernest Mitchell and James Merrick invited George Hobbs of the 1879 Mormon exploring party to join them in search of a secret Navajo silver mine whose ore reportedly assayed at ninety percent. Hobbs fortunately declined. Seven months later, a group of searchers found Mitchell's and Merrick's bodies at the foot of the mesas that bear their names in Monument Valley, victims of a Ute/Paiute faction that resented their presence.[1]

In March 1884 a similar fate befell two prospectors, Samuel Walcott and James McNally, who split from a larger group of miners to try to find silver in the Navajo Mountain region. The two men camped near a group of Navajos and offered to trade for corn and meat. Some of the Indians had lost loved ones in a previous conflict with whites in southwestern Utah a number of years before and so decided this was a good opportunity to repay old debts. The Navajos killed the two men, but not before the prospectors wounded an older Navajo.[2] Mining in Navajo country was risky business for whites traveling in small groups.

Yet Cass Hite, an avid seeker of the "lost" Mitchell and Merrick mine, spent years by himself or with a handful of men stumbling through the canyons of the San Juan and Colorado rivers in search of something he never found. At one point, he so persistently pestered Hashkeneinii, a headman from the Navajo Mountain–Monument Valley area, that the Navajos named him Hosteen Pish-la-ki [Hastiin Beesh Ligai], translated as "Mister Silver." Perhaps "Mister Copper," deposits of which he discovered at the head of Copper Canyon, or "Mister Gold," which he found near the mouth of White Canyon at a place now named after him, would have been a more appropriate title. Following his discovery in 1883, he started a mild rush along the banks of the Colorado River in Glen Canyon that encouraged several hundred miners to search for placer gold—a boom that lasted for the next seven years.[3] Prospectors staked their claims on the gravel bars at the river's edge, by 1889 claiming twenty-one sites from the mouth of White Canyon to Lee's Ferry.[4] Miners drifted in and out to try their hand, but none achieved any dazzling success.

Placer mining at Mexican Hat Rock in the 1890s. Notice the absence along the shoreline of tamarisk and Russian olive trees, first brought into the Southwest at the turn of the century as a means of flood control. (San Juan Historical Commission)

The first large gold rush occurred on the San Juan River with Bluff as the terminus for the claims scattered all the way to the confluence of the San Juan and Colorado rivers. Most of the activity occurred in the region around and below Mexican Hat. The rush started when a trader named Jonathan P. Williams showed some entrepreneurs and railroad men samples of coal and other minerals found where the two rivers met. Word leaked out that it was gold, not coal, that was being sought.[5] Since silver, in the early 1890s, was no longer used as specie to back United States currency, and since a nation-wide economic panic was then occurring, many of the silver miners from Colorado saw the discovery of placer gold as an enticing solution to unemployment.

Overnight, the rivers in San Juan County became their destination and placer or "flour" gold the object of an intense search for wealth. The greatest promoters of the rush were the newspapers that kindled the interest and then fanned the flames of expectancy with headlines such as "Utah's Eldorado," "The San Juan Craze," and "The Utah Gold Fields . . . Everybody Is Excited."[6] Promoters described the land as having "weird wonders" but with a "delightful" winter climate "so mild that snow never lasts more than twenty-four hours."[7] The Denver and Rio Grande Western Railroad offered a special fare of $8.50 for those going from Salt Lake to Thompson and then to Bluff and the goldfields beyond; teams of horses and equipment sold at premium prices to the men in Arizona towns heading north; and Denver papers reported that "The reputation of the Utah gold fields has gone abroad and people from all points of the Union are arriving on every train."[8]

How many people actually came to San Juan will never be known. Near the height of the rush in January 1893 an estimated 2,000 to 3,000 men, "with more arriving every day," scrambled along the banks of the San Juan.[9] Other figures vary from a low of 700 to a high of 5,000 miners with one person claiming that 1,000 miners passed through Bluff on New Year's Day alone.[10] Within a few months, just as many had left the San Juan, poorer but wiser for the experience.

The peaceful Mormon town of Bluff assumed a bustling, mercantile atmosphere as the demand for goods of all types increased.

Freighting from Mancos, Cortez, and Durango took on new proportions, because everything from clothes, tools, and food for miners,
hay for horses, and lumber for flumes, sluice boxes, and rockers was
in short supply. The unruly element that follows any booming enterprise came close on the heels of the goldseekers, bringing alcohol,
gambling, and other vices that the Mormon citizenry felt obligated
to curtail. Albert R. Lyman, then a young boy, watched as the Bluff
city fathers purchased a load of whiskey from a would-be saloon
keeper, locked it in an old shop away from the thirsty throats of a
gathering clientele, and then made the mistake of letting an outsider
ascertain the kegs' location in the building. That night, a man crawled
under the store, drilled through the floor, punctured the barrels, and
filled the jugs passed to him by the waiting crowd. Lyman reports,
"The plot worked like a charm, and before morning, more drunken
men wallowed in the streets than Bluff ever saw before or since."[11]

Some prospectors floated the river to their destination in boats
made in Bluff especially for the occasion. Others blazed trails across
the mesas and through the canyons to a point where they could lower
their supplies down the cliffs to the banks below. Bert Loper, who
came to San Juan in 1893, described the difficulty of supplying the
camps served by the Honaker Trail.

> We freighted our stuff to the rim of the canyon and there two or
> three of us young fellows at that time carried the stuff down from
> ledge to ledge until we got to the last big ledge [which] was about
> 130 or 140 feet down from the rim. We had to let our stuff over
> with ropes, and then when we got our stuff let over the cliff, we
> would go out to the point where the trail now goes over and climb
> down a rope ladder and then come back to the ledge and down to
> the river.[12]

Working on the San Juan provided some of the most difficult mining conditions in the American West.

Yet even at the boom's height, strident voices declared the whole
thing a scam. The Rio Grande Western sent an engineer to examine
the goldfield, which in his estimation was "a fraud"; "there is no possibility of miners making average wages anywhere on the river."[13]
Platte D. Lyman, an original settler in Bluff, sent a letter that made its

way into the *Salt Lake Herald*. In it he cautioned that the continuous stream of travel going west through Bluff to the goldfields below was matched only by the stream of traffic heading east as discouraged miners told their tales of misfortune and sold their equipment at a loss.[14] By the beginning of February, the word had spread sufficiently: the tide began its ebb.

Not that there was no gold. The problem rested in its fine granular nature and extracting it from where it lay in the gravel deposits along the river's course. The exact source of the gold, or its mother lode, is unknown but feeds from mountain streams into the San Juan.[15] Thus, the big question became how to efficiently remove the mineral.

After 1893 the majority of the gold-seekers shifted to Glen Canyon. Some still used the standard equipment of pan, rocker, and sluice, but others invested in more complex, expensive machinery. Entrepreneurs introduced more than one hundred different types of patented apparatus designed to extract the gold, but none proved successful. Robert B. Stanton supervised the Hoskaninni Company that operated a gold dredge on the Colorado from 1898 to 1901. The system was expensive to run, went aground on the shifting sandbars beneath the water's surface, required continuous repair, and turned no profit. The total venture may have lost as much as $100,000 before the owners abandoned it.[16]

At the same time that national interest focused on the goldfields along the river, other speculators looked to Blue Mountain. By December 1892, thirty lode claims made up the newly formed Blue Mountain Mining District whose workers started tunneling into the earth. Mines located at elevations ranging from 8,000 to 11,000 feet soon ceased operation because of heavy snowfall.[17] But with the advent of spring and warmer weather the men returned with picks and shovels in hand. Johnson Creek held a body of ore at its headwaters with placer gold spread along its course, encouraging miners to fan throughout the Abajos as they staked over three hundred claims and spent thousands of dollars to construct shafts, tunnels, and mills.[18]

More serious mining ventures started in 1896 as men from the Four Corners region invested in mines with such picturesque names as the Viking, Log Cabin, Blue Bird, Danish Girl, Dream, and Copper Queen. However, it was the Gold Queen that received the most publicity. Located southwest of Abajo Peak, this mine's small, rich vein of ore gave rise to two tunnels, three shafts, workers' cabins, and a ten-stamp mill built at a cost of $80,000.[19] An ingenious gravity-powered tram brought the ore in buckets from the mine to the mill below, while another part of the system returned the empty buckets and lifted the ore from the main shaft. In 1897, miners extracted ore averaging between $20 and $25 per ton, with some going as high as $400 a ton.[20] Even at this rate and with such a substantial investment, the amount of ore was insufficient and the mine did not pay sufficient dividends. By 1903 the Gold Queen closed for the last time.

Approximately a mile southwest of the Gold Queen lies the Dream Mine, which, like its neighbor, passed through the hands of a number of owners. The most famous of these was Captain George A. Jackson, a Missourian who fought for the Confederacy during the Civil War and is credited with discovering massive gold deposits in the Clear Creek region outside of Denver and the subsequent establishment of the town of Idaho Springs.[21] He arrived from the La Plata Mining District, Colorado, in 1896 and built a five-stamp mill capable of daily processing seven to eight tons which yielded an average mineral content of $33 per ton. Jackson claimed that, "This is the richest free gold district in America."[22] His practiced eye surveyed the location of Camp Jackson with its wood, water, and ore, the proximity of the railroads at Mancos and Thompson, and the beginning of the flow of 5,000 men he prophesied would be there by the end of the season.[23] Blue Mountain held all the potential of another California or Colorado gold rush, in both of which he had participated.

Within a few months, Jackson lay dead in the snow halfway between Piute Springs and Cross Canyon. An accident occurred when he reached into his sled to get his shotgun. The trigger caught on a blanket, sending a load of buckshot into his face, and thus ending the career of a celebrated miner.[24] Control of the Dream Mine then passed through a succession of owners, none of whom and very successful.

For a while, the Dream, Gold Queen, and other mines continued to attract miners. Newspapers reported the creation of a townsite with cabins at Camp Jackson, the services of the Zion Co-operative Mercantile Institution providing general mining supplies in the camps, and the sales in the stores of Monticello. Travelers could arrive by stagecoach on a two-day trip from Dolores with a stopover at Cross Canyon, or could ride the daily circuit from Moab through La Sal, Big Indian, and Monticello to Bluff.[25] Others came by horse, wagon, or "Rocky Mountain canary," a western euphemism for a donkey.

But the boom did not last. From 1897 to 1899, the mines enjoyed moderate success, but by 1900 only a few miners remained on Blue Mountain, with many of their associates going to the La Sal Mountains to try their luck in new diggings. Equipment, including the mill from Camp Jackson, reappeared at the northern end of the county to process the gold and copper in the recently established fields. An article in the *Montezuma Journal* that jokingly explained how gold nuggets grew by attracting particles of their own element did not appear to have any effect on the flow of impatient miners moving away from Blue Mountain.[26] Neither the sporadic headlines of new, rich veins in the Gold Queen, reported during the early 1900s. By 1908 San Juan County reached its highest production of gold for the next thirty years—a measly 209 ounces valued at $4,320.[27] Justification for gold fever had subsided.

Copper was the next mineral to receive attention; deposits of the mineral were found in White Canyon and the Abajos. Both of these locations proved unprofitable to mine because of the deposits' small size, difficulties of access, and expense of processing. Lisbon Valley, however, was initially believed to be a different story. As early as 1897, newspapers discussed copper claims staked out in the area, but it was not until 1916 that the mining and processing of the ore started to become a reality. The Big Indian Mining Company from Provo employed thirty men to extract the copper from its eleven patented and nine unpatented claims spread over 350 acres. An estimated 800,000 tons of two- to four-percent copper seemed to justify the construction of a mill capable of handling three hundred tons of ore every twenty-four hours. Native pine provided fuel for the furnaces, and water flowed to the plant through a pipeline 34,000 feet long that originated near La Sal. The close proximity of the deposits eased the transportation problem of moving ore to the mill, and the company shipped the processed copper by a fleet of trucks to the railroad at Thompson. By July 1918 the plant was operational.[28]

The mine's success, however, was marginal. Part of the problem lay in insufficient deposits of high-grade ore to warrant the expense of processing and then shipping the copper to a railroad that lay one hundred miles away. Another reason for failure lay in the machinery installed in the plant, which was ineffective in dealing with that particular type of copper ore.[29] Whatever the explanation, the dream of wealth that the plant initially offered never reached fruition. Control of the Big Indian Mine passed through the hands of a number of different owners, the mine yielding its last ore during World War II. One report estimated that by 1938, shortly before it closed, less than $50,000 worth of copper had come from this mine and some smaller claims on Blue Mountain during a thirty-seven-year period.[30]

Oil, though more abundant and dependable as a source of wealth than silver, gold, and copper, has had its own long but checkered history in San Juan. The earliest discovery of oil harkens back to 1882, when a band of prospectors in search of the lost Merrick and Mitchell mine crossed the San Juan and noticed the strong smell of petroleum. Cass Hite, Ernest B. Hyde, and other members of the party camped on the north side of the river where they dipped pieces of bark in the oil floating on top of the water and then burned them. Hyde returned and staked the spot, but allowed his claim to lapse. Later, E. L. Goodridge located another seep at John's Canyon where eighteen years later he drilled his first well. The 1892–93 gold rush had brought others into the area, including Melvin Dempsey, A. P. Raplee, Charles Goodman, and Robert Mitchell. These men became intimately familiar with the land and its wealth and participated in the subsequent oil boom.[31]

By 1909, various oil companies had eight drill rigs in operation, had punched twenty-five holes, 80 percent of which were producing, and had established a field that eventually encompassed the lands between Bluff and Slickhorn Canyon. The home and claim site of E. L. Goodridge near present-day Mexican Hat became the freighting terminus and post office for the majority of businesses sprouting up along the river.[32] Promoters in 1910 proclaimed Mexican Hat a

A drill rig belonging to the Aztec Oil Company passes through Bluff in the early 1900s on its way to the oil fields around Mexican Hat. (San Juan Historical Commission)

"thriving village" that boasted a platted townsite; a telephone line that would soon connect through Bluff, Blanding, and Monticello to Thompson with its Western Union terminal; a water system with eight hundred feet of pressure; a hotel and restaurant; and a "goodly number of citizens [estimated by one author at 1,500 people at its height] who propose to make their residence permanent."[33] Once the boom ended, much of this infrastructure fell into disrepair.

Approximately twenty-five miles above the fields, Bluff organized a board of trade to care for the new arrivals. As during the gold rush, this struggling community saw an opportunity to boost its economy through promotional advertisement, road development, and the sale of goods. As one newspaper explained, "Bluff has a number of the finest homes in the state and these will be thrown wide open to visitors."[34] In the same breath, the writer spoke of the developing wagon road extending to Mexican Hat, a new "gusher" capable of pumping an estimated 600 to 700 barrels a day, and of outside experts from Pennsylvania, Ohio, New York, Washington, Illinois, and Colorado who saw nothing but promise in the growing fields.

Gushers pushing oil from forty to seventy feet in the air seemed to symbolize both the hope and promise of the industry. In one sense, they proved that oil was present and could be tapped, but the reality of the situation was that most of the planning and production was up in the air and not beneficial. In spite of the fact that some entrepreneurs raced through the night to Monticello to establish their claims, that the recorder's office hired three more people just to handle the paperwork from the oil fields, that engineers from the Santa Fe and the Denver and Rio Grande railroads were busily surveying routes to Mexican Hat, that some wells were believed capable of producing from 200 to 500 barrels a day, the truth was that oil was not present in large enough quantities to sustain the boom.[35]

The only wells that produced significant amounts of oil were found roughly within a mile-and-a-half radius. These seven wells, clustered around Mexican Hat and Goodridge, gave hope that others would be found. Most, if not all, of the oil derived from the field went for local consumption, burned in the steam engines that powered the drills. Finding the pockets of oil was often accidental; moving heavy, deep-drilling machinery into difficult-to-reach locations often proved impossible; the closest railroad lay more than one hundred miles away; and lack of wood fuel, water, and a convenient road network made work in the oil fields expensive and labor-intensive.[36]

By 1912 most of the boom had ended, though there were those who believed the canyons would still yield a rich treasure in "black gold." Some oil prospectors looked to the reservation, hoping that its boundaries would change. The history of the Paiute Strip reveals the success and failure of that notion. But, in general, drilling took on insignificant proportions in the county with the exception of those sites in the Aneth area that began to pay handsome dividends in the 1950s, as discussed in Chapter 9.

In tallying the results of the early boom-and-bust economy of San Juan, one could easily believe that little was accomplished. Certainly the intended wealth proved ephemeral. Yet one most important development—roads and accompanying communication—burgeoned because of the mining activity. A perusal of the minutes of the San Juan County Commission shows that from its earliest days county leaders invested much of their time and resources in developing a network of roads to nurture a struggling economy.

Within a year of the opening of the Hole-in-the-Rock Trail, the Bluff pioneers had forsaken its use and established ties with the markets of Mancos and Durango, Colorado, to the east, and Salt Lake City via parts of the Old Spanish Trail to the north. Road improvements, in an economy that had little cash flow, became a community responsibility borne by the local Mormons and the county government, which were invariably one and the same. The minutes of the commission meeting held on 4 September 1882, illustrate the importance placed on the development of a road system. In less than a page of handwritten notes the secretary recorded a petition signed by William Hyde and sixteen others asking for an appropriation of two hundred dollars to build a road to Blue Mountain to obtain timber; Jens Nielsen received seventy-five dollars for work on the road to Clay Hills; and selectman Henry Holyoke obtained one hundred twenty-five dollars to improve the road from Montezuma Creek to the Colorado state line. All the other financial business transacted that day totaled only sixty-seven dollars.[37]

Freighting to Colorado, with its consequent dependence on roads, became one of the main sources of cash for the county's inhabitants, until in later years it was matched by livestock sales and dry farming. The road leading to Colorado followed the San Juan River until it reached McElmo Canyon. There a traveler could either journey up the twisting canyon to the foot of Sleeping Ute Mountain or trek farther upstream beyond Aneth where another road stretched around the southern end of the mountain and into Mancos. For people heading north, the earliest road went up Recapture Canyon, passed south of Mustang Mesa, and thence through Devil's Canyon and South Montezuma. In 1888, the route changed to Cow Canyon, the Bluff Bench, and then Recapture; in 1905, with the establishment of Blanding, the present Bluff-Blanding-Monticello route came into common use.[38]

Roads in the western part of the county developed during the gold rush of 1892–93 and the years of oil development in the early 1900s. Freighting along the Honaker Trail to Slickhorn Canyon and to Dandy's Crossing (Hite), along with the improvement of already existing roads in Comb Wash, Clay Hills, and Mexican Hat, helped open for development a vast area traversed primarily by Indian trails.

Spurs poked their way from the main arteries into numerous canyons and across uncounted mesas to new prospecting claims.

The excitement generated by the desired wealth and the necessity of gaining access to it was shown in the road and railroad plans of the time. For instance, in 1909 the Midland Bridge Company received a five thousand dollar contract from the state to build a bridge at Mexican Hat; Moab capitalized on the oil fever and declared that it also needed a bridge to span the Colorado if "Salt Lake is to get the business of San Juan County."[39] On 8 April 1912, the people of Moab dedicated their bridge after they had "begged for it . . . cried for it . . . fought for it and . . . won," but it was the oil, 130 miles to the south, that had been most influential in getting it.[40]

"Commence the Good Work" (13 January 1910) . . . "Let's Build a Railroad" (9 September 1910) . . . "San Juan Will Gladly Help" (30 September 1910) . . . "We Are Building the Montezuma-San Juan Railroad" (8 May 1913) are among the era's headlines of the Cortez and Moab papers. One would think that San Juan County was destined to be a hub for the markets of the West. The Denver and Rio Grande Western and the Southern Pacific railroads each had plans to develop its own network to the oil fields from already existing trunk lines. A vigorous competition arose between the rival factions for the rights to build. One article pointed out that in just the past six months companies had shipped 500,000 pounds of machinery to the fields; that the single store in Bluff had recently handled 100,000 pounds of flour, not to mention other supplies; and that if advantage was not taken within the state of Utah of the opportunities for economic growth railroad interests from New Mexico would take advantage of the opportunity.[41] In reality, no one had to worry about the competition—as the hopes for oil faded, so did the plans for railroads.

This discouragement did not hold true for the owners of a new invention—the car—who began to press for road improvements. Again, the driving force was oil. Newspapers spoke of "Automobile Line to Oil Fields" and "Road Appropriations," signaling the intention to spur the economy by making highways where only wagon tracks existed. This was not an easy task. Old trails were deeply rutted according to the dimensions of the wagons that had traveled them.

One of the first cars in San Juan County, photographed in 1912 in front of the Bluff San Juan Co-op. The stairway leads to the dance hall on the top floor. (Courtesy Inez Conway)

The automobile, with its narrow frame and thin tires, cut into the sides of the center strip and pushed loose sand into the ruts. Cars going too slowly bogged down, wheels rotating too fast dug a shallow grave, while rocks, washouts, and mudholes invited mechanical failure, flat tires, and flaring tempers.[42]

Man with his machine accepted the challenge. Long after the excitement over illusive oil wealth had ended, the roads continued to improve as automobiles carried wide-eyed tourists, expectant homesteaders, government officials, and longtime residents to Moab or Cortez. Albert R. Lyman summarized this process:

> With this era [starting around 1910] came the Ford car. . . . The people gathered around the venturesome creature, stroking its shining fenders and gazing curiously at its funny entrails, and then going back indoors to that novelty, the phone, and began howling after better roads so that the dear thing which had come buzzing into their midst, might never have to go away.
>
> That howl for better roads became so terrific that it moved

sand and rocks and shale, it got appropriations from the legislature, it made new surveys, it put in bridges, made cuts and fills and
swept away many a place which had long been fruitful in thrilling
adventures.[43]

Now it was just a matter of time before the dirt would change to
gravel and then pavement, as San Juan moved further into the twentieth century.

The single greatest force, beyond government funding, that
improved the transportation system in the county came again in the
form of a boom, this one lasting for approximately thirty years. This
time it was uranium. As an "exciter," it stimulated every facet of the
economy as nothing has before or since. Local people as well as outsiders capitalized on this abundant resource, deposited during geologic era long agos. And best of all, it was a closed market, regulated
by the federal government's Atomic Energy Commission. During the
1950s and 1960s, this agency took an active role in controlling prices
and sales of the valuable material for those interested in joining the
race for wealth.

The early history of uranium is tied to the carnotite and pitchblende in which it is found. Starting in the late 1800s, industry found
a variety of uses for these radioactive materials, including as a pig-
ment for dyes and ceramics, an additive to strengthen steel, a treatment for cancer, a glowing paint for luminescent dials, and a claimed
cure for baldness.[44] Fluctuations in the market led to an unstable
industry affected by the economic bounces of World War I, the
Roaring Twenties, the worldwide depression of the 1930s, and a second world war. Uranium did not hold real economic promise until
the end of World War II, when the nuclear age arose in a mushroom
cloud.

The development of the uranium industry in San Juan has been
characterized by a vast and complicated network of individual, family, and large company involvement; government regulation and private initiative; exploration, surveying, and the laying of claims in
hundreds of canyons and mesas; backbreaking labor and instant
wealth. Volumes could be written about the men who traipsed over
the countryside with a "buzz box" or Geiger counter in hand, wait-

ing for the familiar noise to signal a find. Other books could be written about the companies that wheeled and dealed their way into the richest beds of ore.

The symbol of the strike-it-rich miner is well represented in the story of Charles A. Steen and one of his wealthiest mines—the Mi Vida—that lies in San Juan County. Although Steen's activities centered around Moab, his discovery of fourteen feet of high-grade uranium ore on 6 July 1952, changed not only his busted luck but the character of San Juan County. Within a year, Steen was well on his way to becoming a millionaire, providing hope for others that wealth hid just around the next rock formation.[45]

The most dramatic part of the boom lay between the years of 1953 and 1957, when domestic production leaped from 700 tons to 17,800 tons of uranium per year. Prospectors staked an estimated forty percent of San Juan County, and this did not include claims made upon previously established claims, or lands unavailable or requiring special-use agreements, such as reservation land and school sections. Uranium stocks spiraled upward in the market for eighteen months before beginning their downward descent.[46] Everyone wanted a piece of the action.

Hundreds of mines dotted the landscape, each with its own story. Many individuals looked upon the uranium industry as their chance to make a living and possibly strike it rich with one big discovery. From this hope arose the "dog hole" miner: a man armed with shovel, pick, and dynamite who worked out of the back of a pickup truck and burrowed into a hill after a vein of ore. Dog hole miners lacked the equipment and expertise that came with big outfits and so could not afford to be able to move large quantities of rock or create a mine big enough to handle an internal rail or truck system to haul ore. Instead, they snaked their way after the exposed ore, creating just enough space for a man to work in. A bigger vein required a bigger tunnel.

The experience of Grant Lee Shumway and his brothers is representative of that of hundreds of dog hole miners who roamed the county. They mined vanadium and uranium in Monument Valley, Cottonwood Canyon, Montezuma Canyon, and on Shay Mountain next to Blue Mountain. Shumway's typical mine started with an exposed outcrop of ore that looked promising. He would then drill thirteen holes for dynamite with two in the center of a circle whose diameter depended on the desired size of the mine. After the blast, the pick, shovel, and wheelbarrow work started, and the ore was hauled to the mill for sale. Once the uranium petered out, or the mine became too dangerous, or the claim could be sold for a profit the Shumway brothers packed their things and began again the process of prospecting, staking, and working the next find.[47]

Yet it was the large companies that really made the most money. In addition to Steen's holdings, some of the larger companies and mines included the White Canyon Mining Company, the La Sal Mining Company, the Big Buck Claim, and the largest mine in the county—Monument Two on the Navajo Reservation.[48] Another of the larger mines was the Happy Jack, located in White Canyon and owned by three Monticello men—Joseph Cooper, Grant Bronson and Fletcher Bronson. The Duckett brothers, John and Joe, were the first to lay claim to its copper at the turn of the century, after which there were a number of owners, none of whom became rich. In 1946 Cooper and the Bronsons began producing copper heavily "contaminated" with uranium that no one wanted to process. When atomic energy moved center stage, the "waste" from the mine started to pay big dividends when the experimental VCA mill fifteen miles to the west at Hite began to crush and ship the ore. The deeper the miners bore into the earth, the richer and larger the deposit became, with a seam of pitchblende containing one of the highest grades of uranium discovered one hundred feet into the mine shaft.[49]

By 1957 the Happy Jack mine was a proven success. The Texas Zinc Minerals Corporation, composed of two different groups of wealthy businessmen from New Jersey and Texas, for a large sum of money bought nine claims and leased twenty-four others that constituted the Happy Jack. The exact price was not disclosed. Cooper and the Bronsons sold 450,000 tons of ore that was already blocked out for mining, with an estimated 200,000 tons more in reserve, because they felt their own capital and equipment insufficient, their technical expertise lacking for this size mine, and because they anticipated undesirable changes in their tax status.[50]

Five years later, Texas Zinc still employed twenty-seven miners who pulled several thousand tons of ore from the mine each month. The men and their families lived in the twenty-two trailers hauled in by the company, enjoyed a recreation hall and playground for their children, formed a volunteer band to provide entertainment, and had their mail flown in and out from the nearby airstrip. When touring the mine one saw

> yards of narrow gauge mining track winding throughout the tunnels. Getting lost in the maze of drifts would be no problem. . . . Jack hammers rap and whine as they bore into rock; cable guided slushers skid shot ore toward dumping chutes; toy freight cars fill up and head for daylight and the dump pile. Large rooms, kept safe with 14 foot 24 inch diameter spruce logs seem to have no end. The abandoned rooms remind one of an eerie forest with logs split and buckled showing the strain of weight they hold.[51]

Eventually, mining crews stripped part of the overburden off the mine and pulled the pillars of ore, starting from the back of the tunnels, causing part of the mine ceiling to collapse. As late as the early 1980s a skeleton crew worked a portion of the Happy Jack.

A mill, constructed in 1957 at Mexican Hat by Texas Zinc, processed 2.2 million tons of dry ore from the Happy Jack and surrounding mines before it closed in 1970.[52] Other mills that at one time or another received ore from San Juan County included those located at Kayenta, Arizona; Shiprock, New Mexico; White Canyon, Monticello, La Sal, and Moab, Utah; Uravan, Naturita, and Durango, Colorado; and eventually Blanding.

The Monticello mill was an important one. The initial building occurred in 1942 to provide vanadium for the war industries of World War II. The Atomic Energy Commission (AEC) purchased it in 1948 from the Stearns Rogers Company and expanded the mill's capacity to handle two hundred tons of ore a day. The AEC turned the facility over to the Galigher and National Lead companies, which later increased its capacity to six hundred tons a day and created 900,000 tons of low-level radioactive waste before the mill closed in 1959.[53] More than thirty years after its closing and dismantling, the mill still provides indirect employment in the government's cleanup of its toxic waste.

Monticello uranium mill, 1957. At its height the mill employed around 300 people. (Courtesy Frank "Bo" Montella)

Monticello blossomed economically in other ways during the uranium boom. Take a single year—1954—for example. The San Juan County Recorders Office handled more claims registration fees—to the amount of $117,000—than did Salt Lake County. Two years earlier, the revenue from claims registration in San Juan had been only $3,500. In order to handle the avalanche of paperwork, the recorder hired fourteen assistants, who worked in two seven-hour shifts, entered an average of three hundred documents a day, and filled sixty-three claims registration books in a single year.[54]

Monticello doubled its population to 2,500 in three years' time. A million dollars worth of buildings was constructed within city limits and included four motels and six trailer parks. The water and sewer system was expanded at a cost of $500,000 and a dozen new businesses ranging from dry cleaners to investment brokers were established along with an expansion of the mill facilities.[55] Health services, education, and other human services enjoyed a similar growth.

But as with other booms in the past, one of the largest and most permanent contributions of this era was the development of roads. While San Juan County has been interested from its beginnings in road development for economic reasons ranging from timber to tourism and commerce to cars, nothing infused money and heightened interest as mineral extraction did. The roads built to lonely mines and bustling mills were supplemented by those that crossed the desert to isolated oil rigs and shipping points in the Aneth area. Shortened routes, better surfaces, and easier grades became the goal. The Atomic Energy Commission paid for much of the initial establishment of main arteries in the 1950s, with county, state, and other federal coffers providing the rest.

The carving of a highway through Comb Ridge provides a dramatic example of the determination of these road builders. The route through this large sandstone formation was part of an effort to create an all-weather route that bypassed the old road over Elk Ridge on the way to the mines and mill at Hite. The road traversed seven large washes, but the most formidable was the Comb, where the highway dropped at a 10-percent grade for 750 feet over a quarter of a mile. Forty men used two tons of dynamite a day, with an estimated eighty tons total, to blast a series of switchbacks at this and other places along the route to Hite. The cost of the project soared to $250,000. The AEC picked up the tab, the State Road Commission performed the work, and the public reaped the benefit.[56]

Thanks to mineral production, bridges now spanned the San Juan River. On 5 June 1953, Bill Weidman, driving a heavily loaded truck headed for the Last Chance oil well in Emery County, tried to cross the cable bridge at Mexican Hat. Although cautioned about exceeding the bridge's weight limit, forewarned was not forearmed. When he reached the center, the bridge gave way, sending the truck plummeting fifty feet below. Bill swam away from the wreck badly shaken, but he had helped highlight the long standing need for a sturdier structure to bear the ten to twelve trucks that crossed daily with their shipments of uranium. The state repaired the cable bridge temporarily, but within a year, a $180,000 steel and concrete bridge spanned the river, thanks to the AEC.[57] Aneth received its own $300,000 bridge in 1958, primarily paid for by oil companies as they reached full stride in petroleum production.[58] Economic development was the key that unlocked access to much of isolated San Juan County.

The 1940s and 1950s also saw the paving of the main transportation arteries in San Juan. The road from Moab to Monticello

The Happy Jack Mine in White Canyon, one of the more successful mining claims that initially provided copper, then uranium for many years. (San Juan Historical Commission)

had been completed in the early 1940s. In 1952 and 1953 the stretch of highway between Monticello and Blanding was finished, and in 1956 the roads going from Blanding to Bluff and from Bluff to Mexican Hat were completed.[59] Even before these last two additions, in 1954 the county could boast of almost 250 miles of paved county and state roads that tied northern Utah and western Colorado to the oil and uranium industry in southeastern Utah.[60]

The general trend in uranium development in the later part of the 1950s and continuing into the 1960s and 1970s was the takeover by large energy companies of small companies and the holdings of independent miners. Most of the surface finds had been worked; as a result, expensive equipment, technical engineering, and large amounts of investment capital became the order of the day, with cut-throat competition pushing many out of the field. For example, in 1957 there were 184 mining operations in the county, with seventeen of them providing eighty-five percent of the ore.[61]

Uranium continued to play an important role in San Juan's economy until the market declined in a serious slump during the early 1980s. The Rio Algom mine and mill, located in upper Lisbon Valley near La Sal, had started production in late 1972. At its height, the operation employed more than 250 workers, mined ore at the bottom of a 2,500-foot-deep shaft, and earned $30.4 million in just the first quarter of 1980.[62] By 1986 the site had closed because of diminishing ore, worn equipment in need of repair, and the low sale price of "yellow cake" uranium. While Rio Algom was prospering, in 1980 the Energy Fuels mill in Blanding opened its doors to accept ore and did not officially close them until 1991–92.[63] This company had the distinction of operating the last of fifteen mills in the Four Corners area.

In considering the past hundred years of boom-and-bust mining economy in San Juan, one can see a pattern that has played itself out in many areas of the United States. Whether looking at the more fanciful rushes for silver and gold or the more productive ones for oil and uranium, each was fueled by an individual's desire for wealth. Large companies played an increasingly important role as the riches became more and more difficult to extract from a land that did not give up its treasures easily. Sophisticated technology and engineering often provided the best chance at obtaining mineral wealth, but even then it was a gamble that could send large companies to their economic death. There was no guarantee—either as to what was in the ground, or how it could best be retrieved, or in the stability of the market once it was removed, processed, and sold. What was more permanent was the road network and the improvements made in the hub communities supporting the mining population. In general, San Juan County was enriched by its mining experience.

Today, mining for gold and silver is left to the weekend vacationer; individuals and companies still hold copper claims, but no one presently works them; people still cast a hopeful eye at the uranium stock market, but for now, it is dormant; oil is still being pumped from the Aneth field, but the number of barrels is in decline; and the field and refinery in Lisbon Valley and the wells east of Blanding provide the only other significant oil production in the county. What the future holds is just as uncertain today as it was one hundred years ago; however, if and when the phoenix of mineral extraction should arise from its ashes, there will be a network of roads in place and a greater understanding to guide it on the path to success.

ENDNOTES

1. For a more complete account of this incident see Robert S. McPherson, *The Northern Navajo Frontier 1860–1900: Expansion through Adversity* (Albuquerque: University of New Mexico Press, 1988), 41–43.

2. "Report of Sam Boo-Ko-Di," Navajo Agency Records, New Mexico, 19 April 1884, National Archives, Record Group 75, Letters Received, 1881–1907, Bureau of Indian Affairs.

3. C. Gregory Crampton, *Standing Up Country: The Canyonlands of Utah and Arizona* (Salt Lake City: Peregrine Smith Books, 1983,: 123–28.

4. Herbert E. Gregory, *The San Juan Country—A Geographic and Geologic Reconnaissance of Southeastern Utah* (Washington, D.C.: Government Printing Office, 1938), 108.

5. *Salt Lake Tribune*, 28 December 1892, 1.

6. "Utah's New Eldorado," *Salt Lake Tribune*, 18 December 1892, 1; "The San Juan Craze," *Salt Lake Tribune*, 16 December 1892, 4; "The Utah Gold Fields," *Salt Lake Tribune*, 25 December 1892, 1.

7. Ibid., "Eldorado."

8. "All about the Mines," *Salt Lake Herald*, 22 December 1892, 1; "San Juan Craze," 4; "Utah Gold Fields," 1.

9. "Two Thousand There," *Salt Lake Herald*, 4 January 1893, 1.

10. Bryant L. Jensen, "An Historical Study of Bluff City, Utah, from 1878 to 1906," M.A. thesis, Brigham Young University, 1966, 107.

11. Albert R. Lyman, "History of San Juan County 1879–1917," Special Collections, Brigham Young University Library, 77–78.

12. Bert Loper testimony, "Colorado River Bed Case," microfilm, Utah State Historical Society, Salt Lake City, Utah, 969–70.

13. "The Whole Thing a Fraud," *Salt Lake Tribune*, 19 January 1893, 4.

14. "The Senseless Stampede," *Salt Lake Herald*, 18 January 1893, 1.

15. Maureen G. Johnson, *Placer Gold Deposits of Utah*, Geological Survey Bulletin 1357 (Washington, D.C.: Government Printing Office, 1973), 12–13.

16. Crampton, "Standing Up Country," 131–41.

17. "Blue Mountain Strikes," *Salt Lake Herald*, 30 December 1892, 1.

18. Gregory, *San Juan Country*, 108–9.

19. Ibid., 109.

20. Harold Muhlestein and Fay Muhlestein, *Monticello Journal: A History of Monticello Until 1937* (Self-published, 1988): 56, 63.

21. For more information on this early period of Jackson's life see Leroy R. Hafen, "George A. Jackson's Diary, 1858–1859," *The Colorado Magazine* 12 (November 1935): 201–14; "George A. Jackson Dead," Jackson File newspaper clipping, March 1897, Colorado Historical Society, Denver, Colorado.

22. *Mancos Times*, 13 November 1896, 4.

23. "Rush to Blue Mountains," *Denver Republican*, 21 January 1897, 1.

24. "Captain Jackson Dead!" *Mancos Times*, 19 March 1897, 4.

25. "Blue Mountain Free Gold," *Mancos Times*, 14 May 1897, 1; Muhlestein, *Monticello Journal*, 59.

26. "How Gold Nuggets Grow," *Montezuma Journal*, 28 August 1903, 2.

27. "San Juan County Basic Data of Economic Activities and Resources," compiled by Utah State Planning Board, 1940, Special Collections, Brigham Young University Library, 21.

28. "The Mining Prospects," *Grand Valley Times*, 23 April 1897, 1; "Dips, Spurs and Angles," *Salt Lake Mining Review*, 15 December 1916, 40; "Big Indian Statement," *Salt Lake Mining Review*, 15 February 1917, 28; "Wonderful Possibilities of Big Indian Mine and Mill," *Salt Lake Mining Review*, 15 May 1917, 23–27; "Big Indian Looks Good to Colonel Loose," *The Independent*, 4 July 1918, 1.

29. Faun McConkie Tanner, *The Far Country: A Regional History of Moab and La Sal, Utah* (Salt Lake City: Olympus Publishing Company, 1976), 220; Cornelia Perkins, Marian Nielson, and Lenora Jones, *Saga of San Juan* (Salt Lake City: Mercury Publishing Company, 1968), 270.

30. W. L. Dare and R. R. Durk, *Mining Methods and Costs, Standard Uranium Corporation Big Buck Mine, San Juan County, Utah* (n.d.), Special Collections, Brigham Young University Library, 5; "San Juan County Basic Data" (n.p.), map.

31. Charles Goodman, "History of the Oil Fields in San Juan County, Utah," *The Salt Lake Mining Review*, 15 April 1910, 17–18. For information concerning some of the personalities associated with the gold rush and oil industry in the Mexican Hat area, see Doris Valle, *Looking Back around the Hat—A History of Mexican Hat* (Mexican Hat: n.p., 1986).

32. H. E. Gregory, "The San Juan Oil Field, San Juan County, Utah," *Contributions to Economic Geology, 1909*, Part II, Bulletin 431 (Washington, D.C.: Government Printing Office, 1911), 11, 21–23.

33. "Mexican Hat Now a Village," *Grand Valley Times*, 2 December 1910, 1; Valle, *Mexican Hat*, 10.

34. "Oil Boom Continues," *Grand Valley Times*, 22 May 1908, 1.

35. "Monticello Happenings," *Grand Valley Times*, 8 January 1909, 5; "Happenings in San Juan," *Grand Valley Times*, 24 June 1910, 1; "Send Men to San Juan," *Grand Valley Times*, 22 July 1910, 1; "The New Bluff Gusher," *Grand Valley Times*, 1 July 1910, 1.

36. Gregory, *San Juan Country*, 111–13; "Government Report on Oil Resources of San Juan," *Grand Valley Times*, 10 May 1912, 1.

37. "Minutes of County Commissioners of San Juan County," Recorder's Office, County Court House, Monticello, Utah, 14.

38. Perkins et al., *Saga*, 264.

39. "Monticello News," *Grand Valley Times*, 24 September 1909, 5; "Bridge is a Necessity," *Grand Valley Times*, 30 December 1910, 1.

40. "Celebration Is Grandest in History of Moab," *Grand Valley Times*, 12 April 1912, 1.

41. "Commence the Good Work," *Grand Valley Times*, 13 January 1910, 1; "Let's Build a Railroad," *Grand Valley Times*, 9 September 1910, 5; "San Juan Will Gladly Help," *Grand Valley Times*, 30 September 1910, 1; "We Are Building the Montezuma-San Juan Railroad—Stock Subscriptions Rising Daily," *Montezuma Journal*, 8 May 1913, 1; "San Juan Field Trade Tempting," *Grand Valley Times*, 24 February 1911, 1.

42. "Automobile Line to Oil Fields," *Grand Valley Times*, 3 February 1911, 1; "Asks for Road Appropriation," *Grand Valley Times*, 27 January 1911, 1; John Meadows, interview with author, 30 May 1991, transcript in possession of author.

43. Lyman, "History," 110.

44. For an excellent overview of the uranium industry in San Juan County see Gary L. Shumway, "Uranium Mining on the Colorado Plateau," in *San Juan County, Utah*, ed. Allan Kent Powell (Salt Lake City: Utah State Historical Society, 1983), 265–98.

45. For a good overview of the life of Charles Steen and the uranium mining activities in Utah during this era see Raye C. Ringholz, *Uranium Frenzy: Boom and Bust on the Colorado Plateau* (Albuquerque: University of New Mexico Press, 1989).

46. Gary Lee Shumway, "The Development of the Uranium Industry in San Juan County, Utah," M.A. thesis, Brigham Young University, 1964, 77–86.

47. Ruth S. Robinson and Gary Lee Shumway, "The Family of Peter and Mary Johnson Shumway" (Fullerton, Calif.: Oral History Program,

1976): 305–12. This is part of a much larger oral history collection concerning uranium mining and supervised by Gary Shumway, California State University, Fullerton.

48. "Uranium Activities Bring Recorders Work to All Time High in San Juan," *San Juan Record* (hereafter cited as *SJR*), 21 January 1954, 1.

49. "Mine Offers Wealth," *SJR*, 22 March 1951, 8; Albert R. Lyman, "The Old Settler," *SJR*, 5 June 1952, 4.

50. "National Mining and Milling Corporation Purchases 'Happy Jack' Property," *SJR*, 1 December 1955, 1; "Texas Zinc Minerals Complete Purchase of Happy Jack Group," *SJR*, 19 July 1956, 1; Grant Bronson telephone conversation with author, 26 May 1994. Mr. Bronson corrected some of the published statistics and requested that the amount of money paid for the Happy Jack remain confidential, though he said the newspaper accounts were much too high.

51. "Happy Jack Mine Still Going Strong in 1961," *SJR*, 23 March 1961, 3.

52. Robert Sullenberger, "100 Years of Uranium Activity in the Four Corners Region—Part II," *Journal of the Western Slope* 8, no. 1 (Winter 1993): 19–20.

53. Robert Sullenberger, "100 Years of Uranium Activity in the Four Corners Region—Part II," *Journal of the Western Slope* 7, no. 4 (Fall 1992): 55–57.

54. "San Juan County Recording Fees Top Salt Lake County by Approximately $4,619 During 1954," *SJR*, 6 January 1955, 1.

55. "Monticello Uranium Boom Creates Million Dollar Building Program," *SJR*, 23 June 1955, 1.

56. Don Howard, "We'll Take the Scenic Road," *SJR*, 30 April 1953, 1.

57. "Heavily Loaded Truck Breaks Through Bridge on San Juan River at Mexican Hat," *SJR*, 11 June 1953, 1; "San Juan River Bridge Dedication April 24th," *SJR*, 22 April 1954, 1; "State Recognizes San Juan County's Mineral Wealth," *SJR*, 6 May 1954, 3.

58. "Bridge Dedication Opens New Way across San Juan," *SJR*, 12 December 1958, 1.

59. "Highway 160 and 47 Are Scheduled for Surfacing Says State Road Official," *SJR*, 4 September 1952, 1; "The Big Road Heads South from Blanding," *SJR*, 9 August 1956, 1; "Winter Stops Oil on Bluff-Hat Road," *SJR*, 13 September 1956, 1.

60. Jay M. Haymond, "San Juan County Roads: Arteries to Natural Resources and Survival," *San Juan County, Utah*, ed. Allan Kent Powell, 237.

61. Shumway, "Development of . . . Uranium," 92.

62. "Rio Algom Mine in the Making," *SJR*, 5 February 1970, 3; "Rio Algom," *SJR*, 27 November 1980, T6.

63. "Largest Crowd . . . in County at Open House," *SJR*, 17 July 1980, 1; Sullenberger, "100 Years," vol. 8 no.1, 11.

12

Taking Care of Its Own

HEALTH AND EDUCATION IN SAN JUAN COUNTY

John Locke, a seventeenth-century English philosopher, wrote, "A sound mind in a sound body is a short but full description of a happy state in this world." For the residents of newly established San Juan County some two centuries later, no truer sentiment could be expressed. Each culture—Ute, Navajo, and Euro-American—sought to improve their quality of life within their existing circumstances, but each had a very different conception of how to achieve it. Conflict and denial resulted, as shifting worldviews clashed. The subsequent healing helped bring about a new comprehension of how to best achieve the "happy state" of which Locke spoke. Health and education were the core of these concerns.

To the Native Americans, health practices included religious and spiritual curing as much as they did physical medicine. Ute beliefs, for instance, centered around the shaman, usually a man, who received his healing power either through a charm obtained from an older medicine man or through dreams provided by supernatural beings. He often learned healing rites through repeated dreams received in puberty. The dreams gave secret information concerning

A Navajo medicine man sits before a sandpainting of Monster Slayer, drawn in flint armor with shafts of lightning surrounding his body. Once the sandpainting has been blessed, the Holy Beings portrayed participate in healing the sick person and providing a shield of protective power to prevent further harm. (San Juan Historical Commission)

power within animals, plants, and natural elements that the shaman could invoke for good. These supernatural teachings could not be denied but also could not be divulged, charging the shaman with a lifelong responsibility of service.

A typical Ute healing ceremony consisted of a medicine man using his wisdom and the healing paraphernalia he had collected to chant, pray, suck out, or otherwise exorcise the evil afflicting the sick person. Usually he performed at night, either in his or the patient's home. Stripped to the waist, the medicine man used all his wiles, including sleight of hand, dancing, and personal attacks on the illness. Inside the shaman was a small being, or powa'a, who directed the use of power and swallowed the sickness when it was removed from the patient by sucking it out. If the powa'a was misused or became angry, it could turn on the practitioner, calling for blood and causing illness or death.[1]

Herbs and plants also played an important role in healing. Utes believed that a lack of food caused colds, and such patients drank tea brewed from sagebrush leaves; a sore throat was cured by boiling pinyon sap with grease and then applying the mixture externally on the neck; the roots and flowers of sand puff remedied stomach and bowel problems; spearmint leaves cured an upset stomach; and gum plant served as a cough syrup. Non-plant remedies included putting breast milk on a nursing baby's sore eyes; putting sugar on large cuts to stop bleeding; using skunk grease on chapped hands and feet; horse urine on pustules that broke and caused itching; tobacco as a pain reliever for a decayed tooth; and, after the adoption of baking powder, swabbing a sore throat internally with this substance.[2] In a world dominated by spirits and fraught with the possibility of physical harm, the Utes fortified themselves against the trials of life.

The same was true of the Navajos, whose ceremonial system was even more complex. Most illness originated in the mythological underworlds when First Man and First Woman filled a basket with "smallpox, whooping cough, nervousness, paleness or pulmonary diseases, and every fatal disease. Indeed, First Man and his companions were evil people who practiced witchcraft. . . . Their wish alone was sufficient to inflict these diseases and to cause death through them."[3] Thus, physical ailments were in many instances the symptoms of a violated taboo or the curse from a malcontent. The holy beings that pervade the universe knew when a person had not shown proper respect and therefore afflicted the culprit with illness.[4]

Health was restored by recounting and reenacting the mythological events through song, sand painting, and prayer. In a very mechanical sense, if these activities are performed properly, the holy beings are bound to heal or cure the sufferer. When a patient failed to be healed, then the divining of the illness was incorrect, part of the cure was left out, or an additional complication was not considered. Today dozens of different ceremonies are classified into three general types: Holyway ceremonies are directed by holy beings who attract good and restore health, Evilway casts out ghosts and protects from witchcraft, while Lifeway treats injuries from accidents. The result of all three is the restoration of *hozho*, a term generally glossed as being in harmony with the world and oneself.[5]

The Navajos also use plants, herbs, soil, rocks, feathers, and many other objects as medical remedies.[6] Topographical features ranging from mountains to rivers and from rock formations to springs create a sacred, healing geography based upon mythology. For the Navajo, the land and its inhabitants form a web of life that is both physical and supernatural. To disregard this is to ignore the essence of Navajo thought and belief, including their accompanying aid from the holy beings.[7]

Early Euro-American practices in San Juan County shared a number of similarities with those of the Utes and Navajos. Until a clearly defined theory of germ disease became accepted, many healing conventions revolved around herbs, family remedies, and religious teachings. Much early medical treatment was provided by midwives. Jody Woods, a Mormon midwife, accepted her calling as one from God, was set apart by church authority, received some basic training, and administered to the Latter-day Saints as much through prayer as physical remedy. She told of many instances where she believed the Holy Ghost guided her, such as the time a voice clearly told her to remove the umbilical cord from around a strangling baby's neck. She said, "I thought Bishop Nielson had spoken to me but when I turned to look at him, he was not in the room. I knew that the Lord had blessed me, telling me plainly what to do."[8]

Another good example of mixing social, spiritual, and physical care is found in the journal of Mary Jones, who attended a midwives' seminar offered in Bluff in 1896. Hannah Sorenson, from Salt Lake City, taught the class and offered observations sprinkled amid the latest theories about disease control and delivering babies. She wrote: "Skirts should have waists on them and not bands for they injure the development of the generative organs by pressure." "Cold does not prevent menstruation, it is weakness"; and, when two people sleep beside each other, "the more sensitive of the two bed fellows will absorb the poison excretions from the body of the other. . . . Often the languor and nervousness with which certain individuals arise in the morning is directly traceable to the influence of the companion during sleep."[9]

Physical remedies of the pioneers, like those of the Utes and Navajos, sometimes depended upon cures that could be as difficult

Graduates of a six week midwife course held in Bluff, 1896. Instructor Hannah Sorenson standing at the far right. (San Juan Historical Commission)

for the patient as the disease. Some homespun San Juan cures to attack pneumonia included applying a poultice made from camphor, turpentine, and alcohol; hanging bread soaked in milk around the patient's chest; and applying a basic mustard plaster made from mustard, eggs, flour, and water with some additional ingredients like grease, kerosene, vinegar, and eucalyptus oil thrown in for good measure. Kerosene in lemon juice was a prescribed cure for the croup; other beliefs were that a bag of eucalyptus buds hung around the neck prevented the flu; cedar-berry tea remedied kidney disease; sage or oak-bark tea lowered fevers; sticky pine-gum salve prevented infections and promoted healing; and rubbing a wart with a penny or a potato removed the growth.[10]

Perhaps the best way to understand the medical practices of different cultures is to compare their reaction to the same disease. The influenza epidemic of 1918–19 provides a good example.[11] This catastrophic illness was a national and international phenomenon that left an estimated 548,452 Americans dead in its wake.[12] In San Juan County, a quantitative analysis is not possible because statistics about the disease do not exist, but there is a good body of anecdotal information that hints of the trauma caused by the disease.

For example, isolated Monticello and Blanding had nothing comparable to the medical care in Moab with its two doctors and several nurses. Because of these towns' Mormon dominance, the afflicted were cared for through community cooperation. When the owner of the Grayson Co-op became sick, customers stopped by his home, got the key, opened the store, and took what they needed with a promise to pay later.[13] Although most of the townspeople were ill at one time or another, a few healthy men who hauled wood, fed livestock, and performed heavier chores, while the women plied their knowledge as accomplished midwives and nurses.[14] Outside help was limited to infrequent visits from the doctor in Moab. To speed his travel to Monticello, town residents met him approximately halfway with a fresh team of horses.[15] For those in Blanding, there was no doctor.

Preventive medicines were also used, the sick eating wild garlic and hanging asafetida around their necks. This latter substance is an offensive-smelling resinous material extracted from the roots of several kinds of plants of the genus *Ferula*. One survivor of the ordeal of wearing asafetida around his neck swore that "it's the stinkingest stuff you ever seen . . . but it makes a good coyote bait."[16]

The Navajo reaction to the influenza outbreak was steeped in the teachings of mythology. On 8 June 1918, a solar eclipse occurred, presaging misfortune. The sun, an important Navajo deity, hid his light from his people because of his anger, thus warning of a catastrophe about to take place.[17] During the summer and fall, dawns and sunsets had pronounced reddish hues that bathed the landscape in an ominous red. The tips of cedar and juniper trees started to die, a sign indicating that sickness was in the area and would be visiting humans. Some Navajos had bad dreams portending disaster.[18]

Influenza raged across the landscape, destroying entire clusters of people. One eyewitness reported that

> whole families were wiped out, leaving their flocks wandering over the hills at the mercy of the wolves. Several related families living together all died but one small boy who was found herding the

combined flocks of sheep. . . . [A father] and five children crossed the [San Juan] river into the Navajo country with their sheep where they died one by one along the trail. Only one little boy survived and he is so small that he is unable to give his parents' name.[19]

Louisa Wetherill, a trader in Kayenta, reported a constant flow to her trading post of Navajos seeking help with burials. Although it took two weeks for her husband to recover from his own bout with the flu, both she and John spent considerable time burying the dead and nursing the living. John Wetherill estimated that by 6 December, in Kayenta alone, he interred more than one hundred Navajos.[20] Medicine men traveled about, performing ceremonies for the sick; how much of the disease was spread through these unwitting vectors and the close contact required in the rituals will never be known; but, in the mind of the Navajo, these healers saved many lives and performed a valuable service. Prayers, not vaccine, held the cure.

Utes and Paiutes living in the Four Corners region were also affected by the disease, but apparently not to the same extent as the Navajos. The Ute agent, headquartered at Towaoc, reported a population of 300 Indians on his reserve. Many of them traveled off their lands and thus had ample opportunity to contract the disease. But by 27 December 1918, there had been only a few deaths, because the Utes had "yielded readily to medical treatment and seemed to suffer much less than their Indian neighbors."[21] A possible explanation is that in addition to medical help, the curing practices of the Utes, unlike those of the Navajo, did not stress congregating to perform ceremonies. In fact, "when the flu was bad, most of the Indians left the agency, some going to Mesa Verde and some to other parts, and their ponies are so poor and weak they can neither ride or drive them."[22]

The Utes, however, did not escape the effects of the illness entirely. Like the Navajos, they fled from their homes when someone died inside and thus more readily fell prey to the elements and the disease. Many of them had trouble understanding how white men could get sick, take medicine, and get better, while the Indians took the same medicine and died. Apparently by the end of the epidemic,

Early drugstore owned by Arthur Kimball in Blanding around 1920. In addition to selling patent medicines, the store also served as a confectionery and local gathering place. The first drugstore to boast a licensed pharmacist did not appear in Blanding until 1956. (Howard Kimball Collection)

white doctors did not have easy access to the Utes, who suggested "maybeso medicine given Indian was coyote bait [poison]."[23] The Indians turned mistrustful and ran from their camps to hide when a white man approached, fearing he might be a doctor. Fortunately, by February 1919 the epidemic had subsided.

There would be other epidemics, though not as serious or widespread; but conditions in San Juan were changing. Gradually, the county forged stronger ties with the national economy, roads improved, health education increased, and medical knowledge expanded, giving rise to a growing understanding of the germ theory of disease. This is not to suggest that Anglo-Americans had not been aware of it as far back as the late 1800s but only that better information and greater reliance on professionally trained doctors and nurses became increasingly important.

The next problem was how to get doctors to practice in this isolated part of the Four Corners. Monticello's first doctor, a man named Harrison, arrived in 1914 and stayed for less than a year; the next year another doctor, Harry S. Bussey, followed; but he too left after a few years. Doctor C. R. Spearman arrived in 1929 with a monthly income guaranteed by county residents, but the closest hospital was in Moab and medical conditions remained primitive. Blanding had even more difficulty obtaining medical services.[24]

Finally, in 1938 the county struck upon the idea of a cooperative effort to finance health care for its Anglo-American citizens. Enthusiastic support arose as civic and religious leaders endorsed a program to serve the county's 3,700 residents wherein each family could enroll and pay $35 per year for general health care.[25] The plan called for cooperation with the Moab hospital and Dr. I. W. Allen from Grand County who would provide the necessary coverage including surgical operations, laboratory examinations, maternity care, home visits, and hospital facilities (with a one dollar daily fee) after a family signed its annual contract. By the end of the first year, 250 families had enrolled in the program, an additional doctor took up residence in Monticello, and the charges of "communistic," "un-American," and "socialized medicine" levelled by the American Medical Association were ignored. Indeed, one writer "thanked God" for the efforts of the men and women serving in the San Juan Medical Cooperative.[26]

The program was not without its problems. Surprisingly, people were often slow to renew their contracts unless they anticipated an illness. Forty families were so poor that they took out loans to cover the charges. At the same time, however, LDS priesthood quorums and Relief Societies encouraged church members to subscribe. One doctor became ill and was replaced by Wesley L. Bayles, a dedicated, native-son physician who served Blanding. The Army called him to serve during World War II, and it took 1,400 signatures on a petition sent to Washington, D.C., to persuade military authorities to allow him to remain to help care for the 5,000 residents of San Juan County. Because of the county's rural nature and the Vanadium Corporation of America's mill site involved in defense-related work in Monticello, the government allowed Bayles to stay.[27]

One of the biggest hurdles for the county to overcome was obtaining a hospital. As early as 1936 an article appeared in the *San Juan Record* suggesting that the money for such services should not go to Grand County but stay home and that an eighty-mile trip to reach the Moab hospital was excessive. As the San Juan Medical Cooperative plan took shape two years later, Grand County capitalized on the anticipated increase of patients and applied for a $60,000 federal grant for expansion. San Juan residents reasoned that those funds could be put to better use within their own county. By 1945, San Juan residents started a dialogue that two years later resulted in four buildings donated by the War Assets Administration and the VCA for use as a twelve-bed hospital with homes for a doctor and nurses. San Juan County purchased the property for $25,000.[28]

Amid the seeds of success lay the seeds of friction. Doctors' fees increased, competition between Monticello and Blanding for health services intensified, and county politics came into play. In 1952, Monticello residents canceled their medical contracts in favor of supporting a private practice. Soon, Dr. Carroll D. Goon began his work in town. He became highly respected in the community as a physician and then insisted upon better facilities in which to practice. By 1961 the county had built a new hospital in the northwestern section of town, a facility which two years later had treated more than 4,200 inpatient and outpatient cases. Also Blanding built its first clinic in the 1950s. Yet the county ratio of one doctor to approximately 3,000 people still remained well below the national average of one to 830.[29]

In spite of continued problems with recruiting doctors, rising costs, intercity competition for health-care facilities, and contracting with larger, regional organizations to provide administrative and medical services, the general trend has been one of expansion. For example, during 1993 the thirty-six-bed hospital in Monticello admitted 877 inpatients and handled approximately 5,500 outpatient visits.[30] In addition to a $1.5-million remodeling of its building and updating of its equipment, the hospital also provided services in the Dove Creek clinic in Colorado and operated a mobile facility that traveled to remote locations on the Ute and Navajo reservations, as well as to Hite, Halls Crossing, and Bullfrog marinas.

That same year, the Blanding Medical Center, an extension of the hospital, received 1,790 emergency room visitors, 65 percent of whom were Native Americans; the three-bed birthing clinic (built in 1991) admitted 112 expectant mothers; and approximately 1,500 Navajos and Utes from southern San Juan County registered for emergency services at the facility.[31] Located with the clinic is the Four Corners Regional Care Center, started in 1968, with a 104-bed capacity. The white residents of San Juan County have come a long way since the pioneers arrived in Bluff a hundred years ago.

The story of Native American health care has also seen dramatic improvements, though at a generally slower rate. Perhaps the greatest challenge was the conquest of tuberculosis, the leading infectious killer of Navajos until the 1960s. As early as 1949, a medical team went to Bluff to test a portion of the Navajo population, but the doctor and nurses reached too few people within the vast geographical area to make much of a difference.

By the mid-1950s, Health Department officials recognized that San Juan Navajos faced a disease difficult to detect until its last stages and that hundreds of Navajos were infected due to a limited understanding of germ theory and the ease with which the disease could be contracted. San Juan County had the dubious distinction of having the highest tuberculosis rate in Utah and, according to one article, in the United States. Authorities explained this problem by citing an example from Bluff in which three Navajo people had died of the disease in the same hogan with twenty-four others living in close proximity.[32]

Until the 1960s, there were no health facilities on the Utah portion of the reservation, all local medical care being handled by the Indian Health Service in Kayenta, Shiprock, or Tuba City, with more complicated cases sent to Gallup or Albuquerque. In 1964, state, federal, tribal, and private organizations agreed to pool their resources in a united effort to eradicate tuberculosis. Workers held the first of many clinics in Monument Valley and then fanned out to other locations from Aneth to Navajo Mountain. Interpreters, traders, and social workers spread the word, encouraging the reticent Navajos to come for help. Health practitioners examined 775 patients, identified seventy-two active cases, hospitalized six immediately, and returned semiannually for the next five years. The case rate dropped from 534 in 100,000 in 1965 to 69 in 100,000 in 1967 to only one new case reported in 1975.[33]

To provide sustained health care for a variety of other needs, a more permanent form of outreach service was necessary. The answer came in the form of two religious groups—Reverend H. Baxter Liebler's one-room clinic at Saint Christopher's Mission in Bluff,

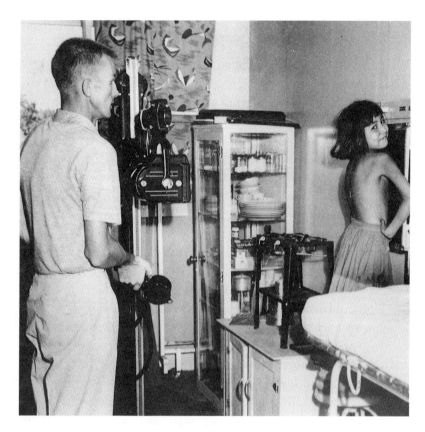

The clinic at Saint Christopher's Mission became an integral part of the fight against tuberculosis and trachoma in the 1950s and 1960s. The girl in the picture does not appear to mind having an x-ray taken, but some older traditional Navajos feared that it would "burn" their insides. (San Juan Historical Commission)

starting around 1945, and the Seventh-Day Adventist hospital in Monument Valley, which opened its doors in 1950. These facilities provided excellent, caring service that expanded over the years. The Adventists especially had a large pool of resources to draw upon in equipping, financing, and staffing their operation.[34]

By 1971–72 a Navajo owned-and-operated system began to provide outreach care. The Utah Navajo Development Council aggressively sought either construction of new clinics or control over ones already existing on the Utah portion of the reservation. Centers of

Navajo population in which clinics were maintained included Montezuma Creek (1971), Navajo Mountain (1971), and Mexican Hat (1976), all of which remained open until 1991. The Seventh-Day Adventists helped provide staffing for both medical and dental programs offered in the clinics, while UNDC contracted with the Indian Health Service and Utah Navajo Trust Funds for money to provide local care.[35]

UNDC furnished transportation for doctors to drive or fly to these remote locations, but the heart of the program was the nurse practitioners and Navajo paraprofessionals who offered programs such as health education, well-baby clinics, prenatal and postpartum care, family planning, and special clinics for screening cancer, treating tuberculosis, and teaching handicapped children. The results were impressive. In fiscal year 1971–72, Navajos made 8,421 visits to the clinics; by 1983 this figure had doubled to 16,845.[36]

UNDC instituted a program that further decentralized services and brought health care into the hogans of some of the most remote camps. Navajo-community male and female nurses traveled over rutted dirt roads in the back country, visiting homes with medicine and advice for those not able to reach the clinics. In 1982 these nurses attained a peak of 2,700 visitations.[37]

The clinic at Navajo Mountain expanded its capacity with an innovative program during the summer of 1983. Assuming the title "Hogan Heroes," the full-time health personnel trained female Navajo high school and college students who were home for the summer to give instruction to the old, the disabled, and the housebound on subjects as varied as first aid, fitness, drug use, and accident prevention. As a result, 122 of the 135 families the clinic had identified as needing such help were contacted and instructed, giving rise to a final report that boasted, "Every family now has someone who can take a temperature."[38] Thus, even the most isolated parts of the reservation have been affected by health care, with the result that disease and infant mortality are no longer the scourge they once were.

Health challenges still lie ahead. The recently recognized Hantavirus, spread by rodents, alarmed reservation residents in 1993. Heart disease, diabetes, and cancer—which have historically been rare among Navajos—are now as prevalent among Native Americans

The first log church and school in San Juan County was built as part of the Bluff Fort, 1880. It served as a meeting house, school, dance hall, and place for public gatherings until torn down in 1894. About forty houses comprised the fort which was approximately 130 yards square. Pictured left to right: Kumen Jones, Platte D. Lyman, Jens Nielson, James B. Decker, and Francis Hammond. (San Juan Historical Commission)

as they are in the dominant population, and alcohol still curses the lives of many. But the general trend in health care has been one of improvement in quality with a subsequent lengthening of the lives of the county's inhabitants.

Education, like health care, has also made slow but steady progress in the county. The first district school started in early November 1880 in Montezuma Creek and was managed by Parthenia Hyde, a teenager; a month later, Ida M. Lyman began a school in Bluff.[39] Both were situated in crude log cabins, had all grades and ages in one room, and reflected the values of the predominantly Mormon community from which they took root. The flood of 1884 swept the Montezuma Creek school down the river, and it was not until 1887, with the establishment of Monticello, that the area settlers held classes other than in Bluff. Two years later, thirty to forty children were attending school in the community log church; by 1894 the number had doubled. Three years later the people of La Sal started their own school. In 1901 the Bluff and Monticello school districts were funded by amounts of $543 and $624, respectively.[40]

Improving education in San Juan has been a struggle against isolation, poverty, and inadequate resources at the same time that the population has grown. The story of the early years of school in Blanding reflects the pattern, on a larger scale, of the roughly two dozen one-room schoolhouses scattered throughout the county. Starting in 1907, Lucretia Lyman taught the first class in Blanding in a tent with double wood walls packed with sawdust. As the town grew, so did the school. From a rough-hewn frame building, to a backroom in the Grayson Co-op, to a donated "chicken coop," to a four-room stone-and-brick facility, the school reflected the life of the financially struggling citizens of Blanding as they sacrificed time, labor, and materials to provide for their children.[41]

The local people appreciated what they had achieved, but to outsiders, it was inadequate. By 1917 the Blanding school was filled to capacity because of the influx of Mormons from Mexico; Monticello had outgrown its three-room facility; La Sal had a new $1,000 structure under construction; and school superintendent J. B. Harris felt "fairly swamped with children demanding teaching and training." He was, however, delighted with the people who responded "nobly with individual contributions of money and labor."[42] But when Professor Mosiah Halls from the state accreditation committee toured these facilities, he offered "a little praise and much drastic criticism." He attacked Blanding's school for its inadequate space; the small, "cold, uncomfortable, unsanitary and disease producing" main building was almost as bad as the "unpardonable" temporary classrooms utilized for excess students. Monticello's facilities fared no better. He "declared them not fit for school use" and threatened to report these conditions to health authorities, who would close the buildings down.[43] He did, however, praise the teachers and ultimately managed to grant accreditation for the schools to continue.

If the situations in Blanding and Monticello were bad, the one-room schoolhouses that dotted the landscape especially between the 1920s and 1940s were even more of a problem. Due to long distances to the schools in the larger towns, poor roads, inclement weather, and numerous other inconveniences, local communities lobbied for their own educational facilities and teachers. Eventually, San Juan County could boast of more than two dozen single-room schools, either private or public, that served its population from La Sal to Aneth and from White Canyon to Ucolo. Many of these would come and go as economic trends and populations shifted.[44]

Obtaining and retaining teachers were among the greatest challenges. The larger the community the better the chance of keeping the teacher. Many teachers were young females, new to the profession, and recruited from outside of the county through mail or personal contact. Take, for example, Hilda Rose Palmer, who taught twenty-one students in eight grades for a year. She arrived in Thompson fresh from her studies at Snow College and ready to start her career in Horsehead, "wherever that was." Her one-room schoolhouse sported wooden desks, benches, and two outside privies. The parents provided wood fuel, the older boys stoked the stove, and everybody drank cold spring water from a common dipper. Miss Palmer boarded with a family who lived two miles from the school. She rode to dances on horseback and enjoyed the artwork of a cowboy who broke into the classroom and left his drawings all over the blackboard. Although she felt her experience to be "special" and "rewarding," a year later, in 1927, she moved on to the bright lights of Blanding.[45]

The educational system gradually improved despite the rollercoaster effects of the economic and political situation. Monticello (1913) and Blanding (1914) enrolled students in the county's first high school programs. Homesteading booms increased the student population; hard times just as quickly depleted it. The county school district in 1944 discussed closing Monticello High School and bussing the students to Blanding to consolidate the small classes, provide an improved curriculum, and conserve resources. A firestorm of protest from Monticello arose in a mass meeting attended by 200 people, resulting in a petition with 350 signatures decrying the action. The school board rescinded the plan.[46]

Teacher shortages persisted until the discovery of uranium deposits in the 1940s and oil in the mid-1950s. Suddenly, San Juan County moved from being one of the poorest to being the richest school district in Utah. The total enrollment skyrocketed from 800

First schoolhouse in La Sal, built in 1909 by the private funds of Fred N. Prewer. The one-room school had all eight grades meet together. In the early years, Prewer provided room and board for the teachers without charge. (San Juan Historical Commission)

students in 1948 to 1,800 ten years later, an increase of 225 percent.[47] By 1959 the tax dollars allocated for education exceeded by $600,000 the required amount necessary to run the program.[48] This money helped build better school facilities and attracted more and better qualified teachers. A 1957 survey examining teacher credentials pointed out that 34 percent of the teachers and principals were properly certified; by 1962, the figure had risen to 93 percent. The next year, the teachers received a $300 raise, making the salary schedule one of the highest in the state.[49]

Fortunately, some of these benefits, especially from the Aneth oil field, spurred change for a group in San Juan County that had previously not received much in the way of education—the Native Americans. Part of the reason for the previous lag was that until livestock reduction necessitated a change, traditional teachings were sufficient for a life and livelihood on the reservation. Both Navajo and Ute traditional education consisted of stories, example, and informal methods that stressed the individual's need to choose certain lifeways. One Navajo woman explained it this way:

They [mother and father] were the only ones to teach me these
things. They said this is the way you walk through life. I found out
it was true. "I will sit here and set examples for you," she said,
"until you can stand up. With my breath of life [for I gave you life]
you will be like that throughout your years." I think sometimes
that this is true. I always hang on to the old words said by her.[50]

However, according to the Treaty of 1868, the government was to
provide formal education to the Navajos through schools and teachers sent to all parts of the reservation. Although this program got off
to a slow start, by the mid-twentieth century large numbers of Navajo
children were enrolled—either willingly or by force—in some form
of educational program. Four general types of schools were available:
the federal boarding school, the Navajo community boarding school,
mission schools, and the Anglo or Navajo community day school. To
serve Native American residents, the BIA established boarding
schools in Shonto, Tuba City, and Kayenta, Arizona; Shiprock, New
Mexico; Towaoc, Colorado; and Aneth and Navajo Mountain, Utah.[51]
Mission schools included the Navajo Faith Mission at Aneth, Saint
Christopher's Mission at Bluff, and the Seventh-Day Adventist school
in Monument Valley.[52] Day schools operated for a short time for the
Utes in Allen Canyon and in Westwater for both Navajos and Utes.[53]
All of these schools generally struggled to obtain sufficient numbers
of students, keep them involved in classroom activities, redirect tra-
ditional Native American values, and maintain a positive attitude
toward learning.

One of the earliest attempts to educate Indian children in the
northern part of the county was undertaken by Albert R. Lyman and
his wife, Gladys. The couple erected a tent across Westwater Canyon
on the outskirts of Blanding and taught both Ute and Navajo children. Their difficult circumstances eventually forced them to move
into town with their students, but not without first meeting local
resistance from the white community. Integration into the regular
school system was slow, and it was not until the 1960s that significant
numbers of Indian students started to remain in school long enough
to complete high school.[54]

Another option available for Ute and Navajo children was the
Indian Placement Program of the Church of Jesus Christ of Latter-

day Saints (LDS). Because Utah was predominantly Mormon, many of the local Native American children remained in the state and attended school in the Salt Lake City area; others went to California for their education. The program was strictly voluntary yet selective, being based on ability and church membership for those children who chose to attend. It is difficult to measure the impact of this placement program since the church has not released reports concerning its success or failure. As time went on, however, the program became smaller and more selective until it ended in 1990.

Still another option was not to attend school at all. A study conducted in 1969 found that the parents of many Navajo students had avoided formal education for one reason or another. Whether they were caught in the web of familial responsibilities, blocked by transportation problems, or simply lacked the desire, these parents were sending their children off to an experience they had never had. The study points out that of the Navajo students attending San Juan High School, 40 percent of their fathers and 59 percent of their mothers had no formal education. Only 5 percent of these parents had completed twelve years of school, and 2 percent of the fathers and 1 percent of the mothers held college degrees.[55] According to the 1990 census, 35 percent of the Utah Navajo population twenty-five years or older now hold a high school diploma or higher, and 4.4 percent have a bachelor's degree or higher.[56]

This increased emphasis on education for the Utah Navajos did not always come easily. Because the northern two-thirds of San Juan County contained the majority of the white population, most of the private businesses, state and federal agencies, and schools were also located there. For those Navajos living on the reservation, the alternative beyond boarding schools and the LDS Placement Program—especially for high school students—lay in traveling to Blanding for an education.

Bussing was the only reliable daily means for getting students to school, but it came at a high price. Indian children, depending upon which part of the reservation they lived in, were transported from 80 to 166 miles (round-trip) each day to get to classes.[57] Translated into travel time, this could mean as much as five or six hours by the time they had walked or been driven by parents to their bus stop. People

The old District grade school in Blanding. Built of cut stone and brick, the school opened in 1912 and was demolished in 1956. (San Juan Historical Commission)

who endured this bussing confirm that it was a trial to get chores done, eat breakfast, and reach a pickup point to meet their means of transportation; it also curtailed extracurricular and study activities after school.

In 1975, parents took steps to help the more than 200 students who found themselves in this situation. Believing these children were products of educational and racial discrimination, forty-eight individuals filed notice with the DNA (Dinebeiina Nahiilna Be Agaditahe—roughly translated as "Winning a Case for the People's Rights") office in Mexican Hat. DNA, an agency that provides legal aid for the Navajo people, in turn filed suit in a case known as *Sinajini v. The Board of Education*. Although Jimmie Sinajini was only one of the students, his case represented both the Oljato and Red Mesa chapters' fight against the school district. Navajos read pertinent documents at chapter meetings, insuring local involvement in the case.[58]

San Juan School District officials sat down with lawyers from both sides and discussed emotionally charged issues. School representatives pointed out that as late as 1958 only 4.4 percent or 120 stu-

dents in the district, were American Indian and that the BIA had
responsibility for the others. By 1974 the figure had changed dramatically. Indian students now numbered 1,235, or 46.5 percent, 431
of whom were involved in secondary education and 220 of whom
were being bussed. Comparative distances traveled by Indian and
non-Indian students showed that the high schools were located so
that the average Navajo student traveled four times as far as his or her
white counterpart. Many Native Americans spent the equivalent of
120 school days physically sitting on a bus just to attend classes for
180 days. For students at the end of the longest bus routes, these figures rose to 30,000 miles each year and the equivalent of 240 school
days on a bus.[59]

The school district eventually came to terms. Both parties agreed
that what was needed were high schools in Montezuma Creek and
Monument Valley. The former opened in 1978, the latter in 1983, and
each has had a larger attendance than the projected 150-person
enrollment initially anticipated. The school district also improved the
three elementary schools on or near the reservation in Bluff, Mexican
Hat, and Montezuma Creek, and initiated bilingual/bicultural programs at each institution. The significance of these developments is
highlighted by information from the 1990 census. San Juan County
had never had as many Navajo students enrolled in elementary and
secondary education—as many as 1,600 on the reservation alone,
with 332 others attending some type of college. These figures support
the general trend established in 1980 of dramatic increases in the
education of Native Americans.

Ironically, it was because of Native Americans, the most educa-
tionally deprived group in the county, that programs for higher education came to improve the lives of all of San Juan's citizens. Colleges
and universities had offered classes sporadically for a number of
years, primarily as an aid to teacher training and recertification in the
school district. By the mid-1970s, the College of Eastern Utah had
contracted with the Utah Navajo Development Council to import
classes on a regular basis for Navajos aspiring toward a college degree.

The program became so successful that by 1977 UNDC had
hired a full-time coordinator, Lynn Lee, who envisioned a greatly
expanded program to provide educational services for county resi-

dents. One year later, the San Juan Campus in Blanding hired its first full-time instructor and began an outreach program that, at one time or another, has offered classes in every community in the county. This "commuting community college" has taught courses as varied as mine training, nursing, truck driving, building trades, and secretarial work, as well as offering the standard two-year associate of science/arts degrees. Starting with an annual composite enrollment of 407 students in 1978, the number had more than tripled by 1993 to 1,461 students. At least half of these were Native Americans.[60] Today, the San Juan Campus, housed in eight buildings in Blanding, still offers classes in Monument Valley and in the Montezuma Creek area. Its program has continuously grown in both the number of students enrolled and the quality of its offerings.

Thus, the history of education and health services in San Juan County reflects a shift from individual, isolated practices based on cultural beliefs to a broad acceptance of dominant, twentieth-century Anglo-American values. This is not to suggest that folk medicines and religious cures have disappeared. Mormon grandmothers still talk of the healing qualities of pine-gum salve, pray for blessings, and teach their grandchildren important lessons of life; Navajo medicine men still heal through ceremonies, apply herbs picked from sacred places, and tell stories on cold winter nights about good triumphing over evil; and a Ute mother still guides her children as she hums and stitches beads onto a piece of leather.

As these people move into the twenty-first century, change will continue. The questions are only in what direction and at what rate. If the past is any indication, much of it will be in improvements that will add intellectual breadth and longevity of life. When Menander, a Greek dramatist before the time of Christ, wrote, "Health and intellect are the two blessings of life," he named two important ideals for the residents of San Juan. Hopefully, as they obtain these blessings, they will not forsake much of the still vital cultural heritage that has preceded them.

ENDNOTES

1. Marvin Kaufmann Opler, "The Southern Ute of Colorado," *Acculturation in Seven American Indian Tribes* (New York: D. Appleton-

Century Company, 1940): 141–45; Harold Lindsay Amoss, Jr., "Ute Mountain Utes," Ph.D. diss., University of California, 1951, 36–38.

2. Amoss, "Ute Mountain Utes," 37–38; Ralph V. Chamberlain, "Some Plant Names of the Ute Indians," *American Anthropologist* 11, no. 1 (January-March, 1909): 27–40; James Jefferson, Robert W. Delaney, and Gregory Thompson, *The Southern Utes: A Tribal History* (Ignacio, Colo.: Southern Ute Tribe, 1972), 72–73.

3. Berard Haile, recorder, *Upward Moving and Emergence Way: The Gishin Biye Version* (Lincoln: University of Nebraska Press, 1981), 6.

4. For a good overview of traditional Navajo religion see Clyde Kluckhohn and Dorothea Leighton, *The Navaho* (Cambridge, Mass.: Harvard University Press, 1946), 178–252.

5. Leland C. Wyman, "Navajo Ceremonial System," *Handbook of North American Indians—Southwest* 10 (Washington, D.C.: Smithsonian Institution, 1983), 543–63.

6. For a good overview of Navajo plant use see Vernon O. Mayes and Barbara B. Lacy, *Nanise—A Navajo Herbal: One Hundred Plants from the Navajo Reservation* (Tsaile, Ariz.: Navajo Community College Press, 1989).

7. For a good overview of these principles see Robert S. McPherson, *Sacred Land, Sacred View: Navajo Perceptions of the Four Corners Region* (Provo: Brigham Young University Press, 1992), 1–75.

8. Frances H. Hoopes, "Josephine Catherine (Jody) Chatterley Wood: Midwife of San Juan," *Blue Mountain Shadows* 2, no. 1 (Fall 1988): 35.

9. Mary Jones, notes entitled "The Woman's Hygienic Physiological Reform Class," held in 1896, in possession of author, 4–9.

10. Laura Shumway, "A Cure for Everything," *Blue Mountain Shadows* 1, no. 2 (Spring 1988): 60–62.

11. The excerpts are taken from an article by the author entitled, "The Influenza Epidemic of 1918: A Cultural Response," *Utah Historical Quarterly* 58, no. 2 (Spring 1990): 183–200.

12. Joseph E. Persico, "The Great Swine Flu Epidemic of 1918," *American Heritage* 27 (June 1976): 84.

13. Margie Lyman interview with Helen Shumway, 11 April 1986, tape in possession of Shumway.

14. Ibid.; Mae Black interview with Janet Wilcox on 15 July 1987, San Juan County Historical Society, 3–4; Ray Redd, interview by Jody Bailey on 16 July 1987, San Juan County Historical Society, 5–6.

15. Redd interview, 6.

16. Ibid.

17. Gladys A. Reichard, *Navaho Religion, a Study of Symbolism*

(Princeton: Princeton University Press, 1963), 19; Ada Black interview with Bertha Parrish on 18 June 1987, San Juan County Historical Society, 1–2.

18. Mae Black interview with Janet Wilcox, 15 July 1987; Rose Begay, interview with Bertha Parrish, 17 June 1987, both tapes in San Juan County Historical Commission office, Blanding, Utah; Tallis Holliday interview with author, 3 November 1987; Fred Yazzie interview with author, 5 November 1987, both tapes in possession of author.

19. Albert B. Reagan, "The Influenza and the Navajo," *Proceedings of the Indiana Academy of Science* 29 (Fort Wayne: Fort Wayne Printing Company, 1921), 246.

20. "Navajo Indians Are Dying by Hundreds," *Grand Valley Times*, 6 December 1918, 1.

21. "The Influenza among the Utes," *The Mancos Times Tribune*, 27 December 1918, 1.

22. "Superstitious Utes," *The Mancos Times Tribune*, 10 January 1919, 1.

23. Ibid.; "Influenza Very Bad among Indians," *The Mancos Times Tribune*, 13 December 1918, 1, 3.

24. Cornelia Perkins, Marian Nielson, and Lenora Jones, *The Saga of San Juan* (Salt Lake City: Mercury Publishing Company, 1957), 257–59; "Monticello Community Development Report," Section II, 17, in possession of author; Albert R. Lyman, *History of Blanding, 1905–1955* (n.p., 1955), 72.

25. "Civic, Religious Leaders Endorse Health Program," *San Juan Record* (hereafter cited as *SJR*), 31 March 1938, 1; "Blanding Chamber of Commerce Active," *SJR*, 14 April 1938, 4.

26. "Co-operation Triumphs Once More in New Field," *SJR*, 7 July 1938, 1; "San Juan Medical Cooperative to Celebrate," *SJR*, 29 June 1939, 4; "Successful Year of Cooperative Medical Program," *SJR*, 6 July 1939, 1.

27. "Medical Contracts Are Now Ready," *SJR*, 4 July 1940, 1; "Medical Program Has Set-Up for Next Year," *SJR*, 10 April 1941, 1; "County Appeals for the Services of Dr. Bayles," *SJR*, 20 August 1942, 1; "Petition to Hold County Physician Receives Support," *SJR*, 31 August 1942, 1.

28. "San Juan County Needs and Can with WPA Grant Build a Hospital," *SJR*, 3 December 1936, 1; "San Juan's Place in the Sun," *SJR*, 14 July 1938, 4; "Townsite Properties Set Aside for San Juan County Hospital," *SJR*, 5 June 1947, 1; "Hospital Assured for San Juan County," *SJR*, 26 June 1947, 1; "San Juan County Hospital Opens," *SJR*, 3 July 1947, 1.

29. "Medical Program in Monticello Area to Be Discontinued," *SJR*, 10 July 1952, 1; "Thousands Receive Treatment at Local San Juan Hospital," *SJR*, 2 January 1964, 1; "2,986 Persons per Doctor in S. J. County," *SJR*, 24

February 1961, 6; Leda Young interview with Dawn Boyle, 15 January 1995, notes in possession of author.

30. Bryan Sisson, Finance Officer—San Juan County Hospital, telephone conversation with author, 22 June 1994.

31. Donna Singer, administrative supervisor of Blanding Medical Center, telephone conversation with author, 27 June 1994.

32. "Health Conditions on the Navajo Indian Reservation," *SJR*, 30 June 1938, 1; Josephine Pehrson, "Mercy Work among the Navajos," *SJR*, 10 November 1949, 6; "T-B Spreads among Indians," *SJR*, 14 May 1953, 4; "San Juan County Has Highest TB Rate in Utah; Seals Go Out," *SJR*, 13 November 1959, 1; "Operation 'Trackdown' to Fight TB," *SJR*, 6 May 1960, 1; "Survey Shows T.B. Common Cause of Indian Deaths," *SJR*, 18 March 1964, 8.

33. "Health Workers Winning Fight on TB in Navajoland," *SJR*, Part I, 30 March 1978, 12, and Part II, 6 April 1978, 11.

34. Nell Murbarger, "White Man's Medicine in Monument Valley," *Desert Magazine* 21, no. 7 (July 1958): 5–10; Catherine Pickett, interview with Daniel Kelly, 11 July 1972, Southeastern Utah Oral History Project, California State University–Fullerton, 5–6. Harry Goulding can take much of the credit for the hospital in Monument Valley, because he provided both land and encouragement for the initial start of the facility.

35. Cleal Bradford, executive director, UNDC, interview with author, 22 June 1994.

36. "Annual Report of the Utah Navajo Development Council—1978–83," on file at UNDC's main office, Bluff, Utah.

37. Ibid.

38. Ibid., 10.

39. Platte D. Lyman, "Journal," Special Collections, Brigham Young University Library, 18, 26; Kumen Jones, "Writings," Special Collections, Brigham Young University Library, 213.

40. Harold Muhlestein and Fay Muhlestein, *Monticello Journal: A History of Monticello Until 1937* (Self-published, 1988), 22, 27, 47, 62, 74.

41. Lyman, *History,* 26–27.

42. "History Recalls Growth of Schools Throughout Years," *SJR*, 7 December 1961, 7; "Early San Juan Educating a Rewarding Challenge," *SJR*, 9 September 1962, 4; "San Juan Schools Are Flourishing," *San Juan Blade*, 9 November 1917, 1.

43. "Prof. Hall's Verdict on San Juan's Schools," *San Juan Blade,* 30 November 1917, 6.

44. "Early San Juan Educating a Rewarding Challenge," *SJR*, 9 September 1982, 4; see also *Blue Mountain Shadows* 9 (Winter 1991).

45. Muhlestein and Muhlestein, *Monticello Journal*, 191; see also "Education," *San Juan County, Utah*, ed. Allan Kent Powell (Salt Lake City: Utah State Historical Society, 1983), 307–52.

46. "Mass Meeting Held Protesting Action of School Board," *SJR*, 20 April 1944, 1; "Citizens Committee Meets with School Board to Present Plea and Petition," *SJR*, 4 May 1944, 1.

47. Reed A. Morrill, "San Juan School District Survey, 1958," Special Collections, Brigham Young University Library, 1.

48. "Rags to Riches," *SJR*, 14 August 1959, 1.

49. "Teacher Survey in SJ District Is Encouraging," *SJR*, 28 December 1961, 6; "$300 Plus Raise Contained in New Teacher Salary Schedule," *SJR*, 25 April 1963, 1.

50. Kitty At'iinni interview with Fern Charley and Dean Sundberg, 13 July 1977, OH 1224 Utah State Historical Society and California State University–Fullerton Oral History Program, Southeastern Utah Project, 8.

51. See K. C. Benedict, "Education and the Navajo Mountain Community," *Blue Mountain Shadows* 9 (Winter 1991): 62–68.

52. See Murbarger, "White Man's Medicine," 8–9; H. Baxter Liebler, *Boil My Heart for Me* (New York: Exposition Press, 1969).

53. See Ryan Roberts and Jenny Hurst, "Indian Education," and Jami Bayles, "The Blanding Ute Dormitory," both in *Blue Mountain Shadows* 9 (Winter 1991): 69–79.

54. Lyman, *History*, 32–36.

55. Kent D. Tibbits, "A Study of Parental Factors Affecting Success or Failure of Navajo Indian Students," M.A. thesis, University of Utah, 1969, 25.

56. Larry Rodgers, *1990 Census—Population and Housing Characteristics of the Navajo Nation* (Scottsdale, Ariz.: The Printing Company, 1993), 48.

57.57 *Sinajini v. Board of Education* case materials on file at DNA Office, Mexican Hat, Utah.

58. Ibid., "Agreement of Parties," Civil Number C–74–346, 7.

59. Ibid., 2.

60. Annual statistics available from Admissions Office, College of Eastern Utah Campus, Price, Utah. These figures were derived by adding up the number of students attending four quarters in 1978 and 1993 and do not necessarily mean that the totals represent all different students.

13

Faiths of the Land

RELIGIOUS EXPRESSION
IN SAN JUAN COUNTY

The land in southeastern Utah has served as an important element in many different people's religions. Anasazi, Ute, Navajo, Mormon, Catholic, Episcopalian, and other branches of Christianity have all sunk their roots deeply into the soil and traditions of this area. This is not to suggest that the major beliefs of each of these groups have been subverted from their main doctrine, only that they have been added to. The focus of this chapter will be on how religious perception has affected the people and their actions in relation to what they have experienced in San Juan County.

The first of these known groups was the Archaic hunters and gatherers, who left behind in their pictographs and petroglyphs an eerie, shamanistic-type of art filled with anthropomorphic forms. Ghostlike figures, animals, and lines in undulating patterns appear to indicate connections with the supernatural in a dream world beyond physical reality. Panels of these anthropomorphic forms march across rockfaces at sites along the San Juan River, at Green Mask ruin in Grand Gulch, and in the Needles District of Canyonlands to remind others of a religious belief long since forgotten.[1]

The Anasazi were the next to leave evidence of their spiritual outlook. Through ethnographic comparison with living puebloan cultures coupled with material remains and ruins, archaeologists believe that religion played a central role in the daily life of the Anasazi. The proliferation of small kivas with their sipapus; the great kivas at Rincon, Edge of the Cedars, and Cottonwood Wash; a series of ceremonial roads stretching from the San Juan River into the interior; paintings and carvings on rock surfaces; surviving medicine pouches, tablitas, and the enigmatic Tchamahias (a hoe-shaped rock blade) all speak of a vital religious life, including ceremonial cycles to ensure rain, crops, and interaction with supernatural beings. Even explanations of the Anasazi's departure from this region—often interpreted as caused by drought, arroyo cutting, enemy depredation, or social dysfunction—appear in the myths and teachings from other tribal memories. The Hopis indicate that supernatural beings or problems forced the abandonment of many Anasazi ruins in the Four Corners region. Only through purifying migrations could the problems be solved, akin to Moses and the children of Israel wandering in the desert for forty years until cleansed of their wrongs.[2] Clan migration stories of the Hopi and Zuni include claims to geographical features in San Juan County as part of their spiritual heritage.

The interaction with the land by the Utes also spoke of deep religious ties. Though not as well documented as some historic groups, the Utes placed names and endowed the land and its creatures with spirituality. Blue Mountain, Standing-Alone-Mountain (Navajo Mountain), and the La Sals have all been identified as Ute places of worship. Sleeping Ute Mountain near Cortez, Colorado, is said to be one of seven giants who protected the Utes from other tribes' gods during the times of the myths. He grew tired, fell into a deep sleep, and there he will remain until he is again needed.

Spiritual beings also reside on the mesas and in the canyons to either hide or show deer and elk to hunters who have prepared themselves through ritual. If these little people are seen, the individual must leave a blanket, food, or some other useful object and then depart. By saying nothing about such an incident, the person is guaranteed good fortune in the future. Utes also held healing rites in what

The Ute Bear Dance is traditionally performed in the spring. Believed to be the only dance to have originated from the Utes, it served as a social gathering at which marriage partners could be selected, and plans for different family groups determined for the following seasons. (San Juan Historical Commission)

is now called Babylon Pasture, Peavine Canyon, and on the Bears Ears, because of the supernatural power invested in the landscape.[3]

The Bear Dance plays an important part in the social and religious life of the Utes. They perform the dance in the spring to symbolically help the animals awaken from hibernation, thus strengthening the relationship between humans and this supernaturally powerful creature. The brush circle in which the dance is performed is constructed of cottonwood limbs, juniper boughs, and sagebrush and is called "cave of sticks." The structure opens to the east and represents a bear's den, and the rasping sound of a wooden stick dragged across another serrated stick represents the noises of a bear.

The Sun Dance, though not of Ute origin, embodies many important teachings derived from supernatural beings. As with the

Bear Dance, it is held in a cottonwood-and-brush enclosure that opens to the east. In the center is a large, erect pole with four attached scarves—red to represent the earth, yellow for the sun, white for daylight, and black for darkness—all of which are offerings to the four directions. Before dancing, the men go to a sacred spot where they fast for four days to determine if the gods have selected them. If a man dreams three times about participating, then he has a special purpose in life to fulfill and will be attended by his guardian spirit. If the supernatural beings are pleased with the sacrifice, the power derived from the performance insures that food will be plentiful and that the sick and afflicted will be healed.[4]

Power, prayers, and protection are also major elements in Navajo beliefs. The complexity of the stories, symbols, and rituals are intricately intertwined and extend far beyond the boundaries of San Juan County, but even in this most northerly part of the reservation, there resides a rich body of lore.[5]

The heart and soul of Navajo beliefs centers on the four sacred mountains—Blanca Peak, Colorado; Mount Taylor, New Mexico; San Francisco Peaks, Arizona; and Hesperus Peak, Colorado. Everything that lies within their boundaries and those established by the four sacred rivers—San Juan, Colorado, Little Colorado, and Rio Grande—is protected and blessed by the holy beings.

The values associated with these formations pervade Navajo life. In every ceremony the powers of mountains and their deities are invoked to render aid in healing the sick, protecting the people and their wealth, bringing rain for crops and livestock, and insuring tranquillity in life. The traditional wedding basket, woven blankets, silverwork, and the tribal seal repeat this central mountain motif.

But what of those mountains in or near southeastern Utah that are not among the four most sacred ones? Navajo Mountain, for instance, is viewed as part of a female anthropomorphic figure that ties in land formations extending across three states. The head of this female is Navajo Mountain, her body Black Mesa, and her feet Balukai Mesa; she grasps a wool twiner, El Capitan, in her fist. The entire formation is known as Pollen Mountain. Her partner, a male, is identified as Goods of Value Mountain, whose head is Chuska Peak, or Tohatchi Mountain, his body the Chuska-Tunicha range, and his lower extremities the Carrizo Mountains. His feet are located at Beautiful Mountain, New Mexico. He holds in one hand a bow or sacred medicine pouch, which is Shiprock.[6]

Blue Mountain is called Furry Mountain by the Navajo. It is a female, with its paired male, the La Sals, to the north. Both ranges are noted for their curative plants. A medicine man explains, "It has sat there since the beginning of time with medicine. When the Navajo are going to have a ceremony, they always go over there . . . for cedar and yucca plants of various sizes."[7] A number of Navajos indicated that Blue Mountain produced a good breed of horses because of the horsehead figure made by trees on the east slope. This male figure is matched by a female horsehead on the west slope, though no specific location for this creature is given. Many mention that Blue Mountain is a good place to hunt deer, while, according to mythology, Black God covered Blue Mountain with elk.[8]

Rock formations are also sacred places of power in which spirits reside; Valley of the Gods is one such place. These imposing monoliths are seen as Navajo warriors frozen in stone who can be appealed to for protection. They are guardians whose power and strength aids young men going to war. When one places a mixture of sacred materials at their base, the spirit inside is pleased and provides supernatural aid to the one whose name is mentioned or whose voice is heard in prayer. People are cautioned against climbing on these rocks so as not to offend the holy beings, since "one does not know to which clan or tribe these frozen warriors belong."[9]

To the southeast lies "Valley in the Rocks," or "Treeless Area amid the Rocks," called by white men Monument Valley. Various explanations exist about the De Chelly sandstone monoliths that cover this area. There is a wide range of sites and stories; for example, some say the large monuments are barrels or pots that store water. The seeps at their bases exist for the people's use. Rain God Mesa has four springs located at its foot in the four cardinal directions, so medicine men collect water there for ceremonies associated with healing and rainmaking. Places where streamers of desert varnish mark the path of water over the edge of rocks are also used for healing purpose.[10]

Nearby stands Totem Pole Rock, a frozen ye'ii, or god, held up by lightning. Because people have climbed on it, the spirit has been offended and, as a result, there now is not as much rain in Monument Valley as there used to be. The rock is also said to be symbolized by the dancing feathers used in the Mountainway ceremony. Underneath is the home of the hadahoniye (mirage) people, who have powers to bless and bring wealth to those who leave offerings there.[11]

One of the most photographed landmarks in Monument Valley is the Mittens, two hands that lie dormant, left behind by the gods as a sign of great power. Some day the holy beings will return and rule from this place. Not far away is Eagle Mesa, a sacred site where the spirit of a dead person may go after burial. One can hear the voices of babies and adults in this area and can see bones and footprints on the mesa.[12]

The beliefs associated with these rock formations and mountains can be multiplied hundreds of times over as many square miles in southeastern Utah, northwestern New Mexico, and northeastern Arizona. Similar attitudes of reverence exist for rivers, springs, and standing bodies of water, the animals that roam over the land, the various elements of weather, and the vegetation of both mountain and desert. The Navajo live in a world recognized as a spiritual creation. Everything has a spirit, is male or female, controls a power, teaches a lesson, deserves respect, and holds a place in the universe. Thus, the land for the Navajo contains a vast array of supernatural beings who serve as guides in surviving the trials of life.

Though Native American religions have deep ties to the land through the myths and holy beings associated with it, Christian denominations would appear not to have those same links.[13] Yet to suggest this in the case of Mormonism would be to say that there is no diversity, no local stories, and no belief that God expects his Saints to reside upon this land. Anyone familiar with Mormonism in San Juan knows this just is not true. From the time of its introduction in San Juan County, the LDS church has fostered the belief that it has an important religious work to do in the land and to ignore that is to risk invoking divine displeasure.

For instance, Kumen Jones, a member of the initial exploring party preceding the Hole-in-the-Rock expedition, told of a dream he had in December 1878 before being called to serve. He saw himself among Indians and white men, most of whom were strangers, but all

of whom were building a large stone structure. Nearby was a river
with muddy water. When he awoke, he asked his mother what it all
meant, and she without hesitation said, "You will be called with others to go and live among the Indians."[14] And that is exactly what
Kumen did in Bluff and then Blanding for most of his life.

Other Latter-day Saints had similar feelings of obeying divine
will. A dream warned James Davis that he would live in the "Arizona
country." Jens Nielson, leader of the San Juan settlers, expressed a
firm conviction underlying his mission call when he said, "It is the
voice of the Lord to me to go and I am going by the help of the
Almighty."[15] And once the settlers had spent a few discouraging years
fighting the San Juan River, Mormon leaders George Smith and
Erastus Snow visited the people of Bluff and pronounced a blessing,
saying, "I promise those who are willing to remain and face this difficult situation that they will be doubly blessed by the Lord." According
to Nielson, "the above prophecy and promise came to pass every
whit."[16]

Perhaps the greatest recorder of spiritual experiences and promoter of the idea of a divinely inspired San Juan mission, especially
to work with Indians, was Albert R. Lyman, a prolific early historian
and church leader. His writings are filled with a righteous certainty
that God has taken a special interest in the county and its people—
both Indian and white—and that when they are in tune with His will,
they will prosper. In 1955 Lyman wrote a brief history of Blanding,
in which he described the role his uncle Walter C. Lyman played in
bringing the Lord's desires to pass. Reminiscent of Puritan theology,
Lyman wrote of the town:

> In the kind providence of the Lord, places had been preparing
> for these homeless refugees, and this was one of those places. The
> Lord had the welfare of these people in mind when in 1897, He
> fired us with desire to begin a town in the wilderness. To me it was
> all very wonderful, for I saw it not at all as the unbelieving and
> indifferent outside saw it; to me it was plainly the farseeing hand
> of Providence.[17]

In almost everything that Lyman wrote, he referred to the San
Juan Mission and its major goal of proselyting to and serving the

Indians. Later, when the days of pioneering were long gone, he still believed that the people had "never once been released nor changed from that status." He went on to say that Mormons were to set the example, that their responsibility was "inseparably connected" with missionary work, and that they would "fail their great purpose if they hinder this work or shirk their responsibility in it."[18] Even the LDS placement program, which sent Navajo children out of the county and, in some instances, out of the state, was considered an aid in fulfilling prophecy.

How successfully, then, has this Mormon mission been fulfilled? By 1882 the initial mission included not only Bluff but also San Luis and Mancos, Colorado; Burnham (Fruitland), New Mexico; and Moab, Utah—with Platte D. Lyman as the first stake president.[19] The record is not clear when those branches and wards outside of Utah were established in their own stakes (though it was probably in the late 1890s or early 1900s); but, during that time, church authorities insisted that the controlling power remain in southeastern Utah. When stake president Francis Hammond once again importuned church authorities to shift the pioneering emphasis away from Bluff to a more desirable location outside of Utah, newly appointed church president Wilford Woodruff reminded Hammond:

> You, yourself, understand how important it is that we should maintain the political control of that county; but if settlements are made in New Mexico or in Colorado instead of in San Juan County, the object in having them go to that region is not answered. Mancos may be a good point in some respects, but it is not the place we want to build up at present as it is in the State of Colorado, and the impression prevails among the brethren who are familiar with the country that there is danger of our folks being outnumbered there and being compelled to move sooner or later.[20]

And so the stake in southeastern Utah grew. A quick survey of facts and figures shows that as towns and communities developed, Mormonism became entrenched as the dominant religion, giving the county to those within and without a distinctive LDS tinge. In 1882 Bluff Ward and the Montezuma Creek Branch boasted thirty-two male tithe payers contributing a total of $760 for the year. Around

The first chapel in Blanding, built 1908–1909. Prior to its construction, LDS meetings had been held in tents and private homes. (San Juan Historical Commission)

this same time, the Bluff Ward selected Kumen Jones and Thales Haskel as special missionaries to its Native American neighbors. Six years later, the town formed its first Relief Society while sending out a feeler in the form of the Blue Mountain Mission to establish present-day Monticello. In 1894 the Monticello Branch became a ward; in 1905, Grayson became a branch of the Bluff Ward, and three years later it became an independent ward.[21] By 1955 Blanding housed two wards and an LDS Indian branch; it also had sent out 125 missionaries to the far corners of the earth.[22] In 1993 there was one stake with four wards in Monticello, with branches in La Sal, Eastland, and Paradox; there were two stakes in Blanding, with eight wards, a ward in Montezuma Creek, and branches in White Mesa (Ute), and Bluff and Mexican Hat (Navajo). Though the Church of

Jesus Christ of Latter-day Saints is still the predominant religion, less than half of the population (5,261) in San Juan County currently belongs to this faith.[23]

The largest single infusion of Mormons in the county other than the Hole-in-the-Rock expedition started shortly after the turn of the twentieth century when families from the polygamous settlements of colonias Diaz, Dublan, Juarez, Pacheco, Garcia, and Chuichupa experienced threats aligned with force to remove them from Mexico. For more than twenty years these Mormons had found sanctuary from the turmoil surrounding polygamy and were now enjoying economic prosperity. But when their farms and fields came under the scrutiny of land-hungry peasants and the Mexican government, many Mormons packed their belongings and trudged north across the border. From there they fanned out to various locations, taking advantage of new homesteading laws and other inducements.[24]

The first settlers from Mexico came to San Juan in 1906, with the major influx occurring between 1912 and 1918.[25] Many took a circuitous route, living elsewhere until they could accumulate enough wealth to continue their move to greener pastures. Blanding attracted most of the newcomers, with an estimated sixty-four families of around 600 people.[26] Initially, they were well accepted and settled unoccupied lands on the outskirts of town.

As time wore on, friction between the "Hole-in-the-Rockers" and the "Pachecoites" festered beneath the calm social surface of the rural community. To some people, the generic term "Pachecoites" not only signified that individuals had come from Old Mexico but also that they were somehow impoverished and inferior. Riley Hurst remembered how baseball teams accentuated these rivalries, as each group sponsored its champions to show who was best.[27] Albert R. Lyman recalled how church leaders had prophesied before the exodus from Mexico that Blanding would receive a large influx of settlers from places "you have never heard" of, that the town would prosper from the skills and work of these people, and that, if the citizens of Blanding failed to harmoniously keep the commandments, the rain and irrigation water would cease to be abundant.[28] Subsequent droughts were blamed by some people upon God's anger over local

Construction of the Monticello LDS church building began in 1905 and was completed in 1912. It replaced the first log church completed in 1888. (San Juan Historical Commission)

jealousy, friction, and unrighteousness, a common theme in the Book of Mormon.

Evidence of this friction is found in the *San Juan Blade* in 1917, when it referred to men who volunteered for the army during World War I. The paper listed twelve recruits, ten of whom were Pachecoites, and then went on to editorialize that "for those who still wonder whether the refugees from Mexico are really loyal to Uncle Sam, here is evidence they should consider. If in addition to this, they take into account the widowed mothers of three of these boys, and the straited [*sic*] circumstances of parents of others, the evidence must be regarded as conclusive."[29] For the most part, it took a full generation to quiet some of this subtle and not-so-subtle animosity.

While the Mormons expanded their communities throughout San Juan County, other Christian denominations quietly arrived to practice their faith. Catholicism appeared with Hispanic herders and their families who came from New Mexico to work as ranch hands in the last decade of the nineteenth and early decades of the twentieth century. Many of the Hispanicized Catholic practices found throughout the Southwest were transported to Monticello, where a small Spanish community flourished. Infant baptism, selection of godparents, different marriage practices, all-night chanting at funerals, and Christmas pageantry were strange sights to see for the Mormons.[30]

Although friendship and respect existed between the two communities, separation characterized their general relationship.

As in other religions, many of these early Hispanic Catholics believed their faith helped them as they interacted with the land. For instance, the Feast of Saint John, held on 24 June, ushered in the time when children could go swimming in the ponds and streams around Monticello, because this was the date that John had baptized Jesus. Water for the crops was also said to be sweeter and more plentiful after this feast. The Feast of San Lorenzo was on 19 August and was a time when the threshing of wheat took place. The workers chanted the short prayer, "Send us a breeze, send us a breeze, Saint Lawrence of the Golden Beard," in order to have the necessary wind to separate the wheat from the chaff. One man reportedly became frustrated when the saint did not hear his plea and shouted, "A breeze, a breeze, Saint Lawrence, beard of a he-goat," and was cursed with a large windstorm that whisked his harvest away.[31] In December, when the visit of the Christ Child was imminent, the Catholic townspeople lit candles that lined the walkways, so that the Savior's feet would be guided to the homes of the righteous. Thus, the daily life of the Spanish community in Monticello was marked with constant reminders of the sacredness of life.

As early as 1917, parishioners tried to obtain a building for the Catholic community, but not until 1935 was St. Joseph's Church in Monticello dedicated.[32] Before that time, most religious activities were held in private homes. The very personal and family-oriented nature of many of the practices did not seem to suffer in intensity because of a lack of facilities or interaction with other religions. As the number of Hispanics dwindled during World War II and again after the closing of the vanadium mill in 1960, so too did the practicing Catholic community. Today, the membership enrollment in Saint Joseph's parish numbers about sixty families.

At one time or another, the people of San Juan have enjoyed the fellowship of members of many different Christian denominations, including Baptist, Methodist, Jehovah's Witness, Assembly of God, Episcopalian, and various Bible-oriented fundamentalists not part of a local organization. Space does not allow discussion of all of these faiths, but only a representative sampling.

Take, for instance, the San Juan Community Church in
Monticello, which illustrates the problems, compromises, and suc-
cesses presented by a small number of diverse faiths spread over a
large geographical area. As early as 1918, a Baptist minister from
Moab came to San Juan to see how practical it would be to unite a
variety of Christian groups under one minister; however, he soon
abandoned the effort. The 1920s and 1930s saw similar short-term
efforts by community volunteers, Presbyterian and Baptist ministers,
members of the Salvation Army, and an itinerant preacher from
Colorado—all trying to bring under one umbrella a diverse number
of Christian faiths. Finally, on 20 October 1940, Baptist minister W. E.
Parks, whose area of service stretched from Grand Junction,
Colorado, through Moab to Monticello, enlisted sixty people from
the county in the establishment of the San Juan Community Church.
The meeting drew people from Horse Head, Ucolo, Monticello,
Boulder, South Canyon Point, Ginger Hill, and Moab—all of whom
agreed upon the desirability of uniting for an interdenominational
Christian experience.[33] Two years later, another minister took Rev.
Parks's place.

The congregation next faced the problem of where to hold its
meetings. The earliest gatherings were in the homes of parishioners
until the group received donated office space provided by the
Vanadium Corporation of America; when that was no longer available, Marie Ogden, who had her own religious faith, provided the
"Ogden building" on Main Street. In 1948 the church started construction on a meeting place, only to suffer a setback when half the
building burned a year later. Soon, through donations and fund-
raising efforts, the meetinghouse was completed and dedicated in
1950. Besides Sunday morning services in Monticello, there was an
evening service for those who worked during normal church hours,
weekday programs for school-aged children and adults, seasonal
pageants, scheduled services in Ucolo, Boulder, and Horsehead, and
the regular visitation of members in 119 homes in the county.[34]

A survey in May 1943 indicated that there were sixteen different
denominations spread among 141 men, women, and children living
within the area; there were another 155 who claimed no membership
in any church, 125 Catholics, and "well over 600" Mormons.[35] All of

Marie Ogden, a native of New Jersey, came with thirty followers to Dry Valley in San Juan County to establish the Home of Truth. (San Juan Historical Commission)

these groups appear to have cooperated with each other. When the San Juan Community Church burned while still under construction, people from Dove Creek, Cortez, and Salt Lake City, as well as many local LDS people and parishioners, provided substantial donations. One newspaper article commented on this cooperation; the writer gave thanks for the "astounding results" of the community fund drive and in the next breath mentioned that the Monticello Ward would soon be doing some building and hoped it would receive the "same enthusiastic response and support that the other church enjoyed."[36]

Approximately fifteen miles down the road, a far different story had unfolded. The Home of Truth, located at Photograph Gap in Dry Valley, was the creation of Marie Ogden. She, like the Mormons, believed that spiritual forces and "destiny" had guided her from New Jersey to San Juan County to establish her commune. Initially, she received "a description and a mental picture of the place and knew it was on virgin soil, far removed from city life," and in the "inter-mountain country." Following a fruitless visit to Idaho, she returned to New Jersey only to receive a letter from a friend who dreamed of a barren land with the word "Utah" above it. Ogden, with the help of some associates, heard of available land in San Juan County, and, after living for a time in Recapture Canyon and near Camp Jackson, visited the area around Church Rock on Highway 191 and knew this was the place she should settle.[37]

Her Home of Truth started with twenty-one followers, swelled to around 100 during its height in 1934–35, and by 1949 had dwindled to eight people. Those who came embraced her teachings and "messages" or revelations received from God in preparation for the fulfillment of Bible prophecy concerning the end of the world. Marie Ogden's prolific writings, her connections with similar groups and individuals throughout the United States, her tight-fisted control of activities within the communal setting, and her ability to interpret the signs of the time through a spiritual medium all speak of a complex personality and vibrant intellect. At a time when women held few significant leadership positions, she enjoyed administrative power over those who joined her commune. After many of her disciples departed, she remained with a handful of the faithful to ponder the signs of the times, operate the *San Juan Record* newspaper, and eke out a bare existence in Dry Valley until old age and their economic situation forced the survivors to move from their sanctuary.[38]

Although religious cults can spring up in many different environments for many different reasons, Marie Ogden chose San Juan County because of her belief that it would serve as a refuge during the cataclysmic last days of the earth. She located her home on what she considered the axis of the earth, a place of safety when "the final catastrophe in the form of the 'great earthquake' will put an end to warfare for all time and will produce that time of great isolation . . . when those who are left on the earth will lose contact with each other for a time and when we who will be in this intermountain country will be able to prove many things. "[39]

Before all of this happened, however, Ogden had to prepare a community to receive the Savior when He came. His first appearance reportedly was going to be on Church Rock.[40] Dry Valley was ideal because the desert was a place where "spiritual strength and courage and renewed faith in the ultimate survival of that which is good and right" could be obtained.[41] Ogden had seen each building in her sagebrush community through a vision, picturing it in its paradisaical glory "beautiful beyond words to express . . . when water will flow through our valley."[42] She established structures in various locations along the road leading to the heart of the community—her home— and named these outlying buildings the Outer Portal and the Inner Portal, respectively. The land was thus imbued with a religious significance—as it was for other religions in San Juan—in that it tied deity and a divine plan through an intense religious experience to those living on the land.

The land and its people affected in a different manner a young Episcopalian minister from Greenwich, Connecticut, who was visiting the area in the summer of 1942. Reverend H. Baxter Liebler stood on the banks of the San Juan River and declared on behalf of the Navajos, "God has brought me here to realize the need of these people. . . . A mission here could perform miracles. I'll build one."[43] A year later he was back with a party of missionaries, searching for a place to start his work. Two miles outside of Bluff he established the Saint Christopher's Mission, not as a bastion of white civilization to change his parishioners but as a meeting point between cultures where one could "learn from the Navajo all the lore and wisdom which will enable them to live simply in this country."[44] Even plans

for the projected chapel reflected "conformity with Navajo practices
... [so as not to] violate the taboos of Navajo lore."

Reverend Liebler kept his word. In fact, some of the local white
people believed that the Navajos had, in part, converted him. He
enjoyed his Navajo name, "The-One-Who-Drags-His-Robe," and
wore his hair in the traditional Navajo bun as a symbol that showed
acceptance of Navajo values.[45] In the summer he held services outside
in a cottonwood shade, while in the winter the home-grown chapel,
constructed from logs and rocks and other local materials, was built
in the form of a cross, with rugs covering the altar and other Navajo
paraphernalia decorating the interior.

Liebler learned the Navajo language, conducting high mass in
both English and Navajo. Next to the altar stood a statue of the Virgin
Mary with brown skin, hair bun, and traditional Navajo clothing,
holding the baby Jesus wrapped in a cradleboard.[46] Music accompa-
nying the service was of Native American origin—the Kyrie set to a
Hopi snake dance melody, the Sanctus and Benedictus based on an
Omaha tune, Agnus Dei incorporating a Zuni song, and part of the
Navajo Night Chant used intermittently with prayers.

Following the conclusion of a service, Liebler occasionally would
do a sandpainting based on a Christian theme and accompanied by
song. He did one reported drawing shortly after the Normandy invasion during World War II and dedicated it to the soldiers participating in the liberation of France, calling its creation an act of prayer.
Participants described the sandpainting as showing "symbolically our
Saviour on the Cross and under him the eucharistic bread and chalice. From the wounds in the Saviour's hands and feet and side were
drawn life-lines to the host and chalice, indicating that from the sac-
rificial death and blood-shedding of Christ on the Cross flow life-
giving sacraments of the Gospel."[47] Shortly after the completion of
the sandpainting, a drenching downpour arrived in the area, con-
vincing the Navajos that the priest held strong supernatural powers
beneficial to his people.

Five years after his arrival, Reverend Liebler could assert that
much of his dream was fulfilled. The mission not only boasted a
church, vicarage, and school but also provided medical services (an
official clinic was completed in 1956) and a meeting hall for com-

H. Baxter Liebler, Episcopalian priest and founder of Saint Christopher's Mission in Bluff, serves the sacrament in a self-made wooden church. Father Liebler was very sympathetic to Navajo values, mixing Christian doctrine with traditional Navajo ceremonial practices. He held services in Bluff, Montezuma Creek, Oljato, and Navajo Mountain. (Courtesy Baxter Benally)

munity life. The site became a focal point for Navajo activities north of the river, as Liebler became a trusted spokesman and advocate for everything from attempts to expand reservation lands to helping Native Americans understand a new tuberculosis vaccination program.[48] The success of the mission was reflected in the success of its twentieth anniversary celebration when an estimated 2,000 people convened for the day's activities of races, Navajo dancing, craft contests, and the eating of a 150-pound cake, all to the accompaniment of the Navajo Tribal band from Window Rock.[49] By the time Liebler left St. Christopher's Mission, 5,000 people had claimed membership in his parish over a twenty-year period.[50]

In June 1962 Reverend Liebler officially retired, although he actually stayed on as an adviser for four years and then changed locations. He next went to Oljato and founded Saint Mary of the Moonlight Water, where he lived until his death in 1983.[51] His legacy survived his passing. Today there are three Episcopalian churches—Saint Christopher's, Saint Mary, and Saint John the Baptizer (Montezuma Creek)—with a combined membership of 1,500 on the rolls. Presiding over them at present is Steven T. Plummer, ordained in 1990 as the first Navajo Episcopalian bishop in the history of the church.[52] He lives at Saint Christopher's, walking on the paths that Liebler blazed.

While Reverend Liebler was modifying Episcopalian beliefs to fit with traditional Navajo culture, the Native American Church was also making inroads on the reservation by offering a system of more generalized Indian teachings. As part of the Pan-Indian movement, the Native American Church has its roots in Kiowa and Commanche tribal practices of the late nineteenth century. These Plains tribes provided the tepee, feather fan, drum, waterfowl, crescent-shaped altar, fire, and poker as standardized symbols of this church, while peyote, a hallucinogenic cactus button common in Mexico, became the driving force within the ceremony. It provided the means through which God and his powers could be made manifest to the participants involved in all-night ceremonies.[53]

The Native American Church entered San Juan County from Oklahoma via the Ute Mountain Ute Reservation. Two anthropologists, David F. Aberle and Omer C. Stewart, conducted an extremely detailed study of this phenomenon between 1946 and 1951 and identified four phases of development of these beliefs in the northern part of the Navajo reservation.[54] They concluded that Towaoc Utes introduced the practices in the Mancos Creek and Aneth area, followed by a second phase where Navajos working alongside Utes in the Civilian Conservation Corps, as well as others traveling to Towaoc for curing rites, encountered Native American Church practices. These phases encompass the years between 1914 and 1938. Starting in 1936, peyote priests, or "Road Chiefs," next started visiting reservation communities south of the San Juan River, so that by 1951 there was an open flow of religious leaders from Oklahoma, Towaoc, and the Mancos/Aneth area throughout San Juan County. Aberle and Stewart inferred that more than half of the population in certain districts, which include Aneth, Montezuma Creek, and the region south of Bluff, were practitioners in the Native American Church by this time.[55] It remains still one of the fastest growing denominations on the reservation today, with an estimated fifty percent of the tribe subscribing to its tenets.[56]

According to Aberle, there are also differences between the practices of members in the northern part of the reservation, which includes Utah, and those living in the south. The northerners emphasize the mystical, magical power of peyote. Revelation, insight, and good fortune through divine intervention are all some of the fruits of this faith. Although many elements of Christian doctrine are entwined in the ceremony, strong antiwhite sentiments are also characteristic of this northern orientation. Aberle believes the more aggressive nature in the north fits a pattern of confrontation that has historically characterized white-Navajo relations.

Navajos living in the southern part of the reservation tend to be more contemplative and less expectant of revelation. A belief that hard work is necessary for success, a greater emphasis on the "teachings" of peyote, and less antiwhite sentiment also characterize these southern views. Because of their more peaceful nature, sometimes members are accused by northerners of being "half-white." Again, historically, the southern part of the reservation, according to Aberle, has enjoyed more peaceful relations, even during such periods as livestock reduction.[57]

In summarizing the variety of religious expression in San Juan County, one is struck by the complexity, beauty, and diversity of thought. Each of the faiths has a much longer story to be told, yet a thread that passes through each of them, either tangentially or through the core, is the land. Whether one looks at the Navajos and Utes visiting sacred sites, the Mormons traveling through the Hole-in-the-Rock, the Hispanics blessing the waters of Monticello, Marie Ogden waiting for the Savior to appear, Reverend Liebler creating a Christian sandpainting, or a Road Chief worshipping with his neighbors in Aneth, one cannot help but feel that the land has encouraged a deep spirituality played out in many forms. The county's size alone has created the need for compromise and cooperation, as in the San Juan Community Church. Yet, despite the ethnic diversity, the geographical dimensions, or the predominant social orientation, people of San Juan County have generally shown restraint and tolerance for others' beliefs—an important accomplishment for any mix of neighbors.

ENDNOTES

1. See Sally J. Cole, *Legacy on Stone: Rock Art of the Colorado Plateau* (Boulder: Johnson Books, 1990), 42–108.

2. See Harold Courlander, *The Fourth World of the Hopis* (Greenwich, Conn.: Fawcett Premier, 1971); Frank Waters and Oswald White Bear, *The Book of the Hopi* (New York: Viking Press, 1963); and Charlie R. Steen, "The San Juan Anasazi in the 13th Century," in *Proceedings of the Anasazi Symposium–1981* (Mesa Verde National Park: Mesa Verde Museum Association), 169–73, for an explanation of clan formation and migration due to religious reasons.

3. Carla Knight, "The Utes and Their Environment," unpublished paper, used with permission, in possession of author.

4. Mary Jane Yazzie, "Life and Traditions of the Utes of Avikan," unpublished manuscript, used with permission, in possession of author.

5. For a more complete explanation of Navajo sacred geography see Robert S. McPherson, *Sacred Land, Sacred View: Navajo Perceptions of the Four Corners Region* (Provo: Brigham Young University Press, 1992).

6. Editha L. Watson, *Navajo Sacred Places* (Window Rock, Ariz.: Navajo Tribal Museum, 1964), 9; Charlie Blueeyes, interview with Robert S. McPherson and Baxter Benally, 28 August 1988, manuscript in possession of author; Stephen Jett, "Preliminary Statement Respecting the San Francisco Peaks as a Sacred Place" (n.p.), in possession of author, 11–12.

7. Slim Benally interview with Robert S. McPherson and Baxter Benally, 8 July 1988, manuscript in possession of author.

8. Ibid.; Mary Jim interview with Robert S. McPherson and Baxter Benally, 7 June 1988; Hashk'aan Begay interview with Robert S. McPherson and Baxter Benally, 1 July 1988; Tallis Holiday interview with Robert S. McPherson and Jessie Holiday, 3 November 1987, manuscripts in possession of author; Curly Toaxedlini, as cited in Karl Luckert, *The Navajo Hunter Tradition* (Tucson: University of Arizona Press, 1975), 94.

9. Billy Yellow interview with Robert S. McPherson and Evelyn Yellow, 6 November 1987; Martha Nez interview with Robert S. McPherson and Baxter Benally, 2 August 1988, manuscripts in possession of author.

10. Editha L. Watson, essay presented 17 March 1968, Doris Duke Oral History Project no. 796, Special Collections, University of Utah Library, 18; Richard F. Van Valkenburgh, *Dine Bikeyah* (Window Rock, Ariz.: Office of Navajo Service, U. S. Department of the Interior, 1941), 101; Billy Yellow interview; Tallis Holiday interview; Fred Yazzie interview with Robert S. McPherson and Marilyn Holiday, 5 November 1987, manuscript in possession of author.

11. Tallis Holiday interview; Watson, essay, 15.

12. Ibid., 15.

13. For an expanded comparison between Mormon and Navajo beliefs see Robert S. McPherson, *The Northern Navajo Frontier, 1860–1900: Expansion through Adversity* (Albuquerque: University of New Mexico Press, 1988), 21–37.

14. Kumen Jones, "Writing of Kumen Jones," Special Collections, Brigham Young University Library, 140.

15. David E. Miller, *Hole-in-the-Rock* (Salt Lake City: University of Utah Press, 1966), 3, 12.

16. Kumen Jones, "The San Juan Mission to the Indians," Special Collections, Brigham Young University Library, 28.

17. Albert R. Lyman, "History of Blanding, 1905–1955," unpublished transcript, in possession of author.

18. Ibid., 2.

19. Cornelia Perkins, Marian Nielson, and Lenora Jones, *Saga of San Juan* (Salt Lake City: Mercury Publishing Company, 1968), 62.

20. Wilford Woodruff to Francis A. Hammond, 3 October 1887, "Francis A. Hammond Collection," Special Collections, Harold B. Lee Library, Brigham Young University.

21. Albert R. Lyman, "History of San Juan County, 1879–1917,"

unpublished manuscript, Special Collections, Brigham Young University Library, 29, 35, 58, 89, 107.

22. Lyman, "Blanding," 19.

23. Telephone conversation of the author with LDS stake clerks from the Monticello and Blanding stakes on 7 September 1993.

24. Karl Young, "Brief Sanctuary," *The American West* 4, no. 2 (May 1967): 4–11.

25. Lyman, "Blanding," 36.

26. William Riley Hurst telephone conversation with author on 13 September 1993. Finding an exact figure for the number of people in this Mormon migration is difficult because it occurred over a six-year period, was not recorded, and members of this group came and went. Mr. Hurst, a long-time resident of San Juan, was able to reconstruct by name and family a list of community members in Blanding during 1918. He used as his criteria for a family any man who was married before he came to Blanding; four men had two wives and so this constituted eight families because each wife had her own dwelling. Widows who came in alone or with children were also counted as a family.

27. William Riley Hurst interview with Robert S. McPherson, 23 January 1992, manuscript in possession of author; Hurst telephone conversation with author, 16 September 1993; see also Jessie L. Embry, "The Role of LDS Polygamous Families—Blanding: A Case Study," *Blue Mountain Shadows* 1, no. 1 (Fall 1987): 23–27.

28. Albert R. Lyman, "The Old Settler," *San Juan Record* (hereafter cited as *SJR*), 11 November 1971, 2.

29. "13 Volunteers from Blanding," *San Juan Blade* 10 August 1917, 1.

30. For a more complete treatment of Hispanic religious practices in Monticello see William H. Gonzalez and Genaro M. Padilla, "Monticello, the Hispanic Cultural Gateway to Utah," *Utah Historical Quarterly* 52, no. 1 (Winter 1984): 9–28.

31. Ibid., 25–26.

32. "Catholic Church Proposed for Monticello," *San Juan Blade*, 10 August 1917, 1; "Anniversary of Catholic Church in Monticello Celebrated Here," *SJR*, 7 August 1959, 1.

33. "Community Church History," *SJR*, 21 December 1961, 8; "Community Church Organized in San Juan County," *SJR*, 24 October 1940, 1.

34. "San Juan Community Church Opening," *SJR*, 10 September 1942, 1; "Community Church Makes Fine Progress," *SJR*, 1 October 1942, 1; Community Church Progress Noted," *SJR*, 10 December 1942, 1.

35. "Baptists to Observe 60th Anniversary," *SJR*, 13 May 1943, 1.

36. "Community Church History," *SJR*, 21 December 1961, 8; "Community Church Ravaged by Fire," *SJR*, 9 June 1949, 1; "Editorial," *SJR*, 28 July 1949, 4.

37. "Subject Files—San Juan County," no author (most likely Frank Silvey), n.d., Utah State Historical Society, Salt Lake City, Utah.

38. Ruby Bronson interview with Robert S. McPherson, 2 October 1992, transcript in possession of author.

39. Marie Ogden, "Home of Truth Message," 4 August 1942, Utah State Historical Society, Salt Lake City, Utah.

40. Rusty Musselman interview with author, 23 September 1992, manuscript in possession of author.

41. "Editorial," *SJR*, 30 January 1947, 4.

42. Marie Ogden, *Home of Truth Cooperative Settlement*, Booklet 3, 18 February 1941, Utah State Historical Society, Salt Lake City, 14.

43. Marian H. Talmadge and Iris P. Gilmore, "Padre of the San Juan," *Desert Magazine* 11, no. 10 (August 1948): 6.

44. "Missionaries Arrive in Bluff from East," *SJR*, 22 July 1943, 1.

45. For information concerning Rev. Liebler's attempt to mesh Christianity with Navajo traditional beliefs see H. B. Liebler "Christian Concepts and Navaho Words," *Utah Humanities Review*, 2 no. 2 (April 1948): 169–75.

46. Cleal Bradford conversation with author, 24 September 1993.

47. Talmadge and Gilmore, "Padre," 9; "Corpus Christi Day at St. Christopher's," *SJR*, 15 June 1944, 1.

48. "Spotlighting Utah," *SJR*, 26 December 1946, 1; Josephine Pehrson, "Mercy Work among the Navajos," *SJR*, 10 November 1949, 6; for a detailed account of Liebler's activities from 1943 to 1962 see H. Baxter Liebler, *Boil My Heart for Me* (New York: Exposition Press, 1969).

49. "2,000 Attend Mission Celebration," *SJR*, 1 August 1963, 6.

50. Bishop Steven T. Plummer telephone conversation with author, 24 September 1993.

51. "St. Mary of the Moonlight Dedicated Sunday at Oljato," *SJR*, 26 August 1971, 1.

52. Ibid.

53. For a very detailed explanation of the growth of the Native American Church see David F. Aberle, *The Peyote Religion among the Navaho* (Chicago: University of Chicago Press, 1982).

54. See David F. Aberle and Omer C. Stewart, *Navaho and Ute*

Peyotism—A Chronological and Distributional Study, University of Colorado Studies, Number 6 (Boulder: University of Colorado Press, 1957).

    55. Ibid., 25–27, 90.

    56. See John J. Wood, "Western Navajo Religious Affiliations," 176–86, and David F. Aberle, "The Future of Navajo Religion," 219–31, in *Navajo Religion and Culture: Selected Views,* ed. David M. Brugge and Charlotte J. Frisbie, Museum of New Mexico Papers in Anthropology Number 17 (Santa Fe: Museum of New Mexico Press, 1982).

    57. Aberle, *Peyote,* 190–93.

14

Taming San Juan

THE ESTABLISHMENT OF LAW, ORDER, AND GOVERNMENT

On 14 February 1880, acting Utah Territorial Governor Arthur L. Thomas signed a bill that officially created San Juan County from parts of Sevier, Kane, Iron, and Piute counties. In spite of a land mass that encompassed roughly its present-day boundaries in addition to those of Grand County, San Juan was still among the poorest of the counties in Utah, a fact that still holds to this day.[1] When Grand County, sliced from the lands of northern San Juan and eastern Emery, became a reality on 13 March 1890, the grounds for a local boundary dispute began, elements of which continued for almost a hundred years. So it is with many San Juan political issues that are deeply embedded in the history of government relations on various levels—local, state, and federal.

In 1894 nascent Grand County fired the first salvo in its effort to obtain more land from San Juan. However, the state legislature's committee on counties believed that because there was such a small revenue already coming out of San Juan, to remove any part of the land base would create an "[in]sufficient amount of taxable property in the remaining portion of San Juan County to support a county government."[2] The Utah House unanimously defeated the bill.

Three years later, San Juan commissioners entertained the idea of willingly annexing the county to Grand, whose tie with the railroad at Thompson, mining wealth, and livestock ventures helped it weather the depression of the 1890s better than its neighbors. The commissioners argued that consolidation would relieve San Juan's financial burden because the county was too impoverished to pay claims against it, had reached its debt limit, and lacked operating funds because of the decline in the cattle industry.[3] For four years the dialogue continued. Many of the people in Monticello and Verdure opposed the idea, fearing that they would lose the "protecting influence of the district court, which has been so instrumental in ridding the country of the lawless element" infesting it. They also felt that it would become too difficult for miners to file on claims and abide by government regulations and that a number of new industries associated with mining were soon going to create a financially solid base for the government. Citizens in Moab countered that new mining roads in the La Sal Mountains would run through San Juan and that their neighbor's county school system would greatly benefit by receiving some of the tax dollars coming from the Denver and Rio Grande Western Railroad. The decision, depending on a majority vote from each, was left to the counties; most San Juan voters rejected the idea, thus defeating the bill.[4]

Boundaries continued to play an important part in the political process. When the Great Depression reached its height in 1932–33, San Juan again toyed, tongue-in-cheek, with the idea of attaching itself to Wayne and Garfield counties. The reasoning was that the three could make one "whopping big" county, ideally suited for the time and place—all were "God-forsaken," ignored by the federal government, and could not pay their debts.[5]

This was hardly the case in the 1950s as uranium, oil, and other mineral developments peaked. In 1958 the boundary between Grand and San Juan counties again became an issue when the latter filed suit for a strip of land two-thirds of a mile wide and fifty-four miles long. Deposits of potash, estimated to yield 1,000 tons a day for forty-one years would make a nice addition to San Juan's $93 million valuation—the county now prospering because of its oil and mineral industries. For Grand County's approximately $20.5 million valuation, the potash revenue could make an even bigger financial difference. The bartering tables were now reversed. The state supreme court ruled in favor of San Juan, holding the counties to the original boundary established in 1880.[6]

In 1986, more than a hundred years after the establishment of the first county boundary, another issue arose. This time it was some of the people in Spanish Valley who desired to be annexed to Grand County because of their close proximity to Moab. They felt removed from the services and concerns of San Juan County and so tried to reach an agreement where both counties concurred—one to receive, the other to relinquish control of this area. Grand County readily accepted the proffered acquisition, but San Juan, in a resounding vote of 429 for and 2,000 against, refused to let the land go.[7] The potash deposits again played a significant part in this decision-making process.

The county boundary issue is one example of many that show the primary influence of economic development in the governance of San Juan, or any county, for that matter. Indeed, one of the responsibilities of government at all levels is to provide services that promote economic and social well-being. Certainly Silas S. Smith, as the first probate judge, and his selectmen, Platte D. Lyman, Zechariah B. Decker, and Jens Nielson were concerned with these issues, though on a limited scale, when they held their first county court session in Bluff on 7 June 1880.

For thirteen years, the county's government resided in Bluff. The attempt to build a courthouse with a jail served as the catalyst to remove the county seat to the more central location of Monticello. Even though the local government had appropriated $1,500 for construction, selected plans for a building 25 feet long and 21 feet wide, and purchased a site for fifty dollars, the county fathers had to reconsider when they received a petition signed by twenty-three citizens asking that the seat of authority be moved north. The judge and selectmen recognized that the power should be closer to the middle of the county, that "the greatest economy should be used in the expenditure of public as well as private money," and that members of

Construction on the San Juan County Courthouse at Monticello began in 1920 and was totally completed in 1938 at a cost of $47,937. (San Juan Historical Commission)

the court who had received money for the work did not have the right to be on the committee that decided what was to be done. They consequently halted construction, paid for what had already been accomplished, and left the final decision to the people in the next general election. On 5 March 1895 the court learned that more than two-thirds of the populace had voted that the county seat be moved to Monticello. On 5 April 1895, fifteen years to the day after the Mormons first arrived in Bluff, the county government moved to Monticello, where it remains.[8]

Less than a year later, another momentous change occurred—statehood—and with it a shift in county government. The new state constitution did away with the system of judge and selectmen and in its place required that three county commissioners be elected by the people. In the interim, Frederick I. Jones served as chairman of the board of county commissioners; the first elected county commissioners assumed office in 1897: F. H. Hyde, chairman; T. B. Carpenter;

and D. L. Goudelock.[9] The driving force of county government still rests in the hands of its three commissioners, elected every four years by the county's residents.

During the early, formative years of government, the problems of handling taxation, road building, water rights, law enforcement, Indian relations, federal legislation, and sheer survival loomed large.[10] The solution to some of these issues, such as developing a transportation network or gaining access to water, carried obvious rewards. Other situations were more mixed, such as the problems caused by the roughneck cowboys of the Carlisle outfit, who proved a constant source of friction but who also herded thousands of taxable cattle that boosted the county's economy. All these various matters were in some way related to the land base and the money derived from it.

One service of interest to everyone was the delivery of mail. At first the mail came with anybody headed in the right direction, but soon established routes crossed the county. In 1879 postmaster Tom Ray of La Sal received the first scheduled mail delivery. His stop was one of many on a 350-mile trail that originated in Salina, Utah, and then went to Green River, Moab, and La Sal before continuing on to Naturita and Ouray, Colorado—the route serving fewer than 100 people and taking as long as six weeks to traverse.[11] As Moab grew in importance and the railroad made delivery more practical, the northern end of the county obtained more regular service, and by 1890 Monticello was receiving mail three times a week.[12]

Bluff, Aneth, and settlements in McElmo Canyon, on the other hand, initially forged their postal ties with Mancos and, later, Cortez, Colorado. The first scheduled mail arrived on 26 October 1882, coming along a route that threaded its way through McElmo to Aneth and then along the San Juan River to Bluff.[13] Later, a shortcut six miles beyond the mouth of McElmo Canyon took the mail rider onto Mail Trail Mesa, then Ismay, and into Colorado.[14] This route remained in service until 1910, when George and Benjamin Perkins received the contract for a mail route stretching from Moab to Bluff.

The towns of southwestern Colorado also vied for government mail contracts to serve the communities of San Juan County. They created enough political pressure to open routes from Mancos to

Bluff and from Dolores to Monticello in 1916.[15] By 1918 most communities had mail a minimum of three times a week and, in the larger towns of Monticello and Blanding, six days a week. Now it became a matter of streamlining the system to increase efficiency.

A problem arose in 1914 when parcel post became part of the regular service, straining the resources of the carriers. For instance, one week it took six wagon teams just to haul packages from Monticello to Blanding. The number, weight, and size of this type of mail forced an increase in both the capacity of the vehicles and the cost of delivery. Three times the government advertised for bids by contractors to carry the mail, yet few wanted to tackle the unknown factors posed by the parcel-post system. Finally, some businessmen from Moab took the contract, established a stage service, and made arrangements to haul packages heading south as far as Blanding. Within two years they also replaced their wagons with cars and trucks.[16]

The evolution of the mail system reflected not only changing government views about delivery but also shifts in technology. This can be illustrated through the life of C. R. Christensen, who in 1895, started carrying the U.S. mail in a light sack slung over his saddle-horn or in specially made pouches that fit over his saddle. He covered the route between Moab and Monticello by meeting Nick Wilson in Dry Valley, exchanging his sack of outgoing mail for the incoming, and then returning to Monticello. The pair later created a specially built buckboard with extra-wide wheels to prevent their sinking in the sand. In the winter, however, this type of vehicle was impractical because of road and snow conditions, so Christensen would turn to a sleigh, skis, or snowshoes to work his way from Verdure to Devils Canyon, where he handed the mail to a rider heading for Bluff. He was also the first to introduce a motor vehicle on the mail route when, in 1914, he fired up a "hard-tired chain driven truck" to bounce along the rutted, sandy road between Thompson and Monticello. In 1950, at the age of seventy-five, he still held a four-year contract to carry Uncle Sam's mail.[17]

Besides delivering mail, the government provided law enforcement as a service. Part of the mystique about San Juan County is the idea that the Mormon settlers were called to this region to wrest it from the grasp of a lawless element inhabiting its canyons and secluded places. If the pioneers' mission was, in the words of one writer, to serve as a "point of interception of bank robbers, horse thieves, cattle rustlers, jail breakers, train robbers and general desperadic [*sic*] criminals . . . terrorizing and plundering inland settlements," then they were woefully unprepared for the undertaking.[18]

The first decade was more a desperate attempt to control the tough cowhands brought in by the various cattle companies to tend the herds. The general policy of the Mormons was to sit passively by until a situation became intolerable, at which time they were forced to take some type of action. When something was done, it took the form of an impromptu law-abiding vigilance committee composed of church members, who administered justice until the particular problem was solved.[19]

More important is the growth in law enforcement once the government had matured sufficiently to compel miscreants to live by the law on a more regular basis. This trend started around 1890, as the large non-Mormon cattle companies began to leave the county. At about this same time, San Juan received its first sheriff, Willard "Dick" Butt, and the services of Joe Bush, a federal marshal, who became involved in solving some of the more difficult crimes.

Although both of these men helped bring law and order to the county, Bush was particularly impressive. He stood six feet tall, weighed 200 pounds, had steel blue eyes, a gruff voice, and packed a sawed-off shotgun, all of which allowed him generally to intimidate his quarry as he walked directly up to disarm them. Although he rarely used his weapon, on one occasion, while arresting John Gibson in Monticello, he shot the cattle thief as he emerged, pistol in hand, from behind a curtain. Gibson's wounds required the services of a doctor from Grand Junction before the prisoner could be taken to Salt Lake for trial.[20]

In contrast with heroic lawmen like Bush, there were also some well-known outlaws who frequented San Juan. One of the most famous groups, whose history has been shrouded in myth and folktale, was the "Wild Bunch," composed of such luminaries as Butch Cassidy (Robert Leroy Parker), the Sundance Kid (Harry Longabaugh), Matt Warner, Tom McCarty, and others. Their connection to the county was real but has been coated with hearsay that ranges from simplified fact to pure fiction. Members of the gang, especially Tom McCarty, had definite ties to the community of La Sal, knew the geographical region well, received aid from cowboys working at the Carlisle ranch, and traveled in the area to and from various illegal activities.[21] There is also no doubt that the Utah legislature placed a $5,000 reward on Tom McCarty's head, "either on or off the shoulders of that outlaw."[22]

Other elements of the gang's history are not as easily substantiated. Frank Silvey, who claimed to have known members of the gang, suggested that they used a trail that crossed the Colorado River at Spanish Bottom, traversed near Elk Ridge, and over to Monticello.[23] They also supposedly planned the Telluride bank robbery of 1889 while living in San Juan County. Of no credibility is the report that in the "fastnesses of Blue Mountain," they would rendezvous in

> an enormous cave well up in the mountains hollowed out by natural and artificial means with avenues leading out in different directions to the several slopes. The cave is fitted up with all modern conveniences, and said to have a well-equipped electric light plant, and that wires from the plant run down the slopes to great deposits of dynamite sufficient to annihilate an invading regiment.[24]

The Wild Bunch often received more credit than was due them.

San Juan County has had its share of lawbreakers throughout its history. State criminal files indicate that in the county's early days, livestock theft and assault were among the most common crimes, and murder also has been a factor. Two incidents, in particular, have gained notoriety. The first concerns the murder in 1935 of William Oliver, a former sheriff, and his grandson, Norris Shumway, by Clinton James Palmer from Texas. A dispute erupted over the rangelands of John's Canyon, leased by Oliver for his cattle. Palmer, an itinerant on the run for another murder, herded sheep for Harry Goulding in the neighboring Valley of the Gods. Available water and grass encouraged Palmer to intrude on Oliver's and Shumway's range. The two collided over the land's use, and Palmer attacked, killed, and then beheaded Shumway; he then went in search of Oliver, whom he shot. He dragged and rolled Oliver's body partway down a cliff. Palmer and his young wife fled to Texas, where they were eventually caught. He stood trial for the previous murder of a Texan and spent the rest of his life in prison.[25]

The second notorious incident involved the killing of forest ranger Rudolph E. Mellenthin when he tried to arrest Ramon Archuleta, a deserter from the army. Archuleta had made his way from Kansas to New Mexico, where he was apprehended. He escaped to the Navajo Reservation and then took up residence in a sheep camp in the La Sal Mountains. His father-in-law, Ignacio Martinez, helped hide him until the afternoon of 23 August 1918 when Mellenthin and two other men arrived in the camp to arrest Archuleta. Conflicting testimony as to the sequence of events has blurred what happened, but when the smoke cleared, the ranger lay dead on the ground with three mortal wounds.

Shortly after, both men were apprehended and charged with murder, stood trial in Manti, and were sentenced—Archuleta to life imprisonment and Martinez, an older man, to fifteen years hard labor. Two years later, the courts freed Martinez because of doubts as to his guilt; six years later Archuleta was out of prison on parole. The people of San Juan and Grand counties were irate but unsuccessful in reversing the legal process. They received some satisfaction with the naming of a peak in the La Sals in San Juan County—Mount Mellenthin—as a memorial to a good man killed in the wartime service of his country.[26]

The killings in John's Canyon and in the La Sals suggest some of the problems of providing law enforcement in San Juan County. Among the most obvious is the vast territory into which a lawbreaker could flee. The rugged topography, abundant springs and seeps for water, and the network of backcountry roads helped make escape and evasion a real possibility. With limited communication facilities until fairly recently and a small population, a criminal's movements and activities could go relatively unnoticed. Finally, many of the men providing law enforcement, though well-intentioned, often lacked extensive training.

Yet San Juan County's problems with criminal activities also reflected problems faced by the government on a national level. Take, for instance, the Roaring Twenties and the issue of bootlegging illegal liquor.[27] Problems encountered in law enforcement in rural southeastern Utah had about as much variety as there were names and recipes for moonshine: bathtub gin, busthead, hooch, mountain dew, white lightning, white mule, and bug juice, to name a few. Closet drinkers in Blanding made malt beer and wine out of home-grown grapes. Peaches were a favorite in the Bluff area. On the Navajo Reservation any kind of available fruit was used, especially raisins. Monticello residents liked the chokecherries that grew on Blue Mountain, while homesteaders in Eastland brewed some of their dry farm crops of wheat and corn.[28] In each area there were those who looked forward to a seasonal harvest and a forthcoming year of drinking and sales.

The battle of wits between federal prohibition officers and bootleg traffickers resulted in the development of some ingenious methods of concealing and transporting the liquor. Producers hid boxes of liquor in hollowed-out bales of hay or on the side of a wash, or they buried their wares in streambeds. Adults often used children to help them evade the law. A seller might stack his liquor under quilts for his children to sleep on inside cars transporting the alcohol.[29] Frequently, older children were either knowingly enlisted or unwittingly duped into becoming accomplices. Because of their age, they often were not suspected by the law; but an adult caught involving a minor was guilty of an even greater crime. According to one story, a young boy who was helping to haul whiskey to Moab had his arm out the car window when another car hit him and broke it. He let the arm heal crooked because he was a fifteen-year-old minor and afraid that if he went to a doctor he would be turned in to the authorities.[30]

East of Monticello lived William "Old Man" Long, who mastered the technique of hiding his brew and never getting caught, even though he was a notorious bootlegger. He built his house, which was part log cabin, out of cases of beer cans that he stacked on the outside and plastered over on the inside. This made a good thick wall and kept his house better insulated. Alfred Frost of Monticello reminisced about Long: "After he died a few years ago, I was out showing some people the place. We got to looking around. There were underground tunnels all under his place. They went clear out to the trails in the back and his chicken coop. There were long cross tunnels under the ground all over."[31]

Other bootleggers were not as fortunate in avoiding detection, and often a chase ensued. One of the locals in Monticello was peddling his whiskey in town when federal officers arrived. The bootlegger speedily loaded his wares into his car and left, but as he passed the small settlement of Boulder he took a shortcut that went from the main road to the schoolhouse. By a stroke of luck he became high-centered on the muddy, rutted road, which saved him from the officers traveling down the main road.[32]

Though moonshining and bootlegging were illegal activities, there was considerable tolerance for them in the rural communities. A partial explanation lies in the unpopularity of Prohibition. The controversial nature of the Eighteenth Amendment was mirrored in the ambiguous actions of the public. For example, one man in Monticello was informed on for selling gallons of whiskey but at the same time was also warned that the law had been notified and so was able to make a successful escape.[33]

Because of vacillating views about Prohibition, the grand social experiment did not succeed as planned. The feeling of southeastern Utahns reflected the attitudes of the nation. One person remembers that when the government legalized alcohol there was a big celebration and everybody quite easily found something to drink. Once the fervor died down, people bought liquor much as they had before Prohibition was enacted.[34]

As this era came to an end, the towns and counties in Utah cast their votes for or against legalizing the sale of alcohol. In November 1933 the majority of San Juan County residents voted against ending Prohibition. The driving force came from Blanding, "throwing almost the entire town's strength" against repeal, while half the town of Monticello voted "wet."[35] Moab and other less Mormon towns readily accepted the reintroduction of legal liquor, thus giving the impression that where Mormon influence was weakest and where bootleggers had been most active, alcohol was more acceptable. Although San Juan County voted against repeal of the Eighteenth Amendment, Utah became the thirty-sixth and deciding state to vote for repeal, an action that openly brought the tavern back to the state's rural districts.[36]

In San Juan, the issue was still not over. A look at how the problem continued serves as an example of the types of concerns the county commissioners have faced in their daily management of local government. Two months after county residents cast their votes in favor of Prohibition, Monticello established its right to sell beer within city limits. This was possible because the decision to sell alcohol in incorporated towns was left to local residents. Blanding rejected any type of licensing or sale of alcohol.[37]

Liquor issues lay dormant until the 1960s and 1970s, when new concerns arose. The first question centered around the sale of beer on Sunday. Early Mormon attitudes had influenced the local laws forbidding this activity on the sabbath, but with the influx of oil-field workers and uranium miners into the county, some people felt the laws needed to be changed. Delegations for and against the purchase of beer on Sunday petitioned the commissioners, who held out until August 1988 before agreeing to its sale on Sundays.[38]

Another issue concerned the operation of bars in various locations such as Bluff and Mexican Hat that were close to the reservation. These establishments came under county control because they were not in incorporated towns. Approvals and denials followed, giving rise to a policy in which the residents of a community were allowed to vote on the issue.[39] However, this was not before more than 100 residents in Montezuma Creek went to the local trading post and smashed forty cases of beer in protest of the sale of alcohol near the new Whitehorse High School on the reservation.

By the time the results of the election were in, residents of Aneth, Montezuma Creek, and Red Mesa had voted five-to-one to eliminate bars and alcohol vendors in their area. Accordingly, the county commission terminated three beer licenses, affecting businesses that claimed a combined yearly profit of $90,000 from the sale of alcohol. These entrepreneurs saw this action as a violation of civil rights and sued for $1.5 million in damages. When county voters registered their sentiments in the next general election in 1982, 58 percent (2020 of 3501 votes) were against restricting the sale of beer in unincorporated areas. Thus, alcohol could be sold as long as the store or bar was not on the reservation or within a city's limits, such as in Blanding, where its residents had voted to remain "dry."[40]

Although San Juan County may not have followed the national desire to reintroduce alcohol, it certainly paralleled mainstream support of World War I and World War II.[41] Between 1917 and 1918, patriotic sentiments ran high, as San Juan filled draft quotas established by the government. For instance, the induction board screened eighty men in the county to fill its commitment of twenty-seven men. What the review board encountered was surprising. Every inductee was required to pass a physical examination, but a large proportion of the unmarried men were "rejected on some minor defect" while the married men "went through with flying colors."[42] Twenty-four of the eighty men from San Juan passed the physical examination; nineteen of them filed for exemption because of dependent relatives. The final summary of the first draft notice in San Juan eventually listed sixteen eligible, fifty-six discharged, five already enlisted, and three unaccounted for. A second call for eighty-five men netted thirty-one eligible.[43] After an initial introduction to the military, they went to their branch specialty school where they learned a trade in artillery, infantry, or some other skill. Training sites included Fort Riley, Kansas; Camp Kearney, California; Camp Lewis, Washington; and Camp Mills, New York.

While the draft cast the largest net of procurement, there were many who volunteered, especially as a spirit of national service affected the communities. Omni Porter, the foreman at the Grayson [Blanding] Cooperative Company's sawmill, could attest to that. His entire crew of five men attended a farewell dance for some enlistees. Early the next morning they also went to enlist, leaving their foreman with 150,000 feet of logs waiting to be cut. Porter complained that he had lost his engineer, his ratchet setter, two off-bearers, and the planing-machine man. A solution was proposed: hire women—but he never did.[44]

For those who did not don a uniform, there were other means of promoting the cause. Donations to Soldier's Welfare and the Red Cross, the purchase of war stamps and liberty loans, and food rationing were important symbolic as well as real means for every individual and community to express support for the war. Federal,

World War I veterans marching in a Fourth of July parade in Blanding. (San Juan Historical Commission)

state, and local governments established quotas and expected them to be filled. A good example of this approach is seen in the federal government's attempt to raise $10 million for Soldier's Welfare work. Of this amount, Utah's share was to raise $100,000 and San Juan County $190. The Council of Defense for San Juan, a local organization that coordinated a variety of war-related activities, took on the task of raising the sum and allocated the amount as follows: Bluff $30, Blanding $70, Monticello $70, and La Sal $20. To create a fund of twenty dollars for contingent expenses, the Council added an additional five dollars to each community's assessment.[45] The towns and county achieved their goals.

Like the county's men, women also readily enlisted for local war service. Each female registrant received a card with different activities from which to choose. In Blanding, seventy married and single women appeared at the registrar's door, filled out the fifty available registration cards, and indicated their willingness to sew, knit, and do work that would not take them from home. Thirteen of the seventy offered to join the Red Cross nursing program, requiring them to be ready to leave on twenty-four-hours' notice.[46]

When news of the armistice reached southeastern Utah in November 1918, it tore through the communities like unexpected lightning in the crisp fall air. Rapid demobilization allowed many of the men in the service to be home within three months. The towns held official welcome-back-and-thank-you-for-serving celebrations that rivaled the occasions of the soldier's departure. One festivity in Monticello started at three o'clock in the afternoon and lasted into the early morning hours. The obligatory banquet, speeches, and dance had a new wrinkle added when the returning soldiers and a lieutenant staged a drill exhibition during intermission.[47] Following the conclusion of this display of patriotic fervor, uniforms were hung in closets or consigned to mothballs, only to be resurrected for the annual Fourth of July or Pioneer Day celebrations in the future.

Following more than a decade of relative prosperity, San Juan again plunged into a national crisis—this time an economic depression. Part of Franklin Delano Roosevelt's "alphabet soup" legislation of the WPA (Works Progress Administration), PWA (Public Works Administration), FERA (Federal Employment Relief Act), CCC (Civilian Conservation Corps), NRA (National Recovery Administration), and CWA (Civic Works Administration) made their way to the county to help bring relief to an already depressed economy dependent on the agriculture and livestock industries for its cash flow. It was now the government's turn to reciprocate for the support rendered during World War I.

The general concept behind all of these programs, too numerous to delineate here, was to put money back in the pockets of the county's citizens through either direct relief (in which the government handed out money to stimulate production) or work relief (where the government employed people for various jobs). The important point is that the county actively sought its fair share of help from the federal government.

The *San Juan Record* testifies of the strong desire of residents to

CCC bridge construction project on Recapture Wash southeast of Blanding. (Courtesy Frank "Bo" Montella)

have help with projects that affected every aspect of life from the paving of roads to the issuance of food stamps and from placing farmlands in the Federal Land Bank to petitioning for CCC camps to be established and continued. Headlines indicate the ardor of this courtship: "San Juan Must Get Its Share of Reconstruction Funds Now," "People Demand NRA Money for Monticello Public Works," "Town and Planning Board Ask PWA Funds," and "Stockmen Stress Need of CCC Camp on Colorado."[48]

The response of the government was gratifying, but never enough. Its money, involvement, and control at this point in San Juan history was very desirable; forty years later, the county's enthusiasm for the funds remained, but the other elements became a source of intense friction.

One of the most important factors in raising the county and the nation out of the depths of the depression was the beginning of World War II. Twenty-two years after the end of the First World War, San Juan County again started to prepare, with characteristic zeal, to wage another. Even before Japanese bombs fell on Pearl Harbor, 337

CCC facilities near Baker Ranger Station west of Monticello in 1937. (San Juan Historical Commission)

local men had registered in just one day with the Selective Service board in different districts in the county. Monticello and Blanding again sported an "atmosphere of holiday spirit . . . with flags displayed" prominently throughout the towns, while the Monticello high school band marched up Main Street serenading the onlookers. Three months later the first six recruits left San Juan County; by 1944, Blanding alone could boast of 150 of its "boys" in the service, 40 percent of whom were overseas.[49]

As in World War I, the economic side of the conflict waged by the county coupled sacrifice with stimulation. Keeping in mind that San Juan was one of the poorest of Utah's counties, a few statistics from 1943 provide a glimpse of the part residents took in achieving victory. For example, the government quota for county war bond sales was $60,000—the amount subscribed was a little more than double that figure; the Red Cross War Fund drive established a goal of $700 for Blanding and Bluff, which in a few days' time was surpassed; residents exceeded a county Red Cross goal of $1,000 by contributing

$1,600; a year later, citizens again topped the projected sum for the Red Cross Fund of $3,300.[50]

The government also encouraged thrift and industry. By establishing annual quotas of farm products—such as 6,000 acres in wheat, 6,000 acres in dry beans, and 3,500 acres in barley— the government moved the county into greater productivity with a decrease of idle acreage from 4,072 to 2,116.[51] Gasoline ration cards limited a normal driver to 2,880 miles per year unless on business essential to the war effort, which included war workers, doctors, and farmers, whose mileage then increased to 5,000. Scrap metal, especially tin, became important in a recycling program in which discarding a can became an "unpatriotic act." At one point it was written that, "For every can of new goods purchased, an old can [was] required . . . no goods will be sold without the exchange."[52]

Fifteen families from the Topaz Japanese relocation camp, near Delta, Utah, came to southeastern Utah and enjoyed a degree of freedom. Charlie Redd saw their arrival as an opportunity to employ them on his ranch in La Sal in every capacity from truck gardening to teaching music and dance to his children. He hired a dozen men and women, who stayed for less than a year because they felt isolated from city life and did not get along well with some of the cowboys.[53]

The county quietly rejoiced when news of Victory in Europe (V-E) day arrived on 8 May 1945. Owners closed their stores at 1:00 p.m. for a half-day holiday, and the town siren blew for a few minutes; but the residents realized that there was still a tough fight ahead in the Pacific. Four months later, with the Japanese surrender, the same siren in Monticello blew again, horns honked for an hour, "cars filled with young folks [drove] around town, staging their own kind of celebration," while the "more seriously minded folks" used the time for "prayer and thanksgiving."[54] The county and its residents had earned a well-deserved rest from war.

The Cold War, however, soon made its influence felt. San Juan men and women willingly served in the frozen rice paddies of Korea, as well as in the mountains and coastal plains of South Vietnam, although these conflicts did not elicit the same fervor as had the previous wars. At home, Civil Defense groups organized for emergencies ranging from enemy sabotage and hosting regional evacuees to nuclear war. The National Guard even sponsored a ground observer program in which Boy Scouts and interested adults devoted two hours each week to manning an observation post near Monticello, where they reported sightings of any aircraft. In 1957, Blanding youth made a "listening" or "detector" post with sensitized microphones to notify residents of potential enemy aircraft. The air force issued plane description cards so that when the alarm sounded in a boy's home, the defender could go out and identify what type of enemy aircraft was in the vicinity.[55] A few families even built bomb shelters.

The most dramatic form of federal, state, and local government involvement came to San Juan through the U.S. Army missile program located on Black Mesa, southwest of Blanding. Starting in 1963, the army began a testing program for Pershing medium range missiles fired at targets in White Sands, New Mexico, a distance of 350 miles. At the same time, launchings from a site near Green River placed Hatch Mesa, Indian Creek, Blue Mountain, La Sal and other parts of San Juan County beneath the trajectory of the four-stage Athena missile and other types of armament. Since different parts of these missiles were expended and discarded in flight, safety precautions required that parts of the county be evacuated during launch times.[56] Suddenly, San Juan had rocketed into the business of national defense in a way not believed possible twenty years before.

The arrival of the army in August 1963 was anything but subtle. A 185-vehicle convoy stretched more than fifty miles and was manned by a battalion of 400 soldiers. If this spectacle was not enough, the army staged a mock missile firing by thirty helicopter-borne troops during halftime at a high school football game. On 24 September the army fired the first of five missiles that flew the distance in four minutes and impacted safely in the soil of New Mexico. In a few weeks the 800-man military contingent and civilian employees were gone with a promise to return and a thanks for the warm hospitality offered by the county.[57]

The military continued to shoot missiles from San Juan each year through 1974, with a return engagement in 1980. The Green River site, because of its more permanent, larger facilities and longer distance to the target, enjoyed much more intense use up to 1977, with a reopening for a short period in 1982 and discussion of its being uti-

Pershing missile fired from Black Mesa near Blanding on the afternoon of
23 September 1963. The target site was White Sands, New Mexico, approximately 350 miles away. (Courtesy Carolyn Black)

lized again in the mid 1990s.[58] If the past repeats itself, some residents of San Juan County will again be evacuated as missiles fly over its borders. How much of a hazard this type of program presents needs to be considered by county and state government, but in the past errant missiles or their parts fell near Bluff, Blanding, and Durango, Colorado, much to the chagrin of the military.[59] However, there was no large protest from the citizenry, who generally accepted it and went on with life.

The more recent suggestion of having missiles fired over San Juan were not as calmly accepted. Meetings between government officials and citizens raised environmental and safety questions that were not as great a concern in the past. Some people feared that archaeological remains would be destroyed, that the tourist industry would decline, and that irreparable damage would be done to the environment. The army suggested alternative flight paths for the missiles, but those protesting the plans were still not convinced. Other residents believed the issues were blown out of proportion and welcomed the testing program from a sense of patriotism and a belief that little harm would be done to the county physically or economically. At present, the military has declined the use of San Juan County for its program.

In summarizing federal, state, and San Juan County government relations in the past, one finds a general pattern of interest, involvement, and cooperation. Strongest evidence of this surfaced during the two world wars and the Depression, where all groups were mutually supportive. Patriotism and sacrifice were common beliefs held by county residents, who worked hard to surpass what was asked of them individually and collectively. And when tough times arrived, such as in the Depression, they expected the government to turn about and help this isolated, rural community to get back on its economic feet.

This attitude is important to grasp in order to understand the more recent conflict between the county and the federal government. Its roots also lie in the past and are deeply embedded in a view of personal and government responsibility. What caused this schism and its results is the topic of the next chapter.

ENDNOTES

1. *Journals of the Legislative Assembly of the Territory of Utah*, 24th Session, 1880, Utah State Archives, State Capitol, Salt Lake City, Utah, 285; *Laws of the Territory of Utah*, 24th Session, 1880, State Capitol, Salt Lake City, Utah, 10.

2. *House Journal of the Legislative Assembly of the Territory of Utah*, 31st Session, 1894, Utah State Archives, State Capitol, Salt Lake City, Utah, 112, 120.

3. "Shall San Juan County Be Annexed to Grand?" *Grand Valley Times* (hereafter cited as *GVT*), 2 July 1897, 4.

4. "Monticello Notes," *GVT*, 15 March 1901, 1; "Editorial Notes," *GVT*, 26 April 1901, 1; "Editorial Notes," *GVT*, 3 May 1901, 1; "Editorial Notes," *GVT*, 7 June 1901, 1.

5. "San Juan Must Have Help Now Neglect Has Gone Too Far," *San Juan Record* (hereafter cited as *SJR*), 10 August 1933, 1.

6. "Survey to Settle Land Dispute Between Counties," *SJR*, 13 June 1958, 4; "Grand County Wants Border Suit Dropped," *SJR*, 18 March 1960, 1; "Potash Mine Heats Boundary Dispute," *SJR*, 6 May 1960, 1; "State Supreme Court Will Hear Boundary Dispute," *SJR*, 5 April 1962, 1; "San Juan County Wins Boundary Line Case," *SJR*, 31 May 1962, 1. The figure for Grand County's assessed valuation was obtained from Grace Eastin, Grand County Treasurer, telephone conversation with author, 14 October 1994.

7. County Commissioner Bill Redd telephone conversation with author, 29 July 1994. Statistics housed in San Juan County Courthouse, Monticello, Utah.

8. "Minutes of the County Commission of San Juan County, Utah, From April 26th 1880 to March 5th 1900," Recorder's Office, County Courthouse, Monticello, Utah, 142, 144, 146, 153–154, 183.

9. Ibid., 201, 218.

10. See Thomas E. Austin and Robert S. McPherson, "Murder, Mayhem, and Mormons: The Evolution of Law Enforcement on the San Juan Frontier, 1880–1900," *Utah Historical Quarterly* 55, no. 1 (Winter 1987): 36–49.

11. Frank Silvey, "History and Settlement of Northern San Juan County," unpublished manuscript, Utah State Historical Society, 9–10.

12. LaRaine Redd, "Mail Service," *Blue Mountain Shadows* 8 (Summer 1991): 59.

13. Kumen Jones, "Writings," Special Collections, Brigham Young University Library, 29.

14. Charles Stiles to author, 3 July 1991, letter in possession of author; Oliver W. Harris, "Carrying the Mail," *Blue Mountain Shadows* (Summer 1991): 61.

15. "News Notes from San Juan County," *GVT*, 17 March 1916, 10; "New Mail Route Out of Mancos," *Mancos Times-Tribune*, 12 January 1917, 1.

16. "Around Town," *GVT*, 3 June 1910, 1; "Monticello-Bluff Logical Route for Mail Service," *GVT*, 19 January 1912, 1; "Grayson, Utah," *Montezuma Journal*, 12 March 1914, 1; "Have Meeting With Official," *GVT*, 20 March 1914, 1; "Parcel Post Scares Bidders on Moab-Bluff Mail Route," *GVT*, 15 May 1914, 1; "Allred Bros. Get Monticello Mail Contract," *GVT*, 12 June 1914, 1.

17. "Rounding Out 40 Years of Mail Delivery," *SJR*, 27 April 1950, 1.

18. Morgan Amasa Barton, "Back Door to San Juan," 9, as cited in David E. Miller, *Hole-in-the-Rock* (Salt Lake City: University of Utah Press, 1959), 8.

19. This era of "wild West shoot-em-up" has been documented sufficiently elsewhere and so will not be developed further here. In addition to Austin and McPherson, "Murder, Mayhem," 36–49, see Albert R. Lyman's works such as *Indians and Outlaws* (Salt Lake City: Bookcraft, 1962) and his "Fort on the Firing Line," published serially in *The Improvement Era*, October 1948 to 1950; Cornelia Perkins, Marian Nielson, and Lenora Jones, *Saga of San Juan* (Salt Lake City: Mercury Publishing Company, 1968); and Harold Muhlestein and Fay Muhlestein, *Monticello Journal: A History of Monticello Until 1937* (Self-published, 1988).

20. Frank Silvey, "Rambling Thoughts of a Rimrocker," *SJR*, 21 April 1938, 1.

21. See Faun McConkie Tanner, *The Far Country: A Regional History of Moab and La Sal, Utah* (Salt Lake City: Olympus Publishing Company, 1976), 147–71.

22. "Tom McCarthy [sic]," *Montezuma Journal*, 5 May 1899, 4.

23. Pearl Baker, *The Wild Bunch at Robbers Roost* (Lincoln: University of Nebraska Press, 1989), 9; Frank Silvey, "Rambling Thoughts of a Rimrocker," *SJR*, 6 August 1936, 1.

24. Ibid.

25. Helen N. Shumway, "The Ingredients of Violence in the Murders of William E. Oliver and Norris Shumway," *Blue Mountain Shadows* 1, no. 1 (Fall 1987): 46–52.

26. "Murderers of Ranger Get Heavy Sentences," *GVT*, 13 June, 1919, 1; "Confessed Murderer of Ranger Paroled," *Times-Independent*, 1 October 1925, 1.

27. For a more complete discussion of this era see Jody Bailey and Robert S. McPherson, "'Practically Free from the Taint of the Bootlegger': A Closer Look at Prohibition in Southeastern Utah," *Utah Historical Quarterly* 57, no. 2 (Spring 1989): 150–64.

28. J. P. Gonzales interview with Laura Shumway and Janet Wilcox on 6 July 1987, tape located in the San Juan County Historical Commission [hereafter SJHC], Blanding, Utah; Erv and Beth Guymon interview with Janet Wilcox on 17 July 1987, SJHC; J. Glen Shumway interview with Janet Wilcox on 25 July 1987, SJHC; Pearl Butt interview with Jody Bailey on 2 July 1987, SJHC.

29. Butt interview.

30. Cloyd Johnson interview with Jody Bailey, 14 July 1987, SJHC.

31. Alfred Frost interview with Regina Yazzie on 6 July 1987, SJHC.

32. Ibid.

33. Ibid.

34. Ibid.

35. "Utah Votes for Repeal: San Juan against Wet Law," *SJR*, 9 November 1933, 1.

36. Ibid.

37. "Beer Licenses Now Available," *SJR*, 11 January 1934, 1.

38. "Beer Ordinance Amended," *SJR*, 20 April 1961, 1; "Group Meets with Commission, Ask 'No Sunday Beer,'" *SJR*, 27 April 1961, 1; "Officials Oppose Sale of Beer on Sunday," *SJR*, 15 April 1965, 1.

39. "Delegation Protests Hat Beer Request; Bluff License Revoked," *SJR*, 24 January 1963, 1; "Hat Beer License Approved," *SJR*, 21 February 1963, 1; "Disturbance at Montezuma Creek," *SJR*, 14 September 1978, 2; "Beer Election Policy Extended County Wide," *SJR*, 28 September 1978, 1.

40. "$1.5 Million Suit over Beer Issue," *SJR*, 18 January 1979, 1; "57.7 Percent Say No to Beer Ordinance," *SJR*, 4 November 1982, 1.

41. For a more complete treatment of World War I see Marcia Black and Robert S. McPherson, "Soldiers, Savers, Slackers, and Spies: Southeastern Utah's Response to World War I," *Utah Historical Quarterly* 63, no. 1 (Winter 1995): 4–23.

42. "74 Men Drawn from County," *GVT*, 27 July 1917, 1;"San Juan Men Are Called to Colors," *San Juan Blade*, 11 August 1917, 1; Justin A. Black interview with Louise Lyne, 11 July 1972, Utah State Historical Society and California State University–Fullerton, Southeastern Utah Project, 9.

43. "16 Eligibles for Service," *San Juan Blade*, 24 August 1917, 1; "47 Eligibles for Service," *San Juan Blade*, 31 August 1917, 1.

44. "Sawmill Crew to Volunteer," *San Juan Blade*, 10 August 1917, 1.

45. "San Juan County Again to the Front," *San Juan Blade*, 6 November 1917, 1.

46. Catherine Moore interview with Jessie Embry, 23 April 1979, Charles Redd Center Southeastern Utah Oral History Project, Brigham Young University, Provo, Utah, 13; "Women of San Juan Register," *San Juan Blade*, 9 November 1917, 1; "Seventy Blanding Women Register," *San Juan Blade*, 16 November 1917, 1.

47. "Returned Soldiers to Receive Royal Reception Friday Eve," *San Juan Blade*, 26 February 1919, 1.

48. "San Juan Must Get Its Share of Reconstruction Funds Now," *SJR*, 14 September 1933, 1; "People Demand NRA Money for Monticello Public Works," *SJR*, 2 November 1933, 1; "Town and Planning Boards Ask PWA Funds," *SJR*, 7 February 1935, 1; "Stockmen Stress Need of CCC Camp on Colorado," *SJR*, 11 July 1935, 1.

49. "U.S. Registration for Selective Service Gets Under Way in San Juan County," *SJR*, 17 October 1940, 1; "First Recruits to Leave San Juan Given Send-off," *SJR*, 23 January 1941, 1; Grace Shumway, "Blanding News," *SJR*, 27 April 1944, 6.

50. "Blanding and Bluff Score in Red Cross War Fund Drive," *SJR*, 18 March 1943, 1; "Sale of War Bonds in San Juan County Is Doubled," *SJR*, 7 October 1943, 1; "San Juan Tops Its Quota Drive," *SJR*, 2 December 1943, 1; "Red Cross War Fund Drive Is Completed," *SJR*, 20 April 1944, 1.

51. "San Juan's Food Production Program," *SJR*, 15 April 1943, 1.

52. "Car Owners Register for Gasoline," *SJR*, 19 November 1942, 1; "Tin to Be Gathered in Next Drive," *SJR*, 29 October 1942, 1; "Salvage Drive for Tin, Fats and Rags," *SJR*, 25 February 1943, 1.

53. "La Sal Rancher to Employ Japanese," *SJR*, 25 March 1943, 1; Annaley Redd, telephone conversation with author, 15 August 1994.

54. "V-E Day Observed Quietly in Town," *SJR*, 10 May 1945, 1; "Victory over Japan Is Proclaimed," *SJR*, 16 August 1945, 1.

55. "Civil Defense Program Set Up," *SJR*, 7 January 1951, 1; "Civil Defense Field Officer Cautions on A-Bomb Hazards," *SJR*, 10 March 1955, 1; "Ground Observer Program to Begin Soon," *SJR*, 16 February 1956, 1; "Youngsters Take Over Civil Defense Duty at Detector Post in Blanding," *SJR*, 24 October 1957, 1.

56. "Missile Site to Be Near Blanding," *SJR*, 19 July 1962, 1; "Missile 'Dropout Zone' Detailed," *SJR*, 25 April 1963, 1.

57. "Missile Battalion, Convoy Arrives Here Next Thursday," *SJR*, 29 August 1963, 1; "First Pershing Firing Now Set for Late in September," *SJR*, 12 September 1963, 1; "Pershing Missiles Fired Successfully," *SJR*, 26 September 1963, 1; "Missile Men Like Area," *SJR*, 3 October 1963, 1.

58. "Missile Site at Black Mesa to Continue," *SJR*, 30 November 1967, 1; "Missile Launch Planned in Blanding Area," *SJR*, 13 September 1979, 1; "Air Force Concludes Tests in Area," *SJR*, 29 May 1980, 1; "Missile Testing Will Return to Green River," *SJR*, 2 April 1981, 12; "Army Plans to Drop Missile Boosters between Monticello and Navajo Nation," *SJR*, 10 March 1994, 2.

59. "Misguided Missile Drops in Colorado," *SJR*, 13 February 1964, 1; "Wayward Pershing Missile Falls in Vicinity of Blanding," *SJR*, 7 October 1965, 1; "Missile Malfunctions, Falls Near Bluff," *SJR*, 1 May 1969, 1.

15

From "Blank Spot" to "Sagebrush Rebellion"

THE RISE OF FEDERAL HEGEMONY IN SAN JUAN COUNTY

The discovery of San Juan—or at least the southern part of it—
occurred in the summer of 1933. At any rate, that is what a *San Juan
Record* headline intimated, announcing that the "blank spot" was
finally going to be "explored by California."[1] Teams of specialists from
many universities, including Stanford, Cornell, Princeton, Illinois,
Minnesota, Pittsburgh, and others, descended on the Monument
Valley-Rainbow Bridge area to record its geology, archaeology, ethnology, flora, fauna, and topography. The ultimate goal was to make
it possible for the government to "reach a decision as to which parts
of this vast wilderness, if any, are of outstanding significance . . . [in
order to] form the basis for any plans which may be projected for the
future administration of the area."[2] To the Navajos, Paiutes, Utes, and
some of the local whites, this whole exercise must have seemed a silly
formality about something with which they were intimately familiar.

Yet there were some important things to be learned from this
undertaking. The intent was to acquire knowledge, but for what purpose? From a local perspective, San Juan residents were more concerned about surviving the Depression than about what kinds of

345

insects lived in Monument Valley or what the shape was of Navajo Mountain. But the fact of "outside experts" coming into the county to advise the government about what was "best" for the land and its people suggested that local involvement and decision-making would be kept to a minimum. This pattern has been repeated on numerous occasions throughout the history of San Juan—a county whose residents control only 16 percent of its land base with federal (78 percent) and state (6 percent) holdings composing the remainder.[3] Thus, what appeared to be relatively inoffensive held the potential to foster resentment against government intervention and outside influence.

As discussed in the previous chapter, the county had shared friendly relations with both state and federal governments in the past. The reason for a gradual shift away from this attitude lies in the ever-tightening control of the land and its resources by forces outside of San Juan. The historical roots of this controversy creep in from many directions, but they all feed the main trunk of dissension concerning who has the final voice in deciding what is to be done. The general pattern of discovery, promotion, development, and control summarizes what has occurred over this last century, as the county came under increasing federal hegemony.

The first national park area established in San Juan County was Natural Bridges National Monument. In keeping with the American penchant for determining first, last, biggest, and best, the first recorded right of discovery goes to Cass Hite, Scotty Ross, Edward Randolph, and Indian Joe, who in 1883 found three arches located in White Canyon and its tributary, Armstrong Canyon. The men named the arches President, Senator, and Congressman in order of decreasing size and then thought no more of them.

As the livestock industry spread throughout the canyons of San Juan, cowboys such as James Scorup chased stray cattle beneath the arches, but it was not until March 1903, when mining engineer Horace J. Long accompanied Scorup to the arches, that the rock formations started to gain notice. The men renamed the arches after people they knew—the President became Augusta after Long's wife, the Senator became Caroline for Scorup's mother, and the Congressman became Edwin after Edwin Holmes, a former president of the Commercial Club, which sponsored the visit.[4]

Edwin, now Owachomo, Bridge in Natural Bridges National Monument, 1907. (San Juan Historical Commission)

Word spread. In 1907 the University of Utah sent a formal expedition to report on the archaeological and natural wonders of White Canyon, while a government surveyor, William B. Douglass, mapped the area the following year. Douglass also renamed the monuments: Augusta became Sipapu (a Hopi term for the place of emergence into this world), Caroline became Kachina (named after figures pictured on a nearby rock art panel), and Edwin became Owachomo (meaning Flatrock Mound, for a neighboring rock formation). Based on the two reports, President Theodore Roosevelt proclaimed the arches a national monument in 1908, and his successor, William Howard Taft, set aside 2,420 acres of unsurveyed land to surround it.[5]

The characteristics of these rock formations lent themselves to spectacular promotion. Sipapu, the largest of the arches, spans 261 feet across White Canyon and is 222 feet high. Pictures showing the nation's capitol building, large contemporary buildings, or a giant sequoia nestled beneath the span sent graphic messages about the size of these formations. The next problem was how to get the public to see them. Local people, especially men like Ezekiel "Zeke" Johnson, custodian for the monument until 1941, and J. Wiley Redd, custodian until the mid-1950s, worked hard to obtain roads.

As early as 1917, tourists complained about the fatiguing travel to the monument by horseback, and residents hoped that "purse strings governing road expenditures" would loosen. The first road wound its way from Blanding through the canyons to the Bears Ears and then dropped down to the monument. The Forest Service and workers from Blanding labored together, starting in 1920, to make the road a reality, but both groups lacked sufficient funds. Seven years later, impetus in the form of oil exploration on Elk Ridge pushed the project closer to completion. Suddenly an economically minded state legislature found $10,000, and the road was completed. Soon there was talk of tying Zion and Bryce national parks to the Bridges and Mesa Verde to the east, although no such direct route materialized.[6]

The uranium industry of the 1950s also fostered change. Mining in White Canyon and the surrounding area created a need for better, more direct roads, one of which went right by Natural Bridges. In order to protect the monument and its periphery, the Bureau of Land Management transferred 4,916 acres of land to the monument in 1961, bringing the total to 7,435 acres. The federal government also provided additional funds for roads, a visitor center (completed in 1968), and trail improvements.[7] Naturally, with increased access and facilities, the number of tourists increased. In 1949, 1,800 tourists registered at the monument; in the 1950s, roughly 3,000 to 4,000 made their way to the park each summer; in 1993, there were 151,504 visitors.[8]

A similar pattern was true of Canyonlands, north of Monticello. Although Captain J. N. Macomb is credited with the first detailed account of the Canyonlands area in 1859, and although there were local individuals, such as Kent and Alfred Frost, who brought travelers into the area to marvel at the rock formations and scenery, it was not until the late 1950s and early 1960s that the government gave serious consideration to setting these lands aside as a national park.[9] Unlike the creation of Natural Bridges as a monument, accomplished through executive order, the establishment of a national park requires an act of Congress. Not surprisingly, the birth of Canyonlands emerged only through a tortuous process of state and federal politics.

Significant, complex issues fueled the controversy. Briefly, in 1961 U.S. Senator Frank Moss introduced legislation to create a 300,000-acre park encompassing the Needles District, Island in the Sky, and the Maze.[10] Arrayed on his side were Bates Wilson, Superintendent of Arches National Park; Secretary of Interior Stewart Udall, and Utah's Democratic members of the U.S. House of Representatives, David King and M. Blaine Peterson. Governor George D. Clyde and U.S. Senator Wallace Bennett, both Republicans, opposed suggested elements of the plan. Their main reason for opposition lay in their philosophy of resource development—mining, hunting, and grazing—which they believed would end if these lands became a national park. Compromises between the "scenery purists" and the "resource hogs" assumed many forms of give-and-take as each side offered to add or subtract lands, toyed with limited and full-blown multiple land use ideas, and appealed to various organizations for support.[11] Finally, on 3 September 1964, Congress passed the bill creating the 337,258-acre Canyonlands National Park, with only limited grazing rights, which were later phased out.

Local sentiment generally favored park development. For instance, the county commissioners received "100 percent credit" for promoting a sight-seeing trip on the Colorado River and in Canyonlands with Udall in 1961; they fought to have the park headquarters in a central location in the county and not in the Neck, located near Grand County; and they hosted a regional conference to gain support for the park from southwestern Colorado residents. The county commission encouraged the formation of a nonpartisan committee that promoted the concept of limited multiple-use, with the understanding that certain parts of the park, what Bennett called a "string of pearls," would come under normal park regulations, which automatically denied any form of resource development. However, the surrounding areas would be open to mining, hunting, and grazing.[12] Even when asked if they still supported having the park without any resource development, the commissioners went on record as being generally in agreement, one of them saying that "the park would do more good for San Juan County than anything he knew of."[13]

Federal money started to roll towards San Juan even before passage of the bill creating the park. The Department of the Interior planned to spend $400,000 in creating facilities and roads to meet the anticipated onslaught of tourists. By the end of 1969, the government had spent $8 million for road and campground improvements in the Needles District alone, yet Senator Bennett complained that a drop in visitation had occurred because the area needed to be more accessible.[14] Even though the money continued to flow to Canyonlands—another $8.5 in 1977 alone—there began to be a hardening of attitudes against federal control. New management plans called for a decrease in development and an increase in restricting access to prevent "irreversible environmental damage."[15] The basis of what has been called the "Sagebrush Rebellion," a movement discussed later, was now laid.

The increase of visitors to Canyonlands and its surrounding features has been dramatic. For instance, in 1968 there were 26,300 tourists scrambling around the monuments in the park; ten years later the number rose to 86,307; and in 1993 there were 434,844.[16] Greater numbers of visitors have necessitated increased federal control, much of it in opposition to county desires.

The general trend in visitation to Canyonlands has been one of steady increase. One factor that brought travelers into the area was the creation of state parks. Deadhorse Point near the northern county boundary officially joined the tourist industry as a state park in 1959 and became seasonally staffed starting in 1964; Newspaper Rock, south of Canyonlands, was dedicated in 1961. The following year, the ten-acre Goosenecks of the San Juan State Park near Mexican Hat became one more registered drawing feature to the county. This last site is a classic example of what geologists call an entrenched meander, and photographs of it appear in many geography texts throughout the world. In 1993, this park attracted 65,347 visitors, a seventeen percent increase from the previous year.[17]

The dramatic landscape was not the only drawing card to San Juan. Beginning in the 1950s, interest in preserving and displaying Anasazi sites and relics fostered important legislation concerning the

Four Corners region. The Bureau of Land Management (BLM) gave ten acres of land surrounding Newspaper Rock to the Utah Division of State Parks and Recreation for the protection of the significant rock art panel. This small plot of land became an attractive tourist site, with interpretive materials and picnic areas. The state applied to the BLM for an additional thousand acres in 1983 to encourage more camping and site development, which, ironically, became so overwhelming that by 1993 the lands reverted back to the BLM, which has since drafted plans to restrict access and limit growing environmental impact of the area.[18]

The love of tourists for the remnants of Anasazi culture that prompted a desire to control access to sites may be seen in other areas throughout the county. Hovenweep became a national monument in 1923 and has shown a steady increase of visitation. For instance, in 1983 there were 14,328 tourists; ten years later the figures had almost doubled to 26,000.[19] The ruins in Grand Gulch have experienced similar visitation growth. Starting in the 1960s, the BLM began stabilizing and inventorying the larger sites. The Secretary of the Interior, through two different acts, one in 1970 and the other in 1977, created a 37,807-acre primitive area that enhanced tourism but excluded traditional economic activities such as grazing cattle. Rangers, either full-time, part-time, or volunteer, have worked with the ever-increasing flow of tourists who backpack to the ruins to enjoy the sites and mystery of the Anasazi.

The rangers' job is not easy. Vandalism and looting of artifacts are far too common at the archaeological sites, spread over a large geographical area. An exact count of the growing number of visitors is difficult because there are many different ways of entering the canyons. In 1992 there were 9,497 registered tourists, and in 1993 there were 12,041; but BLM rangers estimate that these figures represent only half of those hiking in the area.[20] There has been nothing but a steady increase in use. Consequently, a Grand Gulch management plan, developed in 1993, restricts access by a permit system, controls the number of visitors, and charges higher visitation fees to pay for an increased staff of rangers.[21]

To encourage a greater understanding of the Anasazi and promote a larger flow of tourists, four agencies—San Juan County, the

Utah Navajo Development Council, the Navajo Tribe, and the Utah State Legislature—worked hard to create the Edge of the Cedars Museum State Park in Blanding. The $600,000 museum opened its doors in December 1978 to people interested in prehistoric and historic Native American and early Anglo American cultures within the county. Fifteen years and $1.6 million later, the museum had increased its space by one third with the addition of a repository for artifacts coming from San Juan County, as well as laboratory and storage space. Approximately 22,000 people visit the museum each year.[22]

While the government created many monuments, parks, and museums in the northern end of the county, the southern part, composed primarily of the Navajo reservation, was not far behind in its efforts to increase tourism. Credit for being the first promoter of tourism in this area goes to John Wetherill, who not only led expeditions to explore Anasazi ruins—such as Betatakin, Keet Seel, Inscription House, and others throughout the Four Corners area—but also guided the expedition initially credited with discovering Rainbow Bridge in 1909.[23] A year later it became a national monument administered by the National Park Service. Controversy followed over which white man was actually first to see the 275-foot-wide and 290-foot-high arch, some claiming the honor as early as 1884; but there is no debate about the monument's popularity.[24]

As information spread about the arch, hundreds of people made their way to the site. Sections of the trail that wound its way around the south and west sides of Navajo Mountain became a road in 1924, and, the next year, Hubert Richardson opened Rainbow Lodge, where tourists could obtain meals, a night's rest, and guides with pack animals for the remainder of the trip to the bridge. Over the years, many famous personalities, including Theodore Roosevelt, Zane Grey, Everett Ruess, and Barry Goldwater, have stood in awe at the base of the arch.[25]

Today, the 160-acre national monument is visited by thousands of people each year. Few of them travel the trail, however; rather, they arrive by boat on Lake Powell, the waters of which have been backed up to the site since 1965. Park managers are concerned that water is

Rainbow Bridge at the northern base of Navajo Mountain. (Photo by author)

undermining the arch's base, that too many tourists are affecting Navajo worship practices, and that recreational activities are spoiling the aesthetic experience. Again, the proposed solution to these problems has been to eliminate overnight camping and sports activities, limit the number of visitors, and increase park supervision.[26]

Scenery and Navajo culture have played major roles in the development of Monument Valley as a mecca for sightseers. At the turn of the century, the Wetherills were in the area to promote individual tours and to encourage early motorists to chance an overheated radiator or wheels buried to their axles in sand in order to see the dynamic monoliths that tower over the valley floor. But it was Harry Goulding who did the most to inform Americans about this rugged beauty. The story of how Goulding left his trading post for Hollywood, armed only with some photographs, and how the landscape's beauty sold itself to casts, crews, and directors has become well known. Harry and his wife became major promoters for these various ventures, and the trader on a number of occasions has recounted the story of the film industry's genesis in San Juan County.[27] Starting in 1938 and continuing for the next twenty-six years, director John Ford appeared in Monument Valley on a fairly regular basis to create such film classics as *Stagecoach, Fort Apache, The Searchers, She Wore a Yellow Ribbon, My Darling Clementine,* and *Cheyenne Autumn.*

The film industry brought about changes for both the people and the land. Over 260 miles of road were either constructed or improved, a great deal of which was done by Navajo labor. The tribal headquarters in Window Rock, Arizona, took responsibility for issuing permits to movie companies for filming activities on the reservation, while the Bureau of Land Management handled the off-reservation permits. Eventually, the tribe also sent Navajo inspectors to insure that the countryside was not damaged.[28]

Yet, the land, more than any other feature, was the thing that Ford loved and was willing to pay for. In 1946 he said:

> I think you can say that the real star of my Westerns has always been the land. . . . My favorite location is Monument Valley; it has rivers, mountains, plains, desert. . . . I feel at peace there. I have been all over the world, but I consider this the most complete, beautiful and peaceful place on Earth.[29]

Indeed, Ford made the land synonymous with the Indian in a thematic statement that pitted basic survival and wilderness against the white man and civilization. The former qualities mesh with the timeless, pure landscape of natural beauty that also portrays an ever-present threat. The image of the land and the Indian were inseparable.[30]

Cheyenne Autumn, filmed in 1964, was the last of the Ford films produced in Monument Valley. The end of an era had arrived. By 1973, the year that Ford died, the Navajo Tribe opened a department of film to handle requests by moviemakers who wished to photograph the lovely backdrop of red rocks and sand. Charging $1000 a day or more for professionals, the department keeps much of the money that used to trickle down to the people.[31] Movies like *Back to the Future III,* and commercials of everything from cars to batteries to cigarettes take advantage of the wide open spaces to sell an image, in some respects not so different from the ones that Ford created— wilderness, freedom, and the Native American. Despite all this exposure, there is still a magical feeling when a person first enters Monument Valley, the same feeling that fostered its early film history.

The Navajo tribal government saw an opportunity to capitalize on this feeling in 1960 when it created the Monument Valley Navajo Tribal Park. Development of the 94,000-acre park initially cost $275,000, which included a visitor center, campgrounds, and a network of roads that wind between and around some of the most heavily photographed monoliths and mesas in the world—the Mittens, Totem Pole Rock, Three Sisters, and Merrick Butte. The growing number of visitors attests to the park's popularity: in 1960 there were approximately 22,000 fee-paying tourists; in 1983 there were 100,000; in 1993, 292,721.[32] Today, local Navajos are faced with the questions of what type and how much more development they desire in Monument Valley. The general attitude, however, has been favorable towards the park and the economic boost it has given to the area.

The northern boundary line of the reservation near Monument Valley is the San Juan River, another notable tourist attraction. While Monument Valley had its promoters in Wetherill and Goulding, the river had its advocate in Norman Nevills. He officially started his river-running business in 1936, which peaked in the late 1940s at the time of his death.[33] Norman and his wife, Doris, rowed, fed, and entertained hundreds of vacationers on a variety of trips down the San Juan and Colorado rivers. From their headquarters in the Nevills' Mexican Hat Lodge, they launched a promotional campaign that took them throughout the Four Corners region and beyond, bringing tourists from all parts of the United States.

In addition to being physically fit, safety conscious, and an avid salesman of his product, Nevills was creative and had a flare for the dramatic. His repertory of entertainment ranged from storytelling to balancing upside down on his hands on a floating log, and from vocally exhorting his river god, "Yogi," for help to relating facts and figures about the San Juan gleaned from his river statistics project for the government.[34] He appealed to all audiences from the Monticello high school students he guided down the San Juan to such notables as Barry Goldwater, Reverend H. Baxter Liebler, Ernie Pyle, and numerous authors, editors, and scientists who later wrote of their experiences.[35]

Norman Nevills (in third boat bending over) preparing for a launch in June 1945. Headquartered at Mexican Hat, he led tourist groups on river-running expeditions from the mid-1930s to the end of the 1940s. (Special Collections, University of Utah Library)

Nevills's personal daring and creativity encouraged him to improve upon what was successful. In his early days, he tried carrier pigeons as a means of communicating with his home base, and he coordinated his river trips with the owners of Rainbow Lodge. When commercial airplane flights from Mexican Hat became feasible, he bought a Piper Cub and then replaced it with two other planes to give local scenic tours. This last addition was literally his downfall. On 19 September 1949, Norman and Doris Nevills died in a fiery plane crash caused by engine failure, causing his plane hit the rim of a canyon during take-off. Following their funeral and the cremation of their bodies in Grand Junction, a friend scattered their ashes over canyon country, a fitting farewell to a pair who had made the land and its rivers so popular.[36]

At the time of Norm Nevills's death, he had floated some 13,000 miles and had "done much to awaken interest in our scenic wonders and possibilities for vacation trips in southeastern Utah," according to a newspaper account[37] His work lived on through those who bought his equipment and continued his operation and others who formed their own professional river-running outfits.[38] Today there are approximately a dozen professional companies that ply their trade on the San Juan River. Private groups and individuals make up the vast majority of the river traffic, which has become so popular that the BLM restricts by permit and fee the number of visitors to 12,000.[39]

The tourist industry has also mushroomed at Lake Powell, created by the Glen Canyon Dam in 1963. The 1.25-million-acre Glen Canyon National Recreation Area, stretching primarily over southern Utah, is controlled by the National Park Service and feeds on tourist dollars. Bullfrog, Hite, Hall's Crossing, Rainbow Bridge, and Dangling Rope, located in or near San Juan County, sport marinas, stores, campgrounds, airstrips, and docking facilities in varying degrees of complexity and sophistication. The Bureau of Reclamation and the National Park Service completed the $1.25-million visitors center at Page, Arizona, in 1968, and it attracts increasing numbers of tourists. In 1992 more than 3.6 million vacationers visited the recreation area.[40]

The overall impact of this type of development has brought more people to the county, created more need for control, and fostered a greater interest in the government's utilization of its resources. Roderick Nash, a scholar who has studied this phenomenon on a national level, calls the results the "irony of victory" as he points out that Americans have so commercialized yet sanctified the outdoor experience that they stand in danger of "loving" their wilderness to death.[41] This is certainly true of San Juan, where more people come each year to "get away from it all," only to find that some of what they were trying to escape has come with them.

In summarizing the growth of parks, tourism, and recreation discussed so far, one sees clearly the pattern of discovery, promotion, development, and control. With the exception of three national monuments—Natural Bridges, Rainbow Bridge, and Hovenweep—that were introduced in the early part of the twentieth century and had relatively little acreage, the creation of parks, scenic-access roads, and tourist facilities occurred primarily in the 1960s. The government withdrew access to and use of large sections of public domain to make this possible, through actions generally supported by the people of San Juan.

San Juan was a part of the larger, national trend of the 1960s during which an increased awareness of the environment, a growing utilization of leisure time, and the expansion of the nation's economy were coupled with a desire of many to experience nature and return to a slower-paced lifestyle. In its most extreme form, the hippie movement embodied the ideals of casting off social convention and returning to the way it felt humans were meant to live—in harmony with nature. San Juan County received part of the subsequent exodus of health-seeking visitors who fled from the cities to the glories of the outdoors. Word spread on a formal level as brochures, magazines, and dramatic photographs reached the public eye and also spread informally as vacationers returned to tell of the wonders they had encountered. San Juan's popularity catapulted the county from being a back eddy in the main flow of national interests into an environmental showpiece as thousands flocked to see for themselves what the land had to offer. Government promotion and control followed.

For the National Park Service and other government agencies, the 1960s was the honeymoon period before economic reality set in. The picture started to change dramatically by the mid-1970s, when the uranium business had faltered and almost stopped; when limitations on grazing livestock, building roads, and cutting timber affected the livelihood of residents; and when the county's infrastructure of schools and community services that had blossomed during the boom times now started to shrink painfully with decreasing revenue.

County government officials realized that to support residents with necessary services, the county needed to have a strong tax base. With only 16 percent of county lands controlled by private interests, the leaders were very concerned about how the government utilized the remainder. In 1975 Calvin Black, a county commissioner who throughout his career reminded the government of its obligations to rural communities, sent a bill to the national government for $2,000,000 for "taxes" on federal land. His thinking, with that of others throughout the West, stirred the bureaucracy to action, with the result that, starting in 1976, a new program called "Payment-in-Lieu-of-Taxes" (PILT) began. It was designed to help rural counties obtain

Calvin Black, San Juan County Commissioner and champion of local access to natural resources, receives an award from James Watt, Secretary of the Interior, in June 1983. (Courtesy Carolyn Black)

revenue from untaxable lands controlled by federal organizations such as the BLM, National Forest Service, National Park Service, Fish and Wildlife Service, and various water projects. The first payment came in 1977 and added $292,896 to the county coffers; each successive year usually saw a slight increase, so that, in 1993, the county received $400,847.[42]

Yet these annual payments were only part of the picture. Multiple use of the land for everything from mining, logging, and hunting to water development, grazing, and recreation was the real economic lifeblood of the county. Therefore, in 1972, when the government selected 60,000 acres of Forest Service land in the Woodenshoe-Dark Canyon area for consideration as a wilderness area, many county residents felt uneasy at the suggestion. To qualify as a wilderness area, the land under review had to have a roadless tract of at least 5,000 acres, "solitude," and "opportunities for primitive and unconfined recreation."[43] What that meant in laymen's terms was that all economic activity would cease once identified areas were inventoried and approved.

Eventually, the commissioners' unrest turned to anger. Other areas appeared on the list of lands to be studied for wilderness designation. Arch Canyon, Hammond Canyon, Lockhart Basin, Bridger Jack Mesa, Butler Wash, Slickhorn Canyon, Fish Creek, Mule Canyon, Grand Gulch, and many others came under scrutiny. Of the 2.6 million acres of BLM-controlled lands within the county, the government inventoried 2 million, but due to either unsuitability or public pressure actually considered only 11 percent or 312,902 acres.[44]

The issues were real: dramatic times calling forth dramatic lines. Calvin Black protested what he considered this part of federal "colonialism" of the West. He wrote to Utah Senator Jake Garn and proposed that while President Jimmy Carter was giving control of the Panama Canal back to the Panamanians, he might just as well give all the federal lands in the West back to the states so that they too could chart their own destiny.[45] A lawsuit entitled *Kleppe v. New Mexico* (1976) granted the government extensive powers, both as a "proprietor" and as a "legislature," over federal lands within a state. In a sense, the government could do what it wanted despite the state's and county's desire to do differently.[46]

But it was the environmentalist, often labeled a "backpacker," who became the archenemy to many residents, "trying to bring the country to its knees economically." Black publicly warned in a newspaper report that the citizens of San Juan were frustrated with federal agencies and "are actually considering committing acts of vandalism on areas of land being considered for possible wilderness designation 'if they [the federal government] don't start paying attention to us. People might get hurt.'"[47]

The San Juan County Commission was not the only vocal grassroots organization opposing government control of land during what has been called the Sagebrush Rebellion. In Utah, farm and ranch organizations, Husky Oil, the Utah Mining Association, and the Public Lands Council, among others, expressed their sentiment that "the federal land agencies have gone too far" in protecting the environment and in creating wilderness areas. The Western Interstate Region of the National Association of Counties, 400 delegates strong, met in Boise, Idaho, to reaffirm its position that the states should receive ownership of federal lands. That same year, 1980, the western states submitted the Sagebrush Rebellion Bill calling for transfer of 460 million acres to their control.[48] It was not passed.

The key to winning the "rebellion" lay in mustering the most political support on one's side. The National Forest Service Regional Director Vern Hamre pointed out that of the 264,000 responses received nationally concerning wilderness, those opposing it stood three to every one who favored it; in Utah, it was ten to one.[49] San Juan commissioners urged their people to "out-organize" their opponents, sponsoring workshops in Blanding and Monticello to increase citizen awareness. The main gist of their argument was that with so many parks, monuments, and recreation areas already preventing multiple use of much public land, why should more land be added to the list; that many of the areas now under review held known, valuable mineral deposits; and that by designating an area a wilderness, the lands would be overrun and ruined by avid "backpackers." Those favoring wilderness countered that this rhetoric was a "smoke screen" to weaken federal regulations in order to open areas to further exploitation.[50]

The BLM realized that on the local level it faced a very real "credibility gap." To counter the growing opposition, the government began to espouse the concept that "residents of an area should have a 'fairly significant say'" as to what happened in their region. Federal representatives came to San Juan County and in public programs and luncheons explained their position in softened tones. In 1981 the San Juan commissioners signed an agreement with the BLM's Moab District manager which pledged coordinated planning on a local level. The "New Beginning," as it was dubbed, eased tension, but the issues remained. By 1983 Commissioner Black said he would "accept, not support" the BLM's wilderness designation of Dark and Woodenshoe canyons, Grand Gulch, Butler Wash, and other locations. Eleven years later, ten wilderness areas in San Juan County, totaling 359,910 acres, are still pending, waiting for congressional recognition.[51]

County government officials also fended off an attempt by the federal government to add 260,000 acres of land to the Navajo

Reservation as part of the settlement of the Navajo-Hopi land dispute under discussion in Arizona. The roots of this problem go back to the 1880s, but the issue centers on establishing aboriginal rights to lands near the Hopi Reservation and then resettling displaced Navajo occupants to another area. The San Juan commissioners outlined their reasons for not wishing to expand the Navajo Reservation northwards at the expense of county lands. Their concerns included the fact that the government wanted to use Utah resources to solve what the Utah commissioners considered an "Arizona problem"; the land selected would not support the estimated 3,500 people to be placed upon it; the oil-royalty money designated for Utah Navajos would be diluted and spread among a much larger number of people; reservation lands did not qualify for PILT funds, thus decreasing county revenues while county services such as health care, education, roads, etc., would only increase; and the 21,000 acres of private land, 24,000 acres of state land, and many tracts of land leased for mineral development would be lost for future use.[52] Following further investigation, the relocation committee dropped San Juan County from its list of possibilities.

The Utah Navajos, however, have enjoyed an increase in political power. The most notable gain occurred in 1984, when the United States Department of Justice directed the county to redraw its voting districts to create a political voting bloc on the reservation. Traditionally, Navajo residents had never been significantly involved in county politics, many of them looking to Window Rock for whatever help was required. The tribal government was often slow, and sometimes deaf, when it came to hearing pleas for aid. But now the county commission would have one of its three members come from the reservation as a spokesman for those people.

In 1985, the Navajos elected Mark Maryboy from Aneth as their first representative. As a Democrat in a conservative, Republican-dominated county, Maryboy has received off-reservation support from environmental groups and organizations in Utah's urban areas. For example, University of Utah students have driven hundreds of miles of reservation back roads to register Navajo voters. Maryboy was reelected to the county commission in 1990. He has also held a position on the Navajo Tribal Council, was appointed by President

Bill Clinton to serve on the National Indian Education Advisory Committee, and offered the opening prayer in Navajo at the 1992 Democratic National Convention in New York City.[53] The voice of Native Americans in San Juan County will grow ever stronger as education, political organization, and community involvement become increasingly prominent parts of their way of life.

Changing issues have always faced county government officials as priorities concerning people, land, the economy, and legislation shift with the times. The general concern voiced by many residents recently, however, expresses a fear that the federal bureaucracy is growing beyond its constitutional powers; that many residents will not be able to derive an income from the land because of increasing government control; that those who live in an area have a greater right to land-use decisions than outsiders; and that the federal government has reneged on previous agreements such as building promised roads into Canyonlands or allowing the county to build highways on unreserved public domain, and so cannot be trusted.[54] The result when the parties meet seems to be endless wrangling.

Perhaps one of the most interesting debates occurred in the late 1970s as the Sagebrush Rebellion gathered steam. This time, however, the controversy concerned the storage of nuclear waste in Gibson Dome, ten miles from the entrance to the Needles District of Canyonlands National Park. By 1979 the federal government had selected nine possible national sites to evaluate for their suitability of storage of radioactive materials. Lavendar and Davis canyons, a part of Gibson Dome, had deep salt deposits that would safely protect the materials once they were embedded in the earth in durable containers. A one-mile-wide facility with a three-mile buffer zone would receive the material from twenty-two truck shipments by highway per week, would consume ten tons of coal an hour and utilize 1,000 gallons of fresh water each minute. For the flagging San Juan economy this meant the possibility of creating jobs for 1,600 workers during the five-year construction phase, an additional 1,200 employees to operate the facility for thirty years, and the possibility of 1,800 secondary service jobs. An estimated annual cash flow of $100 million made the possibility all that much more enticing.[55]

The county commissioners saw the economic benefits and went

on record early in the fight as being unequivocally in favor of evaluation of the sites with the hopes that the repository would eventually
be in San Juan County. With mines and mills closing on the Colorado
Plateau and one-third of the county's assessed valuation coming
from the uranium business, the commissioners felt that to vote otherwise would be foolish. The opposing side received heavy support
from environmental organizations active on both regional and
national levels, from the superintendent of Canyonlands, Peter Parry,
and from three different Utah governors holding office during this
period.[56]

The point-counterpoint of both sides' attempts to influence the
outcome was dramatic. For example, fifty people participated in a
sixty-mile hike from Canyonlands to Moab, where a relay of runners
then jogged to Salt Lake City to deliver to the legislature an anti-
repository petition; four months later, a seventy-five-car caravan
delivered to Governor Scott Matheson a petition with 1,700 signatures from Grand and San Juan County residents favoring the repository and chastising the governor for not meeting with them to
discuss the issue. Matheson ordered state offices to refuse licenses and
permits for exploratory work relating to the project; the county commissioners staked 111 mining claims all over Gibson Dome so that
the county could authorize permits to the Department of Energy to
continue its studies. To tweak the governor's nose, they named two
of the claims "Governor" and "Scott."[57]

Local meetings and newspapers received wide support but failed
to bring the sides together. San Juan County residents generally fell
in line with their commissioners in supporting exploration, while
Moab in Grand County had a stronger following against it. The San
Juan commissioners charged that the governor's advisory staff was
composed of "political hacks who are environmental extremists"
using federal money to fight a federal project. They even wrote to the
Department of Energy requesting that it deny a grant to the state
until it could be impartial in its evaluation process. When the newly
elected Republican governor, Norman Bangerter, assumed the same
stance as the out-going Democrat Matheson, the commissioners felt
even more betrayed.[58]

In December 1984 the federal government announced that San

Juan County was fourth in a ranking of five possible sites for the repository. When the Secretary of Energy made the announcement, he mentioned that "veto power held by the states is a 'powerful option,'" no doubt alluding to the political furor accompanying the exploration phase. For a few years, the feud languished behind the scenes, but it received new life in the 1990s when the federal government renewed its interest in San Juan. Governor Mike Leavitt, like his predecessors, had no desire to revitalize the drama and so on 14 January 1993 announced his decision to disapprove San Juan's application for a study grant for a monitored retrievable storage facility for nuclear waste.[59] It was hoped that state and county could at last bury their animosity over the nuclear issue, which had held potential for destruction akin to that of the spent nuclear rods waiting to be stored.

The love-hate relationship between San Juan County and state and federal government agencies offers an interesting study in subordinate/dominant relationships. The growing federal hegemony has presented recent challenges that have been met by resistance. While money, power, and control remain center stage, there has also been a strong desire evidenced to meet the wishes of local residents even at great cost. The tradition of service and loyalty has been evident from the start and has helped the county. Aspiring politicians in the future will do well to look at the county's servants in the past.

ENDNOTES

1. "The Blank Spot to Be Explored by California," *San Juan Record* (hereafter cited as *SJR*), 18 May 1933, 1.

2. Ansel Franklin Hall, *General Report on the Rainbow Bridge-Monument Valley Expedition of 1933* (Berkeley: University of California Press, 1934), 5–6.

3. Rick Bailey, assistant executive to the San Juan County commissioners, telephone conversation with author, 15 August 1994.

4. W. W. Dyar, "The Colossal Bridges of Utah, *Century Magazine* 68 (August 1904): 505–11; John W. Van Cott, *Utah Place Names* (Salt Lake City: University of Utah Press, 1990), 269–70.

5. Byron Cummings, "The Great Natural Bridges of Utah," *Bulletin of the University of Utah* 3, no 3 (November 1910): 4–16; Neil M. Judd, "On Some Names in Natural Bridges National Monument," *National Parks*

Magazine 4, no. 241 (October 1967): 16–19; "National Monument," *Grand Valley Times*, 15 October 1909, 1.

6. "Tourists Are Enthusiastic," *San Juan Blade*, 16 November 1917, 1; "San Juan Working for Road to Natural Bridges," *Times-Independent*, 2 September 1920, 1; "Asks $15,000 for Road to Natural Bridges," *Times-Independent*, 3 February 1927, 1; "Sum of $10,000 for Bridge Road," *Times-Independent*, 10 March 1927, 1; "Auto Road to Natural Bridges Completed," *Times-Independent*, 27 October 1927; "The Old Settler," *SJR*, 6 February 1936, 1.

7. Lloyd M. Pierson, "Natural Bridges, A.Z. (After Zeke) 1956–61," *Blue Mountain Shadows* 10 (Summer 1992): 56–61; "Propose Withdrawal 4,841.55 Acres for Nat'l Monument," *SJR*, 3 February 1961, 1; "Construction Step-up at Natural Bridges," *SJR*, 3 October 1963, 1; "Museum Completed at Natural Bridges," *SJR*, 2 May 1968, 3; Steven H. Mehls, "Canyonlands National Park, Arches National Park, and Natural Bridges National Monument Historic Resource Study," National Park Service, 15 July 1986, on file in the Utah State Historical Society, Salt Lake City, Utah, 182.

8. Josephine Bayles, "Record Number of Tourists Visit Natural Bridges," *SJR*, 17 November 1949, 2; Pierson, "Natural Bridges," 57; "Blanding News," *SJR*, 26 December 1952, 4; statistics located in the San Juan County Economic Development Office, County Courthouse, Monticello, Utah.

9. For delightful accounts of individual exploration and tour guiding in the predevelopment days of Canyonlands National Park see Kent Frost, *My Canyonlands* (New York: Abelard-Schuman Press, 1971); C. Alfred Frost, *Rattlesnakes and Wild Horses and Other Campfire Tales* (Conway, Ark.: River Road Press, 1993).

10. For an excellent explanation of this controversy on a federal and state level see Thomas G. Smith, "The Canyonlands National Park Controversy, 1961–64," *Utah Historical Quarterly* 59, no. 3 (Summer 1991): 216–42.

11. Ibid., 228.

12. "Interior Secretary Stewart Udall Here July 1–6," *SJR*, 15 June 1961, 1; "Canyonlands and San Juan County," *SJR*, 8 February 1962, 2; "Combined Chambers to Discuss Canyonlands," *SJR*, 15 February 1962, 1; "Canyonlands Committee Urges Unified Effort," *SJR*, 5 April 1962, 1.

13. "Senators Impressed by Canyons' Scenery," *SJR*, 26 April 1962, 1.

14. "San Juan to Receive $400 Thousand," *SJR*, 17 January 1963, 1; "Canyonlands Road Nearing Completion," *SJR*, 11 December 1969, 1; "Parks Visits in State Up 12%," *SJR*, 21 May 1970, 3.

15. "Canyonlands Gets 8.5 Million," *SJR*, 3 March 1977, 3; "Canyonlands Plan Renews Protest," *SJR*, 13 October 1977, 1.

16. "Park Visits in State Up 12%," *SJR*, 21 May 1970, 3; "Canyonlands Visitors Increase," *SJR*, 1 March 1979, 10; San Juan County Economic Development Office, County Courthouse, Monticello, Utah.

17. Statistics on file at Edge of the Cedars State Park, received from Steven Olsen, director, telephone conversation with author, 22 August 1994.

18. "Newspaper Rock Turned to State," *SJR*, 21 December 1961, 8; "Newspaper Rock Park Expansion Approved," *SJR*, 10 November 1983, 1; Draft of "Partnership Plan—Indian Creek Canyons," Bureau of Land Management, 1994, in possession of author.

19. Statistics on file in "Hovenweep Monthly Public Use Report," Chief Ranger's Office, Mesa Verde National Park, Colorado.

20. Statistics on file in BLM office in Monticello, given by Kay Wilson, recreation technician, telephone conversation with author, 22 August 1994.

21. "Grand Gulch Plateau Cultural and Recreation Area Management Plan," Bureau of Land Management, 14 April 1993, in possession of author, 2–3.

22. "Rampton Signs Museum Bill," *SJR*, 14 February 1974, 1; "Edge of Cedars Plans Advance," *SJR*, 18 September 1975, 1; "Edge of Cedars Dedication Set," *SJR*, 26 October 1978, 2; Steven Olsen, museum director, telephone conversation with author, 17 August 1994.

23. See Frances Gillmor and Louisa Wetherill, *Traders to the Navajos* (Albuquerque: University of New Mexico Press, 1934).

24. For the most complete discussion and documentation concerning the discovery of Rainbow Bridge see Stephen C. Jett, "The Great 'Race' to 'Discover' Rainbow Natural Bridge," *Kiva* 58, no. 1 (Fall 1992): 3–66; see also James E. Babbitt, *Rainbow Trails* (Page, Ariz.: Glen Canyon Natural History Association, 1990).

25. John Stewart MacClary, "Shortcut to Rainbow Bridge," *Desert Magazine* (May 1939): 3–6; "Guest Book of Rainbow Lodge," *Arizona Highways* 22, no. 6 (June 1946): 26–29.

26. For Navajo views concerning the monument see Karl W. Luckert, *Navajo Mountain and Rainbow Bridge Religion* (Flagstaff: Museum of Northern Arizona, 1977); "Management Plan Set for Rainbow Bridge," *SJR*, 6 January 1994, 5.

27. For accounts of Goulding's role in the film industry see Samuel Moon, *Tall Sheep: Harry Goulding, Monument Valley Trader* (Norman: University of Oklahoma Press, 1992), 144–63; Richard Klinck, *Land of Room Enough and Time Enough* (Salt Lake City: Gibbs M. Smith, 1984): 74–85, William R. Florence, "John Ford . . . The Duke . . . and Monument

Valley," *Arizona Highways* (September 1981): 22–37; and Todd McCarthy, "John Ford and Monument Valley," *American Film* 8, no. 7 (May 1978): 10–16.

28. Rusty Musselman interview with author, 6 November 1991, transcript in possession of author.

29. Florence, "John Ford," 37.

30. Michael N. Budd, "A Critical Analysis of Western Films Directed by John Ford from *Stagecoach* to *Cheyenne Autumn*," Ph.D. diss., University of Iowa, 1975, 436–79.

31. Todd McCarthy, "John Ford and Monument Valley," *American Film* 8, no. 7 (May 1978): 16; John Holiday interview with author, 9 September 1991, transcript in possession of author; Seth Clitso interview with author, 20 January 1992, transcript in possession of author.

32. O. F. Oldendorph, "Monument Valley—A Navajo Tribal Park," *National Parks Magazine* 40, no. 227 (August 1966): 4–8; "2,000 Attend Valley Park Dedication," *SJR*, 13 May 1960, 1; "Navajos Dedicate Tribal Park Gateway," *Denver Post*, 9 May 1960, 31; Marsha Keele, "Monument Valley Park Celebrates 25th Year," *SJR*, 28 July 1983, 1; Statistics on file in San Juan County Economic Development Office, County Courthouse, Monticello, Utah.

33. See P. T. Reilly, "Norman Nevills: Whitewater Man of the West," *Utah Historical Quarterly* 55, no. 2 (Spring 1987): 181–200; Roy Webb, "Never Was Anything So Heavenly—Nevills Expeditions on the San Juan River," *Blue Mountain Shadows* 12 (Summer 1993): 35–50.

34. Randall Henderson, "River Trail to Rainbow Bridge," *Desert Magazine* 8, no. 11 (September 1945): 17–24; Alfred M. Bailey, "Desert River through Navajo Land," *National Geographic* 92, no. 2 (August 1947): 149–65; Doris Valle, *Looking Back around the Hat: A History of Mexican Hat* (n.p., 1986), 37–44.

35. "Interesting Lecture by Norman Nevills," *SJR*, 20 June 1940, 9; "San Juan Boat Trip Thrilling Experience," *SJR*, 7 May 1942, 1; "Nevills Lodge Fire Obliterates Part of Mexican Hat History," *SJR*, 16 January 1964, 5.

36. "Nevills Has New Piper Cub," *SJR*, 23 October 1947, 1; "Nevills Expedition," *SJR*, 2 June 1949, 1; "Norman and Doris Nevills Die in Plane Crash at Mexican Hat," *SJR*, 22 September 1949, 1; Reilly, "Norman Nevills," 200.

37. Reilly, "Norman Nevills," 199; "Norman D. Nevills Returns from Lecture Tour," *SJR*, 19 November 1942, 1.

38. Frank Wright, a Blanding resident who had worked with Nevills, purchased the equipment and formed a company with James Rigg from

Grand Junction. See Randall Henderson, "Glen Canyon Voyage," *Desert Magazine* 15, no. 10 (October 1952): 7–12.

39. Linda Richmond, San Juan River ranger, telephone conversations with author, 10 June and 19 August 1994.

40. Jean Duffy, "Glen Canyon National Recreation Area," *Arizona Highways* 40, no. 1 (January 1964): 42–43; Walter Meayers Edwards, "Lake Powell, Waterway to Desert Wonders," *National Geographic* 132, no. 1 (July 1967): 44–75; "Center Opens Sunday," *SJR*, 11 April 1968, 9.

41. Roderick Nash, *Wilderness and the American Mind* (New Haven: Yale University Press, 1967), 316.

42. "County Gets $292,896 in Lieu of Taxes," *SJR*, 6 October 1977, 1; "PILT Payments Distributed through BLM to Counties," *SJR*, 28 October 1993, 13.

43. "Dark Canyon Is Wilderness Possibility," *SJR*, 1 June 1972, 1; "Wilderness Procedure Outlined," *SJR*, 5 October 1978, 1; "Wilderness Inventory to Begin December 1 in Utah," *SJR*, 16 November 1978, 1.

44. "San Juan Potential Wilderness Reduced," *SJR*, 20 November 1980, 1.

45. "Protests 'Colonialism' of West," *SJR*, 8 September 1977, 3.

46. David E. Engdahl, *Constitutional Federalism in a Nutshell* (St. Paul: West Publishing Co., 1987): 228–31

47. "Critical of 'Wilderness Area,'" *SJR*, 10 August 1978, 2; "Plan to Fight 'Wilderness,'" *SJR*, 26 April 1979, 1.

48. "Farm Groups Oppose 'Wilderness,'" *SJR*, 9 August 1979, 12; "Western Officials Draft Resolution," *SJR*, 1 May 1980, 15; "Sagebrush Rebellion Bill to Transfer Land," *SJR*, 4 September 1980, 4.

49. "'Wilderness' Acreage 48,400 in San Juan," *SJR*, 11 January 1979, 1.

50. "'Wilderness' Foes Urged to 'Out-organize' Proponents," *SJR*, 25 January 1979, 1; "Small Crowd at Wilderness Meet," *SJR*, 28 June 1979, 1; "Commission Opposes Wilderness Tag," *SJR*, 29 March 1979, 1; "West and East Fight Over 514 Million Public Acres," *SJR*, 3 September 1981, 17.

51. "Cites 'Wilderness' as Major Problem," *SJR*, 29 November 1979, 1; "BLM and County Sign Historic Agreement," *SJR*, 3 September 1981, 1; statistics on pending wilderness areas obtained from *Utah BLM Statewide Wilderness Final Environmental Impact Statement*, vol. 1 (November 1990), 49, located at Bureau of Land Management Office, Monticello, Utah.

52. "Commission Opposes Land Plan," *SJR*, 10 March 1977, 1.

53. Florence Williams, "Revolution at Utah's Grassroots: Navajos Seek Political Power," *High Country News* 22, no. 15 (30 July 1990): 1, 10–11; "Maryboy Appointed by Pres. Clinton," *SJR*, 15 June 1994, 1.

54. Bill Redd, county commissioner, conversation with author, 2 September 1994.

55. "San Juan Area Being Considered for Nuclear Waste Disposal Site," *SJR*, 26 July 1979, 12; "Nuclear Waste Poses Storage Problems," *SJR*, 28 August 1980, 2; "Overflow Crowd Attends Nuclear Meeting," *SJR*, 12 November 1981, 1.

56. "Commissioner Urges Positive Response to Nuclear Repository," *SJR*, 15 January 1981, 19; "Nuclear Site Concerns Park Superintendent," *SJR*, 12 November 1981, 4; "Two Agencies Act to Counter BLM Permit," *SJR*, 22 July 1982, 1.

57. "Hikers Protest Nuclear Repository," *SJR*, 25 March 1982, 8; "Citizens Appeal Ban on Repository Permits," *SJR*, 29 July 1982, 1; "Legal Action Underway in Nuclear Controversy," *SJR*, 5 August 1982, 1; "County Stakes Mining Claims at Gibson Dome," *SJR*, 20 June 1984, 1.

58. "Nuclear Staff 'Hacks' Says County Commissioner," *SJR*, 18 January 1984, 1; "Governor Moves to Axe Repository Study," *SJR*, 9 May 1984, 1; "Local Government Challenges Governor on Nuclear Waste Study," *SJR*, 27 June 1984, 1; "San Juan Asks DOE to Deny Grant to State," *SJR*, 1 August 1984, 1; "Anti-repository Stance Infuriates Commission," *SJR*, 5 December 1984, 1.

59. "Gibson Dome Fourth: Nevada, Washington, Texas Top Three Repository Ranking," *SJR*, 26 December 1984, 1; "San Juan County Approved for Study Grant," *SJR*, 6 May 1992, 3; Western Network Consultants, "An Invitation to Participate in the Feasibility Study of a Monitored Retrievable Storage Facility (MRS) in San Juan County, Utah," Issue 2 (December 1992), in possession of author, 4.

16

San Juan in the Imagination

A WRITER'S PARADISE, A PHILOSOPHER'S DREAM

Amid all of the economic development, cultural conflict, and political strife, San Juan County has still spoken to a poetic side of the human soul. Few geographical regions on the earth enjoy such a wide variety of natural beauty, from sandstone monoliths in a high country desert to alpine splendor basking in the glow of a radiant sunset. Throughout the ages, people have expressed their appreciation for the land in paintings on cliff walls, in myths and stories told around the campfire, and in written songs, poems, and prose. The Four Corners region has been a spawning ground for raconteurs, writers, and philosophers who have shared with the rest of the world their experiences with the land and people of San Juan County.

Many stories from the Utes look at the land through religious and philosophical eyes. The tales are tinged with supernatural and mystical teachings that imbue the Four Corners region with a power and sense of divine meaning. For instance, in the time of the myths, the chief of all the Utes lost his wife and did not know where to look for her. Ta-vwoats, a supernatural being, answered the chief's prayers by taking him to the land of the dead to locate his wife. The god

371

rolled a great magical ball of fire before them, cutting the earth and its mountains, creating a path upon which the two could walk. The husband arrived in the land of the dead, saw how happy his wife was, and returned to the living after being cautioned that he should not walk upon this trail again. Ta-vwoats insured that the humans kept this law by forming a river in the trail—known today as the Colorado River and the Grand Canyon.[1]

Another story tells of how the gods gave the Indians fire by placing it in every physical form. When a tree or grass burns, it is the fire coming out, and when sparks fly from a rock, the power trapped long ago is being released. Yet another story tells how pieces of petrified wood are the remains from a fight between the sun and another supernatural being. The two battled on the ground and in the air; their lightning arrow shafts turned into petrified wood, while the missiles hurled by the sun remain as cobblestones. Since the rainbow was the weapon used against the sun, it is now found on the other side of the sky, away from the fiery orb. In another legend, a bear tells the Utes that he is heading to the Bear Ears country because that is where he will find "bull-grass, strawberries and good eating."[2] Thus, physical forms upon the land often held a deep, mythological significance for the Utes.

The same is true of the Navajos. Take, for instance a story about the Bears Ears that starts with a beautiful young woman who had refused wedlock to many suitors. She lived with her twelve brothers, kept a neat home, and lived a decorous life. Coyote, the trickster, asked for her hand in marriage, successfully completed a series of challenges, and married the girl. As she learned some of her husband's sinister knowledge, however, she began to assume qualities of evil and disorder along with the ability to change into a bear—hence her name, Changing Bear Maiden.

Her brothers became increasingly concerned about the strange behavior of their sister and sent the youngest boy to spy on her. He watched as she secretly performed rituals that turned her into a bear. When her brothers left to the four directions to go hunting, she methodically tracked them down and killed them all, except for the youngest one, who hid in a hole in the ground covered with rocks and dirt. Changing Bear Maiden returned to her camp in search of the sole survivor and eventually unearthed him.

The wind served as the boy's guardian, warning him that he should sit so that the sun would cast a shadow of his sister that he could watch. Just before she bent close to bite his head, he sprang to his feet, ran to a bush where she had hidden her vital organs, and let fly a lightning arrow. Blood gushed forth from the bush as well as from the bear. Wind warned that if the two separate streams of blood should meet, she would revive and be even harder to kill, and so the brother took a knife and made a deep furrow to keep the liquids apart.

He next addressed the body and said, "You shall live again but no longer as the mischievous bear-woman. You shall live in other forms, where you may be of service to your kind and not a thing of evil." He cut off body parts and tossed them in different directions. The pieces became various natural things such as a porcupine, pinyon nuts, acorns, yucca fruit, sorrel, dock, and other plants. Her paunch he dragged to the water, which became alkaline, while her limbs became different types of bears which he sent off with a strict warning to behave. The head, which he threw away, is now the Bears Ears, while the furrow dug with his knife is Comb Ridge and Comb Wash.[3] By these actions, good triumphed over evil, and the slain brothers came back to life.

This story, like dozens of others in Navajo lore, illustrates important values, such as good triumphing over evil. The rugged landscape lends itself to this theme, and, ironically, so did the Native American in the eyes of white writers. Although fiction, by definition, is not fact, it nevertheless mirrors feelings and attitudes that represent a perspective of reality. So, as writers mingled with the Navajos and Utes, they sometimes used fiction based on fact to express how they felt about a contemporary situation.

Albert R. Lyman, who penned both factual and fictionalized history, has achieved prominence as one of the chief writers about San Juan. In such books as *Indians and Outlaws*, *Edge of the Cedars*, and *The Outlaw of Navaho Mountain* he blended historical events with literary license to tell stories about sacrifice in achieving Mormon ideals.[4] His main theme, prompted by faith-promoting beliefs, cen-

Albert R. Lyman, a prolific recorder and writer of San Juan history, photographed in the 1940s. (San Juan County Historical Commission)

tered on the struggle of Mormons and the hardships of pioneering in a rugged land. Chapter titles in *Indians and Outlaws* serve as a good indicator of this view. Each one expresses either a positive or negative attitude toward the fulfilling of the San Juan mission. Starting with "Dangerous Mission," titles on the negative side are "Navajo Fury Quenched by Courage," "Human Rattlesnakes," "Cruel Indian Sport," and "Scoff Law Killers," while on the positive side are chapters entitled "Fearless Sentinel," "Light Breaks through the Clouds," and "Gallant Men Face a Grim Future." These leave little doubt as to the author's view, which concludes with "Mission Accomplished."

On one hand, Lyman performed the yeoman's task of recording historical events that by now would have been long since forgotten; on the other hand, his writings were filtered through strong emotions associated with contemporary events. In *The Outlaw of Navaho Mountain*, for instance, he tells about Posey and the Ute/Paiute faction. To Lyman, they were a childish people who "committed no sins, for nothing was forbidden. No haunting specter was raised before them of a life too indolent or too unsanitary." They normally lived like "leeches on the struggling Mormon settlement," stealing "anything, everything, till the colony's existence became a vexed and bitter problem." The land provided the "wild solitudes which they loved . . . [which] had been a security of their fathers for unwritten ages past. Each of the charted death-traps [ambush sites] through which they led their prey had a cherished legend handed down from the past." And forty years after the final struggle between this perceived good and evil ended in the "Posey incident," Lyman wrote that when he died, he was going to "seek out Posey from the great multitude and offer such help as I can give him to grasp the essentials which earth denied."[5] Although some of these writings appear unbalanced, Lyman also often served as an advocate for Native American causes under attack from local prejudice. And regardless of how much fact or fancy some of his writings contained, no other writer from the county has had a greater impact in the formulation of Latter-day Saint thought concerning the San Juan mission.

While Lyman most often presented the Anglo view, other white authors have tried to portray a Native American perspective. The

most notable writer to present the Navajo point of view is Frances
Gillmor, author of *Traders to the Navajo*, a history of John and Louisa
Wetherill in Monument Valley and Kayenta, and *Windsinger*, a novel
about a medicine man living in the same geographical area.[6] Gillmor
attempts in both works to view events as would the Navajo. As with
Oliver LaFarge in *Laughing Boy*, Gillmor has studied the culture, is
sympathetic to Navajo practices, and tries to present an anthropo-
logically accurate work that reflects Indian values. She has been fairly
successful at achieving these results.

Windsinger is the story from birth to death of a Navajo man who
identifies with the supernatural beings. He struggles as a boy and
young man to determine where he belongs in Navajo society, but he
eventually learns that he is destined to be a medicine man. Along the
way, he marries a lovely woman who takes care of the material side
of life, allowing him to immerse himself in spiritual and ceremonial
lore. Only later does he realize that he is losing her because of his
practice. Still, he believes that he is destined to talk to the gods and
works to achieve that end. He eventually suffers the ridicule of those
he has helped because his prophecy of a flood is not fulfilled. The
people shun him, withdrawing their respect, and it is only shortly
before his death that he finally achieves inner harmony and understanding in relation to the gods and his wife.

Gillmor succeeds in blending culture with landscape. A feeling of
harmony and respect, important concepts in Navajo beliefs, pervade
the novel. For example, at the end of Windsinger's life, he realizes that
the gods he sought in far off places were really close at hand. Gillmor
writes:

> But on the desert he knew the gods were moving. . . . There in the
> wide light of the morning, in the breathing of desert earth. There
> without voice as in the Night Chant, or body as in the sand paint-
> ings. Unheard and unseen, but surely there, living and a part of
> life. . . . Windsinger in that moment was still, sensing the breath-
> ing of mountain and desert. Into rock and pinon his spirit moved;
> he and the earth and the wind, and the wide light of morning were
> one, and one with the moving presence of the holy ones.[7]

A similar approach of interpreting the land through Native

American values is found in the works of Frank Waters, a Colorado-born writer enchanted by the cultures and history of the Southwest. His philosophical perspective and interpretation is filtered through what he conceives to be the beliefs of the Anasazi and Navajo people, which he consolidates under the general rubric of Four Corners culture.

To Waters, this land is "physically and metaphorically" the "heartland of America. Squared astronomically to space and time by sacred peaks in the [four] directions, it is still rigidly defined by legend and nature alike." He sees a "Rock in a weary land" upon which the people of the Southwest live. It is oriented to the cardinal points and composed of the sacred colors of the Navajo—white, blue, yellow, and black. The early Anasazi inhabitants, and later the Navajos and Utes, clung to this Rock's nooks and crannies for security and developed cultural beliefs and practices to reflect this reality. Waters says,

> That was the symbol of their lives as it was the shape of their vast complex cities. Their safety depended upon it. Their social structure derived from it. Their ritualistic religion was built upon it. And the sacred kivas reflected all this in their shape and ceremonials; the very heart of the Rock in which the people validated the strength of their faith and lives.[8]

He extends his mystical beliefs to the San Juan River, a "savage red flood," which, like John the Baptist, "cries alone in the wilderness," as it flows through one of the "loneliest, wildest regions in America."[9] Thus, Frank Waters bonds man with the land through a mystical spirituality often associated with Native Americans.

But Waters, as persona, remains distant; the "I" is consistently implied but never stated. This is very different from the personal explorations of Terry Tempest Williams, who in 1983 published *Pieces of White Shell*, an extended lyrical essay about her experiences in Montezuma Creek.[10] As a Salt Lake City-based Mormon, Williams is interested in "journeying into one culture, Navajo, and back out again to my own." To do this she joins previously translated stories from various sources with her own thoughts to reflect upon philosophical ideas. For instance, in the title chapter the author moves from a clam shell she gives to a Navajo friend to the recounting of a myth about Changing Woman (a deity associated with the earth and nature), to cycles of nature and their significance in other cultures, to an experience with a woman removing vegetation in a park in Salt Lake City.[11] These personal wanderings lead the reader to his or her own introspective musings.

Williams uses mythological characters to help explore her inner psyche. While camped at Hovenweep, she watches a coyote, an animal associated with trickery and witchcraft, disappear into the sagebrush and then later finds some of its fur. The author uses these events to explore both ends of a spectrum that portrays the coyote as a cultural hero and as a somewhat sinister being associated with witchcraft. In another instance, she contemplates the land with its ruins:

> Silence. That is time you are hearing. We are in Anasazi country. This is a place where canyon walls rise upward like praying hands. Veins of water run between them. . . . These are the canyons, cool refuges from exposed heat, dripping with red mimulus and ferns. This is the landscape that gave these people birth.[12]

After examining a pottery shard with which she is able to peel back layers of civilization, Williams realizes that instead of keeping it, that "somehow we need to acquaint ourselves with the art of letting go, for to own a piece of the past is to destroy it."[13] According to her, thought and the journey it takes you on is the essence of real life— the piece of white shell that each person holds or discards.

Terry Tempest Williams is one of the latest of a string of writers who have interacted and philosophized, not only with Native Americans but also about the land. One of the earlier authors was a president of the United States, Theodore Roosevelt, who crossed the "Navajo desert" in August 1913 to visit Rainbow Bridge. John Wetherill guided the expedition that passed by Navajos and Utes characterized by the writer as "pleasant-faced, silent men" living near Navajo Mountain. Camping at its base, the party enjoyed a "night [that] was lovely and the moon, nearly full, softened the dry harshness of the land." But, during the day, the "pitiless" sun beat down on a "contorted wilderness of scalped peaks and ranges . . . and twisted valleys of sun-baked clay." The group traveled like "pygmies through the gloom of the great gorge" until they spied the "triumphal arch" that held more majesty than "any arch ever reared by the mightiest conquerors among the nations of mankind." As for the Navajos and Paiutes, they remained stereotypically "silent" and stoic throughout the expedition.[14]

Another traveler was a young artist and philosopher named Everett Ruess, who concentrated his thoughts and visits in the Monument Valley–Navajo Mountain region. In his words, he was "roaring drunk with the lust of life and adventure and unbearable beauty."[15] He sporadically wandered alone in the deserts of the Four Corners region from 1930 to 1934, when his short life presumably ended. Yet the beauty he experienced in that brief period was more than many enjoy in a lifetime.

He had experienced a hectic life in Los Angeles and San Francisco, California, and did what he could to forsake it. The desert, away from the cities, provided "the happiest days of [his] life." His travels through Monument Valley were a "beautiful dream, sometimes tranquil, sometimes fantastic, and with enough pain and tragedy to make the delights possible by contrast." He journeyed alone, not because he did not enjoy friendship but because he "disliked bringing into play the aggressiveness of spirit which is necessary with an assertive companion."[16] Alone, he could contemplate.

Ruess, unlike some writers and philosophers, was not in search of fame or fortune. Part of his philosophy was revealed when he wrote, "Live blindly and upon the hour; the Lord, who was the future, died full long ago."[17] Christianity held little significance for him. But he was more than an itinerant atheist, wandering with a pack burro in search of a scene to paint, a place to write. He was in search of a different deity, which he found in the rocks, streams, and sky of San Juan County. "Beauty has always been my god; it has meant more than people to me. And how my god, or goddess, is flouted in this country which to me is the most beautiful I've known in all my wanderings!"[18]

Ruess's letters encourage the reader to reflect. He uses descriptive prose to create a picture, a mood, and causes the reader to reexamine his or her priorities. Who has not felt or thought like Ruess when he described his experience at War God Spring on Navajo Mountain:

A high wind is roaring in the tops of the tall pines. The moon is just rising on the rim of the desert, far below. Stars gleam through the pine boughs and the filmy clouds that move across the night sky. Graceful, slim-trunked aspens reach upward under the towering pines. Their slender, curving branches are white in the firelight, and an occasional downward breeze flickers their pale green leaves.

The beauty of this place is perfect of its kind; I could ask for nothing more. . . . There are a hundred delightful places to sit and dream. . . . No human comes to break the solitude. . . .

The perfection of this place is one reason why I distrust ever returning to the cities. Here I wander in beauty and perfection. There one walks in the midst of ugliness and mistakes. All is made for man, but where can one find surroundings to match one's ideals and imaginings?[19]

And that is why in his last letter before his disappearance, he could write, "This has been a full, rich year. I have left no strange or delightful thing undone which I wanted to do."[20] At twenty, he disappeared in the wilderness, never to be seen again.

Other philosophers, like Joseph Wood Krutch, recognized but could not immerse themselves in the intense beauty in which Ruess visually bathed. Krutch came to San Juan in 1951 towards the end of a sabbatical leave from Columbia University. He had spent the previous year living a contemplative life in the desert outside of Tucson, Arizona. A sensitive man, Krutch studied the workings of plants, animals, and life in a land that outsiders viewed as lifeless, wringing personal wisdom from his observations and experience. His contemplations produced *The Desert Year* and laid the philosophical foundation for three later books about the desert.

But the canyonlands of southeastern Utah were not the Sonoran deserts of Arizona. To Krutch, there was a "terror" in "a country where the inanimate dominates and in which not only man but the very plants themselves seem intruders. We may look at it [the land] as we look at the moon, but we feel rejected. It is neither for us nor for our kind."[21] Even traveling in a landscape with monuments that appeared as "abandoned cities of some race of prehistoric giants" was unsettling compared to his "cozy" desert experience near Tucson. The

Colorado Plateau was a part of the earth that "defies man to live upon it, and for the most part he has not challenged the defiance."[22]

Krutch did, however, see some positive aspects. For the traveler seeking instant adventure in an isolated area, "one could hardly feel more remote anywhere in the world." When moving at a high speed (sixty miles an hour for Krutch), the panoramas "cannot be made to pass other than slowly. One does not look at a landscape, one passes through it, and in no other that I have seen is the pure sensation of space so beautiful or so overwhelming."[23]

As with all his mental meandering, Krutch found a philosophical meaning or truth to share with others. For canyon country, it lies in the beauty through which man glimpses eternity. One should not contemplate either this land or the stars too long, but rather take "refuge from them with the small and the familiar." Otherwise, we dwell on the "platitude that man is small and that life is precarious. . . . Such truths are among those which no one should either totally forget or be too constantly aware of."[24]

Another person, Marie Ogden, came to the high desert for the same reason that Krutch rejected it. Throughout history there have been "voices crying in the wilderness," calling the world to repentance, and waiting for the last days of earth to arrive. Marie Ogden and her Home of Truth provided just such a millennial community, whose message derived from traditional Christian teachings supplemented by her personal revelations. In addition to being a religious leader, Ogden was also a writer and philosopher who reacted toward the land in her own fashion. Forsaking her roots in New Jersey, she still beckoned her "eastern friends" to better understand her love for the West.

Her location in Dry Valley provided two advantages that could not be obtained elsewhere. First, the pioneering conditions her colony encountered in wresting a living from the land taught the people to "accommodate to conditions that may seem impossible to city folks to accept," but increased their feelings of camaraderie in preparation for future trials. Cities provided the antithesis of this experience. In the wilderness there was a "closer contact with God and nature, which is impossible to do in the crowded centers where millions of people seem to prefer to live and rear their children in order to contact the material pleasures which such an environment may have to offer."[25]

A second and less tangible reason was the aesthetic, wholesome feeling found in a desert environment. Marie Ogden often wrote of her "quiet and peaceful existence here in this lovely San Juan County, which is so conducive to spiritual advancement." She abhorred the smoke of furnaces and automobiles and the bustle associated with the city. At the Home of Truth the people enjoyed the "beauty of the great open spaces by day and the great expanse of heaven by night when the stars and planets shine forth with a great and glorious light, making of our desert country a thing of beauty and a joy forever."[26] This beauty was a physical manifestation of the "Spirit force of power" that was behind every blessing that the colonists "enjoyed in this, [their] desert home."[27]

The Mormons, whose earlier history was greatly influenced by the settling of the desert, shared some similar beliefs. Few writers voiced more eloquently the hardships of this settlement than Wallace Stegner, a non-Mormon author of world renown, who was raised and educated in Utah.[28] He became a master of regional literature ranging from Canada to the Southwest and from California to New England. Whether writing historical fiction, novels, or introspective essays, Stegner maintained an intimate grasp of the land and the people he portrayed.

His discussions of San Juan County, the Mormons, and the desert reveal this. In *Mormon Country* he selected the Hole-in-the-Rock expedition and the settling of Bluff as his point of departure.[29] Stegner believed that "San Juan was then, and is now, the most barren frontier in the United States." As soon as the pioneers pointed their wagons towards the Four Corners, they started fighting their way over "waterless plateaus" and "skidding wildly down slick rock," as "the heavy wagons . . . coasted like otters on a mud slide." "Give those Mormons credit," he proclaimed. "Every mile was enough to make anyone but an automaton weep."[30]

For what purpose? The result was one "constantly-unsuccessful colony" that was "snatched from the encroaching gentiles," yet was just "one more bit of debris in the path of the San Juan floods."[31] But Stegner respected the Mormons he found in the county when he vis-

Part of Al Scorup's Dugout Ranch on Indian Creek with Train Rock in the background. Like so many writers who come to San Juan County, David Lavender was overwhelmed by what he found on the landscape when he visited the area. He wrote, "Here stood the ranch: a few whispering cottonwoods, a sway-backed corral, and a flimsy, open-sided shed for the farm machinery. . . . For more than a hundred and fifty miles [to the west] this is all. This and the measureless unmapped miles of sandrock." (San Juan Historical Commission)

ited. They were far different from Marie Ogden, whom Stegner saw representing the "lunatic fringe" that had "lost its hold on the things of the earth." True, the Mormons had the same notions of "divine guidance," the same "unorthodox . . . theological and social experimentation"; but, unlike Marie, Mormonism was a "practical religion, dedicated to the affairs of the world." It would long be a force to be "reckoned with" in a country that "breeds the Impossible."[32] While Albert R. Lyman likely would not agree with most of Stegner's analysis, on this last point, he would concur.

Another writer/historian in much the same vein as Stegner is David Lavender, who wrote of his experiences in southwestern Colorado and southeastern Utah. In his eyes, "The good earth of [this region] . . . is not so good. Yet there it is, and its people have to do with it whatever they can."[33] Lavender crossed into Utah in search of Al Scorup and found him headquartered at Indian Creek. Describing the descent from Marie Ogden's settlement, Lavender noted that "Slick rock is a Utah staple." He encountered the difficulty of negotiating some of San Juan's sandstone as he and his companion wound their way to the bottom of Indian Creek. He wrote, "The maze unraveled, we nose-dived into a subsidiary gulch, wallowed through sand, and reached the main canyon." There he found the creek running, a few "whispering" cottonwoods, cowboys described as "thirty villainous-looking creatures, gaunt and sun-blackened," and unflappable Al Scorup. Lavender colorfully describes the activity he surveyed with deep respect and admiration for those who struggled on a daily basis to wrest a living from a harsh land.[34]

Even when the land was tempered and kinder, it still offered challenges. To Lavender, Dark Canyon was a "cool fairyland in a blistered waste," but it was still "backwards." In normal places in San Juan, one takes cattle up to the mountains in the summer, while in Dark Canyon, from Lavender's perspective, one had to move them down to grass and water.[35] But the land, in spite of its harshness and surprises, was still beautiful to the point of being awe-inspiring. To watch dawn from a canyon rim as a "golden glow models buttes and trees in high light and shadow," while below "purple shadows stir and swirl," creates the illusion that "your very eyes were sculpturing them [canyon walls], as the great ribs and pinnacles and buttresses take their form."[36] The contrast in colors and lighting accentuates the beauty of the land.

Yet for all of the love and respect that philosophers, religious seekers, and writers have felt towards San Juan, none reached as high a fever pitch as did Edward Abbey, who spoke for the environmentally conscious generations of the 1960s, 1970s, and 1980s. No more strident voice called from the desert than his, proclaiming a "hands-off" policy towards developers, tourists, residents—anyone affecting what he considered a pristine canyon country on the verge or in the midst of destructive exploitation. His writings became the cornerstone of activists' beliefs that range from peaceful noncompliance to militancy. The Four Corners area became the battleground for much of Abbey's fight.

An early book, *Desert Solitaire—A Season in the Wilderness*, digs the trenches for what was to come. The text is loosely based on his employment at Arches National Monument in the mid-1950s where Abbey develops his opposition to the entrepreneurial spirit he saw infecting everyone from Park Service personnel to the residents. Like others, he came to what he considered the "most beautiful place on earth" to "evade for a while the clamor and filth and confusion of the cultural apparatus."[37]

But, for Abbey, "there [was] a cloud on the horizon. A small dark cloud no bigger than my hand. Its name [was] progress."[38] He believed humans had an innate need to have the opportunity to enjoy an untrammelled wilderness experience, "a refuge even though we may never need to go there. . . . We need the possibility of escape as surely as we need hope; without it the life of the cities would drive all men into crime or drugs or psychoanalysis."[39] San Juan County provided such a sanctuary.

The extent to which Abbey was committed to putting his beliefs into practice is found in one of the last chapters in *Desert Solitaire*, when he and a friend explore "Terra Incognita," the Maze in Canyonlands. At one point, the author tells of how his imagination ran rampant over the rock formations, naming them as they washed into view. As Abbey struggled to name a certain monolith, his companion challenged the concept of naming it at all. Abbey immediately agreed and attacked his harmless pastime by declaring, "Vanity, vanity, nothing but vanity: the itch for naming things is almost as bad as the itch for possessing things. Let them and leave them alone—they'll survive for a few more thousand years, more or less, without any glorification from us."[40] And as he stopped at a BLM visitor's register at the conclusion of his experience in the Maze, he scrawled, "For God's sake leave this country alone—Abbey," to which his companion added, "For Abbey's sake, leave this country alone—God."[41]

Desert Solitaire hints at the direction taken by his most famous novel, *The Monkey Wrench Gang*. In the first, he tells of pulling up surveyors' stakes marking a future road, of considering Canyonlands as a place to hide from the government, and of using the wilderness to establish "bases for guerrilla warfare against tyranny."[42] *The Monkey Wrench Gang* is a novel in which Abbey dreams into print what he would like to do to stop economic development in a land which he felt was endangered.[43] The story revolves around four personalities—a doctor, an ex-special forces soldier, a jack-Mormon, and a former dancer (female)—all of whom for one reason or another fall in love with the Four Corners region and want to protect it. Most of the action occurs in San Juan County and northeastern Arizona, where the characters wage a relentless war against any developmental encroachment upon nature.

The plot may be seen as a how-to manual of guerilla warfare against the local, state, and federal agencies responsible for law, order, and growth. Theft, destruction of property, and harassment of officials take various forms in the book and include driving construction equipment off the cliffs near Lake Powell, blowing up bridges and facilities at the Peabody Coal Company, and ruining logging equipment in the Kaibab National Forest. Various chase-and-escape episodes thread throughout the book, written by an author who knew the land intimately. And not surprisingly, the Maze serves as the hideout for the finale of the story. Thus, through the *Gang*, Abbey became, as one reviewer heralded, a new "underground cult hero." He was a product of his time, when many wanted to take on the "establishment" in a place where environmental concerns were of great importance.

Other works by Abbey embellished these ideas. He became popular as a literary spokesman for organizations such as the Sierra Club and the Southern Utah Wilderness Alliance, which shared sympathetic views. During one of his less radical moments, Abbey summarized his beliefs when he wrote:

> The moral I labor toward is that a landscape as splendid as that of the Colorado Plateau can best be understood and given human significance by poets who have their feet planted in concrete—concrete data—and by scientists whose heads and hearts have not lost the capacity for wonder. Any good poet, in our age at least, must begin with the scientific view of the world; and any scientist worth listening to must be something of a poet, must possess the ability to communicate to the rest of us his sense of love and wonder at what his work discovers.[44]

Much of his work, whether about rafting down the San Juan or climbing Mount Tukuhnikivats, does just that.

Moving from philosophy back to fiction, one finds three other famous authors—Zane Grey, Louis L'Amour, and Tony Hillerman—who have used San Juan County in their writings. Each traveled through the land, met its people, and used that material with varying degrees of success. Zane Grey, for instance, based his most popular novel, *Riders of the Purple Sage*, in San Juan County. He used literary license to rearrange the landscape to suit his purposes, but the town of Cottonwood is obviously Bluff, and many of the geographical features he portrayed in Utah and northern Arizona are still recognizable.

Published in 1912, the book melodramatically revolves around the disclosure of different characters' identities and the falling in love of two couples, while being set against a backdrop of sinister Mormons and cattle thieves. The two heroes—Bern Venter and James Lassiter—eventually liberate and woo two women—Bess Erne and Jane Withersteen—away from the dominating evil found in their social environments: Bess rode for cattle thieves and Jane was a virtual prisoner in a Mormon community that treated women as brainless property whose only responsibility was to obey. The foreboding landscape paralleled the tension of the people. Grey constantly referred to characters (especially Mormons), places, and things as being "dark" or "black." He also colored the reader's vision with purple—purple sage, purple hills, purple rocks, purple sand, purple clouds, purple leaves. Thus, in Grey's view, the people reflected a set of values that seemed admirably suited to each other and the land.

Through Lassiter, he summarized this view in a conversation the hero has with Jane. Lassiter believed that qualities like goodness and mercy "can't be lived up to on this Utah border. Life's hell out here. You think—or you used to think—that your religion made this life heaven. Mebbe them scales on your eyes has dropped now. . . . You'd think churches an' churchmen would make it better. They make it worse. You give names to things—bishops, elders, ministers, Mormonism, duty, faith, glory. You dream—or you're driven mad."[45] Thus, it was a harsh land, settled by stubborn, harsh people whose values did not reflect the real meaning of life, but gave only a false sense of security.

In a sequel to *Riders*, Grey painted the Mormons in the same hues. *The Rainbow Trail*, published in 1915, portrays Mormons as dark, sinister characters who felt allegiance only to their fellows. Grey does have a better grasp of distance and topography in this book, primarily because much of what he wrote was based on a trip he made to Rainbow Bridge in the spring of 1913.[46] John Wetherill and Nas ta Bega (Nasja Begay, or Ne'eshjaa' Begay) guided the expedition and two years later appeared in the novel. Perhaps more important is the way a reader can see how Grey sculpts a scene, a personality, or a mood from a real experience to fit the impression he wants to create.

This process becomes clear in an article entitled "Nonnezoshe, The Rainbow Bridge," published the same year as the novel, telling of Grey's visit.[47] Little difference exists between book and article, though one is supposedly fact and the other fiction. The Paiute Nas ta Begay, that "dark and silent Indian," had a "dark, inscrutable face" even when praying, "with all that was spiritual of the Indian suggested by a somber and tranquil knowledge of his place there." Grey writes of how he had a "strange mystic perception that this rosy-hued, tremendous arch of stone was a goal [he] had failed to reach in some former life, but had now found." As for the land he passed through, "Here the canyon was full of purple smoke. It turned, it closed, it gaped, it lost itself and showed again in that chaos of a million cliffs. And then it faded, a mere purple line, into deceiving distance." So much for writer of the purple prose.

Another author of fiction, Louis L'Amour, has been more successful in keeping rein on his diction. Like Grey, he could spin a yarn and did not fear using his literary license; but, unlike Grey, he spent weeks and weeks researching a topic before setting pen to paper. L'Amour wrote at least five books whose settings are anchored in the landscape of San Juan and approximately twenty others that allude to some of its features. One of his last long works, *The Haunted Mesa*, is set almost entirely in the county at places such as No Man's Mesa and Johnny's Hole near Navajo Mountain.[48] Although the critics consider the text as one of his lesser works, it is a good example of how he studied the landscape, knew its history, and attempted to tie fiction to reality.

The plot is simple. L'Amour, in an attempt to write about a mystical world beyond this concrete, measurable one, uses the Anasazi and Mayan beliefs to explore a time warp that can be crossed in certain locations at certain times. He has the hero, Mike Raglan, go in search of a missing friend and client, Erik Hokart, who started to build a house near an old Anasazi ruin and then disappeared. Many different characters drift into the story to help Mike discover the means to rescue Erik. By the end of the novel, both men return to this world, having encountered the lost civilization of the Anasazi as well as a ruling elite described in Mayan mythology of the underworld.

As fantastic as the story is, L'Amour knows the land. He includes dozens of geographical locations and describes them accurately. One person, who helped him with research, stated that L'Amour went at least seven times between 1981–83 to the No Man's Mesa area by various means—fixed-wing aircraft, helicopter, car, and on foot to make sure his understanding of the land was accurate.[49] He took slides, marked springs and petroglyphs on maps, followed trails, and consulted local people about what was and was not possible.

Another person who accompanied L'Amour on some of his fact-finding tours noted how excited the author was when he first saw the location. He exclaimed, "That's my mesa! That's my Haunted Mesa, the mesa in the book I plan to write. Look south across the San Juan—there's No Man's Mesa. It's perfect." And when he tried to find a trail to the top and failed a number of times, his companion suggested that in the book, that particular issue need not create a problem, to which L'Amour replied, "Jackson, I couldn't do that. My readers want to know that every place is real. To say that there was a trail, when none exists, would be dishonest."[50]

Accuracy in geographical and cultural landscapes are also important to the third writer of fiction, Tony Hillerman. Using the Four Corners as his stage, he specializes in portraying Navajo culture and beliefs through two Navajo policemen—Officer Jim Chee and Lt. Joe Leaphorn. While all of his novels are set in the same general locale, none are more entrenched in San Juan than *A Thief of Time*.[51] The accuracy of his presentation of land and people is noteworthy.

The story revolves around the disappearance of an anthropologist named Eleanore Friedman-Bernal who was working on the San Juan River between Bluff and Mexican Hat. As the plot unfolds, Chee and Leaphorn unravel the mystery of her disappearance as they work through three murders, the theft of a backhoe, the sale of Anasazi pottery in New York City, professional jealousy between archaeologists, and some of Chee's romantic problems. Eleanor's disappearance is solved when she is found alive in some ruins after her attempted murder by another anthropologist involved in illegal excavations. Leaphorn saves her, the anthropologist is killed, and Chee appears in time to fly the injured woman back to medical care.

Hillerman weaves throughout this tale Navajo beliefs concerning the dead, the Anasazi, the Beauty Way ceremony, and traditional social practices. He has done extensive research into the culture, and the Navajo Tribe has recognized him for this accomplishment and the way it has spurred the younger generation into learning more about their heritage. His description of Anasazi sites, the petroglyphs and pictographs, and artifacts are equally accurate.

In terms of painting a realistic landscape, Hillerman has traveled every inch of ground he writes about. Not only does he speak with authority about geographic locations, but he also mentions real businesses ranging from river-runners to hotels found in Bluff. His fictional characters are also believably real because of the research of their author. This is one of the reasons Hillerman has enjoyed such success.

Thus, the people and land of San Juan County have appealed to writers of many different persuasions. Whether through religious beliefs, personal philosophy, or fiction, men and women have been awed by the geography and cultural circumstances, forming from it a work of art, a philosophical belief, or both. Just as the miners tore minerals from the earth, the settlers dug ditches for water, and cattle grazed upon the grasses, writers and philosophers have taken the land and turned it into fodder for contemplation, enjoyment, and moral guidance. Some have been economically enriched, others aesthetically enhanced, while others spiritually guided. But none have left impoverished. San Juan in the imagination still has many fertile fields to plow for the fiction-writer and mountains to climb for the philosophical mind. Each generation will leave its own contribution on the intellectual landscape that the people of San Juan call home.

ENDNOTES

1. Don D. Fowler and Catherine Fowler, *Anthropology of the Numa: John Wesley Powell's Manuscript on the Numic People*, Smithsonian Contributions to Anthropology, Number 14 (Washington, D.C.: Smithsonian Institution, 1971): 76–77.

2. William R. Palmer, "The Pahute Fire Legend," *Utah Historical Quarterly* 6, no. 2 (April 1933): 62–64; Albert B. Reagan, "Mother Nature," Albert B. Reagan Collection, Special Collections, Brigham Young University Library, 64–65; Uintah Ouray Tribe, *Stories of Our Ancestors: A Collection of Northern Ute Indian Tales* (Salt Lake City: University of Utah Press, 1974), 22.

3. A number of versions with textual differences are found in Berard Haile, *Upward Moving and Emergence Way* (Lincoln: University of Nebraska Press, 1981); Leland Wyman, *The Red Antway of the Navajo* (Santa Fe: Museum of Navajo Ceremonial Art, 1973); and Raymond F. Locke, *The Book of the Navajo* (Los Angeles: Mankind Publishing Company, 1976).

4. Albert R. Lyman, *Indians and Outlaws—Settling of the San Juan Frontier* (Salt Lake City: Bookcraft, 1962); Albert R. Lyman, *The Edge of the Cedars—The Story of Walter C. Lyman and the San Juan Mission* (New York: Carlton Press, 1966); Albert R. Lyman, *The Outlaw of Navaho Mountain* (Salt Lake City: Publishers Press, 1986).

5. Lyman, *Outlaw*, 8, 47, 61, 232.

6. Frances Gillmor and Louisa Wetherill, *Traders to the Navajos* (Albuquerque: University of New Mexico Press, 1934); Frances Gillmor, *Windsinger* (Albuquerque: University of New Mexico Press, 1930).

7. Gillmor, *Windsinger*, 210–11.

8. Frank Waters, *Masked Gods—Navaho and Pueblo Ceremonialism* (New York: Ballantine Books, 1950), 4, 6, 8, 14.

9. Frank Waters, *The Colorado* (New York: Holt, Rinehart and Winston, 1946), 10–11.

10. Terry Tempest Williams, *Pieces of White Shell—A Journey to Navajoland* (New York: Charles Scribner's Sons, 1983).

11. Ibid., 39–46.

12. Ibid., 121.

13. Ibid., 125.

14. Theodore Roosevelt, "Across the Navajo Desert," *The Outlook*, 105 (11 October 1913): 309–17.

15. This and the following quotations are taken from Ruess's letters published in W. L. Rusho, *Everett Ruess—A Vagabond for Beauty* (Salt Lake City: Peregrine Smith Books, 1983), 145.

16. Ibid., 39, 143.

17. Ibid., 146.

18. Ibid., 152.

19. Ibid., 158–60.

20. Ibid., 180.

21. Joseph Wood Krutch, *The Desert Year* (New York: Penguin Books, 1952), 251–52.

22. Ibid., 240.

23. Ibid., 243.

24. Ibid., 250, 252–53.

25. Marie Ogden, "Home of Truth News," *San Juan Record*, 28 April 1938, 8; *San Juan Record*, 27 December 1945, 4; "Readers Column," *San Juan Record*, 26 December 1940, 4.

26. "Special Activities of Home of Truth and San Juan County," *San Juan Record*, 5 November 1936, 1.

27. Marie Ogden, "Home of Truth News," *San Juan Record*, 27 January 1938, 5.

28. For a good overview of Stegner's life and work see Merrill and Lorene Lewis,*Wallace Stegner*, Boise State College Western Writers Series—Number 4 (Caldwell, Idaho: Caxton Printers, 1972).

29. Wallace Stegner, *Mormon Country* (New York: Hawthorn Books, 1942).

30. Ibid., 229–32.

31. Ibid., 232.

32. Ibid., 342, 349.

33. David Lavender, *One Man's West* (New York: Doubleday and Company, 1956), iii.

34. Ibid., 164–72.

35. Ibid., 174.

36. Ibid., 175.

37. Edward Abbey, *Desert Solitaire—A Season in the Wilderness* (New York: Ballantine Books, 1968), 6, 1.

38. Ibid., 48.

39. Ibid., 148–49.

40. Ibid., 288.

41. Ibid., 250.

42. Ibid., 48–50, 287, 149.

43. Edward Abbey, *The Monkey Wrench Gang* (New York: Avon Books, 1975).

44. Edward Abbey, *The Journey Home—Some Words in Defense of the American West* (New York: E. P. Dutton, 1977): 87.

45. Zane Grey, *Riders of the Purple Sage* (New York: Bantam Books, 1912), 281.

46. Zane Grey, *The Rainbow Trail* (New York: Pocket Books, 1915).

47. Zane Grey, "Nonnezoshe, The Rainbow Bridge," *Recreation* 52, no. 2 (February 1915): 63–67.

48. Louis L'Amour, *The Haunted Mesa* (New York: Bantam Books, 1987).

49. Thomas Austin, friend and research consultant for Louis L'Amour, telephone conversation with author, 16 September 1994.

50. H. Jackson Clark, *The Owl in Monument Canyon* (Salt Lake City: University of Utah Press, 1993): 132, 134.

51. Tony Hillerman, *A Thief of Time* (New York: Harper and Row, Publishers, 1988).

Through a Glass Darkly

ONE HISTORIAN'S VIEW OF THE FUTURE

In counseling the Christians of Corinth during the first century after Christ, the Apostle Paul expressed the dilemma of a historian who understands the past but can only anticipate the future. He wrote, "For now we see through a glass darkly ... now I know in part; but then [in the future] shall I know."[1] Relating this to San Juan County's past, there are certainly distinct patterns that suggest what the future may hold. Yet around each historical corner there lurk, waiting to surprise the unsuspecting, the quirks of fate with their allies, invention and change. These elements can unravel the best predictions, but they also provide the most interesting material for future analyses.

Barring the unforeseen, there are certain issues that promise to be important to San Juan in the years ahead. Starting with the most basic, water will continue to dictate what, where, and how economic development can be sustained. In spite of all the technological advances, nature's control of water still prescribes the type of industry and population growth possible in a high desert environment. Melting snow, summer rains, and underground aquifers will nurture

394

life, just as they have in the past, but their waters also will need to be meted out with greater precision, as a lavish American lifestyle and increased population makes greater demands.

Indeed, the control of many aspects of San Juan growth will become both a necessity and a point of contention. The biggest question is who will wield the greatest power. The answer most likely will be the federal government. With its growing bureaucracy and financial resources, government money, agencies like the BLM, Forest Service, and National Park Service will continue increasingly to restrict entrance to and use of the parks, rivers, canyons, and archaeological sites within the county. As tourism pushes at the limits of access to the land, greater regulation will ensue, excluding local people as well as some tourists from savoring the land they consider their right to enjoy.

An example of this is found in the process of obtaining a San Juan River permit today. There are now two different types of application for a float trip—commercial and private. Commercial outfitters receive an established number of passengers and days on the river, which may account for as much as forty percent of the allowable traffic; private river-runners have their applications drawn out of a hat in a lottery-type system. No provision is made for local residents as opposed to those who travel from outside of the county. Variables are involved, such as the heaviest time of use (May to July), the launch sites (Sand Island or Mexican Hat), and the number of people allowed in any single group; but the fact remains that local people receive no special concessions from the BLM. If this and other types of restriction are imposed on a land base, 84 percent of which belongs to some form of government, then it is conceivable that San Juan residents may either have to stay home because they lack the permits to use their own county lands or go to the Wasatch Front or elsewhere for their vacations. Whether or not this will ever happen is questionable, but many residents fear the possibility.

Another concern is with natural resource development. Renewable and nonrenewable resources in the county have led to such extractive industries as mining and timber, while government regulation is an important issue to its residents. Both of these industries at present are moribund and will remain so until the economy shifts and government control fosters their growth. Ecosystem management, the buzz-word for the politically correct people of the 1990s, must also take into account the economic base of people who live in the region.

Other extractive industries, such as oil and gas, are starting to peter out in the area. If one compares oil revenues of 1984 to those of 1994, one sees a marked decline that decreased the county valuation by 64 percent over the ten-year period.[2] In 1992, San Juan ranked the lowest of all twenty-nine counties in Utah in per capita personal income ($9,609), which was only 62 percent of the state average ($15,573). The largest county industries in descending order of importance were state and local government (27 percent), services (19 percent), and mining (12 percent).[3] Obviously, if this trend continues, fewer and fewer people will find it profitable to make a living directly from the land.

One means by which this drab economic picture may be improved in the future would be to have the federal government contribute a "piece of the gate," or part of the entrance/use fees paid by tourists on county public lands. At present, tourism has not provided a taxable base of income for the county, while roads, power lines, health care services, and other parts of the infrastructure that are used by everyone, including tourists, are maintained primarily by local revenues. A sales tax to provide money that stays in the county would be a nice addition to the higher PILT (Payment-in-Lieu-of-Taxes) formula recently passed to help rural counties. But whatever form the government chooses to use to assist the financial concerns of the county, one can be assured that the day of the open range, gold rushes, and homesteading, when the land was the commodity, is over.

Not that the land will lie idle. San Juan still remains one of Utah's richest counties in such resources as archaeological sites, scenic vistas, and historic landmarks. Attractions such as Poncho House Ruin, Grand Gulch, Newspaper Rock, Hole-in-the-Rock Trail, the Oljato and Goulding's trading posts, Monument Valley, Rainbow Bridge, Canyonlands and Glen Canyon national park areas, and the Edge of the Cedars Museum will continue to lure tourists along the county's roads. An interstate plan, agreed upon by Utah, Colorado, New Mexico, and Arizona, will stimulate and help link the tourist trade on a network of roads known collectively as the Trail of the Ancients. San Juan prehistory, history, and culture will attract visitors and their dollars.

To meet the growing needs of tourism and services for those from outside the county, education will become increasingly important. More than ever before, knowledge will become the key for unlocking and keeping the wealth and people of San Juan at home. In a technologically expanding world, the isolation that in the past was one of San Juan's biggest problems has begun to fade as an obstacle. Computers, the Internet, teleconferencing, satellite relay, and televised education will shrink distances and promote the expansion of learning and business communications. Already, the College of Eastern Utah–San Juan Campus as well as the San Juan School District have the means to communicate throughout the county and the state to receive and provide educational services. Compare that to two generations ago, when a country schoolmarm huddled around her woodburning stove in La Sal wondering about her family in Salt Lake City and hoping spring would soon end her dreadful isolation.

Changes in education also bring financial rewards. An estimated $3 million annually enters the local economy from college students.[4] San Juan Campus recently received $8 million from two federal grants to add technology and televised classes to its curriculum. Financial aid for virtually any county resident who desires to enroll in higher education classes is now made possible by interest payments from an endowment fund of $6 million dollars. Other grants help to meet the needs of low-income and ESL (English as a Second Language) students once they cross the threshold of a college classroom. Now, no one in the county need go without educational opportunity.

Increased participation by Native Americans in formal education is another trend that continues to grow. The San Juan School District in October 1994 reported that Native Americans (along with a small group of Hispanics and Asians) composed 54 percent of its student body.[5] Schools both on and off the reservation are producing bright, talented students ready for the twenty-first century. Thirty years ago, it was a rare sight indeed to see a Native American walk down the aisle in a high school graduation ceremony.

Education has also led to increased political awareness. The expanding Navajo population is a slumbering giant ready to awaken and make its way to an election booth. In sheer numbers alone there are more potential Navajo voters than whites. Power through government could be obtained by concerted efforts to grasp the reins of leadership. Although the traditional decision-making process of the Navajo differs from that of the Anglo, as more and more Native Americans become involved in the dominant society, this will change, and greater competition for control may arise on both sides of the San Juan River. Already some Native Americans have suggested that reservation schools with their funds should come under Navajo management.

These types of issues will continue in San Juan and change will always occur. Yet tomorrow, like today, the county's residents will only be able to select what is best by maintaining a strong, integrated system of values. From these values and the heritage of the county's various people springs a pride connected with the land. That is what keeps people returning to the county, year after year, for the Fourth of July, Pioneer Day, and Bluff celebrations; the four-wheel drive vehicles rumbling over the Hole-in-the-Rock Trail; the families picnicking on Blue Mountain; the Ute people moving in the Bear Dance; and the Navajos giving and sharing through their ceremonies. The county may struggle to find its economic place among the others of Utah, but in its strong heritage and a sense of place, San Juan is second to none.

ENDNOTES

1. 1 Cor. 13:12.

2. "San Juan Statistics," *San Juan Record*, 31 August 1994, 2.

3. "San Juan County 'Bearfacts,'" *San Juan Record*, 24 August 1994, 1. Jim Keyes, a Utah State Extension Agent, wrote an article entitled "Cattle by the Wayside . . . Then the Communities?" *San Juan Record*, 18 May 1994, 1, in which he states that the livestock industry is second only to government expenditure in bringing money into San Juan County.

4. "College a Boon to Local Economy," *San Juan Record*, 3 August 1994, 5.

5. "San Juan Statistics," *San Juan Record*, 19 October 1994, 2.

Selected Bibliography

The following selected bibliography lists the most easily accessible books and periodicals used to write this book. For a more extensive catalog of works, the reader is referred to the endnotes accompanying each chapter.

Abbey, Edward. *Desert Solitaire: A Season in the Wilderness.* New York: Ballantine Books, 1968.

———. *The Journey Home: Some Words in Defense of the American West.* New York: E. P. Dutton, 1977.

———. *Monkey Wrench Gang.* New York: Avon Books, 1975.

Austin, Thomas E., and Robert S. McPherson. "Murder, Mayhem, and Mormons: The Evolution of Law Enforcement on the San Juan Frontier, 1880–1900." *Utah Historical Quarterly* 55, no. 1 (Winter 1987): 36–49.

Baars, Donald L. *The Colorado Plateau: A Geologic History.* Albuquerque: University of New Mexico Press, 1983.

Babbitt, James E. *Rainbow Trails.* Page, Ariz.: Glen Canyon Natural History Association, 1990.

Bailey, Alfred M. "Desert River through Navajo Land." *National Geographic Magazine* 92, no. 2 (August 1947): 149–65.

Bassett, Carol Ann. "The Culture Thieves." *Science* 249 (July/August 1986): 22–29.

Beckstead, James H. *Cowboying: A Tough Job in a Hard Land*. Salt Lake City: University of Utah Press, 1991.

Black, Marcia, and Robert S. McPherson. "Soldiers, Savers, Slackers and Spies." *Utah Historical Quarterly* 63, no. 1 (Winter 1995): 4–23.

Blue Mountain Shadows Issues 1–15 published semiannually by the San Juan County Historical Commission between 1987 and 1995.

Chavez, Fray Angelico, and Ted J. Warner. *The Dominguez-Escalante Journal: Their Expedition through Colorado, Utah, Arizona, and New Mexico in 1776*. Provo: Brigham Young University Press, 1976.

Clark, H. Jackson. *The Owl in Monument Canyon*. Salt Lake City: University of Utah Press, 1993.

Cole, Sally J. *Legacy on Stone: Rock Art of the Colorado Plateau and Four Corners Region*. Boulder: Johnson Books, 1990.

Crampton, C. Gregory. *Standing Up Country: The Canyonlands of Utah and Arizona*. Salt Lake City: Peregrine Smith Books, 1983.

———. "Utah's Spanish Trail." *Utah Historical Quarterly* 47, no. 4 (Fall 1979): 361–82.

Cutter, Donald C. "Prelude to Pageant in the Wilderness." *Western Historical Quarterly* 8 (January 1977): 4–14.

Fletcher, Maurine. *The Wetherills of the Mesa Verde: The Autobiography of Benjamin Alfred Wetherill*. Norman: University of Oklahoma Press, 1977.

Florence, William R. "John Ford . . . The Duke . . . and Monument Valley." *Arizona Highways* (September 1981): 22–37.

Fradkin, Philip L. *A River No More: The Colorado River and the West*. Tucson: University of Arizona Press, 1984.

Frost, C. Alfred. *Rattlesnakes and Wild Horses and Other Campfire Tales*. Conway, Ark: River Road Press, 1993.

Frost, Kent. *My Canyonlands*. New York: Abelard-Schuman Press, 1971.

Gillmor, Frances. *Windsinger*. Albuquerque: University of New Mexico Press, 1930.

——— and Louisa Wade Wetherill. *Traders to the Navajo: The Story of the Wetherills of Kayenta*. Albuquerque: University of New Mexico Press, 1953.

Gonzalez, William H., and Genaro M. Padilla. "Monticello: The Hispanic

Cultural Gateway to Utah." *Utah Historical Quarterly* 52, no. 1 (Winter 1984): 9–28.

Grey, Zane. *The Rainbow Trail.* New York: Pocket Books, 1915.

———. *Riders of the Purple Sage.* New York: Bantam Books, 1912.

Handbook of North American Indians—Southwest, Volumes 9, 10, 11. Washington, D.C.: Smithsonian Institution, 1979, 1983, 1986.

Hillerman, Tony. *A Thief of Time.* New York: Harper and Row Publishers, 1988.

Klinck, Richard E. *Land of Room Enough and Time Enough.* Salt Lake City: Peregrine Smith Books, 1984.

Kluckhohn, Clyde, and Dorothea Leighton. *The Navaho.* Rev. ed. Cambridge: Harvard University Press, 1974.

Kroeber, Clifton B. "The Route of James O. Pattie on the Colorado in 1826—A Reappraisal by A. L. Kroeber." *Arizona and the West* 6, no. 2 (Summer 1964): 119–36.

Lambert, Neal. "Al Scorup: Cattleman of the Canyons." *Utah Historical Quarterly* 32, no. 3 (Summer 1964): 301–20.

L'Amour, Louis. *The Haunted Mesa.* New York: Bantam Books, 1987.

Lavender, David. *One Man's West.* New York: Doubleday and Company, 1956.

Liebler, H. Baxter. *Boil My Heart for Me.* Salt Lake City: University of Utah Press, 1994.

Luckert, Karl. *Navajo Mountain and Rainbow Bridge Religion.* Flagstaff: Museum of Northern Arizona, 1977.

Lyman, Albert R. *The Edge of the Cedars: The Story of Walter C. Lyman and the San Juan Mission.* New York: Carlton Press, 1966.

———. "Fort on the Firing Line." *Improvement Era*, serially, October 1948 to March 1950.

———. *Indians and Outlaws: Settling the San Juan Frontier.* Salt Lake City: Publishers Press, 1962.

———. *The Outlaw of Navajo Mountain.* Salt Lake City: Publishers Press, 1986.

McNitt, Frank. *Richard Wetherill: Anasazi.* Albuquerque: University of New Mexico Press, 1957.

McPherson, Robert S. "The Influenza Epidemic of 1918: A Cultural Response." *Utah Historical Quarterly* 58, no. 2 (Spring 1990): 183–200.

———. "Naalye'he'Ba Hooghan—House of Merchandise: Navajo Trading Posts as an Institution of Cultural Change, 1900–1930." *American Indian Culture and Research Journal* 16, no. 1 (Winter 1992): 23–43.

————. *The Northern Navajo Frontier: Expansion through Adversity, 1860–1900.* Albuquerque: University of New Mexico Press, 1988.

————. "Paiute Posey and the Last White Uprising." *Utah Historical Quarterly* 53, no. 3 (Summer 1985): 248–67.

————. *Sacred Land, Sacred View: Navajo Perceptions of the Four Corners Region.* Provo: Brigham Young University Press, 1992.

Miller, David. E. *Hole-in-the-Rock: An Epic in the Colonization of the Great American West.* Salt Lake City: University of Utah Press, 1959.

Muhlestein, Harold George, and Fay Lunceford Muhlestein. *Monticello Journal: A History of Monticello until 1937.* Self-published, 1988.

Parkhill, Forbes. *The Last of the Indian Wars.* New York: Crowell-Collier Publishing Company, 1961.

Perkins, Cornelia, Marian Nielson, and Lenora Jones. *Saga of San Juan.* Salt Lake City: Mercury Publishing Company, 1968.

Peterson, Charles S. "Cowboys and Cattle Trails: A Centennial View of Emery County," in *Emery County: Reflections on Its Past and Future,* ed. Allan Kent Powell. Salt Lake City: Utah State Historical Society, 1979.

————. *Look to the Mountains: Southeastern Utah and the La Sal National Forest.* Provo: Brigham Young University Press, 1975.

————. "San Juan in Controversy: American Livestock Frontier vs. Mormon Cattle Pool." *Charles Redd Monographs in Western History: Essays on the American West, 1972–73,* No. 3. Provo: Brigham Young University Press, 1974.

Powell, Allan Kent. ed. *San Juan County: People, Resources and History.* Salt Lake City: Utah State Historical Society. 1983.

Powell, John Wesley. *The Exploration of the Colorado River and Its Canyons.* New York: Dover Publications, 1961.

Reay, Lee. *Incredible Passage Through the Hole-in-the-Rock.* Salt Lake City: Publishers Press, 1980.

Reilly, P. T. "Norman Nevills: Whitewater Man of the West." *Utah Historical Quarterly* 55, no. 2 (Spring 1987): 181–200.

Riis, John. *Ranger Trails.* Richmond, Va.: Dietz Press, 1937.

Ringholz, Raye C. *Uranium Frenzy: Boom and Bust on the Colorado Plateau.* Albuquerque: University of New Mexico Press, 1989.

Rusho, W. L. *Everett Ruess: A Vagabond for Beauty.* Salt Lake City: Peregrine Smith Books, 1983.

Stegner, Wallace. *Mormon Country.* New York: Hawthorn Books, 1942.

Sullenberger, Robert. "100 Years of Uranium Activity in the Four Corners Region—Part II." *Journal of the Western Slope* 7, no. 4; 8, no. 1 (Fall 1992, Winter 1993).

Tanner, Faun McConkie. *The Far Country: A Regional History of Moab and La Sal, Utah*. Salt Lake City: Olympus Press, 1976.

Thompson, Gregory C. "The Unwanted Indians: The Southern Utes in Southeastern Utah." *Utah Historical Quarterly* 49, no. 2 (Spring 1981): 189–203.

Valle, Doris. *Looking Back Around the Hat: A History of Mexican Hat*. Mexican Hat: Self-published, 1986.

Walker, Don D. "The Carlisles: Cattle Barons of the Upper Basin." *Utah Historical Quarterly* 32, no. 3 (Summer 1964): 268–84.

———. "Cowboys, Indians, and Cavalry: A Cattleman's Account." *Utah Historical Quarterly* 34, no. 3 (Summer 1966): 252–62.

Waters, Frank. *The Colorado*. New York: Holt Rinehart and Winston Company, 1946.

———. *Masked Gods: Navaho and Pueblo Ceremonialism*. New York: Ballantine Books, 1950.

White, Richard. *Roots of Dependency: Subsistence, Environment and Social Change among Choctaws, Pawnees, and Navajos*. Lincoln: University of Nebraska Press, 1983.

Williams, Terry Tempest. *Pieces of White Shell: A Journey to Navajoland*. New York: Charles Scribner's Sons, 1983.

Young, Norma Perkins. *Anchored Lariats on the San Juan Frontier*. Provo: Community Press.

Index

Antes, Howard, Methodist missionary
   at Aneth, 18, 127–29, 130–31
Antiquities Act of 1906, 45
Arch Canyon, 360
Archaeological Mitigation, Recapture
   Reservoir Site, 233
Archaeological Resources Protection
   Act of 1979, 45
Archaeologists in the county, 40–46,
   233
Archaic Indians 29, 294, rock art, 14,
   29–31, 294
Archuleta, Diego, Ute agent, 66
Archuleta, Don Juan Andres, 1839
   expedition against Navajos, 59–60
Archuleta, Ramon, army deserter—
   kills forest ranger, 327
Arnais, Carlos, 1661 inscription, 75
Arny, W.F.M., Ute agent, 67, 145
Arviso, Jesus, interpreter, 146
Arze, Mauricio, Spanish trader in Utah,
   77–78
Athabascans, 53–54
Athena Missiles, 337
Atomic Energy Commission, 255, 258,
   260
Automobiles, first on Navajo
   Reservation, 204–05; in county,
   253–55
Ayers, John, trader, 146
Aztec Oil Company, 250

Back to the Farm Movement, 187
Back to the Future, 354
Bailey, Mercantile, (Monticello), 115
Bailey, Jesse, farmer, 186
Balukai Mesa, 297
Bangerter, Norman, 364
Barrier Canyon Rock Art Style, 30
Bars, operation of, 330
Basketmaker, see Anasazi Indians
Bayles, Wesley, L., medical doctor, 276
Beadwork and crafts, among Utes, 199
Bear Dance, 296
Bears Ears, 21
Beautiful Mountain, 298
Beef Basin, origin of name, 22

Beer, sell of, 330
Benally, Clyde, Navajo Historian, 3
Bennett, Wallace, 349
Benow, Johnny, Ute leader, 149, 151,
   153, 159
Berlin, S.J., trader, 125
Bernheimer, Charles, leader of
   archaeological group, 42–43
Bicknell, Thomas W., naming of
   Blanding, 23
Big Buck Mine, 257
Big Indian Mining Company, 248–49
Billings, Alfred, leader of Elk Mountain
   Mission, 87
Black Mesa, 297, coal mines, 12;
   missiles fired from, 337, 338
Black, Benjamin D., delivers power
   poles, 115
Black, Calvin, colonialism of the West,
   360; criticism of archaeological site
   mitigation, 44–45; "Payment-in-
   lieu-of-taxes," 358–59; receives
   award from James Watt, Secretary
   of the Interior, 359; wilderness
   issues, 361
Black, Edwin Z., government farmer,
   199, 200
Blanding, barbed wire compound to
   hold Indians in 1923, 161–62;
   bootleggers, 328; churches, 302;
   district school, photograph, 287;
   education, 282; electrical power,
   115–17; Energy Fuels Uranium Mill,
   262; first church, 302; Fourth of July
   parade, 332; future townsite, 109;
   high school, 283, 286; Indian
   branch, 302; medical center, 277;
   rainfall and temperature, 12; origin
   of name, 23; volunteers, World War
   II, 335; votes for prohibition, 329;
   water development, 228–33;
   watershed, 232
Blankets, (Navajo), 197–99
Blue Bird Mine, 247
Blue Goose Saloon, 171
Blue Mountain (Abajo Mountains),
   cattle range, 105; copper mining,